Social Media, Criminal Law and Legality

I0885385

Utilising Lon Fuller's conception of legality, this book argues that current legal provisions often used to control online abuse aided by social media do not conform to the basic principles of legality in the criminal law, in turn, threatening freedom of expression. How we regulate inappropriate behaviour online, often referred to as online abuse, particularly online abuse aided by social media, is a contemporary concern for governments across the globe. Tragedies, such as the death of a celebrity following a campaign of online abuse, often hit the headlines, followed by the same echo: there should be a law against this. Yet, in England and Wales, numerous laws exist to control, prosecute, and convict individuals who use the likes of social media to harass, intimidate, and abuse others online. So why is the law failing to keep pace with modern technology? This monograph critically examines this fundamental question, from the perspective of legality. Applying criminal law to three growing areas of concern, it covers: (1) racist speech, (2) cyberharassment/cyberstalking, and (3) the sending of abusive messages online. It then turns to examine the latest attempts by UK officials to tackle these issues through the implementation of the Online Safety Act 2023 and France's, Germany's, and India's attempts to regulate social media. The book will be of interest to researchers in the field of criminal law and cyber law, as well as online abuse, harassment, and discrimination.

Laura Higson-Bliss is a Lecturer in Law at Keele University, United Kingdom, joining Keele School of Law in 2021. Her interests, broadly conceived, are in the interaction between social media and the criminal law, legality, freedom of expression and law and new technologies. Laura is an author of several blogs and a regular contributor to wider discussions on social media regulation on the radio and television, both nationally and internationally.

Routledge Research in the Law of Emerging Technologies

Regulating Artificial Intelligence
Binary Ethics and the Law
Dominika Ewa Harasimiuk and Tomasz Braun

Cryptocurrencies and Regulatory Challenge
Allan C. Hutchinson

Regulating Artificial Intelligence in Industry
Edited by Damian M. Bielicki

The Law of Global Digitality
Edited by Matthias C. Kettemann, Alexander Peukert and Indra Spiecker gen. Döhmann

Internet of Things and the Law
Legal Strategies for Consumer-Centric Smart Technologies
Guido Noto La Diega

Regulating the Metaverse
A Critical Assessment
Ignas Kalpokas and Julija Kalpokienė

The Regulation of Digital Technologies in the EU
Act-ification, GDPR Mimesis and EU Law Brutality at Play
Vagelis Papakonstantinou and Paul de Hert

Privacy, Data Protection and Data-driven Technologies
Edited by Martin Ebers and Karin Sein

Social Media, Criminal Law and Legality
Laura Higson-Bliss

For more information about this series, please visit: https://www.routledge.com/Routledge-Research-in-the-Law-of-Emerging-Technologies/book-series/LAWTECHNOLOGY

Social Media, Criminal Law and Legality

Laura Higson-Bliss

Routledge
Taylor & Francis Group
LONDON AND NEW YORK

First published 2025
by Routledge
4 Park Square, Milton Park, Abingdon, Oxon OX14 4RN

and by Routledge
605 Third Avenue, New York, NY 10158

Routledge is an imprint of the Taylor & Francis Group, an informa business

British Library Cataloguing-in-Publication Data
A catalogue record for this book is available from the British Library

ISBN: 978-1-032-30155-6 (hbk)
ISBN: 978-1-032-30156-3 (pbk)
ISBN: 978-1-003-30368-8 (ebk)

DOI: 10.4324/9781003303688

Typeset in Times New Roman
by Deanta Global Publishing Services, Chennai, India

This one's for you Dad. We miss you.

Also, to Walt, who has heard me read this monograph out loud dozens of times during the proofreading process. You are loved beyond words.

Contents

Figures

Acknowledgements

This monograph has been a long time coming and would never have been made possible without the support of so many people. I would firstly like to thank Routledge for their support throughout the writing process and for being understanding when asking for extensions following the many occasions the Online Safety Act 2023 was delayed during its passing through Parliament!

This monograph is loosely based on my PhD thesis, submitted to Edge Hill University in 2019. I would like to thank my examiners, Professor Richard Parrish, and Dr Holly Powell-Jones for their constructive and supportive feedback during the viva process.

I am also grateful to my colleagues at Keele School of Law for their support and advice, with particular thanks to Dr Emma Allen, Dr Stella Coyle, Dr Bleddyn Davies, Dr Elizabeth Faulkner, Eve Lakin, Lisa Mountford, Professor Yossi Nehushtan, Dr Abigail Pearson, Dr Sotirios Santatzoglou, and Professor Anthony Wrigley. A special thank you to my mentors, Dr Kathryn Simpson and Professor Alannah Tomkins for all their support whilst I have been at Keele University. I am also grateful for the support I have received from the Foundation Year Team, alongside all of our admin staff at Keele, and the support of so many colleagues during my teaching fellowship at the University of Birmingham.

This monograph would not have been possible without the continued support of my PhD supervisor Adam Pendlebury – he really has gone above and beyond as a PhD supervisor. I am also incredibly lucky that I had Dr Grace Robinson walking the long journey of completing a PhD by my side. Having you made those days that felt never-ending so worthwhile. You truly are the most wonderful person. It takes a lot to get inside the trenches of grief when you are at your happiest moment. But you did that for me, and that I will always be thankful for.

I have also been heavily supported by my friends. Kelly Wilson, Janette McMillan, Steph Farish, and Charna Paton, you really have been my lifelines since school. We may all have grown up and have families of our own, but I know you will always be there for me. Michelle Cliffe, Liz Attwood, and Nic Chatterley – I owe all three of you so much. The next Saturday coffee after the gym is on me.

To James Bliss, my not-so-little brother. You have grown into one of the most wonderful human and your strength of character makes me so proud every single day. We lost our Dad in 2013, and things were difficult for us both.

But none of this would have been possible without my husband, Jonathan Higson-Bliss. You are my rock, and I am forever grateful to have you next to me. I am excited for our next big adventure as parents to Walt, who is already loved so much, following the loss of our twins in December 2023 – we carry them both with us in our hearts.

Finally, to my Dad – everything I do is for you. I love you. I miss you. Always.

Cases

Legislation

Part I

Setting the Scene

This section provides the contextualisation of the key arguments made throughout this monograph. It is broken down into three chapters. The first chapter provides an introductory overview of the monograph, highlighting the dominance of social media today. Chapter 2 discusses at length the right to freedom of expression, an important democratic right, alongside that of the right to privacy. The chapter highlights why freedom of expression is important in the digital world and why we need to be careful in using the coercive nature of the criminal law to limit our online expressions. Chapter 3 provides the theoretical positioning which will be used to critique the criminal law in later chapters, legality. The key arguments put forward in these chapters, the dominance of social media, the importance of freedom of expression in a digital world and the significance of ensuring the principle of legality is maintained in the criminal law, provides the grounding for future arguments made in this monograph.

DOI: 10.4324/9781003303688-1

1 Introduction

1.1 Introduction

The 'harms' associated with the online world have become the moral panic of the digital era. It is very rare for a week to go by without a story emerging in the mainstream media discussing a negative event that has taken place online, both inside and outside of the United Kingdom. From cyberbullying, to harassment, to suicides which can be linked back to a person's interactions with content on the internet, the online world is often portrayed as the 'wild west' which needs to be tamed.[1] But the idea that the internet is beyond regulation is untrue. The law can, and does, apply to conduct carried out online. The issue remains, however, in how far the law should intervene. This becomes an even more prominent question when it comes to communications sent *via* the use of social media platforms.

Today anyone in the world can become a publisher. Indeed, any social media user who actively posts online, is a publisher, just without the legal training. The ease of access to the online world means that communications sent online are rising year-on-year, resulting in more content being published than ever before. The key difference today is that when a comment is made online it can be recorded in a form that can be searched and examined long after the statement was made, even if the message only took seconds to write.[2] It can also reach millions of people from across the globe in a matter of seconds. Nothing has caused as much of a headache for governments globally, then attempting to make the online world a safer environment.

At the point of writing, the regulation of the online world, in particular social media platforms, is a top priority for governments across the globe, with the United Kingdom leading the way in attempting to become 'one of the safest places to go online' through the creation and implementation of the Online Safety Act 2023

1 David Omand, 'The dark net: Policing the internets underworld' (2016) Winter 2015/16 World Policy Journal <https://worldpolicy.org/2015/12/09/the-dark-net-policing-the-internets-underworld/> accessed 13 January 2020.

2 Jacob Rowbottom, 'To Rant, Vent and Converse: Protecting Low Level Digital Speech' (2012) 71(2) C.L.J. 355, 367.

DOI: 10.4324/9781003303688-2

(OSA).[3] At the same time, pressure is being felt across police forces as social media related complaints are on the rise.[4] Not only are the police being asked to patrol the physical streets, there is now a growing expectation that the virtual streets also need to be monitored. As eloquently put by Rowbottom:

> [T]wenty years ago where a person made a racist remark in a social setting, the chances of the police ever hearing about it were small. Now a recipient can direct the police to the statement made online and allow them to witness it first hand.[5]

We are now witnessing a growing trend in the application of the criminal law framework to conduct carried out on the likes of Facebook, X (formally Twitter),[6] Instagram, TikTok, Snapchat, and YouTube, to name but a few. This is especially true for England and Wales, which will be the primary jurisdiction explored in this monograph.

Yet the application of the criminal law to conduct carried out on social media platforms does not necessarily adhere to the basic principle of legality in the criminal law—an important underlying principle which should underpin any legal provision, as set out in Chapter 3. This will be the thesis of this monograph—the criminal law framework, as it currently stands, when applied to certain conduct carried out on social media does not uphold the very basics of legality. In turn, the right to freedom of expression, as protected under both national and international law, as discussed at length in Chapter 2 is under threat. The discussion of legality and freedom of expression form Part One of this monograph.

To illustrate this thesis, Part Two focusses on three key 'harms' associated with the online world and social media:

- Racist comments made online, focussing primarily on s.18 and 19 of the Public Order Act 1986 (POA), alongside discussing s.66 of the Sentencing Act 2020 (SA) and s.31 and 32 of the Crime and Disorder Act 1988 (CDA) in Chapter 4;
- Cyberharassment and cyberstalking with reference to the Protection from Harassment Act 1997 (PfHA) in Chapter 5; and
- More broadly what can be defined as communication offences, as prohibited under both the Malicious Communications Act 1988 (MCA) and s.127 of the Communications Act 2003 (CA) in Chapter 6. In addition, following

3 Technology Secretary Michelle Donelan. See, Department for Science, Innovation and Technology, 'UK children and adults to be safer online as world-leading bill becomes law' (*Gov.uk*, 26 October 2023) <https://www.gov.uk/government/news/uk-children-and-adults-to-be-safer-online-as-world-leading-bill-becomes-law> accessed 1 November 2023.

4 The BBC, 'Teenager's life "ruined" by Live.me and Twitter "trolls"' *The BBC* (London, 24 October 2017) <http://www.bbc.co.uk/news/uk-england-41693437> accessed 30 January 2018.

5 Rowbottom (n 2).

6 Throughout this monograph, where reference is made to Twitter, this is because the content of the discussion relates to something that happen prior to the Twitter rebrand. Otherwise, X will be used.

the passing of the OSA in October 2023, some of the 'new' communication offences will be discussed in Chapter 7.

Each of these chapters will set out the law, focussing on the *actus reus* (the criminal conduct), the *mens rea* (the mental element of the offence) and where appropriate defences, before turning to examine their application in a social media context against the principle of legality and the right to freedom of expression.

Whereas Part Two focuses on the application of the criminal law to certain types of conduct carried out on social media, Part Three turns to examine the regulation of social media companies themselves. Chapter 8 starts by outlining some of the key elements of the OSA against the principle of legality, before turning to examine in Chapter 9, how France, Germany, and India have attempted to regulate social media platforms. This allows for comparisons to be made between different jurisdictions. The final chapter will draw the arguments made in this monograph to a close. Section 1.4 below, provides an overview of each chapter.

However, before setting out each chapter, it is important to contextualise the arguments made in this monograph. To do this, the following discussion will provide a brief overview of the rise in social media platforms. First, what is meant by the term social media will be discussed, before turning to provide a brief overview of the creation and dominance of the World Wide Web (WWW), commonly referred to as the internet. Next, the rise in social media will be outlined. Finally, a discussion will take place exploring the 'good' and the 'bad' when it comes to social media.

1.2 The Development of Social Media

It is hard to imagine a world today without social media. In fact, we are now living in a time where some individuals do not know a world without the internet, let alone social media. These individuals are commonly referred to as digital natives.[7] But like many of the abstract concepts that will be explored in this monograph, such as online abuse, harassment, or offensive commentary, there is no one true definition of social media. The term social media can cover a range of online interactions, for instance, blogging, video sharing, and virtual world reality games can all be considered a form of social media.[8] Many of us, when considering what social media is, will think of Facebook, owned by Meta. Less will consider WhatsApp (another platform owned by Meta) as a traditional form of social media, but it is, for the purposes of regulation, considered a social media platform.

Despite there being no true definition of social media, it has come to be accepted that social media is 'the ability to share, to co-operate, with one another, and to take collective actions, all outside the framework of traditional institutions and

7 Marc Prensky, 'Digital Natives, Digital Immigrants' 2001 9(5) Horiz 1.

8 Laura Scaife, *Handbook of Social Media and the Law* (Routledge 2015) 8–9.

organisations'.[9] As outlined by the Law Commission during their 2018 scoping report into the criminal law and online abuse, there are several fundamental characteristics associated with social media,

> including users being invited to provide data to generate a 'profile', and to share information such as status updates, videos, photographs, and music, so as to facilitate interaction with other users.[10]

Indeed, the OSA does not define the term social media, nor mentions the term social media. This is despite discussions inside and outside of Parliament, at its time of enactment, primarily focussing on regulating social media platforms, in a bid to stop them from 'marking their own homework'.[11] Instead, such platforms are termed user-to-user services, defined as,

> an internet service by means of which content that is generated directly on the service by a user of the service, or uploaded to or shared on the service by a user of the service, may be encountered by another user, or other users, of the service.[12]

For the purposes of this monograph, the term social media is used to refer to platforms which allow users to create their own profiles (either in their own name or under a pseudonym), interact with others (either as a lurker or someone who actively engages with the platform), generate or view content and are created and run by private organisations for the purposes of generating a profit.

1.2.1 The World Wide Web

Surprisingly, the internet, which can be defined as 'a telecommunications system for computer networks',[13] was created in response to the first man-made object entering outer space in 1957. The announcement by the Soviet Union that they had achieved what was considered the impossible in launching an object into space came as a shock to those living in Western society at the time. As a result, the then President of the United States Dwight Eisenhower, in a bid not to be taken by surprise at the emergence of new technology in the future, created the

9 Clay Shirky, *Here Comes Everyone* (Penguin 2008) 20. For a discussion on different definitions of social media see, Christian Fuchs, *Social Media a Critical Introduction* (Sage Publications 2014) 35–37.

10 Law Commission, *Abusive and Offensive Online Communications: A Scoping Report* (Law Com No 381, 2018) [2.32].

11 Lorna Woods, William Perrin and Maeve Walsh, 'It's (nearly) here: a short guide to the Online Safety Act' (*Carnegie UK*, 19 September 2023) <https://carnegieuktrust.org.uk/blog-posts/its-nearly-here-a-short-guide-to-the-online-safety-act/> accessed 27 September 2023.

12 Online Safety Act s.3(1).

13 Andrew Murray, *Information Technology Law: The Law and Society* (5th edn, Oxford University Press 2023) 21.

Advanced Research Projects Agency.[14] It was this research body that created the world's first successful computer network, known as ARPANET (the Advanced Research Projects Agency Network) in the late 1960s.[15] Following the success of ARPANET, further networks were manufactured including the Transmission Control Protocol, which allowed networks to be created between local computers.[16] In 1988 computers based in Canada and France were linked to networks created in the United States, paving the way for the creation of the WWW.[17]

The WWW consists of millions of interlinked web pages which use the internet to connect. The foundations for the WWW were created in 1989 by Sir Tim Berners-Lee.[18] Berners-Lee envisioned a database where users would be able to obtain any information they desired with minimum fuss. In 1990 the first website went 'live'.[19] By 1993, the WWW or Web 1.0 as it is commonly referred to, was made available to the wider public. The purpose of Web 1.0 was to allow users to actively search between static websites.[20] Web 1.0 was, to put it simply, an information database, where users were considered consumers.[21]

By the turn of the next millennium, the advancement of changing technology had altered Web 1.0 completely. Internet users went from consumers to content creators.[22] By 2005 it had been accepted that a new version of the WWW had been created, Web 2.0:

> The term Web 2.0 [...] is said to describe the period in which websites became more interactive, collaborative, and social. This is typically contrasted with more passive website interactions, where users simply viewed or downloaded content from websites.[23]

Web 2.0 unlike its predecessor, was much more interactive, dynamic, and user-driven.[24] The expansion of the WWW changed the job market, altered how individuals communicated, and has become integral to how society functions. At the time of writing, there is an ongoing debate in the wider literature that we are

14 Ibid., 22.
15 Ibid., 32.
16 Jeffrey C. Jackson, *Web Technologies: A Computer Science Perspective* (Pearson Education 2007) 2.
17 Ibid., 3.
18 Kevin M. Rogers, *The Internet and the Law* (Macmillan International Higher Education 2011) 3
19 Madhumita Murgia, 'The world's first website went online 25 years ago today' *The Telegraph* (London, 21 December 2015) <https://www.telegraph.co.uk/technology/internet/12061803/The-worlds-first-website-went-online-25-years-ago-today.html> accessed 2 November 2018.
20 Rogers (n 18) 213.
21 Matthew Allen, 'What was Web 2.0? Versions as the Dominant Mode of Internet History' (2012) 15(2) New Media Soc. 260, 263.
22 Ibid.,
23 Law Com No 381 (n 10) [2.29].
24 Rogers (n 18) 213.

perhaps moving away from Web 2.0 towards Web 3.0,[25] driven by the creation of the Metaverse.[26]

Since its creation, the WWW and the internet have grown in terms of websites and online users.[27] In the United Kingdom in 2018, 90% of adults were regular internet users, an increase of 1% on the previous year. By 2020, this figure had risen to 92%.[28] Of those aged between 16 and 34, 99% were regular users of the internet.[29] Similarly, internet usage has increased across the world. In 2017 it was reported that 3.58 billion people worldwide were users of the internet, an increase of 190 million on the previous year.[30] By July 2023, this figure reached 5.19 billion, of which 4.88 billion were also social media users.[31]

The WWW has therefore gone from static websites, whereby users were able to use the internet as an information database, to interactive websites, which allow for, though not limited to, instant communication, political debate, and the selling of goods online.[32] Today, the internet can be considered 'messy, dynamic, and constantly changing'[33] whilst facilitating the exchange of information on a scale unprecedented in human history.[34] Consequently, the purpose of the internet has expanded, as illustrated in the work of Bernal. Bernal suggests that the purpose of the internet can be split into six categories: the use of the internet as an information database, the use of the internet as a business platform, the use of the internet as a political platform, the internet as a public space, the internet as a communications

25 'Web 3.0 entails an integrated Web experience where the machine will be able to understand and catalogue data in a manner similar to humans'. See, Riaan Rudman and Rikus Bruwer, 'Defining Web 3.0: opportunities and challenges' (2016) 34(1) Electron. Libr. 132.

26 The Metaverse is considered 'the idea of integrating real and digital worlds ever more seamlessly, using technologies such as virtual reality (VR) and augmented reality (AR)'. See, Marcus Carter and Ben Egliston, 'Facebook relaunches itself as "Meta" in a clear bid to dominate the metaverse' (*The International Forum for Responsible Media Blog*, 20 October 2021) <https://inforrm.org/2021/10/30/facebook-relaunches-itself-as-meta-in-a-clear-bid-to-dominate-the-metaverse-marcus-carter-and-ben-egliston/> accessed 27 September 2023.

27 Websites have since expanded from 130 in 1993 to 17,087,182 by the end of 2000. See, Internet Live Stats, 'Total number of websites' (*Internet Live Stats*, 2018) <http://www.internetlivestats.com/total-number-of-websites/> accessed 2 November 2018.

28 Office of National Statistics, 'Internet users, UK: 2020' (*Office of National Statistics*, 6 April 2021) <https://www.ons.gov.uk/businessindustryandtrade/itandinternetindustry/bulletins/internetusers/2020> accessed 27 September 2023. At the time of writing, there are no updated national statistics on internet access in the United Kingdom.

29 Ibid.

30 Statista, 'Number of internet users worldwide from 2005 to 2017 (in millions)' (*Statista*, 2018) <https://www.statista.com/statistics/273018/number-of-internet-users-worldwide/> accessed 2 November 2018.

31 Statista, 'Number of internet and social media users worldwide as of July 2023 (in billions)' (*Statista*, 22 September 2023) <https://www.statista.com/statistics/617136/digital-population-worldwide/> accessed 27 September 2023.

32 Note, this is not a definitive list.

33 Paul Bernal, *The Internet, Warts and All: Free Speech, Privacy and Truth* (Cambridge University Press 2018) 2.

34 Law Com No 381 (n 10) [1.41].

device, and the use of the internet in being integral to society.[35] It is the use of the internet as a communications device, to which this chapter will now turn to examine.

1.2.2 The Early Days of Online Communications and Social Media

The expansion of changing technologies has not only changed how we obtain information, adapted political campaigns, or indeed altered how we shop, but it has also transformed how members of a society interact with each other:

> Technological advancement in the 19th century sparked a revolution in the speed of communication. The invention of the telegraph was the first form of electrical telecommunication that had this effect. Subsequent innovations such as the telephone, radio, television, the internet, and most recently, the emergence of social media, have radically transformed the way we communicate.[36]

In 1971 the first email between two computers was transmitted.[37] Since then, technological advances have continued to revolutionise how we communicate. We have gone from being able to send written or verbal communications to one another, to being able to share pictures, videos, memes, emojis, newspaper articles etc., instantly, at the click of a button, with social media playing a pivotal role in the revolution of online communications.

The first form of social media as society knows it today emerged in 1997, 'SixDegrees.com', in which users of the site could connect with friends and family.[38] Following the initial success of SixDegrees, which boosted around 3.5 million users, other websites started to emerge based on a similar format, such as 'Friendster', 'LinkedIn', and 'MySpace', which all launched in 2002.[39] By 2015 it was estimated that there were over 200 different social media platforms across the globe.[40] However, the biggest turning point for the revolution of social media was the creation of 'TheFacebook' in 2004, which was rebranded as Facebook in August 2005. And despite it being considered 'old', Facebook still, to this day, is the biggest social media platform worldwide.[41]

35 Bernal (n 33) 5–19.

36 Law Com No 381 (n 10) [2.29].

37 Centre for Computing History, '1971: First Network Email Sent by Ray Tomlinson' (*Centre for Computing History*, 2016) <http://www.computinghistory.org.uk/det/6116/First-e-mail-sent-by-Ray-Tomlinson/> accessed 27 November 2018.

38 Scaife (n 8) 4.

39 Broadband Search, 'History of social media (It's younger than you think)' (*Broadband Search*, 10 May 2023) <https://www.broadbandsearch.net/blog/complete-history-social-media> accessed 27 September 2023.

40 Scaife (n 8) 4.

41 Josh Constine, 'Facebook now has 2 billion monthly users … and responsibility' (*Tech Crunch*, 2017) <https://techcrunch.com/2017/06/27/facebook-2-billion-users/> accessed 29 November 2018.

1.2.3 Social Media as We Know It Today and Its Global Reach

On 4 February 2004 Mark Zuckerberg, a college student at Harvard University, alongside several other students, launched Facebook. The initial purpose of Facebook was to create a communications mechanism for students at Harvard University, with the site later being made available to all higher education students in the Boston area.[42] In 2006, Facebook was released to the world, with anyone who claimed[43] to be over 13 years of age being able to create a Facebook page.

Facebook, 'operates as a social networking site based on interconnection[s] with other users to generate content'.[44] Here users must register with the site and build personal profiles of themselves, which can include, likes and dislikes, a picture of themselves, their date of birth, and other unique information such as where they were educated. In fact, Facebook is built on the premise of getting its users to reveal private information about themselves.

By 2016 Facebook had expanded to become the sixth-most valuable public company in the world.[45] In June 2017 Mark Zuckerberg announced, *via* Facebook, that Facebook had 2 billion users, averaging around 580,000 new users each day.[46] In the United Kingdom alone, 48.5 million citizens are active Facebook users.[47] Meta, who owns Facebook, have also extended the number of other social media platforms in its portfolio including, WhatsApp (with a usership worldwide of 2 billion in 2023);[48] Instagram (with a usership worldwide of 1.21 billion in 2021);[49] and most recently, Threads (which surpassed 100 million users in its first 5 days of launch)[50] as a direct response to the decline of X, which until recently was one of its biggest competitors.[51] Other platforms have emerged since the launch of Facebook, but none have surpassed its reach, as illustrated in Figure 1.1.

42 Sarah Phillips, 'A brief history of Facebook' *The Guardian* (London, 25 July 2007) <https://www.theguardian.com/technology/2007/jul/25/media.newmedia> accessed 26 November 2018.

43 Very little is done to verify the age of users on Facebook. However, under the Online Safety Act 2023 platforms will have to do more to ensure those who should not be on the platform, cannot access it through age-verification and age-estimation. See Chapter 8.

44 Scaife (n 8) 9.

45 Ursula Smartt, *Media & Entertainment Law* (Taylor & Francis 2017) 79.

46 James Titcomb, 'Facebook now has 2 billion users, Mark Zuckerberg announces' *The Telegraph* (London, 27 June 2017) <https://www.telegraph.co.uk/technology/2017/06/27/facebook-now-has-2-billion-users-mark-zuckerberg-announces/> accessed 29 November 2018.

47 Statista, 'Distribution of Facebook users in the United Kingdom as of April 2023, by age group' (*Statista*, 22 May 2023) <https://www.statista.com/statistics/1030055/facebook-users-united-kingdom/> accessed 27 September 2023.

48 Statista, 'WhatsApp – Statistics & Facts' (*Statista*, 30 August 2023) <https://www.statista.com/topics/2018/whatsapp/#topicOverview> accessed 27 September 2023.

49 Statista, 'Number of Instagram users worldwide from 2020 to 2025 (in billions)' (*Statista*, 29 August 2023) <https://www.statista.com/statistics/183585/instagram-number-of-global-users/> accessed 27 September 2023.

50 The BBC, 'Threads app signs up 100m users in less than a week' *The BBC* (London, 10 July 2023) <https://www.bbc.co.uk/news/technology-66153244> accessed 27 September 2023.

51 Josh Taylor and Josh Nicolas, 'Twitter traffic sinks in wake of changes and launch of rival platform Threads' *The Guardian* (London, 10 July 2023) <https://www.theguardian.com/technology/2023

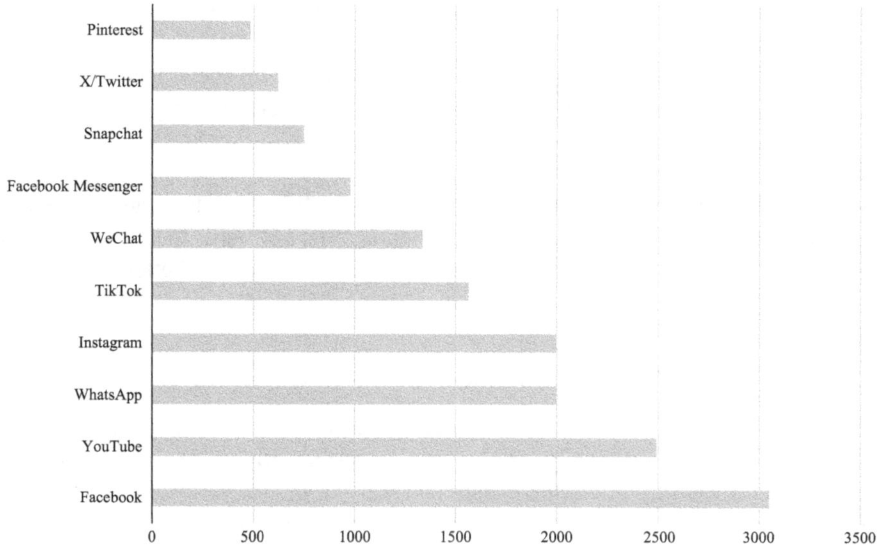

Figure 1.1 Most popular social networks worldwide as of January 2024, ranked by number of monthly active users (in millions).

Note: Statista, 'Most popular social networks worldwide as of January 2024, ranked by number of monthly active users (in millions)' (*Statista*, 31 January 2024) <https://www.statista.com/statistics/272014/global-social-networks-ranked-by-number-of-users/> accessed 1 March 2024.

To put the dominance of social media into context, in 2023:[52]

- An estimated 4.9 billion people globally used at least one form of social media;
- The average user had between six and seven social media platforms, many of which were easily accessed *via* a mobile phone at the click of a button;
- The average person spent around 145 minutes a day on social media;
- 84% of those aged 18 to 29 and 81% of people between 30 to 49 actively used at least one social media site; and
- 77% of businesses worldwide used at least one form of social media.

Whilst in the United Kingdom, in January 2023:[53]

/jul/10/twitter-traffic-sinks-in-wake-of-changes-and-launch-of-rival-platform-threads-elon-musk> accessed 23 September 2023.

52 Belle Wong, 'Top social media statistics and trends of 2023' (*Forbes,* 18 May 2023) <https://www.forbes.com/advisor/business/social-media-statistics/> accessed 27 September 2023.

53 Simon Kemp, 'Digital 2023: Global overview report' (*Datareportal*, 26 January 2023) <https://datareportal.com/reports/digital-2023-global-overview-report> accessed 23 September 2023.

- 57.10 million individuals were social media users (84.4% of the total population);
- The average UK citizen spent 116 minutes each day on social media;
- The average user in the United Kingdom had six social media platforms; and
- 51.6% of UK social media users were female.

Social media therefore dominates much of everyday life, with its usage increasing dramatically during the global COVID-19 pandemic.[54] In turn, the way in which humans interact with each other, has also changed, both for the better and for the worse.

1.3 Social Media: The Good and the Bad

There is no doubt that social media has changed many aspects of everyday life—both positively and negatively. However, it is the negative side of social media that is often raised by government officials and the media when discussing such forms of communication. It is this continued rhetoric around the 'darker' side of the online world which has traditionally led to calls for stronger regulation, to control and punish those who use such platforms to abuse others. Though as noted by Rowbottom:

> [t]he legal responses can, however, seem heavy-handed for what might have been a statement made with little thought while the speaker was sat at a desk at home. Words typed in seconds followed by hitting the enter key can lead to a criminal record or costly civil litigation.[55]

Recently, as discussed in Chapter 8, there has been a change in direction, with emphasis being placed on regulating social media platforms.

There is no doubt that social media can be used to abuse others, with regular research being published highlighting the 'darker' side of social media. From research exposing the use of such platforms to target those in the public domain, including athletes,[56] politicians,[57] and celebrities,[58] to research indicating a rise in

54 Stacey Jo Dixson, 'Social media use during COVID-19 worldwide – Statistics & Facts' (*Statista*, 31 August 2023) <https://www.statista.com/topics/7863/social-media-use-during-coronavirus-covid-19-worldwide/#topicOverview> accessed 23 September 2023.

55 Rowbottom (n 2) 356.

56 Professional Footballers' Association, 'AI research study on online abuse' (*Professional Footballers' Association*, 2021) <https://www.thepfa.com/news/2020/10/21/pfa-charity-ai-research-study> accessed 21 September 2023.

57 Laura Bliss, 'Abuse of women MPs is not just a scandal – it's a threat to democracy' *The Conversation* (London, 17 July 2017) <https://theconversation.com/abuse-of-women-mps-is-not-just-a-scandal-its-a-threat-todemocracy-80781> accessed 9 December 2018.

58 Christopher Hand, 'Why is celebrity abuse on Twitter so bad? It might be a problem with our empathy' *The Conversation* (London, 4 March 2021) <https://theconversation.com/why-is-celebrity-abuse-on-twitter-so-bad-it-might-be-a-problem-with-our-empathy-154970> accessed 23 September 2023.

the use of such platforms to target children.[59] Indeed, anyone can become subjected to horrific forms of abuse online. And although this monograph does not justify the abuse that some individuals experience online, it does dispute the use of the criminal law in this area, particularly criminal law provisions which are incompatible with the principle of legality when applied in a social media context.

Further, as will be noted throughout Chapters 4, 5, and 6, the statistics provided to justify why we need stronger criminal legal provisions to tackle the 'harms' associated with the online world, need to be considered with caution. Many studies use vague definitions of the 'harm'. For instance, as discussed in Chapter 5, cyberharassment and cyberstalking are often used interchangeably and even when applied correctly, studies define such behaviours differently. Additionally, research conducted by The Alan Turing Institute, as noted in Chapter 6, estimates that only 0.001% to 1% of content online can be considered so highly abusive, that further action should be taken.[60] Indeed, research by OFCOM (the UK communications regulator) with adults on 'harmful' content they have seen online, found those who took part in the study, had witnessed in the four weeks prior:

- 'Alternative viewpoints' (14%);
- 'Offensive/upsetting language' (10%); and
- 'Offensive/upsetting videos/images' (7%).

Those who took part in the study considered these behaviours to be 'harmful'.[61] Yet, such content, as discussed in Chapter 2, falls within the right to freedom of expression.

It is studies like these that are often used to justify the paternalistic approach undertaken by governments to regulate individuals' conduct online, where it has come to be accepted that self-regulation is no longer working (if it ever did) and therefore the law must intervene. As highlighted by Gillespie, it is not a defence to say, 'it's only Twitter'.[62] But there is a 'brighter' side to social media, and it's this 'brighter' side that is often missed in conversations. For instance, as noted in Chapter 2, social media can be used as a modern form of protest to challenge state coercion or abuse; it allows individuals to keep updated with loved ones;

59 Nick Stripe, 'Online bullying in England and Wales: year ending March 2020' (*Office of National Statistics*, 16 November 2020) <https://www.ons.gov.uk/peoplepopulationandcommunity/crimeandjustice/bulletins/onlinebullyinginenglandandwales/yearendingmarch2020> accessed 23 September 2023.

60 Bertie Vidgen, Helen Margetts, and Alex Harris, 'How much online abuse is there? A systematic review of evidence for the UK. Policy Briefing – Full Report' (*The Alan Turing Institute*, 2020) 4 <https://www.turing.ac.uk/sites/default/files/2019-11/online_abuse_prevalence_full_24.11.2019_-_formatted_0.pdf> accessed 3 May 2023.

61 OFCOM, 'Ofcom pilot online harms survey 2020/21' (*OFCOM*, 2021) 18 <https://www.ofcom.org.uk/__data/assets/pdf_file/0014/220622/online-harms-survey-waves-1-4-2021.pdf> accessed 23 September 2023. The sample range in total was 4,242 internet users aged 13–84 in the United Kingdom.

62 Alisdair A. Gillespie, 'Twitter, Jokes and the Law' (2012) 76(5) J. crim. law 364 (note).

it can bring people together; and for some, it's the only place they can truly be themselves,[63] but to name just a few examples. In fact, further research by OFCOM around young people's perceptions of the online world and social media, directly opposes much of the current rhetoric that the online world is 'bad' for children:

> Specifically, in relation to social media, a majority of children aged 8 to 17 using these apps or sites were able to identify the benefits of these apps or sites, *all or most of the time.* About seven in ten said they felt safe using these types of apps (73%). There was a positive year-on-year shift in the proportion of children aged 8–17 claiming that these platforms made them feel happy (67%, up from 59% in 2021), while 66% thought that it helped them stay close to their friends (up from 61% in 2021).[64]

And although those who took part in the study acknowledged that there were 'downsides' to being online, overall the good outweighed the bad.[65]

It is vital therefore that we strike a balance when it comes to regulating individuals' conduct online, in which the criminal law should only intervene in the most extreme cases and only when such legal provisions are compatible with the principle of legality. This is because 'for democracy to flourish, we need informed citizens, accountability, transparency, [and] inclusive public debate'.[66] It is only through having difficult conversations, that change can be enacted. We need to be careful to ensure we are not shutting down the voices of the minority to suit the needs of the majority. To put it bluntly 'there [will] always [be] stupid people and now they are all in one place'.[67] Arguably, many of the 'negative' aspects of social media are inherent within society, and social media is just a magnification of conversations that happen every day in the physical world, which can now be documented and searched for, long after the exchange took place. We therefore need to ensure that the law is only applied in extreme circumstances and does not become the go-to option for every little dispute that takes place online. And where such provisions are applied, we need to ensure legality is maintained—something we are currently failing to adhere to.

63 Daria Kuss, 'How social media affects children at different ages – and how to protect them' (*LSE Blog*, 4 May 2022) <https://blogs.lse.ac.uk/parenting4digitalfuture/2022/05/04/social-media-at-different-ages/#:~:text=Engaging%20with%20social%20media%20can,health%20and%20wellbeing%20as%20well> accessed 23 September 2023.

64 OFCOM, 'Children and parents: Media use and attitudes' (*OFCOM,* 29 March 2023) 34 <https://www.ofcom.org.uk/__data/assets/pdf_file/0027/255852/childrens-media-use-and-attitudes-report-2023.pdf/> accessed 23 September 2023.

65 Ibid., 35.

66 Select Committee on Democracy and Digital Technologies, *Digital Technology and the Resurrection of Trust* (HL 2019-21, 77) [10].

67 City University, 'City law school webinar: The law of Facebook' (*YouTube*, 21 April 2021) <https://www.youtube.com/watch?v=zjaOFPmm8wo> accessed 18 October 2023.

1.4 Chapter Overview

The proceeding chapters are split into three parts. Part One sets the contextual background for later discussions in Part Two of this monograph and consists of this chapter and two other chapters: Chapter 2 – Freedom of Expression: The Online Context and Chapter 3 – Regulating Social Media: Theoretical Positioning.

Chapter 2 provides a discussion on the right to freedom of expression and the right to privacy in the online world. First, Article 19 of the Universal Declaration of Human Rights is outlined, before turning to examine aspects of the European Convention on Human Rights which by way of the Human Rights Act 1998 has been incorporated into the legal framework of the United Kingdom. Of focus are Articles 10 (the right to freedom of expression), 8 (the right to privacy), and 17 (the prohibition of abuse rights). Next, why freedom of expression is essential in a digital world is outlined, focussing on the 'good' that can come from social media usage, which is often neglected in wider discussions; before turning to examine the often-misunderstood concept of privacy online, and how, despite what some may think, privacy does exist even in the virtual world. Chapter 2 concludes by reenforcing the importance of protecting freedom of expression online and how ultimately the use of the law to govern inappropriate communications on social media sites, will not change social norms and instead, such use merely threatens the right to freedom of expression.

The overall premise of Chapter 3 is to provide the framework which will be used to critically examine legal provisions and their use to curtail social media abuse in Part Two of this monograph—the principle of legality. To do this, the first half of Chapter 3 explores four theoretical concepts of online regulation: (1) cyber-libertarianism; (2) cyber-paternalism; (3) network communitarianism; and (4) the governance model. It is argued that regardless of the theoretical positioning you take to the regulation of social media platforms, legality needs to be maintained. The second half of Chapter 3 introduces the concept of legality outlining with reference to legal provisions and case law examples, legality in international criminal law, followed by a further in-depth discussion on legality from a European Human Rights perspective. The final section of this chapter explores Lon Fuller's[68] eight principles of legality, with reference to other scholars in the field, such as Joseph Raz,[69] Cian Murphy,[70] and Tom Bingham.[71] It is Fuller's conception of legality which is used to critique the law in the proceeding chapters.

Part Two provides the substantive discussions for this monograph and its split into four chapters; each exploring a different area of the criminal law and its application to a social media context: Chapter 4 – Online Racism and the Criminal Law;

68 Lon L. Fuller, *The Morality of Law* (Yale University Press 1964).

69 Joseph Raz, 'The Rule of Law and its Virtue' (1977) 93 L.Q.R. 195.

70 Cian C. Murphy, 'The Principle of Legality in Criminal Law under the European Convention on Human Rights' (2010) 2 Eur. Hum. Rights Law Rev. 192.

71 Tom Bingham, *The Rule of Law* (Penguin 2011). See also, Lord Bingham, 'The Rule of Law' (2007) 66(1) Camb. Law. J. 67.

Chapter 5 – Harassment and Stalking Online; Chapter 6 – Abusive Communications Online: The Development of Communication Law; and Chapter 7 – The Future of Communication Law.

Chapter 4 starts by outlining the rise in online hate crimes, before turning to examine the use of such sites to send racial abuse—the hate characteristic which will be the focus of this chapter. Reference will be made to the growing concern that social media sites are increasingly being used to spread racial hatred. Following on from this, Chapter 4 examines how the criminal justice system is attempting to tackle the rise in racial abuse on social media sites by examining three legal provisions which prohibit such behaviour: s.66 of the SA, s.31 and 32 of the CDA and s.18 and 19 of the POA. Using a narrative review and case law examples, each provision is taken in turn, looking specifically at the language used within these provisions and their application to a social media context. It highlights, with reference to the Crown Prosecution Service guidelines on hate crimes, the failure of the law to keep pace with digital technology. The final section of Chapter 4 contextualises and demonstrates how the application of these provisions, to a social media context, breaches the fundamental principles of legality.

Cyberharassment and cyberstalking are the focus of Chapter 5. This chapter provides a narrative review, with reference to case law examples and statistics, on the application of the PfHA to cyberharassment and/or cyberstalking. Taking a similar structure to Chapter 4, it starts by contextualising the growth in the use of social media sites to harass and stalk individuals online, before turning to examine the PfHA. Taking harassment and stalking in turn, the *actus reus* and *mens rea* of each offence is critically examined, looking at the language used within the Act, before turning to look at the PfHA and the principle of legality. Chapter 5 concludes by demonstrating how the Act, when applied in a social media context, does not uphold the principle of legality and in turn, freedom of speech is under threat.

Whereas Chapters 4 and 5 focus on substantive criminal offences, Chapter 6 turns to examine communication offences in the criminal law framework of England and Wales. Until very recently, two communication offences existed: the MCA and s.127(1) and (2) of the CA. Chapter 6 starts by briefly outlining the historical development of these two Acts, before discussing the rise in online abuse—a term that is often thrown around and used to justify the coercive nature of the criminal law but lacks any definitive definition. Next, like that of the previous chapters, the MCA and s.127(1) and (2) of the CA are outlined, examining the offences which were originally prohibited under these provisions. Of focus will be the vague terminology used in both provisions—highlighting significant issues with legality, and showing why these provisions were, and still are, considered the most controversial approach to regulating speech. Therefore allowing, in Chapter 7, direct comparisons between the 'new' communication offences and the 'old' offences.

Chapter 7 explores the future of communication law, following the Law Commission in 2021 making several radical recommendations to revamp this area of the criminal law. Many of these recommendations were included in the OSA, others were not. The passing of the OSA has made some small amendments to both the MCA and s.127(2) of the CA. Of note and as discussed in Chapter 7 are offences related to the sending of harmful, false, and threatening communications. Each is taken in turn, discussing the *actus reus* and *mens rea* of each offence, before turning to examine the right to freedom of expression and the principle of legality in the criminal law. This chapter will conclude by demonstrating how these 'new' offences have not addressed previous issues with the application of communication law to conduct carried out on social media platforms.

Whereas Part Two of this monograph focussed primarily on three significant 'harms' associated with the online world from a criminal law perspective, Part Three turns to examine the regulation of social media platforms themselves as opposed to individuals. Part Three is made up of two substantive chapters, followed by the conclusive chapter: Chapter 8 – Regulating Online Behaviour in the United Kingdom: Beyond the Criminal Law; and Chapter 9 – International Perspectives on Social Media and the Law.

Chapter 8 explores and critically examines the United Kingdom's OSA. Under the Act, platforms which fall within its scope, including most social media companies, are legally obliged to do more to tackle the 'harms' associated with the digital world. Including, though not limited to, doing more to reduce the behaviours discussed in Chapters 4, 5, 6, and 7 on their platforms. Chapter 8 starts by outlining the background to the OSA, before turning to critically discuss the Act from the perspective of legality. The rationale for including a separate chapter looking at the regulatory context, beyond just the criminal law, is to situate the discussions and arguments made in previous chapters, within the wider political, ethical, and legal context of online regulation.

The final substantive chapter, Chapter 9, provides a comparative chapter exploring how other countries have attempted to regulate online (mis)behaviours including, France, Germany, and India. Each State is examined in turn, with a narrative review of the key provisions used by each jurisdiction to regulate both individual behaviours online, and social media companies themselves. Through a narrative review of these legal provisions, issues with legality and freedom of expression are exposed. In fact, in France, legislation enacted to tackle online hate has previously been struck down by the French Constitutional Court for being incompatible with the right to freedom of expression. The rationale for focussing on these States, as opposed to others, is due to the similarities in approaches, but the outcomes have varied. The purpose of Chapter 9 is to demonstrate how other countries have attempted to tackle online abuse to aid further discussions, particularly in the conclusive chapter, Chapter 10, on how we can better regulate online behaviours, whilst upholding the principle of legality and protecting freedom of expression.

Reference list

Allen M, 'What was Web 2.0? Versions as the dominant mode of internet history' (2012) 15(2) New Media Soc 260

Bernal P, *The Internet, Warts and All: Free Speech, Privacy and Truth* (Cambridge University Press 2018)

Bingham T, *The Rule of Law* (Penguin 2011)

Bliss L, 'Abuse of women MPs is not just a scandal – it's a threat to democracy' *The Conversation* (London, 17 July 2017) https://theconversation.com/abuse-of-women-mps-is-not-just-a-scandal-its-a-threat-todemocracy-80781

Broadband Search, 'History of Social Media (It's Younger Than You Think)' (*Broadband Search*, 10 May 2023) https://www.broadbandsearch.net/blog/complete-history-social-media

Carter M & Egliston B, 'Facebook Relaunches Itself as "Meta" in a Clear Bid to Dominate the Metaverse' (*The International Forum for Responsible Media Blog*, 20 October 2021) https://inforrm.org/2021/10/30/facebook-relaunches-itself-as-meta-in-a-clear-bid-to-dominate-the-metaverse-marcus-carter-and-ben-egliston/

Centre for Computing History, '1971: First Network Email sent by Ray Tomlinson' (*Centre for Computing History*, 2016) http://www.computinghistory.org.uk/det/6116/First-e-mail-sent-by-Ray-Tomlinson/

City University, 'City Law School Webinar: The Law of Facebook' (*YouTube*, 21 April 2021) https://www.youtube.com/watch?v=zjaOFPmm8wo

Constine J, 'Facebook Now Has 2 Billion Monthly Users … and Responsibility' (*Tech Crunch*, 2017) https://techcrunch.com/2017/06/27/facebook-2-billion-users/

Department for Science, Innovation and Technology, 'UK Children and Adults to Be Safer Online as World-Leading Bill Becomes Law' (*Gov.uk*, 26 October 2023) https://www.gov.uk/government/news/uk-children-and-adults-to-be-safer-online-as-world-leading-bill-becomes-law

Dixson S J, 'Social Media Use During COVID-19 Worldwide - Statistics & Facts' (*Statista*, 31 August 2023) https://www.statista.com/topics/7863/social-media-use-during-coronavirus-covid-19-worldwide/#topicOverview

Fuchs C, *Social Media a Critical Introduction* (Sage Publications 2014)

Fuller L L, *The Morality of Law* (Yale University Press 1964)

Gillespie A A, 'Twitter, Jokes and the Law' (2012) 76(5) J Crim Law 364 (note)

Hand C, 'Why is celebrity abuse on Twitter so bad? It might be a problem with our empathy' *The Conversation* (London, 4 March 2021) https://theconversation.com/why-is-celebrity-abuse-on-twitter-so-bad-it-might-be-a-problem-with-our-empathy-154970

HM Government, 'Internet Safety Strategy – Green Paper' (*Gov.uk*, October 2018) https://assets.publishing.service.gov.uk/government/uploads/system/uploads/attachment_data/file/650949/Internet_Safety_Strategy_green_paper.pdf

Internet Live Stats, 'Total Number of Websites' (*Internet Live Stats*, 2018) http://www.internetlivestats.com/total-number-of-websites/

Jackson J C, *Web Technologies: A Computer Science Perspective* (Pearson Education 2007)

Kemp S, 'Digital 2023: Global Overview Report' (*Datareportal*, 26 January 2023) https://datareportal.com/reports/digital-2023-global-overview-report

Kuss D, 'How Social Media Affects Children at Different Ages – and How to Protect Them' (*LSE Blog*, 4 May 2022) https://blogs.lse.ac.uk/parenting4digitalfuture/2022/05/04/social-media-at-different-ages/#:~:text=Engaging%20with%20social%20media%20can,health%20and%20wellbeing%20as%20well

Law Commission, *Abusive and Offensive Online Communications: A Scoping Report* (Law Com No 381, 2018)

Lord Bingham, 'The Rule of Law' (2007) 66(1) Cam Law J 67

Murgia M, 'The world's first website went online 25 years ago today' *The Telegraph* (London, 21 December 2015) https://www.telegraph.co.uk/technology/internet/12061803/The-worlds-first-website-went-online-25-years-ago-today.html

Murphy C C, 'The Principle of Legality in Criminal Law Under the European Convention on Human Rights' (2010) 2 Eur Hum Rights Law Rev 192

Murray A, *Information Technology Law: The Law and Society* (5th edn, Oxford University Press 2023)

OFCOM, 'Children and Parents: Media Use and Attitudes' (*OFCOM*, 29 March 2023) https://www.ofcom.org.uk/__data/assets/pdf_file/0027/255852/childrens-media-use-and-attitudes-report-2023.pdf/

OFCOM,'Ofcom Pilot Online Harms Survey 2020/21' (*OFCOM*, 2021) https://www.ofcom.org.uk/__data/assets/pdf_file/0014/220622/online-harms-survey-waves-1-4-2021.pdf

Office of National Statistics, 'Internet Users, UK: 2020' (*Office of National Statistics*, 6 April 2021) https://www.ons.gov.uk/businessindustryandtrade/itandinternetindustry/bulletins/internetusers/2020

Omand D, 'The Dark Net: Policing the Internets Underworld' (2016) Winter 2015/16 World Policy Journal https://worldpolicy.org/2015/12/09/the-dark-net-policing-the-internets-underworld/

Phillips S, 'A brief history of Facebook' *The Guardian* (London, 25 July 2007) https://www.theguardian.com/technology/2007/jul/25/media.newmedia

Prensky M, 'Digital Natives, Digital Immigrants' 2001 9(5) *Horiz* 1

Professional Footballers' Association, 'AI Research Study on Online Abuse' (*Professional Footballers' Association*, 2021) https://www.thepfa.com/news/2020/10/21/pfa-charity-ai-research-study

Raz J, 'The Rule of Law and its Virtue' (1977) 93 LQR 195

Rogers K M, *The Internet and the Law* (Macmillan International Higher Education 2011)

Rowbottom J, 'To Rant, Vent and Converse: Protecting Low Level Digital Speech' (2012) 71(2) CLJ 355

Rudman R & Bruwer R, 'Defining Web 3.0: Opportunities and Challenges' (2016) 34(1) Electron Libr 132

Scaife L, *Handbook of Social Media and the Law* (Routledge 2015)

Select Committee on Democracy and Digital Technologies, *Digital Technology and the Resurrection of Trust* (HL 2019-21, 77)

Shirky C, *Here Comes Everyone* (Penguin 2008)

Smartt U, *Media & Entertainment Law* (Taylor & Francis 2017)

Statista, 'Most Popular Social Networks Worldwide as of January 2024, Ranked by Number of Monthly Active Users (in Millions)' (*Statista*, 31 January 2024) https://www.statista.com/statistics/272014/global-social-networks-ranked-by-number-of-users/

Statista, 'Number of Internet and Social Media Users Worldwide as of July 2023 (in Billions)' (*Statista*, 22 September 2023) https://www.statista.com/statistics/617136/digital-population-worldwide/

Statista, 'WhatsApp - Statistics & Facts' (*Statista*, 30 August 2023) https://www.statista.com/topics/2018/whatsapp/#topicOverview

Statista, 'Number of Instagram Users Worldwide from 2020 to 2025 (in Billions)' (*Statista*, 29 August 2023) https://www.statista.com/statistics/183585/instagram-number-of-global-users/

Statista, 'Distribution of Facebook users in the United Kingdom as of April 2023, by Age Group' (*Statista*, 22 May 2023) https://www.statista.com/statistics/1030055/facebook-users-united-kingdom/

Statista, 'Number of Internet Users Worldwide from 2005 to 2017 (in Millions)' (*Statista*, 2018) https://www.statista.com/statistics/273018/number-of-internet-users-worldwide/

Stripe N, 'Online bullying in England and Wales: Year Ending March 2020' (*Office of National Statistics*, 16 November 2020) https://www.ons.gov.uk/peoplepopulationandcommunity/crimeandjustice/bulletins/onlinebullyinginenglandandwales/yearendingmarch2020

Taylor J & Nicolas J, 'Twitter traffic sinks in wake of changes and launch of rival platform Threads' *The Guardian* (London, 10 July 2023) https://www.theguardian.com/technology/2023/jul/10/twitter-traffic-sinks-in-wake-of-changes-and-launch-of-rival-platform-threads-elon-musk

The BBC, 'Threads app signs up 100m users in less than a week' *The BBC* (London, 10 July 2023) https://www.bbc.co.uk/news/technology-66153244

The BBC, 'Teenager's life "ruined" by Live.me and Twitter "trolls"' *The BBC* (London, 24 October 2017) http://www.bbc.co.uk/news/uk-england-41693437

Titcomb J, 'Facebook now has 2 billion users, Mark Zuckerberg announces' *The Telegraph* (London, 27 June 2017) https://www.telegraph.co.uk/technology/2017/06/27/facebook-now-has-2-billion-users-mark-zuckerberg-announces/

Vidgen B, Margetts H & Harris A, 'How Much Online Abuse Is There? A Systematic Review of Evidence for the UK. Policy Briefing – Full Report' (*The Alan Turing Institute*, 2020) https://www.turing.ac.uk/sites/default/files/2019-11/online_abuse_prevalence_full_24.11.2019_-_formatted_0.pdf

Wong B, 'Top Social Media Statistics and Trends of 2023' (*Forbes,* 18 May 2023) https://www.forbes.com/advisor/business/social-media-statistics/

Woods L, Perrin W & Walsh M, 'It's (Nearly) Here: A Short Guide to the Online Safety Act' (*Carnegie UK*, 19 September 2023) https://carnegieuktrust.org.uk/blog-posts/its-nearly-here-a-short-guide-to-the-online-safety-act/

2 Freedom of Expression

The Online Context

2.1 Introduction

As potently put by Newman:

> Words can be hurtful. They can antagonize [*sic*], they can wound. But words also inform and educate. They can dispel prejudice and reveal unanticipated affinities. We need strong laws to protect us from violence and discrimination, but laws that protect us from hurtful words tend to silence us as well as our antagonists, because they close down rather than open conversations and because they teach good citizens to call the police rather than do the hard work of combating hateful ideas.[1]

Indeed, you cannot discuss the limits of online communications without first discussing the right to freedom of expression. It is a right that intertwines with several fundamental human rights, including, thought, association, and assembly, with these rights often being described as 'closely related civil and political rights'.[2] And '[a]lthough the right to freedom of expression is not in every case the ace of trumps, it is a powerful card'.[3] In fact, for Bernal, freedom of expression is prized above all other freedoms.[4] It is both an individual right, in that citizens have the freedom to speak their own mind and a collective right, in that we have the right to exchange ideas and listen to others' viewpoints. It can be traced back to ancient Greece and Socrates.[5] Since, elements of freedom of expression have been found in various legal instruments in one way or another, including the British Bill of Rights written in 1689 which guaranteed freedom of expression within Parliament.

1 Stephen L. Newman, 'Finding the Harm in Hate Speech: An Argument against Censorship' (2017) 50(3) CJPS 679, 693.

2 Kevin Boyle, 'Thought, Expression, Association, and Assembly' in Daniel Moeckli, Sangeeta Shah, and Sandesh Sivakumaran (eds), *International Human Rights Law* (Oxford University Press 2010) 257.

3 *Douglas v Hello! Ltd* [2001] QB 967 per Brooke L.J. at 982.

4 Paul Bernal, *The Internet, Warts and All: Free Speech, Privacy and Truth* (Cambridge University Press 2018) 102.

5 For an in-depth discussion on the history of freedom of expression, see, Jacob Mchangama, *Free Speech: A Global History from Socrates to Social Media* (Basic Books 2022).

DOI: 10.4324/9781003303683-3

The right to speak freely, without interference, plays a pivotal role in any democratic society.[6] It allows us to challenge state authority, aids in the discovery of truth and can be considered a necessary element of self-fulfilment. There are some states, in which the right to freedom of expression does not exist, but these are states in which many of us would not want to live. But the right to freedom of expression is not absolute, nor has it ever been, with human rights provisions allowing governments to restrict the right to freedom of expression when certain criterions are met, discussed further in Section 2.3. Even as early as 1857 there are examples of individuals having their speech restricted in the United Kingdom, such as the prosecution of a person for writing offensive words relating to Christianity on a gate.[7] Indeed, up until 2008, blasphemy was a criminal offence in England and Wales. In fact, it was not until 2021 that blasphemy was decriminalised in Scotland.

Despite the weight given to freedom of expression, there are clearly limits. The issue lies in what constitutes an exception and it is evidently difficult to find the line between protected and non-protected speech. Nothing has demonstrated this more than the increased usage of social media sites, where internet users have gone from consumers to content creators.[8] Today we live in a world where we share our most personal and intimate information online—but at what point does our behaviour on social media sites go beyond what is legally acceptable, and therefore within the boundaries of freedom of expression, to wholly unacceptable and therefore warrants state interference? Indeed, '[t]he internet is the conduit for communications in the digital age, making it the heart of any system of free expression'.[9] Today, anyone with an internet connection can 'become a town crier with a voice that resonates farther than it could from any soapbox'.[10]

For the UK House of Lords Select Committee on Freedom of Expression, abusing another online was considered to fall outside the scope of freedom of expression.[11] Yet for the UK's Divisional Court 'free speech encompasses the right to offend, and indeed to abuse another'.[12] At the same time, it has come to be accepted that although the online world is inherently public, privacy does exist online—an expansive right that encompasses more than just a private life away from the public domain. It includes the right to personal autonomy.[13] A right that is infringed when a person is subjected to online abuse. As potently put by Bernal '[t]he problem with the internet is that the boundaries between what is public and what is private have

6 *Handyside v The United Kingdom* (1976)1 EHRR 737.

7 John Stuart Mill, *On Liberty* (first published 1859, Enhanced Media 2016) 25.

8 Newman (n 1) 680.

9 Emily B. Laidlaw, *Regulating Speech in Cyberspace: Gatekeepers, Human Rights and Corporate Responsibility* (Cambridge University Press 2015) 280.

10 *Reno v ACLU*, 521 U.S. 884, 896-97 (1997).

11 Communications and Digital Committee, *Free for All? Freedom of Expression in the Digital Age* (2021–22 HL 54) 3.

12 *Scottow v CPS* [2020] EWHC 3421 (Admin) per Justice Warby [43].

13 *Pfeifer v Austria App* no 125561/03 [2007] ECTHR 935 [33].

been more than just blurred; they have been all but obliterated'.[14] A balance must therefore be struck, even in the digital world, between freedom of expression and the right to privacy.

The following chapter will outline how freedom of expression is currently protected through international treaties, focussing on Article 19 of the Universal Declaration of Human Rights (UDHR) and regional human rights instruments, with emphasis on Article 10 of the European Convention on Human Rights (ECHR). The right to privacy as protected under Article 8 of the ECHR will also be explored, alongside Article 17. By way of the Human Rights Act 1998 (HRA), the ECHR has since been incorporated into the legal system of the United Kingdom. The final parts of this chapter will explore the balance between freedom of expression and the right to privacy in a digital age—in which it will be argued throughout this monograph that current approaches to online regulation are a serious threat to freedom of expression. Indeed, if we truly want to eradicate online abuse, societal norms need to be altered first, before legal norms will take effect.

2.2 Article 19 and the Universal Declaration of Human Rights

In 1948 the UDHR was adopted by the United Nations General Assembly to create a unilateral understanding of all aspects of human rights. It was drafted as a response to the travesties of the Second World War and set out for the first time on an international scale, fundamental rights to be universally protected, with 48 states signing the declaration. Though not legally binding on states, it has been incorporated into several further legal provisions and is widely considered as paving the way for other human rights treaties, including, the International Covenant on Civil and Political Rights; the International Convention on the Elimination of all forms of Racial Discrimination; the Convention on the Rights of the Child'; and the Convention on the Rights of Persons with Disabilities—each of which protects freedom of expression.

Under Article 19(1) and (2) of the UDHR:

> Everyone shall have the right to hold opinions without interference. Everyone shall have the right to freedom of expression; this right shall include freedom to seek, receive, and impart information and ideas of all kinds, regardless of frontiers, either orally, in writing, or in print, in the form of art, or through any other media of his choice.

Article 19 of the UDHR is embodied further in Article 19 of the ICCPR—in which the United Kingdom is party to and ratified in 1976—with the United Nations clarifying when this right maybe restricted: '(a) For respect of the rights or reputations of others; (b) For the protection of national security or of public order (ordre public), or for public health or morals'.[15] For the United Nations General

14 Bernal (n 4) 18.
15 International Covenant on Civil and Political Rights Article 19(3).

Assembly, such weight is given to the right to speak freely as it contributes 'to the full development of a person', it 'is essential for any society' and can be considered the 'foundation stone for every free and democratic society'.[16] Indeed, freedom of expression is now considered to be a norm of customary international law and is further instilled in Article 10 of the ECHR—in which its creation was heavily influenced by the UDHR.[17]

2.3 The European Convention on Human Rights

The ECHR came into force on 21 January 1959 and was signed by all 47 Member Sates of the European Council, including the United Kingdom. The ECHR itself consists of several Articles protecting what is considered basic human rights, including the prohibition of torture, the right to life, freedom of expression and the right to privacy. As noted above, by way of the HRA, the ECHR has been incorporated into UK law, taking legal effect in October 2010.

Under the HRA, all public bodies in the United Kingdom are under a lawful obligation to protect human rights, with section 6(3) of the Act defining public bodies as: '(a) a court or tribunal, and (b) any person certain of whose functions are functions of a public nature'. Here, public bodies within the criminal justice system, including the courts, the police, and the Crown Prosecution Service, are under a legal duty to consider human rights when coming to a decision. For example, if a matter were to go before a court of law concerning if a particular message sent online was contrary to law, the court must also consider the right to freedom of expression, alongside other rights contained in the ECHR, such as that of privacy. Further, the courts of the United Kingdom must consider the jurisprudence of the European Court of Human Rights (ECtHR) when coming to a judgment as set out in s.2 of the HRA. However, it does not necessarily mean the court will follow the jurisprudence of Strasbourg, as exceptions have been created through the Common Law.[18]

All rights contained in the ECHR can be split into three types: absolute, qualified, and limited. Absolute rights are considered those basic human rights which the state cannot infringe under any circumstances. So, for instance, the prohibition of torture is an absolute right, which cannot be breached even in times of national emergency or during times of war.[19] Whereas Article 5, the right to liberty, is a limited right whereby it can be restricted under the exceptions contained within

16 Human Rights Committee, 'United Nations International Covenant on Civil and Political Rights: General comment No. 34 – Article 19: Freedoms of opinion and expression' (*United Nations*, 2011) [2] <https://www2.ohchr.org/english/bodies/hrc/docs/gc34.pdf> accessed 8 July 2022.

17 Laidlaw (n 9) 87.

18 The English courts may decline to follow the jurisprudence of the European Court of Human Rights if it is clear that the European Court did not sufficiently appreciate the particular nature of the English Legal System (as per *R v Horncastle* [2009] UKSC 14) or if they are bound by the doctrine of precedent (*Leeds v Price* [2005] W.L.R. 1825).

19 The European Convention on Human Rights Article 15(2).

the Article itself. For instance, an individual can be deprived of their liberty when detained following a court conviction.[20]

The right to freedom of expression and the right to privacy are qualified rights:

> A public authority can sometimes interfere with your rights if it's in the interest of the wider community or to protect other people's rights. These rights are qualified. Qualified rights may need to be balanced against other people's rights or the rights of the wider community to achieve a fair outcome.[21]

All qualified rights can be restricted when three criterions are met: the restriction is prescribed by law (the legality element), the restriction fulfils a legitimate aim (contained in the second paragraph of the Article), and the restriction can be considered as necessary in a democratic society (in which the least intrusive method must be taken).

2.3.1 Prescribed by Law

At its very basic, the concept prescribed by law means that there must be a legal rule in place prohibiting the conduct in question and includes both Common Law provisions and Acts of Parliament. However, it is not simply a case of pointing to a legal provision and stating, 'there's the law'. For a provision to be considered as prescribed by law, it needs to encompass key elements of the principle of legality, a fundamental principle of due process which is discussed at length in the following chapter. The ECtHR has identified four key questions in determining if a legal provision can be said to be prescribed by law:[22]

1. Does the domestic legal system sanction the infraction?
2. Is the relevant legal provision accessible to the citizen?
3. Is the legal provision sufficiently precise to enable the citizen reasonably to foresee the consequences which a given action may entail?
4. Does the law provide adequate safeguards against arbitrary interference with the respective substantive rights?

2.3.1.1 Does the Domestic Legal System Sanction the Infraction?

The ECtHR has given a wide definition to sanction and includes Acts of Parliament, the Common Law, international legal obligations, and secondary sources, such as

20 Ibid., Article 5(1)a.

21 Citizens Advice, 'When can a public authority interfere with your human rights?' (*Citizens Advice*, 2018) <https://www.citizensadvice.org.uk/law-and-courts/civil-rights/human-rights/when-can-a-public-authority-interfere-with-your-human-rights/> accessed 5 September 2018.

22 *Huvig v France*, [1990] ECHR, application no. 11105/84, judgment of 24 April 1990; *Kruslin v France*, [1990] ECHR, application no. 11801/85, judgment of 24 April 1990.

royal decrees. In essence, there must first be a legal provision in place as affirmed in *Norman v The United Kingdom*.[23]

2.3.1.2 *Is the Relevant Legal Provision Accessible to the Citizen?*

The issue of accessibility was discussed at length by the ECtHR in *Sunday Times v The United Kingdom*.[24] *The Sunday Times* had run several newspaper articles detailing an ongoing legal dispute between users of the pharmaceutical drug Thalidomide, and the manufacturer of the drug Distillers. Thalidomide had been given to pregnant women in the late 1950s and early 1960s to help with morning sickness. However, it was later discovered that the drug caused significant deformities in the foetus.

The newspaper articles included arguments that Distillers should not mount a legal defence to the allegations against them. In addition, the articles also included suggestions on some of the evidence that may be presented before the Court. Consequently, the Attorney General was granted an injunction by the domestic courts of the United Kingdom for fear that the reports may affect the outcome of the Distillers trial, under the Common Law offence of Contempt of Court. The Sunday Times challenged the decision before the ECtHR on the grounds that the injunction breached their right to freedom of expression. For the ECtHR, freedom of expression could be limited to maintain the authority of the judiciary, however the law limiting Article 10 needs to be accessible: 'the law must be adequately accessible: the citizen must be able to have an indication that is adequate in the circumstances of the legal rules applicable to a given case'.[25] In essence, citizens must be able to understand the legal provision—a concept that underpins legality as discussed further in Chapter 3. An element the ECtHR concluded was missing in the Common Law provision of Contempt of Court. As a result, the ECtHR concluded the legal provisions governing Contempt of Court at the time were not sufficiently clear, breaching the applicant's right to freedom of expression.[26]

2.3.1.3 *Is the Legal Provision Sufficiently Precise to Enable the Citizen to reasonably foresee the Consequences which a Given Action may Entail?*

For a legal provision to be considered compatible with the ECHR, and a principle which also underpins our understanding of legality, as discussed further in the following chapter, it must be 'action-guiding':

> [A] norm cannot be regarded as a 'law' unless it is formulated with sufficient precision to enable the citizen to regulate his conduct: he must be able—if

23 *Norman v The United Kingdom* (Application no. 41397/17), 6 July 2021.

24 *Sunday Times v The United Kingdom* (1979) 2 EHRR 245.

25 Ibid., [49].

26 The decision of the European Court of Human Rights paved the way for the creation of the Contempt of Court Act 1981.

> need be with appropriate advice—to foresee, to a degree that is reasonable in the circumstances, the consequences which a given action may entail.[27]

Though it is accepted by the ECtHR, and indeed, in many legal philosopher's conceptions of legality, that complete precision would be unattainable and therefore some vagueness is inherent in the law, it cannot be so inherently vague that it would be unforeseeable that a person's actions would invoke the law, or it imposes significant discretion by the state on how the legal provision should be applied.[28] A concept upheld by the ECtHR in *Cantoni v France.*[29]

2.3.1.4 Does the Law Provide Adequate Safeguards against arbitrary Interference with the Respective Substantive Rights?

The foundations of the 'prescribed by law' element in the ECHR is to protect individuals from arbitrary interference of their rights by a state. The law should therefore not confer such discretion on members of the executive or, for instance, actors within the criminal justice system, without providing adequate safeguards from abuse:

> [I]t would be contrary to the rule of law for the legal discretion granted to the executive to be expressed in terms of an unfettered power. Consequently, the law must indicate the scope of any such discretion conferred on the competent authorities and the manner of its exercise with sufficient clarity, having regard to the legitimate aim of the measure in question, to give the individual adequate protection against arbitrary interference.[30]

In essence, safeguards need to be in place to stop arbitrary interference by the state with respective substantive rights, not only in theory but also in reality.[31] Indeed, in the joined cases of *Huvig v France*[32] and *Kruslin v France*,[33] the ECtHR found that despite seventeen safeguards cited by the French government as protecting citizens from the abuse of phone tapping by public authorities, these safeguards were not adequate and therefore the actions of the state were incompatible with the ECHR.

2.3.2 Legitimate Aims

If the legal provision under scrutiny can be considered as prescribed by law, next the court must consider if the restriction placed on the substantive right, for instance,

27 *Sunday Times* (n 24) [49].

28 See for example, *Malone v the United Kingdom*, [1984] ECHR, application no. 8691/79, judgment of 2 August 1984.

29 *Cantoni v France*, no. 7862/91, 12 April 1995.

30 *Malone* (n 28) [68].

31 *Gillan v The United Kingdom* (2010) 50 EHRR 45.

32 *Huvig* (n 22).

33 *Kruslin* (n 22).

a legal provision restricting the right to freedom of expression, fulfils a legitimate aim. Under each qualified right within the ECHR a list of aims whereby a right can be restricted is laid out. The legitimate aims differ depending on the right under question. For example, the right to freedom of expression can be restricted when pursuing one of the following aims[34] (alongside fulfilling the criterions set out in Section 2.3.1 above and 2.3.3 below):

1. National security;
2. Territorial integrity or public safety;
3. The prevention of disorder or crime;
4. The protection of health or morals;
5. The protection of the reputation or rights of others;
6. Preventing the disclosure of information received in confidence; or
7. For maintaining the authority and impartiality of the judiciary.

Failure in a restriction to fulfil a legitimate aim will render the restriction unlawful.[35] As discussed in Section 2.3.6 similar aims can be found in Article 8: the right to privacy.

However, it is not simply a case of stating, for example, that by law we will prohibit anti-vaxers from suggesting that vaccinations are being used to track citizens, under the presumption that this would protect the health of those living in a society. Or indeed, we may not mention another person online without permission to protect the rights and freedoms of others (a legitimate aim under Article 8(2)). Instead, the legal provision restricting the substantive right not only needs to fulfil a legitimate aim, but it also needs to be necessary in a democratic society.

2.3.3 Necessary in a Democratic Society

For a restriction to be considered as necessary in a democratic society, it is for the courts to establish:

> whether: (i) the legislative objective is sufficiently important to justify limiting a fundamental right; (ii) the measures designed to meet the legislative objective are rationally connected to it; and (iii) the means used to impair the right or freedom are no more than is necessary to accomplish the objective.[36]

In essence, the state must take the least intrusive method possible to restrict a substantive Article right to render it necessary in a democratic society and in turn, to be

34 The European Convention on Human Rights Article 10(2).
35 *Handyside* (n 6) [49].
36 *de Freitas v Permanent Secretary of Ministry of Agriculture, Fisheries, Lands and Housing* [1999] 1 A.C. 69 (PC) 80.

compatible with the ECHR, as reinforced by the ECtHR in *Dudgeon v The United Kingdom.*[37]

Dudgeon concerned the lawfulness of a legal provision contained in the law of Northern Ireland which criminalised homosexuality. For the applicant who sought leave before the ECtHR, the law breached Article 8(1) of the Convention: the right to privacy. For the ECtHR, the law in question (section 11 of the Criminal Law Amendment Act 1885) was sufficiently clear and pursued one of the legitimate aims contained under Article 8(2) (protection of morals). However, issues arose in relation to the restriction being necessary in a democratic society:

> It cannot be maintained in these circumstances that there is a 'pressing social need' to make such acts criminal offences, there being no sufficient justification provided by the risk of harm to vulnerable sections of society requiring protection or by the effects on the public. On the issue of proportionality, the Court considers that such justifications as there are for retaining the law in force unamended are outweighed by the detrimental effects which the very existence of the legislative provisions in question can have on the life of a person of homosexual orientation like the applicant. Although members of the public who regard homosexuality as immoral may be shocked, offended or disturbed by the commission by others of private homosexual acts, this cannot on its own warrant the application of penal sanctions when it is consenting adults alone who are involved.[38]

Essentially, it was found that criminalising homosexual acts between two consenting adults was not considered necessary in a democratic society therefore breaching Article 8 of the ECHR.[39] As eloquently put in *Olsson v Sweden,* any 'inference [must] correspond to a pressing social need and, in particular, that it is proportionate to the legitimate aim pursued'.[40]

2.3.4 Summary

So long as the three elements discussed above, prescribed by law, fulfilment of a legitimate aim and necessity are met, a state can lawfully infringe on a qualified right protected under the ECHR. It is also important to note that upon making a judgment as to whether a state has impinged upon a substantive right under the ECHR, the ECtHR must have regard to the margin of appreciation whereby the ECtHR often asserts that states are, in principle, in a better position than the courts

37 *Dudgeon v The United Kingdom* (1981) 4 EHRR 149.

38 Ibid., [60].

39 Later parts of this chapter will examine in detail the right to privacy as guaranteed under Article 8 of the European Convention of Human Rights.

40 *Olsson v Sweden* (A/250) (1994) 17 EHRR 134 [67].

to assess the needs of its citizens.[41] Consequently, a state is provided with a degree of discretion on how it fulfils its obligations under the ECHR—including how it protects and balances, the right to freedom of expression and the right to privacy, though the ECHR makes it clear, under Article 17, that you cannot use one right, such as the right to freedom of expression, to disregard another's right, such as the right to privacy.

2.3.5 Article 10

The right to freedom of expression goes beyond just a right to speak freely without state interference. It can include any form of communication, including, though not limited to, art, radio, books, and dance. As outlined at the start of this chapter it is often considered the touchstone of all rights and plays a fundamental role in any democratic society:

> Not only is freedom of expression inseparable from freedom of thought, association, and assembly, it is essential for the enjoyment of all rights, including economic, social, and cultural rights. It is a vital freedom for development, the functioning of a democracy, and modern economies.[42]

The right to freedom of expression is protected under Article 10(1) of the ECHR:

> Everyone has the right to freedom of expression. This right shall include freedom to hold opinions and to receive and impart information and ideas without interference by public authorities and regardless of frontiers.

In essence, every citizen has the right to express an opinion or thought under Article 10 and this does not stop at the borders of a state (the regardless of frontiers element of the right). In fact, in today's digital world, the protection of frontiers would include the prohibition of blocking access to the internet.[43] But as previously acknowledged, the right to freedom of expression can be limited under certain circumstances, though needs to be carefully monitored 'because if wrongly or excessively invoked, they can "chill" the freedom or even eliminate it'.[44] The question remains, at what point does a person's communication or conduct go beyond the right to freedom of expression to warrant state interference?

41 The doctrine of the margin of appreciation has been developed by the European Court of Human Rights as a way to ensure that the Court recognises that the Convention is an international instrument covering 47 countries who may differ in significant ways with regard to their cultural and societal norms and that, therefore, it would not be appropriate for the Court too readily rule against a signatory state for a breach of a Convention right.

42 Boyle (n 2) 266.

43 *Akdeniz v Turkey* (dec.) (no. 20877/10, 11 March 2014).

44 Boyle (n 2).

The jurisprudence of both the ECtHR and the domestic courts of the United Kingdom supports the idea that different types of speech incur different types of protection:

> There are undoubtedly different types of speech, just as there are different types of private information, some of which are more deserving of protection in a democratic society than others. Top of the list is political speech. The free exchange of information and ideas on matters relevant to the organisation of the economic, social and political life of the country is crucial to any democracy. Without this, it can scarcely be called a democracy at all.[45]

Whereas political speech is given the highest form of protection, speech which can be labelled as mere gossip is not necessarily shielded from the law, even in today's digital world.[46] Yet, despite the notion that mere gossip may not be protected under the law, the ECtHR has upheld that the right to freedom of expression includes the right to be offensive in *Handyside v The United Kingdom.*[47]

In the early 1970s, Richard Handyside was prosecuted and convicted under the Obscene Publications Act 1959 and 1964, for the distribution of 'The Little Red School Book'. The book, which was written by two Danish school teachers in 1969, contained several pages on sex, drugs, and alcohol—with the United Kingdom courts upholding that the distribution of the book was contrary to law, resulting in Handyside lodging an application before the ECtHR, claiming his right to freedom of expression had been breached.

Though Handyside's appeal was unsuccessful, with the ECtHR concluding that the restriction did not breach Article 10, the judges did support the concept that freedom of expression encompasses the right to be offensive:

> Freedom of expression constitutes one of the essential foundations of such a society, one of the basic conditions for its progress and for the development of every man. Subject to Article 10(2), it is applicable not only to 'information' or 'ideas' that are favourably received or regarded as inoffensive or as a matter of indifference, but also to those that offend, shock or disturb the state or any sector of the population.[48]

A concept that is further supported by the United Nations who maintain that there needs to be a 'genuine and serious incitement to extremism, as opposed to ideas that simply offend, shock or disturb others'[49] to restrict freedom of expression.

But despite the notion that we do have the right to be offensive under the ECHR, there are limits for the ECtHR, including, speech which can be labelled as holocaust

45 *Campbell v MGN Ltd* [2004] UKHL 22, [2004] 2 A.C. 457 per Lady Baroness-Hale [148].

46 Jacob Rowbottom, 'To Rant, Vent and Converse: Protecting Low Level Digital Speech' (2012) 71(2) CLR 355, 357.

47 *Handyside* (n 6).

48 Ibid., [49].

49 Laura Scaife, *Handbook of Social Media and the Law* (Routledge 2015) 42.

denial,[50] hate speech,[51] and defamatory statements,[52] to name but a few restrictions. In fact, the ECtHR has even upheld that the publication of photographs of Princess Caroline of Monaco was not protected under Article 10 and was an infringement upon her right to privacy, as protected under Article 8.[53]

2.3.6 Article 8

Under Article 8 '[e]veryone has the right to respect for his private and family life, his home and his correspondence'. As discussed earlier, like freedom of expression, the right to privacy is a qualified right and can be restricted when prescribed by law, where it is necessary in a democratic society, and the restriction fulfils one or more of the following legitimate aims:[54]

1. National security;
2. Public safety or the economic well-being of the country;
3. The prevention of disorder or crime;
4. The protection of health or morals; or
5. The protection of the rights and freedoms of others.

But the right to privacy encompasses more than just a right to a private life beyond the public domain, it is one of the most expansive rights under the ECHR and has been interpreted to include, for instance, the protection of reproductive rights,[55] the rights of one's image,[56] police surveillance,[57] and gender identity.[58]

In fact, privacy:

> extends to aspects relating to personal identity, such as a person's name or picture, and furthermore includes a person's physical and psychological integrity; the guarantee afforded by Article 8 of the Convention [ECHR] is primarily intended to ensure the development, without outside interference, of the personality of each individual in his relations with other human beings. There is therefore a zone of interaction with others, even in a public context, which may fall within the scope of 'private life'.[59]

Privacy therefore includes the right for a person not to have their physical or psychological integrity infringed. With Brownsword arguing that, 'privacy is the most

50 *Lehideux and Isorni v France* ECHR 23 September 1998.
51 *Glimmerven en Hagenbeek v Netherlands* [1979] ECTHR 8.
52 *Lingens v Austria* (1986) 8 EHRR 407.
53 *Von Hannover v Germany* (2005) 40 EHRR 1.
54 The European Convention on Human Rights Article 8(2).
55 *A, B and C v Ireland* (2010) Application no. 25579/05.
56 *López Ribalda and others v Spain* (2019) Applications nos.1874/13 and 8567/13.
57 *Shimovolos v Russia* (2011) Application no. 30194/09.
58 *Hämäläinen v Finland* (2014) Application no. 37359/09.
59 *Pfeifer* (n 13).

protean of concepts, with [...] both spatial and informational articulations'.[60] The concept of privacy therefore underpins free speech,[61] complete free speech would limit the speech of the minority,[62] whilst also having significant psychological effects on those subjected to it. Indeed, a right to privacy, even on the internet, does exist—as the Samaritans discovered following the creation, and ultimate backlash, in its 'Samaritans Rader App'.

In 2014 the Samaritans, a UK-based mental health charity, released an App aimed at reducing suicide. The App, once downloaded onto a person's smart device, would link to the users Twitter profile to scan tweets in the user's homepage. Using a list of predetermined keywords, the App would then alert the user if someone who they 'followed' on Twitter indicated possible suicidal tendencies, even if the other person did not have access to the App. Following its launch, the Samaritans came under heavy criticism for breaching Twitter user's privacy. The original stance taken by the Samaritans was to justify the App's usage by arguing that comments made on Twitter were in the public domain, and as a result, there was no expectation to privacy. Two months after the App was launched, the Samaritans suspended its usage.[63]

A balance must therefore be struck between freedom of expression and privacy. In fact:

> any restriction of the right to freedom of expression must be subjected to very close scrutiny. But so too must any restriction of the right to respect for private life. Neither Article 8 nor Article 10 has any pre-eminence over the other in the conduct of this exercise. As Resolution 1165 of the Parliamentary Assembly of the Council of Europe (1998), para 11, pointed out, they are neither absolute nor in any hierarchical order, since they are of equal value in a democratic society.[64]

A concept reinforced in Article 17 of the ECHR.

2.3.7 Article 17

Article 17(1) states:

> Nothing in this Convention may be interpreted as implying for any State, group or person any right to engage in any activity or perform any act aimed at the destruction of any of the rights and freedoms set forth herein or at their limitation to a greater extent than is provided for in the Convention.

60 Roger Brownsword, *Law, Technology and Society: Re-imaging the Regulatory Environment* (Routledge 2019) 303 as inspired by Graeme Laurie, *Genetic Privacy* (Cambridge University Press 2002).

61 Bernal (n 4) 145.

62 Ibid., 106.

63 Samaritans, 'Samaritans rader' (*The Samaritans*, 10 March 2015) <https://www.samaritans.org/how-we-can-help-you/supporting-someone-online/samaritans-radar> accessed 26 October 2018.

64 *Campbell* (n 45) per Lord Hope of Craighead [115].

Put simply, a person cannot rely on the protection of a given Article within the ECHR to the detriment of another right. So, for example, a person cannot spread racial hatred as part of their right to freedom of expression if it is considered to significantly affect other rights contained in the ECHR as illustrated in *Glimmerven en Hagenbeek v Netherlands.*[65]

In *Glimmerven en Hagenbeek* the ECtHR was asked to consider if the Netherlands had breached the applicant's right to freedom of expression by prohibiting them from distributing leaflets. Glimmerven and Hagenbeek, which had previously been declared as a prohibited organisation under the Civil Code of the Netherlands, had distributed leaflets advocating the removal of 'all Surinamers, Turks and other so-called guest workers from the Netherlands'. Before the ECtHR the Dutch Government accepted that they had infringed the applicant's right to free speech, however the Government argued that Article 17(1) prohibited Glimmerven and Hagenbeek from exploiting Article 10 to spread racial hatred:

> The Netherlands' authorities in allowing the applicants to proclaim freely and without penalty their ideas would certainly encourage the discrimination prohibited by [these] provisions of the Convention [… such activities being] contrary to the text and spirit of the Convention.[66]

The arguments put forward by the Dutch government's legal team were accepted by the ECtHR, where the court held that the applicant's right to freedom of expression was lawfully infringed by the state.

2.3.8 Summary

It is evident that both Articles 10 and 8 can, at times, come into conflict with one another. Though in theory, neither provision is more important than the other. However, for Foster:

> [i]nstead of assuming free speech to be good in itself, and only capable of restriction in the most exceptional cases, we are in danger of reversing that assumption and challenging the speaker to prove the overriding good that speech will prevail.[67]

This is even more apparent when it comes to the regulation of the digital world, in particular, the regulation of speech on social media platforms. In recent years, we have seen a drive towards regulating not only social media platforms themselves, through Acts such as the United Kingdom's Online Safety Act 2023 (OSA), but also a continued emphasis being placed on the criminal law to tackle abusive communications on social media sites. Indeed, as will be reflected throughout

65 *Glimmerven en Hagenbeek* (n 51).

66 Ibid., [196].

67 Steve Foster, 'Do We Want Free Speech or Not? Modern Challenges to Free Speech' (2019) 24(2) Cov. L. J 70, 81.

discussions in this monograph, we are at huge risk of restricting freedom of expression and in turn, overcriminalising speech, even though such use of the law can be considered a fundamental breach of the principle of legality. For instance, as will be discussed in Chapter 6, we have seen an alarming increase in the use of s.127(1) of the Communications Act 2003 and the Malicious Communications Act 1988 in criminalising communications, despite the vague terminology used in both provisions. In fact, when it comes to discussions on freedom of expression and social media, society seems to heavily focus on the 'bad' rather than the 'good'.

2.4 Freedom of Expression v the Right to Privacy: The Online Context

The balancing of Articles 8 and 10 is not unique to the digital age. Much of the jurisprudence relating to these two rights stems from traditional forms of media such as the press.[68] In *Campbell v MGN Limited*, the House of Lords had to directly address the issue of freedom of expression versus the right to privacy:

> The present case concerns one aspect of invasion of privacy: wrongful disclosure of private information. The case involves the familiar competition between freedom of expression and respect for an individual's privacy. Both are vitally important rights. Neither has precedence over the other. The importance of freedom of expression has been stressed often and eloquently, the importance of privacy less so.[69]

The continued expansion of the internet and the sheer dominance of social media today, have created further complexities when it comes to balancing freedom of expression and privacy, as the lines between what is considered public and private have been heavily distorted.

As internet usage has grown, how we communicate our thoughts, anger, frustrations, or feelings has evolved, with social media playing a pivotal role. Whereas once-upon-a-time, we would have vented our frustrations to our loved ones, or even our pets, today we can now vent these frustrations to the world at large, in a matter of seconds—with detrimental costs. For example, in 2015 an individual tweeted the following: 'Going to Africa. Hope I don't get AIDS [*sic*]. Just kidding. I'm white!' to her 170 followers just as she got on a plane from JFK Airport to Cape Town. By the time she arrived at her destination, eleven hours later, her name was trending on Twitter, she was making headline news across the world and in the process of her flight, she was dismissed from her employment and was met at Cape Town airport by armed police.[70] Yet, these are extreme cases and it is the extreme

68 Lorna Woods, 'Social Media: It is not just about Article 10' in David Mangan and Lorna E. Gillies (eds), *The Legal Challenges of Social Media* (Edward Elgar Publishing 2017) 109. For Bernal, the use of traditional media law is not necessarily suitable for social media. See, Bernal (n 4) 25.

69 *Campbell* (n 45) per Lady Baroness-Hale [148] and per Lord Nicholls of Birkenhead [12].

70 Jon Ronson, 'How one stupid tweet blew up Justine Sacco's life' *The New York Times Magazine* (New York, 12 February 2015) <https://www.nytimes.com/2015/02/15/magazine/how-one-stupid-tweet-ruined-justine-saccos-life.html> accessed 5 February 2019.

cases that tend to focus the public's attention, resulting in the cry that being able to say such things online 'should be criminal'. There will of course always be cases which should invoke the criminal law, so long as those legal provisions criminalising such conduct comply with the principle of legality, as discussed in the following chapter. But if we focus primarily on the extreme cases, the cases which catch the attention of the media, and use these as the rationale for increasing the criminal law in prohibiting certain types of speech, we run the risk of 'borderline' speech also being caught up in such an approach. We also run the risk of Government's implementing legislation which can be abused for their own political agenda, such as the OSA, which puts pressure on social media companies to remove content that illustrates those crossing the channel in a 'positive' light.[71] In fact, despite, the 'negative' side of social media, which is often the focus of such discussions, freedom of expression on social media platforms plays a significant role within society, and an important one at that.

2.4.1 Freedom of Expression Online

The ability to express oneself freely without fear of being censored is the bedrock of any democratic society. 'If competing views are publicly debated and exposed to public scrutiny the good will, over time, drive out the bad'[72] with social media playing an important role in amplifying the 'wrongs' within a given society. There is no doubt that social media has changed every aspect of everyday life, but this is not necessarily always a bad 'thing'.

Politicians can now directly communicate with their constituents on mass about important matters. Likewise, constituents can contact their local MP with a 'click-of-a-button'. The police can use social media to help locate a person who has been reported missing. Citizens can also use social media to draw attention to campaigns, call for change in society or even hold politicians to account. There are ample examples of how social media has been pivotable in drawing people's attention to social injustice, two of which, #MeToo and Black Lives Matter are explored below. Indeed, for Laidlaw '[w]here the technology of the internet is particularly facilitative is a platform for mobile licence social and political change'.[73]

2.4.1.1 #MeToo

#MeToo is a political movement that started in 2006 on the now debunked social media platform MySpace but gained significant attention in 2017, following the exposure of sexual-abuse allegations against a former Hollywood movie director,

71 See, OFCOM, 'Protecting people from illegal harms online. Volume 2: The causes and impacts of online harms' (*OFCOM*, 9 November 2023) 168 – 178 <https://www.ofcom.org.uk/__data/assets/pdf_file/0019/271243/volume-2-illegal-harms-consultation-1.pdf> accessed 4 January 2024.

72 *Campbell* (n 45) per Lord Bingham [148].

73 Laidlaw (n 9) 25.

Harvey Weinstein. The hashtag, which trended on several occasions in 2017, is used to expose the continued sexual harassment and sexual assault experienced by individuals, in particular women, within society: 'If all the women who have been sexually harassed or assaulted wrote "Me too" as a status, we might give people a sense of the magnitude of the problem'.[74] Here, using the hashtag, individuals spoke publicly on platforms such as Twitter to tell their stories of sexual harassment and assault, allowing those who had been subjected to this abuse, having their voices heard—and in many cases, having their voices heard for the first time.

But the #MeToo movement did not just stop at social media sites, it did create significant changes within society. Widespread coverage of the movement, particularly in Hollywood, led to high-profile dismissals and adaptions of the hashtag emerging to call out sexual harassment in schools, sports, and politics. Through social media, voices could be heard on mass putting pressure on organisations, governments, and the criminal justice system to do more to tackle sexual harassment. Indeed, we have seen the use of social media sites such as Facebook and X used to highlight the everyday sexism that exists within society with #everydaysexism;[75] the use of social media to organise protests to challenge the 'sexism, racism and xenophobia of the Trump Administration';[76] and as a space for women to challenge stereotypical conceptions of rape.[77] Social media has been pivotal in drawing attention to how women are treated within society—it has been a force for good.

Though of course, it must not be dismissed that social media has also been used to target women, as discussed in Section 2.4.2.2 below. However, if we always focus on the 'bad' we risk losing the 'good'—such as the use of social media platforms to evoke wider societal change.

2.4.1.2 Black Lives Matter

Black Lives Matter (BLM) is a movement advocating for non-violent civil disobedience in protest against incidents of police brutality and all racially motivated violence against African-American people. It was founded in 2013 but gained significant attention in 2020, following the death of George Floyd on 25 May 2020

74 Nadja Sayei, 'Alyssa Milano on the #MeToo movement: "We're not going to stand for it any more"' *The Guardian* (London, 1 December 2017) <https://www.theguardian.com/culture/2017/dec/01/alyssa-milano-mee-too-sexual-harassment-abuse> accessed 6 July 2022.

75 Laura Bates, 'The everyday sexism project' (*Everydaysexism*, 2019) <https://everydaysexism.com/> accessed 6 February 2019.

76 Kaitlynn Mendes, Jessica Ringrose and Jessalynn Keller, *Digital Feminist Activism: Girls and Women Fight Back Against Rape Culture* (Oxford University Press 2019) 4.

77 Jessamy Gleeson, '"(Not) working 9–5": The consequences of contemporary Australian-based online feminist campaigns as digital labour' (2016) 16(1) MIA 77 <http://journals.sagepub.com/doi/pdf/10.1177/1329878X16664999> accessed 13 January 2020.

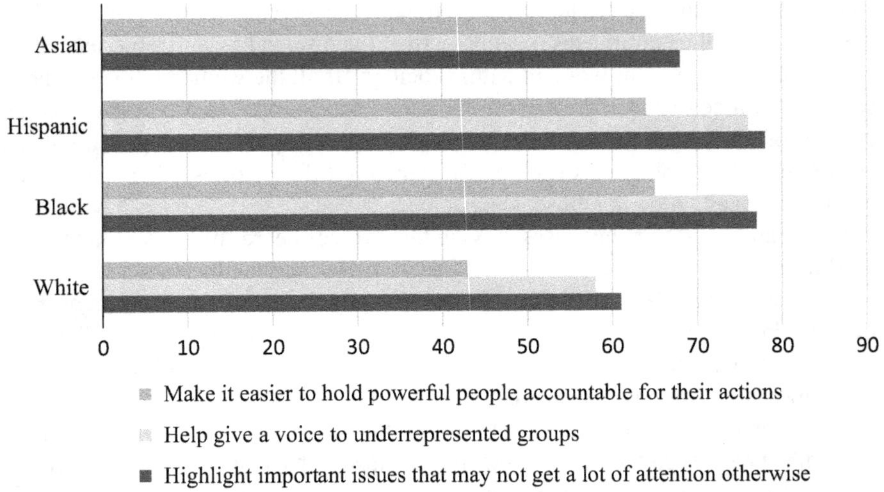

Figure 2.1 Percentages of social media users by race who say the following statements describe social media very or somewhat well.

Note: Brooke Auxier, 'Social media continue to be important political outlets for Black Americans' (*Pew Research Centre*, 11 December 2020) <https://www.pewresearch.org/fact-tank/2020/12/11/social-media-continue-to-be-important-political-outlets-for-black-americans/> accessed 18 July 2022.

at the hands of a Minneapolis police officer.[78] His death made headline news, with video footage of the incident being actively shared across social media sites.[79]

Though the tragic events of that day were also shared through traditional forms of media, such as the press and radio, social media, like that of the #MeToo movement discussed above, played an important role in bringing the events of George Floyd's death to the attention of the public worldwide. In fact, in the following days after the death of George Floyd, nearly 8.8 million tweets contained the hashtag: #BlackLivesMatter.[80] Indeed, social media has played an important role in giving a voice to marginalised groups, with research undertaken by the Pew Research Centre, as shown further in Figure 2.1, finding that for those Black Americans who took part in the study, social media was an 'important political outlet':

> Black social media users have been particularly likely to say that these sites are personally important to them for getting involved with issues they care

78 Kim Parker, Juliana Menasce and Monica Anderson, 'Amid protests, majorities across racial and ethnic groups express support for the Black Lives Matter Movement' (*Pew Research Centre*, 12 June 2020) <https://www.pewresearch.org/social-trends/2020/06/12/amid-protests-majorities-across-racial-and-ethnic-groups-express-support-for-the-black-lives-matter-movement/> accessed 27 July 2022.

79 Brooke Auxier, 'Social media continue to be important political outlets for Black Americans' (*Pew Research Centre*, 11 December 2020) <https://www.pewresearch.org/fact-tank/2020/12/11/social-media-continue-to-be-important-political-outlets-for-black-americans/> accessed 18 July 2022.

80 Ibid.,

about or finding like-minded people. They are also likely to express positive views about the impact of these platforms for holding powerful people accountable for their actions and giving a voice to underrepresented groups.[81]

2.4.1.3 Summary

Freedom of expression on social media sites must be protected from arbitrary government interference. Its use allows users to call out social injustice and express a need for change within society and this should not be forgotten—as noted throughout the discussion above if we always focus on the 'bad' we risk eroding the 'good':

> First, if any opinion is compelled to silence, that opinion may, for aught we can certainly know, be true. To deny this is to assume our own infallibility. Secondly, though the silenced opinion be an error, it may, and very commonly does, contain a portion of truth [...] it is only by collusion of adverse opinions, that the remainder of the truth has any chance of being supplied.[82]

But it is also important to remember that complete free speech online does not exist because complete free speech would, in turn, reduce the speech of the minority and directly affect another's right to privacy.

2.4.2 Privacy Online

There is a 'darker' side to social media, where voices of the minority can be shut down and behaviours such as racism are rife. As evidenced in Article 17 of the ECHR, freedom of expression cannot be used to justify such behaviour(s). In essence, we cannot, and should not, use our own right to freedom of expression to limit another's right to free speech or indeed, to infringe upon another's right to privacy. Social media now forms part of everyday life which cannot be separated from that of the real world.[83] Or as potently put by Bernal, '[t]he internet is now integral to the way society operates'.[84] And even in the digital world, privacy does exist online.

As outlined in Section 2.3.6 privacy is more than just a right to have your private information kept out of the public domain. It encompasses a range of expansive rights, including the right to bodily autonomy, with the ECtHR finding that a person's body is an intimate aspect of a person's private life[85] and includes protection of a person's mental health.[86] When it comes to online abuse, it is clear, that such

81 Ibid.,

82 Mill (n 7) 40.

83 Barry Wellman and Caroline Haythornthwaite (eds), *The Internet in Everyday Life* (John Wiley & Sons 2008) 25.

84 Bernal (n 4) 19.

85 *Y.F. v Turkey* (24209/94, 22 October 2003).

86 *Bensaid v the United Kingdom* (no. 44599/98, 6 May 2001).

behaviours can have a significant effect on a person's mental wellbeing and in turn, breaches that person's right to privacy:

> We have seen that specific harms resulting from being the recipient of abusive and offensive communication[s] online can include: (1) psychological effects and emotional harms; (2) physiological harms; including suicide and self-harm; (3) exclusion from public online space and corresponding feelings of isolation; (4) economic harms; and (5) wider societal harms.[87]

Indeed, like that of freedom of expression, there are ample examples of how a person's right to privacy is infringed in the online world, two examples, cyberbullying and violence against women and girls, are explored in Sections 2.4.2.1 and 2.4.2.2 below.

2.4.2.1 Cyberbullying

Not only has the internet created new and unique ways to taunt another, but behaviours which were once confined to the physical world have now emerged online, with cyberbullying being a prime example.[88] Cyberbullying takes the form of traditional bullying behaviour but is conducted online and unlike bullying, which is commonly associated with the playground, it can occur around the clock.

Each year Ditch the Label, with the help of educational institutions, conducts a survey exposing the extent of bullying in the United Kingdom. In recent years they have included the concept of cyberbullying. In 2016 they found that 65% of participants had experienced some form of cyberbullying, an increase of 3% on the previous year.[89] By 2018, this figure had risen to 66%.[90] However, it is important to note that in the 2020 bullying study by Ditch the Label, this figure had dropped to 27%.[91] Whilst on the other hand, research by OFCOM into the online habits of users in the United Kingdom found that '[a]mong children aged 8–15 who have experienced bullying, more than eight in ten (83%) had experienced it through a

87 Law Commission, *Abusive and Offensive Online Communications: A Scoping Report* (Law Com No 381, 2018) [3.30].

88 Ibid., [1.33].

89 Ditch the Label, 'The annual bullying survey 2016' (*Ditch the Label*, 2016) 14 <http://www.ditchthelabel.org/wp-content/uploads/2016/04/Annual-Bullying-Survey-2016-Digital.pdf > accessed 18 October 2016. See also, Ditch the Label, 'The annual bullying survey 2015' (*Ditch the Label*, 2015) 18 <http://ditchthelabel.org/downloads/abs2015.pdf> accessed 26 February 2016.

90 Ditch the Label, 'The annual bullying survey 2018' (*Ditch the Label*, 2018) 13 <https://www.ditchthelabel.org/wp-content/uploads/2018/06/The-Annual-Bullying-Survey-2018-2.pdf> accessed 12 December 2018.

91 Ditch the Label, 'The annual bullying survey 2020' (*Ditch the Label*, 2020) 16 <https://dtl-beta-website-assets.s3.amazonaws.com/The_Annual_Bullying_Survey_2020_2_a8a474bb3f.pdf> accessed 12 October 2023.

communications device such as a phone or laptop[92].' Indicating, that such behaviour is still present online.

Cyberbullying can have detrimental effects on those who are subjected to it:

> The psychological harm inflicted by cyberbullying, just like bullying, is reflected in low self-esteem, school failure, anger, anxiety, depression, school avoidance, school violence, and suicide.[93]

Further research conducted by John *et al* found that individuals who were bullied online were twice as likely to self-harm or attempt suicide.[94] Clearly, those subjected to such behaviour(s) online are having their right to bodily autonomy violated and in turn, their right to privacy is interfered with. A notion which was supported by the ECtHR in *Buturugă v Romania*,[95] where it was held that the states failure to investigate cyberbullying/cyber-violence in the context of domestic violence, was an infringement on the applicant's human rights under Article 8 (the right to privacy) and Article 3 (the prohibition of torture).

Despite cyberbullying being evidently present on social media sites, as noted above, bullying is not new and no matter how we change the law to prohibit such behaviour, including both in the physical and virtual world, we will never eradicate bullying or cyberbullying as it's embedded within societal norms. Consequently, the law will always fail to tackle these issues, so long as societal norms remain stagnant. As highlighted by Reed and Murray, it is only through changes in societal norms, such as better education, that legal provisions will take effect.[96] However, changing such norms in the online world is inherently difficult:

> In the physical world norms have developed (or have evolved) incrementally over centuries. In the modern world individuals normally live their lives in a mature and stable normative landscape. The norms which defined the landscape do change of course, but they change gradually and over time scales which allow most people to come to terms with their slow evolution. Cyberspace is arguably different because online communities are still in their formative phase […] in human terms, we might see cyberspace as a young adult, taking its origins as being from the mid-1990s. Or we could say that cyberspace really began when the internet became a genuine medium of mass communication, in which case we might set its birthday as Tuesday, 26 August 2008 when Facebook announced that it had 100 million users. If

92 OFCOM, 'Online Nation' (*OFCOM*, 2022) 8 https://www.ofcom.org.uk/__data/assets/pdf_file/0023/238361/online-nation-2022-report.pdf accessed 15 November 2023.

93 Qing Li, 'Cyberbullying in High Schools: A Study of Students' Behaviours and Beliefs about This New Phenomenon' (2010) 19(4) J. Aggress Maltreat 372, 374.

94 Ann John *et al*, 'Self-Harm, Suicidal Behaviours, and Cyberbullying in Children and Young People: Systematic Review' (2018) 20(4) J Med Internet Res <https://www.jmir.org/2018/4/e129/> accessed 12 December 2018.

95 *Buturugă v Romania* (no. 56867/15, 11 June 2020).

96 Chris Reed and Andrew Murray, *Rethinking the Jurisprudence of Cyberspace* (Elgar 2018) 103.

> so, cyberspace is not even a teenager and most of the largest communities therein are around a similar age.[97]

If this is the case, we have yet to set a precedent on what is or is not socially acceptable on social media sites, the law can only do so much—we need to change societal norms first, rather than attempting to restrict the right to freedom of expression or engage in arbitrary use of the criminal law.

2.4.2.2 Violence Against Women and Girls Online

The notion that online abuse is embedded in societal norms is further illustrated in the use of social media to abuse women online. In recent years, we've witnessed an increase in the use of social media sites to send abusive and often misogynistic comments to women online, with research undertaken by Amnesty International exposing that in the United Kingdom, of those women who took part in the study, 1 in 5 had experienced online abuse.[98] The abuse experienced by these women had a direct impact on their right to privacy, shown further in Figure 2.2.

Of those women who took part in the study, 55% of participants in the United Kingdom stated that they had experienced anxiety, stress, or panic attacks as a result of online abuse;[99] with a further 24% of those surveyed across Denmark, Italy, New Zealand, Poland, Spain, Sweden, the United Kingdom and United States feeling that their family's safety was at risk. But it was not just their right to bodily autonomy, as protected under Article 8, that was infringed. The findings of the study also uncovered that 76% of those who said they had been subjected to online abuse had, as a result of the conduct they were subjected to, changed how they used social media. Online abuse which results in the user changing their online habits not only infringes Article 8 but also Article 10—freedom of expression. As noted by Bernal, '[t]o exclude oneself from the internet is to put oneself at a massive disadvantage'.[100]

However, like cyberbullying discussed above, violence against women and girls is not new. In fact, it is rife in every aspect of society, including, for example, the police.[101] This is again another example of a behaviour which is inherent within society and consequently, will also be mirrored in the online world. Without changing attitudes and norms amongst citizens, no legislation will adequately deal with the 'darker' side of social media.

97 Ibid., 108.

98 Amnesty International UK, 'Online abuse of women widespread in UK' (*Amnesty International*, 2017) <https://www.amnesty.org.uk/online-abuse-women-widespread> accessed 3 October 2018.

99 Ibid.,

100 Bernal (n 4) 19.

101 His Majesty's Inspectorate of Constabulary and Fire and Rescue Services, 'An inspection of vetting, misconduct, and misogyny in the police service' (*HMICFS*, 2 November 2022) <https://hmicfrs.justiceinspectorates.gov.uk/publications/an-inspection-of-vetting-misconduct-and-misogyny-in-the-police-service/> accessed 1 February 2023.

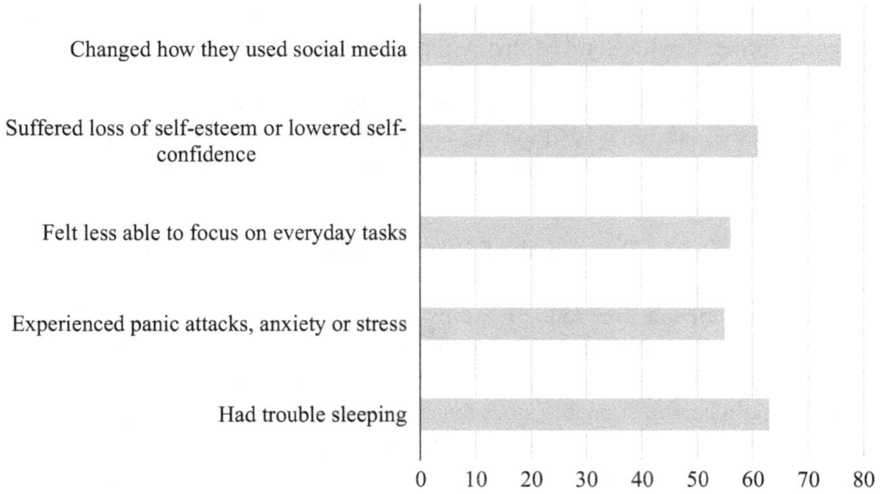

Figure 2.2 The effects of online abuse on women (in percentages) who took part in Amnesty International's research project.

Note: Amnesty International UK, 'Online abuse of women widespread in UK' (Amnesty International, 2017) <https://www.amnesty.org.uk/online-abuse-women-widespread> accessed 3 October 2018.

2.4.2.3 Summary

It cannot be disputed that online abuse does have detrimental consequences and can result in the loss of life;[102] this should never be downplayed. However, it should be that '[i]n a well-functioning liberal democratic society [...] censorship will be the exception and not the rule'.[103] With increasing pressure being placed on governments to tackle the harms associated with the online world, we need to be careful to ensure we are striking an appropriate balance between Articles 8 and 10. In which the criminal law, when underpinned by the principle of legality, should only be used in the most extreme cases to ensure freedom of expression is protected.

2.4.3 Getting the Balance Right

As new technology continues to emerge and evolve, striking the balance between privacy and freedom of expression will play a pivotal role in future regulation. It

102 For example, in 2012 Erin Gallagher (13) took her own life after being continually subjected to anonymous abusive comments on the social media site, ASK.FM. See, Greg Harkin, 'Family devastated after tragic Erin (13) takes own life after vicious online bullying' *Irish Independent* (Dublin, 29 October 2012) <https://www.independent.ie/irish-news/family-devastated-after-tragic-erin-13-takes-own-life-after-vicious-online-bullying-28824852.html> accessed 12 December 2018.

103 Newman (n 1) 680.

is generally accepted today, that there is role for the law in regulating individuals conduct online. But it should be that Articles 10 and 8 work together and:

> [g]etting that balance right is one thing for the policymakers and legislators, but it is also an issue for policing and prosecutors, to make sure that we are not criminalising the trivial, the passionate or those really strongly held views.[104]

A balance, as will be shown in the following chapters, we are currently failing to reach.

It's important that freedom of expression remains an integral concept when making decisions on how to regulate individuals on social media platforms, alongside social media companies themselves. Shutting down voices, for fear that such conduct might be objectionable, does not create change in society. Instead, it drives these voices to other areas of the internet, and this is how echo-chambers are created. We cannot challenge another person's viewpoint if we cannot hear that person's view in the first place—shutting down the conversation does not allow for public debate. As discussed in Section 2.4.1, there is a positive side to social media, which is often forgotten. We need to be able to partake in equal debate and that means, hearing opinions which maybe unfavourable for some. Freedom of expression encompasses challenging 'people by exposing them to opposing points of view'.[105]

That is not to say we should have no limits on our online communications, there is a line. But to draw that line we first need to understand that there is a difference between privacy and harm. Privacy is about protecting significant breaches of a person's personal autonomy. Harm is about reducing the impact of behaviours we may find objectionable. Indeed, the 'harms' associated with the online world means we could slip into the realms of regulating the offensive—and we have the right to be offensive. Second, any restrictions on freedom of expression need to be sufficiently clear and comply with the basic principle of legality in the criminal law, which as will be exposed in later chapters, is not always the case.

2.5 Chapter Summary

As highlighted throughout this chapter, the right to freedom of expression is considered a fundamental aspect of any democratic society. It is a right that is embedded in both national and international provisions across the globe, alongside the right to privacy. In theory, neither right is to be considered more important than the other as both are considered vital to any working and stable society. Instead, a balance must be struck between the two—something that has become extremely complex in the wake of the emergence of new technology.

104 House of Lords, *Select Committee on Communications: Freedom of Expression Online* (HL Deb 2021-04, 23) per David Tucker p.4.

105 Laidlaw (n 9) 31.

As the ways in which we can communicate become easier due to the advancement of modern technology, it has also become simpler to abuse, offend or upset another. A message sent online is a message sent to the world. In turn, as will be shown in further chapters of this monograph, there has been a growing emphasis placed on the criminal law to prohibit such speech. But much of the speech that is objected to online, such as racist and misogynistic commentary, is inherent within society and not unique to the digital world. We therefore need to be extremely careful in how we approach the criminalisation of speech to ensure privacy is maintained, whilst also ensuring we do not excessively infringe on the right to freedom of expression.

The above highlights the importance of protecting the right to freedom of expression—it can, and has been, a force for good. Yet, as noted above, it is often the 'bad' which focuses the attention of policymakers, the press and members of the public, especially when it comes to social media. Even in 'stable' states, such as that of the United Kingdom, it is vital that we do not overstep the mark and prohibit people from saying things they are perfectly within their right to say, through the coercive nature of the criminal law. Especially at a time when other rights are being restricted, such as the right to protest.[106] As will be explored in further chapters of this monograph the studies used to justify the use of the criminal law to restrict the right to freedom of expression, are significantly flawed.

Reference list

Amnesty International UK, 'Online Abuse of Women Widespread in UK' (*Amnesty International*, 2017) https://www.amnesty.org.uk/online-abuse-women-widespread

Auxier B, 'Social Media Continue to Be Important Political Outlets for Black Americans' (*Pew Research Centre*, 11 December 2020) https://www.pewresearch.org/fact-tank/2020/12/11/social-media-continue-to-be-important-political-outlets-for-black-americans/

Bates L, 'The Everyday Sexism Project' (*Everydaysexism*, 2019) https://everydaysexism.com/

Bernal P, *The Internet, Warts and All: Free Speech, Privacy and Truth* (Cambridge University Press 2018)

Boyle K, 'Thought, Expression, Association, and Assembly' in Moeckli D, Shah S & Sivakumaran S (eds), *International Human Rights Law* (Oxford University Press 2010)

Brownsword R, *Law, Technology and Society: Re-imaging the Regulatory Environment* (Routledge 2019)

Citizens Advice, 'When Can a Public Authority Interfere with Your Human Rights?' (*Citizens Advice*, 2018) https://www.citizensadvice.org.uk/law-and-courts/civil-rights/human-rights/when-can-a-public-authority-interfere-with-your-human-rights/

Communications and Digital Committee, *Free for All? Freedom of Expression in the Digital Age* (2021 – 22 HL 54).

Ditch the Label, 'The Annual Bullying Survey 2018' (*Ditch the Label*, 2018) https://www.ditchthelabel.org/wp-content/uploads/2018/06/The-Annual-Bullying-Survey-2018-2.pdf

106 See for example, The Police, Crime, Sentencing and Courts Act 2022 part 3, which has made significant changes to the right to protest in the United Kingdom.

Ditch the Label, 'The Annual Bullying Survey 2016' (*Ditch the Label*, 2016) http://www.ditchthelabel.org/wp-content/uploads/2016/04/Annual-Bullying-Survey-2016-Digital.pdf

Ditch the Label, 'The Annual Bullying Survey 2015' (*Ditch the Label*, 2015) http://ditchthelabel.org/downloads/abs2015.pdf

Foster S, 'Do We Want Free Speech or Not? Modern Challenges to Free Speech' (2019) 24(2) Cov L J 70

Gleeson J, '"(Not) Working 9–5": The Consequences of Contemporary Australian-based Online Feminist Campaigns as Digital Labour' (2016) 16(1) MIA 77 http://journals.sagepub.com/doi/pdf/10.1177/1329878X16664999

Harkin G, 'Family devastated after tragic Erin (13) takes own life after vicious online bullying' *Irish Independent* (Dublin, 29 October 2012) https://www.independent.ie/irish-news/family-devastated-after-tragic-erin-13-takes-own-life-after-vicious-online-bullying-28824852.html

His Majesty's Inspectorate of Constabulary and Fire & Rescue Services, 'An Inspection of Vetting, Misconduct, and Misogyny in the Police Service' (*HMICFS*, 2 November 2022) https://hmicfrs.justiceinspectorates.gov.uk/publications/an-inspection-of-vetting-misconduct-and-misogyny-in-the-police-service/

House of Lords, *Select Committee on Communications: Freedom of Expression Online* (HL Deb 2021-04, 23)

Human Rights Committee, 'United Nations International Covenant on Civil and Political Rights: General Comment No. 34 - Article 19: Freedoms of Opinion and Expression' (*United Nations*, 2011) https://www2.ohchr.org/english/bodies/hrc/docs/gc34.pdf

John A *et al*, 'Self-Harm, Suicidal Behaviours, and Cyberbullying in Children and Young People: Systematic Review' (2018) 20(4) J Med Internet Res https://www.jmir.org/2018/4/e129/

Laidlaw E B, *Regulating Speech in Cyberspace: Gatekeepers, Human Rights and Corporate Responsibility* (Cambridge University Press 2015)

Laurie G, *Genetic Privacy* (Cambridge University Press 2002)

Law Commission, *Abusive and Offensive Online Communications: A Scoping Report* (Law Com No 381, 2018)

Li Q, 'Cyberbullying in High Schools: A Study of Students' Behaviours and Beliefs about This New Phenomenon' (2010) 19(4) J Aggress Maltreat 372

Mchangama J, *Free Speech: A Global History from Socrates to Social Media* (Basic Books 2022)

Mendes K, Ringrose J & Keller J, *Digital Feminist Activism: Girls and Women Fight Back Against Rape Culture* (Oxford University Press 2019)

Mill J S, *On Liberty* (first published 1859, Enhanced Media 2016)

Newman S L, 'Finding the Harm in Hate Speech: An Argument against Censorship' (2017) 50(3) CJPS 679

OFCOM, 'Protecting People from Illegal Harms Online. Volume 2: The Causes and Impacts of Online Harms' (*OFCOM*, 9 November 2023) https://www.ofcom.org.uk/__data/assets/pdf_file/0019/271243/volume-2-illegal-harms-consultation-1.pdf

OFCOM, 'Online Nation' (*OFCOM*, 2022) https://www.ofcom.org.uk/__data/assets/pdf_file/0023/238361/online-nation-2022-report.pdf

Parker K, Menasce J & Anderson M, 'Amid Protests, Majorities Across Racial and Ethnic Groups Express Support for the Black Lives Matter Movement' (*Pew Research Centre*, 12 June 2020) https://www.pewresearch.org/social-trends/2020/06/12/amid-protests-majorities-across-racial-and-ethnic-groups-express-support-for-the-black-lives-matter-movement/

Reed C & Murray A, *Rethinking the Jurisprudence of Cyberspace* (Elgar 2018)

Ronson J, 'How one stupid Tweet blew up justine Sacco's life' *The New York Times Magazine* (New York, 12 February 2015) https://www.nytimes.com/2015/02/15/magazine/how-one-stupid-tweet-ruined-justine-saccos-life.html

Rowbottom J, 'To Rant, Vent and Converse: Protecting Low Level Digital Speech' (2012) 71(2) CLR 355

Sayei N, 'Alyssa Milano on the #MeToo movement: "We're not going to stand for it any more"' *The Guardian* (London, 1 December 2017) https://www.theguardian.com/culture/2017/dec/01/alyssa-milano-mee-too-sexual-harassment-abuse

Scaife L, *Handbook of Social Media and the Law* (Routledge 2015)

The Samaritans, 'Samaritans Rader' (*The Samaritans*, 10 March 2015) https://www.samaritans.org/how-we-can-help-you/supporting-someone-online/samaritans-radar

Wellman B & Haythornthwaite C (eds), *The Internet in Everyday Life* (John Wiley & Sons 2008)

Woods L, 'Social Media: It Is Not Just about Article 10' in Mangan D & Gillies L E (eds), *The Legal Challenges of Social Media* (Edward Elgar Publishing 2017)

3 Regulating Social Media

Theoretical Positioning

3.1 Introduction

Since the creation of the internet, and indeed, the expansion of new technology in general, how the internet should be regulated has often been debated in the academic literature, parliament, and society. There is no 'one size fits all' approach to the regulation of new technology, especially when it comes to social media. How we should regulate social media platforms is often debated in the mainstream press. In fact, there does not seem to be a day that goes by without a news story concerning the regulation of social media platforms—often these stories are embedded in the 'darker' side of social media, as discussed in Chapter 2. Much of the response to date has been 'more criminal law, please'.

Consequently, different theoretical positionings have emerged to try and create a universal understanding of how we *should* regulate the online world, with the first concept, cyberlibertarian theory, gaining significant coverage in the early 90s, long before the likes of social media as we know it today. Since then, further theoretical concepts have been created, including cyber-paternalism, network communitarianism, and the governance model. The first part of this chapter will discuss these theoretical concepts. It will be argued that regardless of which theory you associate with, each is underpinned by the concept of legality.

The second part of this chapter will examine the key principles of legality. Here, the chapter outlines how legality is protected on an international scale, with particular reference to the Universal Declaration of Human Rights (UDHR) and International Criminal Law (ICL), before turning to examine how legality is protected regionally by the European Convention on Human Rights (ECHR).[1] Next, Fuller's conception of legality will be outlined, drawing on the works of other legal philosophers. The final parts of this chapter will discuss what the law should strive for to be considered compatible with the principle of legality.

1 The background of the Universal Declaration of Human Rights and European Convention on Human Rights were discussed in the previous chapter.

DOI: 10.4324/9781003303688-4

3.2 Regulating Social Media

The regulation of the internet is not a new phenomenon. Since the early 90s, regulatory frameworks have emerged across the globe suggesting approaches to tackling the problems associated with the online world. Four theoretical positionings have emerged: (1) cyberlibertarianism; (2) cyber-paternalism; (3) network communitarianism; and (4) the governance model. Though each focusses on the regulation of new technology in general, each model is relevant in the wider discussions on regulating social media platforms.

3.2.1 Cyberlibertarian Theory

Early theorists, most notably John Perry Barlow through the Electronic Frontier Foundation, disputed that governments could impose legal obligations in cyberspace. Barlow, following the enactment of the Communications Decency Act 1996 in the United States, published a Declaration of Independence for Cyberspace:

> I declare the global social space we are building [the internet] to be naturally independent of the tyrannies you seek to impose on us. You have no moral right to rule us, nor do you possess any methods of enforcement we have true reason to fear.[2]

For Barlow, the internet represented a space beyond the realms of government interference, free from political gain and outside the reach of the criminal law.[3] Cyberlibertarianism

> refers to a perspective (some would say philosophy) which claims that cyberspace and the internet should be regarded as uncontrolled and unregulated electronic spaces where anyone is free to be whatever they wish and express themselves however they like.[4]

Those who endorse cyberlibertarianism suggest that the internet is a separate entity from that of the physical world, and consequently, beyond state interference. In essence, for cyberlibertarians 'earthbound' laws should not apply to cyberspace, for several reasons.[5] First, the process of law making is the exercise of power over those persons whom the state can control and for this to work, you need the consent

2 John Perry Barlow, 'A declaration of the independence of cyberspace' (*Electronic Frontier Foundation*, 8 February 1996) <https://www.eff.org/cyberspace-independence> accessed 16 November 2018. Note this declaration was originally sent *via* email.

3 For example, see the work of Esther Dyson, George Gilder, George Keyworth and Alvin Toffler, 'Cyberspace and the American Dream: A Magna Carta for the Knowledge Age' (1994) Future Insight <http://www.pff.org/issues-pubs/futureinsights/fi1.2magnacarta.html> accessed 26 September 2018.

4 David J. Bell, Brian D. Loader, Nicholas Pleace and Douglas Schuler, *Cyberculture: The Key Concepts* (Routledge 2004) 35.

5 Paul Bernal, *The Internet, Warts and All: Free Speech, Privacy and Truth* (Cambridge University Press 2018) 20.

of the people to be governed. Whereas unlike in the physical world, 'in cyberspace, physical boundaries no longer function as signposts informing individuals of the obligations assumed by entering into a new, legally significant place'.[6] Second, if the law were to be imposed on cyberspace, whose law should take precedence? You might be entering cyberspace in the United Kingdom but viewing content from the United States, with Dyson, Gilder, Keyworth, and Toffler arguing that the emergence of new technology, such as the internet, has created an 'information superhighway' which should be for the benefit of its users, and consequently beyond the reach of the law.[7] They go as far as arguing that even computer hacking is for the benefit of 'economic growth and trade leadership'.[8] But how then, should the internet be regulated?

For Post and Johnson, who endorse a cyberlibertarian approach, cyberspace should be treated as a separate geographical location, in which 'laws' or rules will evolve naturally. Like that of churches, clubs, and other social organisations, cyber institutions can create their own rules which would govern users of the internet, rather than imposing state-based law. In essence, rules or 'laws' would be created by individuals in cyberspace as opposed to a centralised legal system. Cyberlibertarianism is essentially built on the premise that the lack of borders on the internet means that regulation by states is impossible, with this theoretical perspective gaining momentum within some internet-based organisations. For instance, Wikipedia founder Jimmy Wales has been vocal about the internet being beyond the realms of state intervention.[9] Indeed, for early cyberlibertarian theorists, the internet is *akin* to the Wild West.

But this utopia of internet regulation is unattainable. As the digital world expands and creeps into every aspect of everyday life in the physical world, it is inevitable the law will intertwine with our online conduct. Most notably for Reed,[10] whilst a physical body remains in a place controlled by a government, the law will have no choice but to intervene—and nothing has demonstrated this more than social media.

3.2.2 Cyber-paternalism

Whereas those who endorse a cyberlibertarian approach to the 'regulation' of the online world believe the internet should be free from interference of traditional lawmakers, those who take a cyber-paternalistic approach, believe that the internet can, and is, regulated through its design:

6 David Johnson and David Post, 'Law and Borders: The Rise of Law in Cyberspace' (1996) 48 SLR 1367, 1389.

7 Dyson, Gilder, Keyworth and Toffler (n 3).

8 Ibid.,

9 David Golumbia, 'Cyberlibertarianism: The Extremist Foundations of "Digital Freedom"' (Clemson University, South Carolina, September 2013).

10 Chris Reed, *Internet Law: Text and Materials* (Cambridge University Press 2004) 174–175.

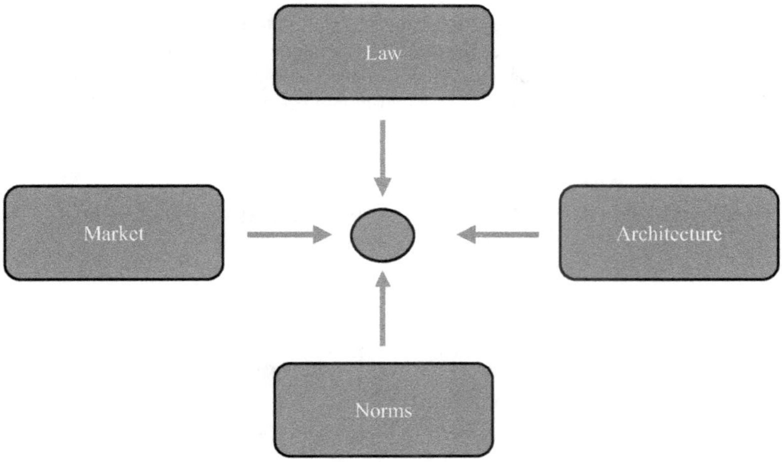

Figure 3.1 Lessig's modalities.

> Cyber-paternalists believe that the guidance of the state, or the elite, achieved through manipulation of software code or network hardware, is necessary to prevent cyberspace from becoming anarchic or simply inefficient.[11]

In essence, the 'internet is regulated by its architecture',[12] whereby we can alter and manipulate the design of an internet platform to regulate the conduct of the user, as supported in the work of Reidenberg who argues that the regulation of the online world occurs in two ways: first, through contractual agreements between internet providers; second, through its own design.[13]

For Lessig, how we regulate behaviour (whether online or offline) is embedded in the four 'Modalities of regulation'—law, markets, architecture, and norms:

> Norms constrain through the stigma that a community imposes; markets constrain through the price they exact; architectures constrain through the physical burdens they impose; and law constrains through the punishment it threatens.[14]

With each 'modalities of regulation' interacting with one another. Lessig uses what he terms a 'pathetic dot' to illustrate his argument, as shown in Figure 3.1. Here the 'pathetic dot' represents an individual, with the four 'modalities of regulation' seen as external forces which puts pressure on the 'pathetic dot' to act in a particular manner. Thereby, rather than the internet being impossible to regulate due to

11 Chris Reed and Andrew Murray, *Rethinking the Jurisprudence of Cyberspace* (Elgar 2018) 144.
12 Ibid., 149.
13 Joel Ridenberg, 'Governing Networks and Rule-Making in Cyberspace' (1996) 45 Emory Law J 911.
14 Lawrence Lessig, *Code Version 2.0* (Basic Books 2006) 124.

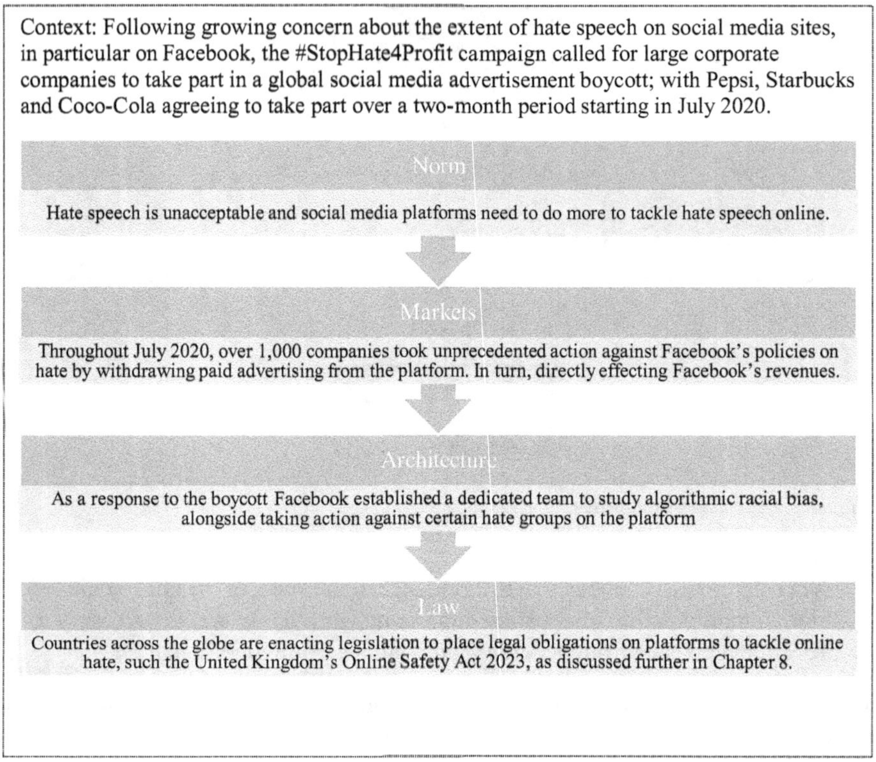

Figure 3.2 #StopHate4Profit.

its design, i.e., no borders as endorsed by cyberlibertarians, it is, in fact, regulated by its own architecture, rooted in the four 'modalities of regulation': law, markets, architecture, and norms.

An example of this can be seen in the #StopHate4Profit campaign, as illustrated in Figure 3.2.

Whereas cyberlibertarians argue that the internet is free from traditional regulation, for instance, free from the coercive nature of the law, cyber-paternalists argue that law and platform design can work together to regulate the online world. An ideal that has gained significant momentum in recent years, with governments across the globe calling for privacy-by-design. Put simply:

> In the same way that law is about control—aiming to instruct people how to behave and providing an incentive for obedience by sanctioning those who do not comply—code also controls behaviour.[15]

Though, it is important to note that for those who endorse a cyber-paternalist approach, the regulation of code should be through governments, rather than private entities.

15 Ibid., 86.

However, this approach is not without fault:

> Lessig's belief assumes three things: first, that lawmakers can always use law to exercise control over those whom it is addressed, a belief [... that is ...] distinctly over-optimistic. Second, that code can be compelled to be written in a particular way in accordance with the designs of lawmakers which [...] cannot be assumed. Third, it assumes that the law's requirements are commands, which are either complied with or flouted.[16]

For Murray, this school of thought fails to consider that 'code is not purely a design or architectural tool it also has a social or communicative function'.[17] Codes can be overwritten. Codes need constant improvement. In essence, the regulation of new technologies is significantly more complex, particularly in a social media context, than both cyberlibertarian and cyber-paternalism theory can comprehend. In fact, cyber-paternalism neglects that humans are not two-dimensional and come with their own 'baggage' which influences the regulatory world.

3.2.3 Network Communitarianism

A further theoretical approach to the regulation of the online world is network communitarianism, as coined by Murray.[18] Stemming from a mix of Actor Network Theory (ANT) (the 'theory of social transactions which accepts a role for non-human actors in any social situation')[19] and Social Systems Theory (SST) (the theory that a person's behaviour is influenced by several factors that work together as a system), Murray argues:

> when taken together they can illuminate much of our understanding of communications and social interaction in a networked environment such as the internet with a variety of actors, both human and non-human.[20]

So, whereas Lessig focussed on one 'pathetic dot', Murray argues, that by applying the theories of ANT and SST, the 'pathetic dot' cannot be considered as an individual in its own right. The individual is influenced by social transactions by non-human actors (ANT). For instance, in a social media setting, the person will be influenced by the content of their social media feed, which is based on algorithms set by the platforms themselves. Alongside being influenced by the system around them (SST), such as a person's political standpoint. In essence, the individual, or the 'pathetic dot' as termed by Lessig, must always be considered in its wider context:

16 Ibid., 151–152.

17 Andrew Murray, *Information Technology Law* (5th edn, Oxford University Press 2023) 68.

18 Andrew Murray, *The Regulation of Cyberspace: Control in the Online Environment* (Routledge 2007).

19 Murray (n 17).

20 Ibid., 69.

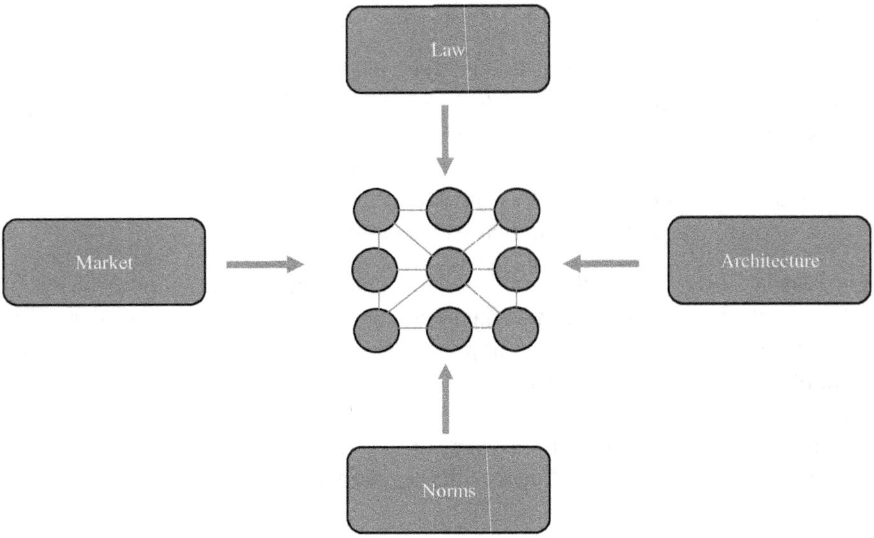

Figure 3.3 Murray's regulatory discourse.

> when one examines the modalities of regulation proposed by Lessig we find that of the four, three of them—laws, norms, and markets—are in fact a proxy for community-based control. Laws are passed by lawmakers elected by the community; markets are merely a reflection of value, demand, supply, and scarcity as reflected by the community in monetary terms; and norms are merely the codification of community values. I [Murray] recognized [*sic*] that these 'socially mediated modalities' reflected an active role for the 'dot' in the regulatory process; far from being a 'pathetic dot' which was the subject of external regulatory forces, the dot was in fact an 'active dot' taking part in the regulatory process.[21]

In essence, whereas cyber-paternalism argues that technology can be regulated and controlled through design, Murray argues that technology enables rather than constrains, in which individuals, considering their social, community, moral, political stances, etc., are active in accepting or rejecting regulation, in which we have gone from one 'pathetic dot' to a 'matrix of dots', all of which influence the four 'modalities of regulation'. See Figure 3.3. A clear example of this, as given by Murray, is the lack of prosecutions under the Obscene Publications Act 1959 and 1964 for privately viewing obscene material using an internet connection,[22] as the morality of the public has evolved to understand that the viewing of pornographic material online, is no longer morally objectionable to the point in which the law should intervene.

21 Ibid., 69–71.
22 Ibid., 62.

For Murray, this approach to online regulation includes the complexity of human nature, and the complex nature of the online world, though he does accept that criminal law is also needed—but this should only be in the most extreme cases. For both Reed and Murray we need to ensure legality in whichever form of regulatory model we subscribe to is maintained to ensure legitimacy in cyberspace.[23] The approach endorsed by both Reed and Murray as to the 'laundry list' of what legality should encompass, is discussed further in Section 3.4.

3.2.4 The Governance Model

Though access to the online world has evolved to be considered a human right in itself,[24] to enter the 'virtual world' you need to go through a gatekeeper. Two types of gatekeepers exist:

1. 'The gatekeeper that controls access to information and acts as an inhibitor by limiting access to or restricting the scope of the information';[25] and
2. A gatekeeper who acts as 'innovator, change, agent, communication channel, link, intermediary, helper, adapter, opinion leader, broker, and facilitator'.[26]

The governance model, as endorsed by Laidlaw recognises the importance of gatekeepers in the regulatory framework of the internet, in which she argues that their approach to regulation needs to be grounded in human rights and corporate responsibility, using the right to freedom of expression to illustrate why this is the case.[27]

The requirements which should be placed on gatekeepers, for Laidlaw, depend wholly on the type of gatekeeper and in particular, the impact it has on democracy, with Laidlaw suggesting that three types of gatekeepers exist:[28]

1. Micro-gatekeepers—these are sites which have some involvement in democratic discussions but are closed and restricted. An example given by Murray is the *Huffington Post*;[29]
2. Authority gatekeepers—these are high trafficking sites (i.e., a high proportion of users) but you do not need to access them to use the internet. Here, some social media platforms would be considered as an authority gatekeeper. Indeed, at the time in which Laidlaw was writing, Facebook would have been considered an

23 Reed & Murray (n 11) 200–230.
24 United Nations General Assembly (47th session) Resolution 47: The promotion, protection and enjoyment of human rights on the Internet (7 July 2021).
25 Emily B. Laidlaw, *Regulating Speech in Cyberspace: Gatekeepers, Human Rights and Corporate Responsibility* (Cambridge University Press 2015) 40.
26 Cheryl Metoyer-Duran, 'Information Gatekeepers' (1993) 28 ARIST 111, 118.
27 Laidlaw (n 25).
28 Ibid., 51–57.
29 Andrew Murray, *Information Technology Law* (4th edn, Oxford University Press 2019) 72.

authority gatekeeper. However, Facebook has grown beyond anything anyone could have expected, and today is more *akin* to a macro-gatekeeper; and
3. Macro-gatekeepers—sites, applications etc., that you must go through in order to access the online world. For example, search engines such as Google.

Using the governance model, Laidlaw accepts that the law on its own is not the most effective way to protect human rights online,[30] such as the right to freedom of expression as discussed in Chapter 2. Instead, she endorses the creation of a corporate governance model for the digital age.

The governance model is built on the acceptance that such platforms have advanced so much, that they have the power to distort public opinion and create codes for their own personal gain. Facebook, which is still the biggest social media platform to date, is a prime example of this and has been heavily criticised for distorting public views on politics, following the Cambridge Analytica scandal.[31] Consequently, the most powerful gatekeepers, such as Facebook, should have a responsibility to protect human rights with Laidlaw stating:

> Whether human rights responsibilities should be incurred and the extent of the responsibilities depends on the extent to which the gatekeeper controls deliberation and participation in the forms of meaning-making in democratic society.[32]

Maco-gatekeepers should therefore have the most responsibility in protecting human rights online. Whereas micro-gatekeepers should have the least. This approach to online regulation, as argued by Laidlaw, would be overseen by an independent digital commission (the regulator and adjudicator of the governance model), consisting of three layers of governance.

The top layer includes education, research, and policy, with emphasis placed on educating gatekeepers about the responsibilities they have in protecting human rights, alongside educating the general public. The middle layer encompasses corporate support, including policies, assessment tools, and audits. The bottom level consists of remedial mechanisms, whereby users or businesses can make complaints to the digital commission, where the complainant has been heavily impacted by the decisions or processes of the gatekeeper. The remedial mechanism would include a complaints procedure consisting of dispute resolution and in some instances, fines issued by the digital commission for a failure to comply with human rights.[33] This is the bedrock of the governance model for Laidlaw.

30 Laidlaw (n 25) 62.

31 See, for example, Nicholas Confessore, 'Cambridge Analytica and Facebook: The scandal and the fallout so far' *The New York Times* (New York, 4 April 2018) <https://www.nytimes.com/2018/04/04/us/politics/cambridge-analytica-scandal-fallout.html> accessed 23 January 2023.

32 Emily B. Laidlaw, 'A Framework for Identifying Internet Information Gatekeepers' 24 (2010) Int. Rev. Law Comput. Technol. 263, 267.

33 Laidlaw (n 25) 266.

This approach endorsed by Laidlaw is somewhat similar to Brownsword, who supports the concept of regulation over that of law, which must be grounded not just in human rights but also the principle of legality.[34] As will be discussed in Chapter 8, Laidlaw's approach seems to have been accepted by the United Kingdom's government in their quest to become one of the safest places in the world to go online—though there are some clear differences between what Laidlaw recommended and the approach undertaken in the Online Safety Act 2023 (OSA).

3.2.5 Summary

There is clearly no 'one size fits all' approach to online regulation and as the internet has advanced, governments across the globe have attempted, and failed, to keep pace. Regardless of which theoretical positioning a person assigns to, legality will underpin all these regulatory frameworks. The 'modalities of regulation' as endorsed by Lessig includes, laws and these legal provisions need to encompass key aspects of legality. Cyber-paternalism would also need to include a consideration of legality, alongside network communitarianism. Indeed, the governance model would need to be underpinned by legality to ensure the digital commission stayed within the boundaries set by Parliament.

As social media usage has increased, we have seen a rise in the use of the criminal law to tackle the 'harms' associated with the online world,[35] despite it being clear that the 'mistake of twentieth-century jurists is to assume that rules and norms are the exclusive keys to social ordering'.[36] In fact, technology can and has been used in situations, where the criminal law has failed to control the behaviours of individuals it deems as inappropriate. Brownsword uses the example of building GPS into golf buggies to stop joy ridders, as was done by Warwickshire Golf and Country Club.[37] For Brownsword, technology is the answer to where law, in particular, the criminal law, is struggling, so long as this technology conforms to legality.[38]

Any form of internet regulation, whether it be cyber-paternalism, network communitarianism or the governance model needs to be grounded in the principle of legality. Even more so, where the regulation of online behaviours is embedded in the criminal law framework.

34 Roger Brownsword, *Law, Technology and Society: Re-imaging the Regulatory Environment* (Routledge 2019).

35 See for example, The BBC, 'Teenager's life "ruined" by Live.me and Twitter "trolls"' *The BBC* (London, 24 October 2017) <http://www.bbc.co.uk/news/uk-england-41693437> accessed 5 October 2023.

36 Brownsword (n 33) 6.

37 Ibid., 7.

38 Ibid.,

3.3 The Principle of Legality

The principle of legality is considered a fundamental right, and though there is no definitive definition,[39] it is underpinned by several guiding principles: (1) society should be governed by law; (2) there should be certainty within legal provisions; and (3) the law needs to be accessible, in which members of the public should be able to govern their behaviour in accordance with clear and distinct rules. Legality is therefore a vital condition of the rule of law (the idea that we should be ruled by law, not by man).[40] It is fundamental in any democratic society and of particular importance when it comes to the criminal law where, as discussed in Section 3.5, at worst, a person's liberty could be at risk, or in some countries, a person's life. Put simply, legality prohibits the use of retrospective criminal law; it strives to ensure that laws are defined with the 'maximum clarity which the imperfect medium of language can attain';[41] it helps to protect against arbitrary punishment; and most importantly, it creates legal certainty—without which, anarchy would prevail.

For Luban legality ensures the law is action-guiding, whilst also curtailing the powers of the state.[42] Similarly, for Fuller, the law should not only be action-guiding but should also encompass a further seven principles in a bid to strive for legal excellence, all of which are discussed in Section 3.4,[43] and will be the theoretical positioning of legality underpinning later chapters. Likewise, Bingham's conception of what constitutes the rule of law encompasses key values associated with legality including the ideal that the law must be accessible and so far as possible intelligible, clear and predictable; legal questions should be answered by law and not by discretion; and the protection of human rights.[44] Legality is a principle enshrined in international and regional legal provisions.

3.3.1 Legality on an International Scale

Though there is no true consensus as to the meaning of legality, it is a principle that dates back to 440 AD. It has been embedded throughout legal provisions across the globe. For instance, the principle is enshrined in Article 11(2) of the UDHR which states that:

> [n]o one shall be held guilty of any penal offence on account of any act or omission which did not constitute a penal offence, under national or international law, at the time when it was committed. Nor shall a heavier penalty be

39 Jason N. E. Varuhas, 'The Principle of Legality' (2020) 79(3) Camb. L. J. 578.

40 Hilaire Barnett, *Constitutional & Administrative Law* (5th edn, Cavendish Publishing 2004) 69.

41 Law Commission, *Report on Conspiracy and Criminal Law Reform* (1976) Law Com No. 76 [1.8].

42 David Luban, 'Fairness to Rightness: Jurisdiction, Legality, and the Legitimacy of International Criminal Law' in Samantha Besson and John Tasioulas (eds), *The Philosophy of International Law* (Oxford University Press 2010) 34.

43 Lon L. Fuller, *The Morality of Law* (Yale University Press 1964).

44 Tom Bingham, *The Rule of Law* (Penguin 2011). See also, Lord Bingham, 'The Rule of Law' (2007) 66(1) Camb. Law. J. 67.

> imposed than the one that was applicable at the time the penal offence was committed.

A similar provision is found in Article 15(1) of the International Covenant on Civil and Political Rights (ICCPR):

> No one shall be held guilty of any criminal offence on account of any act or omission which did not constitute a criminal offence, under national or international law, at the time when it was committed. Nor shall a heavier penalty be imposed than the one that was applicable at the time when the criminal offence was committed.

In essence, the principle of legality under international human rights law prohibits the use of retrospective criminal law—which as discussed further in Section 3.3.2.1 is the ideal that a person cannot be convicted of an offence which was not a crime at the time in which the conduct took place.

The principle of legality underpins many other human rights provisions, including the right to life, the right to liberty and the right to a fair trial—rights which would be at significant risk if legality was not maintained. In fact, for the Human Rights Committee of the ICCPR even in times of national emergency, the principle of legality must be upheld.[45] However, the principle of legality encompasses more than the prohibition of retrospective criminal law. Demonstrated further when examining how legality is maintained and protected in ICL.

ICL is, at its very basic, the application of criminal law across borders,[46] consisting of three types of provisions: domestic criminal law enforced on an international scale; treaty-based criminal law (this is the creation of treaties between states which criminalises certain conduct); and pure ICL which includes crimes such as genocide, aggressive war, and crimes against humanity.[47] Legality must be obtained in the creation, publication, and application of ICL.[48]

For Corsi, who endorses a strict approach to legality in ICL, legality encompasses four key principles:[49]

1. *Nullum Crimen Sine lege*—no crime without law (discussed further in Section 3.4.1);
2. *Lex Praevia*—the prohibition of retrospective criminal law (discussed further in Section 3.3.2.1);

45 UN Human Rights Committee, 'General comment no. 29, States of emergency (article 4): International Covenant on Civil and Political Rights' (*United Nations Digital Library*, 2001) <https://digitallibrary.un.org/record/451555?ln=en> accessed 15 August 2022.

46 Douglas Guilfoyle, *International Criminal Law* (Oxford University Press 2016) 3.

47 Luban (n 42) 19.

48 Darryl Robinson, *The Principle of Legality in International Criminal Law* (Legal Studies Research Papers Series 10-08, 2010) 4.

49 Jessica Lynn Corsi, 'An Argument for Strict Legality in International Criminal Law' [2018] 49 Geo. J. Int'l L. 1321.

3. *Lex Certa*—legal certainty within criminal law provisions; and
4. *Lex Stricta*—strict interpretation of the law.

Though Corsi acknowledges that 'strict legality is not a perfect principle [...] strict legality offers the most just, most effective, most coherent, most persuasive, most legitimate and even the most moral approach to ICL'.[50]

3.3.1.1 Lex Certa

Lex certa is the principle that there should be legal certainty within legal provisions, in which a crime should be 'articulated with sufficiently precise wording so that the criminalized [*sic*] conduct is clear'.[51] The drafting of legal provisions should therefore be clear, tangible, and predictable, allowing citizens to govern their behaviour in accordance with law. In essence, a person should be able to foresee that their given actions may invoke the criminal law, as reinforced by the International Criminal Court (ICC) in *Čelebići*[52] with the ICC confirming the connection between legality and the action-guiding nature of the law: 'The purpose of this principle is to prevent the prosecution and punishment of an individual for acts which he reasonably believed to be lawful at the time of their commission.'[53]

Here the ICC upholds the idea that law must be constructed in a clear and precise manner, which without, 'no process of criminalization [*sic*] would be recognized [*sic*]'.[54] Indeed, in *Vasiljević* it was found that 'violence to life and person, prohibited under Article 3 of the GCs [Geneva Conventions], was insufficiently precise to form the basis of a criminal conviction.'[55] As noted by Bassiouni, '[t]he goals of principles of legality are to provide notice as part of general prevention, as well as notice to the accused as part of fairness'.[56]

3.3.1.2 Lex Stricta

Lex stricta is the idea that when interpreting legal provisions, judges should not over-stretch the meaning of a legal provision and instead, they should endorse a strict approach to interpretation. For Bassiouni, 'the basic rule of interpretation embodying the principle of legality is the prohibition or limitation on the use of analogy in judicial interpretation'.[57]

50 Ibid.,
51 Ibid., 1334.
52 *Čelebići Camp, Prosecutor v Delalić (Zejnil) and others,* Appeal Judgment, Case no IT-96-21-A, ICL 96 (ICTY 2001), 20 February 2001, United Nations Security Council [UNSC]; International Criminal Tribunal for the Former Yugoslavia [ICTY]; Appeals Chamber.
53 *Ibid.*, 313.
54 Robinson (n 48) 4.
55 *Prosecutor v Vasiljević*, Case no. IT-98-32-T, Trial Judgment, (Int'l Crim. Trib. for the Former Yugoslavia 29 November 2002) 193.
56 Mahmoud Cherif Bassiouni, *International Criminal Law* (3rd edn, Brill Nijhoff 2008) 98.
57 Ibid., 73.

Consequently, to adhere to the principle of legality and *lex stricta*, where there is doubt over the meaning of legal provisions, interpretation should always fall in the favour of the accused, to render it compatible with the principle of legality. For Fuller, as discussed further in Section 3.4.3, an over-expansive interpretation of criminal provisions, can result in retrospective criminal law.[58] *Lex Stricta* is therefore built on the principle that judges should not create law. However, as Hall acknowledges, the line between judicial interpretation and judicial legislating can be thin,[59] which is why the four principles endorsed by Corsi in underpinning legality in ICL must all work in tangent.[60]

3.3.1.3 Summary

To adhere to the principle of legality from an international stance, each source of law must be significantly clear to allow citizens to reasonably foresee what a given action would invoke because without clarity, free choice and autonomy are heavily affected. Further, only the law can dictate what is a criminal offence, in which retrospective criminal law is prohibited. In turn, judges need to ensure they are not going beyond reasonable interpretations of the law. But these are principles which ICL should strive to achieve whilst also keeping in mind that complete adherence may not always be achievable. There needs to be some air of flexibility in the law. Or as potently put by Corsi:

> While perfect notice—the idea that all persons know and understand all law—is a legal fiction, law makers and those with the power to punish are instructed by these two tenets to take all steps necessary to ensure maximum notice.[61]

Indeed, no valid legal system or democratic society can exist if it does not conform to legality, as reinforced in the ECHR.

3.3.2 The European Convention on Human Rights: The Fundamental Principle of Legality

The principle of legality is further enshrined in the ECHR in two fundamental ways, which as was discussed in Chapter 2, has been incorporated into UK law. First, as discussed in Section 3.3.2.1, legality has specific protection under Article 7, no punishment without law. Second, when it comes to the restriction of rights under the ECHR, at its very basic, the restriction needs to be prescribed by law, which as discussed in the previous chapter encompasses key provisions associated with the principle of legality and will not be repeated here at length.

58 Fuller (n 43) 73.

59 Jerome Hall, *General Principles of Criminal Law* (2nd edn, Lawbook Exchange Ltd 2010) 173.

60 Corsi (n 49) 1332.

61 Ibid., 1335.

3.3.2.1 Article 7: No Punishment without Law

The fundamental principle of legality has specific protection under Article 7(1), no punishment without law, in which the right is considered absolute. As a result, Article 7 cannot be infringed under any circumstances, even in times of national emergency.[62] Similar to Article 11(2) of the UDHR and Article 15(1) of the ICCPR, Article 7 of the ECHR states:

> No one shall be held guilty of any criminal offence on account of any act or omission which did not constitute a criminal offence under national or international law at the time when it was committed.

As acknowledged by the European Court of Human Rights (ECtHR) in *Kafkaris v Cyprus*:[63]

> The guarantee enshrined in Article 7, which is an essential element of the rule of law, occupies a prominent place in the Convention [ECHR] system of protection [...] It should be construed and applied, as follows from its object and purpose, in such a way as to provide effective safeguards against arbitrary prosecution, conviction, and punishment.[64]

In essence, a person cannot be punished for an offence, which was not an offence at the time in which the conduct took place. With Fuller, as discussed in Section 3.4 below and Corsi as discussed above in Section 3.3.1, going as far as to argue that the law should not be overly stretched beyond its original interpretation that it *could* constitute retrospective criminal law.

Similar to ICL, Article 7 is underpinned by two overriding principles: *nullum crimen sine lege* (no crime without law) and *nulla poena sine lege* (no punishment without law).[65] As outlined by Murphy, the concept of legality within the ECHR consists of three interrelated rules: only the law can define a crime and prescribe a penalty, the prohibition of retrospective criminal law, and no harsher penalties can be given then those that are prescribed in the law at the time the offence was committed.[66] The first rule was restated and affirmed in *Kafkaris v Cyprus*,[67] where the court upheld the concept that only the law can define a crime, affirming that 'law'

62 Cian C. Murphy, 'The Principle of Legality in Criminal Law under the European Convention on Human Rights' (2010) 2 Eur. Hum. Rights Law Rev. 192, 207.

63 *Kafkaris v Cyprus* App no. 21906/04 (ECtHR, 12 February 2008).

64 Ibid., [137].

65 Susana Sanz-Caballero, 'The Principle of nulla poena sine lege Revisited: The Retrospective Application of Criminal Law in the Eyes of the European Court of Human Rights' (2017) 28(3) Eur. J. Int. Law 787, 788.

66 Murphy (n 62) 192.

67 *Kafkaris* (n 63) [137].

consists of both Acts of Parliament and the Common Law.[68] With the second and third rule, affirmed in *Welch v The United Kingdom*:

> The concept of 'penalty' in Article 7(1) is, like the notions of 'civil rights and obligations' and 'criminal charge' in Article 6(1), an autonomous Convention concept. To render the protection offered by Article 7 effective, the Court must remain free to go behind appearances and assess for itself whether a particular measure amounts in substance to a penalty within the meaning of this provision.[69]

A person therefore cannot be punished for conduct that was not considered unlawful at the time in which the behaviour took place and is further enshrined throughout the ECHR and the jurisprudence of Strasbourg under the concept of 'prescribed by law'.

3.3.2.2 Prescribed by law

As previously discussed at length in Chapter 2, the prescribed by law element preserved in the ECHR, encompasses key elements of the principle of legality. Therefore, this will not be repeated here, but as a quick reminder to the reader, legality, from a 'prescribed by law' perspective includes:

1. No punishment without law;
2. The law must be accessible;
3. The law must be action-guiding; and
4. Adequate safeguards must be in place.

If any of the above are missing, it cannot be said that the legal provision is prescribed by law and therefore it will be incompatible with the principle of legality.

3.3.2.3 Summary

The principle of legality as embedded in Article 7(1) and enshrined throughout the ECHR and the jurisprudence of the ECtHR creates legal certainty within the law and is described by Murphy as the 'hidden jewel of the Convention [ECHR]'.[70] It encompasses procedural requirements (i.e., there must first be some legal provision in place), alongside substantive or qualitative obligations, most notably accessibility and foreseeability.[71] However, as acknowledged by the ECtHR strict construction of the law is not always achievable:

68 *Sunday Times v The United Kingdom* (1979) 2 EHRR 245.
69 *Welch v The United Kingdom* App no. 17440/90 (ECtHR, 9 February 1995) 247.
70 Murphy (n 62) 206.
71 *Del Río Prada v Spain* [GC], no. 42750/09, ECHR 2013.

> As the Court has already had occasion to note, it is a logical consequence of the principle that laws must be of general application that the wording of statutes is not always precise. One of the standard techniques of regulation by rules is to use general categorisations as opposed to exhaustive lists. The need to avoid excessive rigidity and to keep pace with changing circumstances means that many laws are inevitably couched in terms which, to a greater or lesser extent, are vague.[72]

To render the legal provision compatible with the principle of legality, it must be 'sufficiently clear in the large majority of cases'.[73] Where a provision is considered overly vague, this will render it incompatible with the ECHR.

Consequently, as society changes there needs to be some form of flexibility with the law—it just cannot go beyond what would reasonably be expected, as noted by the House of Lords, in *R v Rimmington*:[74]

> no one should be punished under a law unless it is sufficiently clear and certain [...] and no one should be punished for any act which was not clearly and ascertainably punishable when the act was done [...] It is accepted that absolute certainty is unattainable, and might entail excessive rigidity since the law must be able to keep pace with changing circumstances, some degree of vagueness is inevitable. [75]

Indeed, 'those who skate on thin ice can hardly expect to find a sign which will denote the precise spot where they may fall in'.[76]

The law therefore needs to be adaptable to reflect the fast-changing nature of society; this is especially true with technology. Technology and the internet have evolved at a significant pace and in some instances, the law has struggled to keep pace.[77] The law needs to maintain some form of openness to resolve legal disputes, but this should not be at the detriment of breaching the fundamental principle of legality—particularly where the criminal law is involved.

3.4 Fuller: Legality in the Criminal Law

Legality comprises of the logic that individuals should be able to partake in any activities knowing whether their behaviour breaches the law and includes both a thin and thick approach.[78] It is closely linked to the rule of law. Scholars have

72 *Cantoni v France,* 15 November 1996, Reports of Judgments and Decisions 1996-V [31].

73 Ibid., [32].

74 *R v Rimmington, R v Goldstein* [2005] UKHL 63, [2006] 1 A.C. 459.

75 Ibid., per Lord Bingham [33].

76 *Knuller (Publishing, Printing and Promotions) Ltd. and Others Appellants v DPP Respondent* [1972] 3 W.L.R. 143, [1973] A.C. 435 per Lord Morris 463.

77 Law Commission, *Abusive and Offensive Online Communications: A Scoping Report* (Law Com No 381, 2018) [10.76].

78 Reed and Murray (n 11).

opposing views on what constitutes legality, though there are some overlaps in approaches. Reed and Murray, taking a 'thin' approach, suggest that the core 'laundry list' of ingredients that make up legality,[79] are as follows:

1. The law must be set forth in advance;
2. The law must be made public;
3. The law must be general;
4. The law must be clear;
5. The law must be stable and certain; and
6. The law must be applied to everyone according to its terms.

'Amongst the best known' approaches to legality is Fuller,[80] who argues that legality encompasses eight key principles:[81]

1. The law must be general;
2. The law must be prospective;
3. The prohibition of retrospective law;
4. The law must be clear;
5. The prohibition of contradictory law;
6. The law must not ask the impossible;
7. Consistency must be maintained in the law; and
8. The law must be fairly enforced.

For Fuller, '[a] total failure in any one of these eight directions does not simply result in a bad system of law; it results in something that is not properly called a legal system at all'.[82] Though, similar to the approach undertaken by the ECtHR, Fuller does accept that '[n]o system of law—whether it be judged made or legislatively enacted—can be so perfectly drafted as to leave no room for dispute'.[83] It will be Fuller's principle of legality which will be used as the foundations of the theoretical positioning, or as potently put by Reed and Murray the 'laundry list', for which future arguments in later chapters will be based.

3.4.1 The Law Must Be General

For the law to be general, it must be in place. A prospective that is further endorsed by the ECtHR as discussed above, and supported by Raz[84] and Reed and Murray.[85]

79 Ibid., 206.
80 Ibid., 202.
81 Fuller (n 43) 33–94.
82 Ibid., 39.
83 Ibid., 56.
84 Joseph Raz, *The Authority of Law: Essays on Law and Morality* (Clarendon Press 2012) 214.
85 Reed and Murray (n 11) 81.

In essence, for the law to be considered as general, there must be a legal provision prohibiting the behaviour under scrutiny. However, for Fuller, for the law to be general, and in turn to ensure fairness in the application of legal provisions, it is more than just being able to point to a legal provision and stating, 'there is the law'. To adhere to generality in the law, citizens must be given advanced notice of the law, in which the law should not be decided on an ad-hoc approach. In essence, for Fuller, we should not proceed on a 'case by case' account of insight into how the law should develop;[86] the law needs to be accessible for all those living within a society, underpinning the principle of fairness in the criminal law.[87]

This is an issue, which is discussed at length in Chapter 6, where it is argued that the current approach to establishing if a communication can be considered as grossly offensive or menacing, as prohibited under s.127(1) of the Communications Act 2003 (CA) is being decided on an ad-hoc basis where there is a lack of consensus amongst those working in the criminal justice system, as to what constitutes a grossly offensive or a menacing message. As a result, as highlighted throughout Chapter 6, it cannot be said that generality is being maintained in the application of current communication offences to conduct carried out on social media sites. Similar arguments are raised in Chapter 7, which explores the recent amendments made to communication law.

3.4.2 The Law Must Be Prospective

Underpinning the concept of generality in the law is the ideal that the law must also be prospective. For the law to be considered as prospective, it must be publicly accessible. For instance, you should not punish another for failure to adhere to the law if say, the law was written on the back of a post-it-note for no one to see. Though as acknowledged by Fuller, it would be impossible to educate all citizens on the meaning of every legal provision within a given legal system, he maintains that prospectivity is important because 'knowledge of the law by a few often influences indirectly the actions of many'.[88]

Luban, influenced by the work of Fuller and Raz, refers to this as 'the fair notice argument'.[89] Those who breach criminal law provisions are subject to punishment. Nonetheless, those who break legal provisions that are incapable of guiding those living in a society, should not be subject to punishment. Similar provisions are endorsed by Raz under his conception of the rule of law, who argued that 'if the law is to be obeyed it must be capable of guiding the behaviour of its subjects. It must be such that they can find out what it is and act on it'.[90] Here, a person must

86 Fuller (n 43) 46.
87 What is considered 'law' is beyond the scope of this book, but there is a wide array of literature available exploring this concept. See for instance, Raz (n 84).
88 Fuller (n 43) 51.
89 Luban (n 42) 40.
90 Raz (n 84). See also, Joseph Raz, 'The Rule of Law and its Virtue' (1977) 93 L.Q.R.195.

be seen to have been given 'constructive notice' that their actions have breached the law, or as potently put by Bingham:

> This is not because bank robbers habitually consult their solicitors before robbing a branch of the NatWest, but because many crimes are a great deal less obvious than robbery, and most of us are keen to keep on the right side of the law if we can.[91]

By adhering to this aspect of legality, it allows citizens to guide their actions in accordance with law and in turn, curtails the power of the state, whilst also allowing citizens to guide their affairs on the basis of knowing what the law is.[92] In fact, 'obedience of the law depends on humans understanding the law'.[93]

Lack of prospectivity in the law and its application to a social media context is a recurring theme throughout this monograph. For example, in Chapter 5 issues are highlighted with the terms course of conduct, harassment, and stalking, particularly where such notions are applied to the online world. It is argued that these elements which make up the offence of cyberharassment or cyberstalking are so inherently vague, it is impossible to see when a person's behaviour online will go beyond what is reasonably expected (with the Law Commission previously noting that the monitoring of a person's social media activity is generally consented to in the online world)[94] to such behaviour that warrants criminalisation.

3.4.3 The Law Cannot Be Retrospective

As a fundamental principle of not just legality, but also international law, as discussed in Section 3.3 and specifically prohibited under Article 7 of the ECHR, as examined in Section 3.3.2.1, you should not enact a law which would change the legal position of the past. For example, you cannot create a legal provision today prohibiting the sending of a communication which contains explicit language and prosecute those who sent messages yesterday which contained such language. A concept that is further supported by Fuller, who goes as far as stating that 'retrospective law is truly a monstrosity',[95] though he does maintain that there is a place

91 Bingham (n 44) 37.
92 Friedrich Hayek, *The Constitution of Liberty* (Routledge 2006) 153–154.
93 Reed and Murray (n 11) 85.
94 Law Com No 381 (n. 77) [8.171].
95 Fuller (n 43) 53.

for retrospective law in some instances, just not in the criminal law.[96] For Raz, 'one cannot be guided by retrospective law'.[97]

As discussed at length by Reed and Murray, retrospective law is not necessarily an issue when it comes to the online world,[98] however, it is not as simple as stating 'we do not create legal provisions that alter the legal position of the past'. It is also, as noted by Fuller and further supported in both the jurisprudence of the ICC and the ECtHR, important to ensure that when provisions are interpreted, they are not so generously interpreted, that they would, in theory, create retrospective criminal law:

> It is an accepted principle of interpretation that a criminal statute should be construed strictly, so that acts falling outside its normal meaning are not to be considered criminal simply because they present the same kind of danger as those described by the language of the statute.[99]

For Fuller, like the approach endorsed by the ECtHR and the ICC, the interpretation of the statute cannot go beyond what would be reasonably acceptable as this would create retrospective criminal law. Supported further by Bingham.[100] Though no matter how

> clearly drafted a legal provision may be, in any system of law, including criminal law, there is an inevitable element of judicial interpretation. There will always be a need for elucidation of doubtful points and for adaptation to changing circumstances. Indeed, in the United Kingdom, as in the other Convention States, the progressive development of the criminal law through judicial law-making is a well entrenched and necessary part of legal tradition. Article 7 of the Convention cannot be read as outlawing the gradual clarification of the rules of criminal liability through judicial interpretation from case to case, provided that the resultant development is consistent with the essence of the offence and could reasonably be foreseen.[101]

With foreseeability relating both to elements of the offence and the applicable punishment. As potently put by Bingham:

96 Fuller uses the hypothetical scenario that a legal provision is enacted declaring that from such a date no marriage will be vailed unless the marriage certificate contains a special stamp on it, provided by the state. Unfortunately, due to technical difficulties, the stamp is not available when the legal provision comes into force. Further, due to a lack of knowledge of changes to the law in this area, marriages continue to take place but without the stamp affixed to the marriage certificate. Here, it would be accepted that retrospective law could be used to alter the position of the past, to ensure the validity of these marriages. Ibid., 53–54.

97 Raz (n 84).

98 Reed and Murray (n 11) 212.

99 Fuller (n 43) 58.

100 Bingham (n 44) 45.

101 *SW v The United Kingdom, CR v The United Kingdom* App no. 20166/92 (ECtHR, 22 November 1995) [36].

> It is one thing to move the law a little further along a line on which it is already moving, or to adapt it to accord with modern views and practises; it is quite another to seek to recast the law in a radically innovative or adventurous way, because that is to make it uncertain and unpredictable.[102]

By prohibiting retrospective criminal law, due process of the law is maintained. This is an issue discussed further in Chapters 4 and 5. For instance, in Chapter 4, concerns are raised that the current use of stirring up offences under the Public Order Act 1986 (POA) in a social media context, is creating retrospective criminal law as the Act is being applied in situations which it was never intended to do, i.e., where public order was never under threat.

3.4.4 The Law Must Be Clear

Clarity is considered an 'essential ingredient'[103] of legality and is highly supported by not only legal philosophers such as Fuller but also the courts. It upholds the ideal that the law needs to be clear to ensure safeguarding 'against arbitrary punishment by governments under a cover of vague, underspecified law'.[104] This is of particular importance when it comes to legal provisions which, by utilising Bingham's argument above, is not as clear cut as robbery. Bingham suggests three essential reasons why we need clarity in the law:[105]

1. 'If you and I are liable to be prosecuted, fined or perhaps imprisoned for doing or failing to do something, we ought to be able, without undue difficulty, to find out what we must or must not do';[106]
2. So, citizens are aware of their rights and obligations; and
3. You need clarity in the law for successful trade, investment and business. No one would invest in a company or indeed, in new technology, which is based in a country that lacks clarity within its legal provisions—an important consideration when examining the OSA, as discussed in Chapter 8.

However, despite its importance in maintaining legality in the criminal law, it is a concept that is difficult to achieve. On the one hand, a strict approach would render the law rigid and difficult to adapt to the changing nature of society, with Fuller supporting in some instances, the best way to achieve clarity is to take advantage of, and incorporate into the law, common sense standards of judgment that have grown up in the ordinary life lived outside legislative halls.

102 Bingham (n 44) 46.
103 Fuller (n 43) 62.
104 Luban (n 42) 37.
105 Bingham (n 44) 37–38.
106 Ibid., 37.

On the other, an overly vague legal provision which lacks any clarity undermines the principle of fairness within the legal system and risks abuse, with Fuller clarifying that

> [i]t is a serious mistake—and a mistake made constantly—to assume that, though the busy legislative draftsman can find no way of converting his objective into clearly stated rules, he can always safely delegate this task to the courts or special administrative tribunals.[107]

Both the ICC and the ECtHR have previously rendered legal provisions incompatible with legality due to the inherent vagueness contained in the principles under scrutiny.[108] They have also come to decisions, that despite some vagueness within a provision, the legal provision under consideration does conform to legality.[109] Clarity is therefore an important principle, but it needs to be balanced. We need to strive for the 'maximum clarity which the imperfect medium of language can attain'[110] in order to render the law compatible with the principle of legality. The lack of clarity in current legal provisions used to restrict online conduct is a recurring theme throughout this monograph. For instance, in Chapter 7, issues are raised with the 'new' communication offences which became legally enforceable on the 31 January 2024. These 'new' offences were enacted following a significant review of communication law and its application to the online world. Yet as demonstrated in Chapter 7, many of the issues highlighted with previous communication offences, which are discussed in Chapter 6, remain, most notably, the inherent vagueness in terms used throughout the provisions.

3.4.5 The Law Must Be Non-contradictory

A further principle of legality as endorsed by Fuller is the prohibition of contradictory law. In essence, we cannot require a person under a legal provision to do one thing but at the same time prohibit that same conduct under another provision. Fuller provides the example of asking motorists under a statute to change their licence plates on January 1st but also prohibiting any form of labour on the same day, under another statute—this would create contradictory law.[111] Although contradictory laws have and do exist, it is important that such situations are avoided, particularly when it comes to the criminal law, to maintain the principle of legality. A contradictory law cannot be considered, at the very least, general, prospective, or clear. In fact, in 1988 and 1995, the Italian Constitutional Court ruled that ignorance of the law may constitute an excuse for the citizen when the formulation of the law is such as to lead to obscure and contradictory results.

107 Ibid.,
108 See for example, *Prosecutor v Vasiljević* (n 55); *Sunday Times* (n 68).
109 See for example, *Kafkaris* (n 63); *Čelebići Camp* (n 52).
110 Law Com No. 76 (n 41).
111 Fuller (n 43) 65–66.

But consistency is difficult to maintain in the criminal law. For instance, in Chapter 4, concerns are raised following a decision by the Crown Prosecution Service (CPS) to prosecute Liam Stacey under the POA for sending racist comments on Twitter.[112] Whereas in a similar case a decision was made to prosecute under s.127(1) of the CA,[113] with the reasoning as to why the CA was preferred over the POA being unclear and impossible to justify.

3.4.6 The Law Must not Ask the Impossible

Though Fuller accepts that his sixth principle, the law must not ask the impossible, is arguably obvious, because 'no sane lawmaker, not even the most evil dictator, would have any reason to enact such law',[114] it is not that simple. Using the example of the 'reasonable man'[115] test found in various legal instruments, including that of the criminal law, Fuller argues that by comparing a person's actions against that of the 'reasonable man', may in some circumstances ask the impossible, as his education or even personal characteristics may not meet such a requirement.[116] Yet imposing the 'reasonable man with the same characteristics as the defendant' as the boundary for criminal liability risks objectivity being lost.[117] These requirements create difficulties as it imposes some form of moral judgement upon the accused, which may be considered impossible to meet.

The use of the 'reasonable person' test in a social media context, is discussed at length in Chapter 5, in which the *mens rea* of the offence of harassment and/or stalking, is based upon knowledge. Here it must be found that the sender of a message knew or should have known that the message sent would cause alarm or distress in another, with knowledge being judged on that of the 'reasonable person'. Chapter 5 demonstrates the difficulties in applying the 'reasonable person' test to a social media context, calling instead, for the notion of the 'reasonable social media' user to be implemented. Impossibility is also discussed in Chapter 7 where it is argued that the 'new' communication offences are asking individuals to do the impossible at times.

3.4.7 The Law Must Remain Consistent

The idea that the law must remain consistent is closely related to the prohibition of retrospective law. In essence, the law should not change so regularly that citizens are unable to govern their behaviour in accordance with the rules of the land. For Murray, to adhere to legality and in turn, the rule of law, the law must have

112 *R v Liam Stacey,* Swansea Crown Court On Appeal From The Magistrates' Court, A20120033.

113 *R v Alison Chabloz,* Westminster Magistrates' Court, 11 January 2018 (unreported).

114 Fuller (n 43) 70.

115 Though Fuller users the notion of the 'reasonable man', it has come to be accepted that the appropriate term is 'reasonable person'. Reasonable person will be used throughout this monograph.

116 Fuller (n 43) 71–72.

117 Ibid.,

Table 3.1 New criminal offences created either through primary or secondary legislation between 1st June 2009 and 31st May 2014

	2010	*2011*	*2012*	*2013*	*2014*
Primary	189	31	36	66	87
Secondary	523	143	256	261	193
Total	712	174	292	327	280

Note: Ministry of Justice, 'New Criminal Offences (England and Wales)' (*Gov.uk*, 11 December 2014) <https://assets.publishing.service.gov.uk/government/uploads/system/uploads/attachment_data/file/385537/new-criminal-offences-june-2009-may-2014.pdf> accessed 22 August 2022.

some form of stability.[118] Similar provisions are endorsed by Raz.[119] For this to be achieved, the law needs to refrain from being decided on an ad-hoc approach of enlightenment, as mirrored in Fuller's first requirement of generality in the law. A key example of failure to adhere to this requirement is shown in Chapters 4, 5 and 6, following an increase in the use of the criminal law to tackle the 'harms' associated with the online world.

As society has evolved, particularly in the United Kingdom, significant weight has been placed on the law to control not only the behaviour of its citizens but to also govern public institutions, such as schools and the NHS. As noted by Sir Menzies Campbell, between 1997 and 2007 there had been '382 Acts of Parliament, including 10 health Acts, 12 education Acts, and 29 criminal justice Acts, and more than 3,000 new criminal offences' enacted.[120] Such reliance on the law, in particular, the criminal law, has continued since, peeking at over 700 new criminal offences being created in 2010 alone, demonstrated further in Table 3.1. Indeed, when it comes to the internet, there have been significant reforms in this area of the law. With research undertaken by Reed and Murray, finding that in 2017, there were 595 reported court cases on the legal database 'WestLaw' mentioning the word 'internet'; 557 containing the word 'online'.[121] As stated by Bingham '[i]t seems that legislative hyperactivity has become a permanent feature of our governance'.[122]

With a continued rhetoric, when it comes to social media, that more criminal law is needed to control what society deems as inappropriate behaviour online, consistency of the law is under significant threat. An issue highlighted further in Chapter 7 which demonstrates the continued problems in consistency and the application of communication offences, which overlap with each other. An issue which has become even more complex, given the increase in the number of communication offences available to prosecutors in the wake of the OSA.

118 Andrew D Murray, 'Mapping the rule of law for the internet' in David Mangan and Lorna E Gillies (eds), *The Legal Challenges of Social Media* (Edward Elgar Publishing 2017) 27.

119 Raz (n 84) 214–215.

120 HC Deb 11 July 2007, vol 462, col 1455.

121 Reed and Murray (n 11) 223.

122 Bingham (n 44) 40.

3.4.8 The Law Must Be Fairly Enforced

Failure in any of the previous principles of legality as discussed above all lead to one clear consequence—unfair enforcement of the law. If a legal provision lacks, for instance, generality, cannot be considered publicly accessible, contradictory and in turn lacks any form of clarity, how can actors within the criminal justice system ensure that the law is enforced fairly across all sectors of society? Unfair enforcement of the law creates criticism in the community and in turn, results in negative attitudes towards the criminal justice system. Due process cannot be maintained, as highlighted throughout various chapters of this monograph.

For Fuller:

> The most subtle element in the task of maintaining congruence between law and official actions lies, of course, in the problem of interpretation. Legality requires that judges and other officials apply statutory law, not according to their fancy or with crabbed literalness, but in accordance with principles of interpretation.[123]

The interpretation of statute law is dependent on the principle of legality being maintained in all legal provisions. Without this, there runs the real risk of the law being unfairly enforced, as discussed at length in Chapter 7 following the increased availability in communication-based offences.

However, for the law to be fairly enforced, it also needs to be accessible for those working in the criminal justice system, which has not necessarily always been the case as

> there is no comprehensive statute law database with hyperlinks which would enable an intelligent person, by using a search engine, to find out all the legislation on a particular topic. This means that the courts are in many cases unable to discover what the law is.[124]

As put by Bingham:

> [i]t must be questioned whether the current volume and style of legislation are well suited to serve the rule of law even if it is accepted, as it must be, but the subject matter of much legislation is inevitably very complex.[125]

As discussed further in various chapters of this monograph, fair enforcement of the law when it comes to social media offences, is currently under threat. What one police force or prosecutor might consider to be, as an example, harassment, another might deem it grossly offensive. A problem discussed in Chapter 5, following a decision by the CPS to prosecute Peter Nunn for sending grossly offensive communications contrary to s.127(1) of the CA as opposed to s.2 or s.4 of the Protection

123 Fuller (n 43) 82.

124 *R v Chambers* [2008] EWCA Crim 2467 per Lord Justice Toulson [68].

125 Bingham (n 44) 42.

from Harassment Act 1997.[126] A decision which the complainant, Caroline Criado-Perez, has been heavily critical of.[127]

3.4.9 Summary

Fuller's eight principles of legality are evidently mirrored in other scholars' approaches to legality and the rule of law. Each intertwine and support each other. And it will be Fuller's conception of legality which will be used to critique the application of current legal provisions to conduct carried out on social media because, as noted above, Fuller's approach to what constitutes legality is '[a]mongst the best known'.[128] However, it is important to note, like that of the approach endorsed by the ICC, the ECtHR and the domestic courts of the United Kingdom in what constitutes legality, it is accepted that it would be impossible to create legislation which is so perfectly enacted it adheres to all eight principles soundly. It is a degree of balance, and as will become apparent in later chapters, this balance is not being met when it comes to the application of the criminal law to social media conduct.

3.5 Chapter Summary

Ultimately, there is no one approach to the regulation of social media. Different theoretical positions have emerged since the creation of the internet. However, as more individuals choose to live out their lives online, significant emphasis is being placed on the criminal law to tackle the 'darker' side of human behaviour. The principle of legality is therefore fundamental in ensuring the protection of freedom of expression and the avoidance of overcriminalisation. It is a basic requirement to ensure due process—regardless of the stance taken to online regulation.

The principle of legality is therefore important in all aspects of the law, but none more so than the criminal law. The use of the criminal law, at its very basic, is a form of social control and by its very nature, it is coercive. Failure to comply can result in heavy penalties, including a loss of liberty. But despite the coercive nature of the criminal law, as discussed by Corsi,[129] societies make use of criminal law provisions for (at least) five important reasons:

1. To restrict conduct, or completely prohibit, such conduct that may cause harm to another or society in general;
2. As a form of social control;
3. To safeguard individuals from conduct that can be considered as criminal;
4. To act as a warning to others that such conduct will not be permitted; and
5. To elaborate to members of society what is considered minor or serious offences.

126 *R v Peter Nunn,* The City of London Magistrates' Court, 29 September 2014 (unreported).

127 Caroline Criado-Perez, 'A brief comment on Peter Nunn, sentenced today for Twitter abuse' (*Week Women*, 2014) <https://weekwoman.wordpress.com/2014/09/29/a-brief-comment-on-peter-nunn/> accessed 29 October 2016.

128 Reed and Murray (n 11) 202.

129 Corsi (n 49) 1340.

In essence, '[t]he wrongdoing which the criminal law seeks to punish is that which threatens the fundamental values upon which a society is founded'.[130]

Legality therefore underpins many theoretical concepts of the criminal law, including:

1. Deterrence—if a person cannot guide their behaviour in accordance with clear and distinct rules, it cannot be said that the law is action-guiding, therefore deterrence does not exist. A concept reinforced in Bingham's understanding of the rule of law, in which he argues that 'one important function of the criminal law is to discourage criminal behaviour, and we cannot be discouraged if we do not know, and cannot reasonably easily discover, what it is we should not do';[131]
1. Expression—social condemnation cannot exist without clarity in the law; and
2. Retribution—if the law is not accessible, punishment becomes random and cannot be justified.

Not only does legality underpin these theories of criminalisation, but it also acts as a shield against arbitrary interference from the state.

Although legality is an important principle when it comes to the criminal law in general, when it comes to the application of the law in cyberspace, it is vital that legality is maintained for the law to be considered as legitimate in the online world. As discussed by Reed and Murray, three factors influence the legitimacy of the law in cyberspace, all of which are underpinned by the principle of legality.[132] First, the law needs to be seen as being addressed to the online user in which the provision needs to communicate what is and is not accessible (the action-guiding nature of the law). For this to occur, the provision needs to be easily understood (clarity within the law) because

> [i]f the legitimacy of the law's claim to authority is conferred on it by the collective acceptance of those to whom it is addressed, it must follow that structuring or wording the law in a way which makes it inaccessible to those addresses will reduce the likelihood of acceptance. Achieving legitimacy requires attention to style as well as substance.[133]

Second, provisions need to be coherent with cyberspace (the consistency element); and third, provisions need to be fair and uphold natural justice (fair enforcement of the law).

Though as noted at the start of this chapter, there is not one approach to the meaning of legality, there are some clear overlaps between different theoretical

130 Carleton Kemp Allen, 'The Nature of a Crime' (1931) 13(1) J. Comp. Legislation and Int'l L.J. 1, 11.
131 Bingham (n 44) 38.
132 Reed and Murray (n 11) 206–225.
133 Ibid., 183.

approaches, including approaches endorsed by ICL and the ECHR. In particular, though not limited to:

1. Generality;
2. Clarity;
3. Prospectiveness;
4. Consistency;
5. Non-retrospective law, including, strict interpretation of legal provisions; and
6. Fair enforcement of the law.

These concepts of legality will be used in the following chapters to evaluate the current application of the criminal law's response to tackling online abuse, with particular regard to hate crime (Chapter 4), cyberharassment and cyberstalking (Chapter 5), and abusive communications (Chapter 6), before turning to evaluate the latest attempts by the former UK government to control online communications (Chapter 7). Part Three will turn to examine the regulation of social media platforms beyond the criminal law and the United Kingdom, against the principle of legality.[134]

Reference list

Allen C K, The Nature of a Crime (1931) 13(1) J Comp Legislation & Int'l L J 1

Barnett H, *Constitutional & Administrative Law* (5th edn, Cavendish Publishing 2004)

Bartlett J, *The People Vs Tech: How the Internet Is Killing Democracy (and How We Can Save It)* (Penguin 2018)

Barlow J P, 'A Declaration of the Independence of Cyberspace' (*Electronic Frontier Foundation*, 8 February 1996) https://www.eff.org/cyberspace-independence

Bassiouni M C, *International Criminal Law* (3rd edn, Brill Nijhoff 2008)

Bell D J, Loader B D, Pleace N & Schuler D, *Cyberculture: The Key Concepts* (Routledge 2004)

Bernal P, *The Internet, Warts and All: Free Speech, Privacy and Truth* (Cambridge University Press 2018)

Bingham T, *The Rule of Law* (Penguin 2011)

Brownsword R, *Law, Technology and Society: Re-imaging the Regulatory Environment* (Routledge 2019)

Corsi J L, 'An Argument for Strict Legality in International Criminal Law' (2018) 49 Geo J Int'l L 1321

Confessore N, 'Cambridge Analytica and Facebook: The Scandal and the Fallout So Far' *The New York Times* (New York, 4 April 2018) https://www.nytimes.com/2018/04/04/us/politics/cambridge-analytica-scandal-fallout.html

Criado-Perez C, 'A Brief Comment on Peter Nunn, Sentenced Today For Twitter Abuse' (*Week Women*, 2014) https://weekwoman.wordpress.com/2014/09/29/a-brief-comment-on-peter-nunn/

Duff A & Green S, *Philosophical Foundations of Criminal Law* (Oxford University Press 2013)

134 Bingham (n 44) 84.

Dyson E, Gilder G, Keyworth G & Toffler A, 'Cyberspace and the American Dream: A Magna Carta for the Knowledge Age' (1994) Future Insight http://www.pff.org/issues-pubs/futureinsights/fi1.2magnacarta.html

Fuller L L, *The Morality of Law* (Yale University Press 1964)

Golumbia D, *Cyberlibertarianism: The Extremist Foundations of "Digital Freedom"* (Clemson University, South Carolina, September 2013)

Guilfoyle D, *International Criminal Law* (Oxford University Press 2016)

Hall J, *General Principles of Criminal Law* (2nd edn, Lawbook Exchange Ltd 2010)

Hayek F, *The Constitution of Liberty* (Routledge 2006)

HC Deb 11 July 2007, vol 462, col 1455

Johnson D & Post D, 'Law and Borders: The Rise of Law in Cyberspace' (1996) 48 SLR 1367

Laidlaw E B, *Regulating Speech in Cyberspace: Gatekeepers, Human Rights and Corporate Responsibility* (Cambridge 2015)

Laidlaw E B, 'A Framework for Identifying Internet Information Gatekeepers' 24 (2010) Int Rev Law Comput Technol 263

Law Commission, *Abusive and Offensive Online Communications: A Scoping Report* (Law Com No 381, 2018)

Law Commission, *Report on Conspiracy and Criminal Law Reform* (Law Com No. 76, 1976)

Lessig L, *Code Version 2.0* (Basic Books 2006)

Lord Bingham, 'The Rule of Law' (2007) 66(1) Cam Law J 67

Luban D, 'Fairness to Rightness: Jurisdiction, Legality, and the Legitimacy of International Criminal Law' in Besson S & Tasioulas J (eds), *The Philosophy of International Law* (Oxford University Press 2010)

Metoyer-Duran C, 'Information Gatekeepers' (1993) 28 ARIST 111

Ministry of Justice, 'New Criminal Offences (England and Wales)' (*Gov.uk*, 11 December 2014) https://assets.publishing.service.gov.uk/government/uploads/system/uploads/attachment_data/file/385537/new-criminal-offences-june-2009-may-2014.pdf

Murphy C C, The Principle of Legality in Criminal Law Under the European Convention on Human Rights (2010) 2 Eur Hum Rights Law Rev 192

Murray A, *Information Technology Law* (5th edn, Oxford University Press 2023)

Murray A, *Information Technology Law* (4th edn, Oxford University Press 2019)

Murray A, *The Regulation of Cyberspace: Control in the Online Environment* (Routledge 2007)

Murray A D, 'Mapping the rule of law for the internet' in Mangan D & Gillies L E (eds), *The Legal Challenges of Social Media* (Edward Elgar Publishing 2017)

Raz J, *The Authority of Law: Essays on Law and Morality* (Clarendon Press 2012)

Raz J, The Rule of Law and its Virtue (1977) 93 LQR 195

Reed C, *Internet Law: Text and Materials* (Cambridge University Press 2004)

Reed C & Murray A, *Rethinking the Jurisprudence of Cyberspace* (Elgar 2018)

Ridenberg J, 'Governing Networks and Rule-Making in Cyberspace' (1996) 45 Emory Law J 911

Robinson D, *The Principle of Legality in International Criminal Law* (Legal Studies Research Papers Series 10-08, 2010)

Sanz-Caballero S, 'The Principle of nulla poena sine lege Revisited: The Retrospective Application of Criminal Law in the Eyes of the European Court of Human Rights' (2017) 28(3) Eur J Int Law 787

The BBC, 'Teenager's life "ruined" by Live.me and Twitter "trolls"' *The BBC* (London, 24 October 2017) http://www.bbc.co.uk/news/uk-england-41693437

UN Human Rights Committee, 'General Comment no. 29, States of Emergency (Article 4): International Covenant on Civil and Political Rights' (*United Nations Digital Library*, 2001) <https://digitallibrary.un.org/record/451555?ln=en>

Varuhas JNE, 'The Principle of Legality' (2020) 79(3) Camb LJ 578

Part II

The Application of the Criminal Law

The second part of this monograph examines three key growing concerns surrounding social media and online abuse: racist commentary online (Chapter 4), cyber-harassment/cyberstalking (Chapter 5) and unlawful communications (Chapters 6 and 7). Each of these areas are explored in separate chapters in which the use of the criminal law to tackle these online 'harms' is critically examined. To do this each chapter takes a very similar format, looking at the rise in these behaviours, the criminal law framework used to prohibit such behaviour(s), followed by its application to a social media context. The final parts of each chapter highlight how the application of each of these provisions, to conduct carried out on social media platforms, creates significant issues with legality and in turn, it cannot be said that freedom of expression is being protected.

DOI: 10.4324/9781003303688-5

4 Online Racism and the Criminal Law

4.1 Introduction

Though there is no universal definition of hate speech, under international law, any advocacy of national, religious, or racial hatred that constitutes incitement to discriminate must be prohibited by law. Hate speech falls within the broad definition of a hate crime, which like that of hate speech, no universal definition exists. A hate crime can however be considered a criminal act aimed at another due to a protected characteristic associated with that person, whether real or presumed. Characteristics can include race, gender, sexuality, religion, or political affiliation, to name but a few—and what characteristics constitute a hate crime differ between states and indeed, between social media platforms.

In England and Wales, a hate crime is defined as a criminal act aimed at another which is 'motivated by hostility or demonstrates hostility towards the victim's disability, race, religion, sexual orientation, or transgender identity'.[1] Hate speech, is the use of words or expressions motivated by hostility or demonstrates hostility towards another because of a protected characteristic (i.e., disability, race, religion, sexual orientation, or transgender identity). Although hate speech constitutes more than racial hatred,[2] this chapter will focus on the use of the criminal law to target the spread of racial hatred on social media sites—something which has become a growing concern for governments across the globe.[3]

The use of the criminal law in prohibiting racist speech is uncontroversial, as restricting this form of speech is designed to protect the vulnerable.[4] In fact, 'bigoted views can be restricted as they bring about harm and add little to public

1 The Crown Prosecution Service, 'Hate crime' (*CPS.gov*, 2018) <https://www.cps.gov.uk/hate-crime> accessed 9 December 2018.

2 Significant criticism has been raised against the current approach to hate crime in England and Wales, where it has been argued that the current approach has created a hierarchy of offences. For further discussion on this see, Catherine Heard 'Hate crime law: more incrementalism or time for reform?' (2014) (7) Arch. Rev 4.

3 See Chapter 9 for an in-depth discussion on different government approaches to combatting hate online.

4 Erick Bleich, 'The Rise of Hate Speech and Hate Crime Laws in Liberal Democracies' (2011) 37(6) J Ethn Migr Stud 917, 918.

DOI: 10.4324/9781003303688-6

discussion'.[5] However, like that of other online expressions, which will be discussed in later chapters, we need to distinguish between racist speech, which is prohibited in many countries across the globe, including England and Wales and offensive speech, which as outlined in Chapter 2, is a protected form of speech. Or as potently put by Murray 'sometimes there is a fine line between political speech and hate speech'[6] and as noted by Newman, there is no bright light to distinguish between the two.[7]

The following chapter will start by exploring the rise in hate crime in England and Wales, before turning to examine hate speech on social media sites which has caught the attention of the public in recent years and, in turn, placed increasing pressure on the government and the criminal justice system to do more. The hate characteristic which will be of focus, is racially motivated incidences. This chapter will then proceed to discuss how the criminal justice system is attempting to tackle racist speech. To do this, the criminal law will be outlined and examined, exploring how legal provisions are currently being utilised to govern racist speech on social media sites, with reference to s.66 of the Sentencing Act 2020 (SA), s.31 and 32 of the Crime and Disorder Act 1988 (CDA) and s.18 and 19 of the Public Order Act 1986 (POA).[8] Although other criminal law provisions exist to prohibit racist speech, focus is placed on these provisions as their use to prosecute comments made online, as will be examined in the final parts of this chapter, poses significant issues with the principle of legality and freedom of expression. Further, the stirring up offences contained in s.18 and 19 of the POA are priority illegal content under the Online Safety Act 2023 (OSA)—discussed further in Chapter 8.

4.2 The Rise in Hate

The number of hate crimes recorded by the police in England and Wales has risen year-on-year, as illustrated further in Figure 4.1, with 124,091 hate crimes recorded in the year ending March 2021, rising to 155,841 by the end of March 2022.[9] Though arguably the rise in the number of recorded hate crime offences could be associated with a drive towards a better understanding of the offence across police forces, certain political events (the EU referendum in 2016; terrorist attacks in 2017; and the COVID-19 pandemic in 2020) have created spikes within the data.[10]

5 Melina Bell, 'John Stuart Mill's Harm Principle and Free Speech: Expanding the Notion of Harm' (2021) 33(2) Utilitas 162, 173.

6 Andrew Murray, *Information Technology Law: The Law and Society* (5th edn, Oxford University Press 2023) 126.

7 Stephen L. Newman, 'Finding the Harm in Hate Speech: An Argument against Censorship' (2017) 50(3) CJPS 679, 681.

8 Though similar provisions are contained in the Racial and Religious Hatred Act 2006, there is little evidence in the literature of its use in cases related to social media.

9 Home Office, 'Hate crime, England and Wales, 2021 to 2022' (*Gov.uk*, 6 October 2022) <https://www.gov.uk/government/statistics/hate-crime-england-and-wales-2021-to-2022/hate-crime-england-and-wales-2021-to-2022> accessed 1 February 2023.

10 Ibid.,

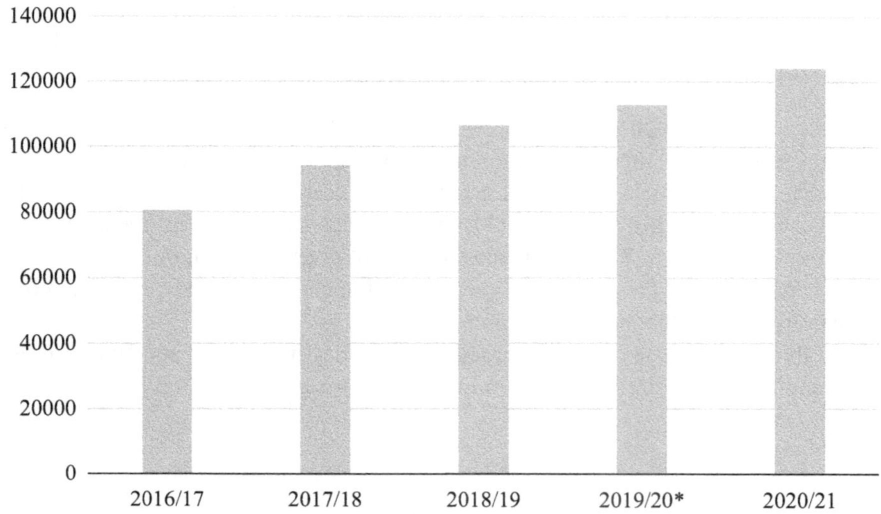

Figure 4.1 Number of hate crimes recorded by the police in England and Wales from 2016 to 2022.

Note: Home Office, 'Hate Crime, England and Wales, 2021 to 2022' (*Gov.uk*, 6 October 2022) <https://www.gov.uk/government/statistics/hate-crime-england-and-wales-2021-to-2022/hate-crime-england-and-wales-2021-to-2022> accessed 1 February 2023. *Does not include figures from Greater Manchester due to technology issues.

Similar trends have also been mirrored in the online world, where the volume of online hate is enormous,[11] with Stephens arguing that:

> [t]here seems to be something about the internet that encourages toxicity in public discourse amongst a small but vocal minority, who seem to have nothing better to do than resort to hateful, racist, misogynistic comments and personal attacks, something that would never be tolerated in the offline world.[12]

Indeed, during the global COVID-19 pandemic, online hate rose by 20%.[13] Reflected further in the high number of posts removed from social media platforms, for breaching hate speech policies. For Minto:

11 Dr Fernand de Varennes, 'Recommendations made by the Forum on Minority Issues at its thirteenth session on the theme "Hate speech, social media and minorities"' (*United Nations*, 26 January 2021) <https://documents-dds-ny.un.org/doc/UNDOC/GEN/G21/017/29/PDF/G2101729.pdf?OpenElement> accessed 19 August 2022.

12 Hugh Stephens, 'Facebook: Who bears responsibility for them?' (*The International Forum for Responsible Media Blog*, 25 November 2021) <https://inforrm.org/2021/11/25/facebook-who-bears-responsibility-for-them-hugh-stephens/> accessed 28 June 2022.

13 Michael Baggs, 'Online hate speech rose 20% during pandemic: "We've normalised it"' *The BBC* (London, 15 November 2021) <https://www.bbc.co.uk/news/newsbeat-59292509> accessed 28 June 2022.

> Gone are the days when far-right information and propaganda were confined to the back rooms of seedy pubs and clubs. This material can now be accessed 24/7 with a few swipes of your phone.[14]

Between January 2020 and December 2021, Facebook removed a total of 192.6 million pieces of content from its site for breaching hate speech policies.[15] In the same period, Twitter removed around 7 million pieces of hateful content;[16] YouTube removed just over 334,000 videos it deemed hateful or abusive;[17] and TikTok removed over 7 million pieces of content considered hateful.[18] Of all hate crimes recorded by the police and removed by social media sites, racially motivated offences are the most common.[19]

Of the 155,841 hate crimes recorded by the police in England and Wales in the year ending March 2022, nearly two-thirds (70%) were racially motivated, with a

14 Rachel Minto found in Sally Weale, 'Children coming across far-right material when researching, teachers say' *The Guardian* (London, 18 April 2022) <https://www.theguardian.com/politics/2022/apr/18/children-coming-across-far-right-material-when-researching-teachers-say> accessed 28 June 2022.

15 Statista, 'Global number of hate speech-containing content removed by Facebook from 4th quarter 2017 to 1st quarter 2022' (*Statista*, 1 June 2022) <https://www.statista.com/statistics/1013804/facebook-hate-speech-content-deletion-quarter/> accessed 19 August 2022. Note, Facebook defines hate speech: 'as a direct attack against people – rather than concepts or institutions—on the basis of what we call protected characteristics: race, ethnicity, national origin, disability, religious affiliation, caste, sexual orientation, sex, gender identity, and serious disease'. See, Meta 'Hate speech' (*Meta*, 2022) <https://transparency.fb.com/en-gb/policies/community-standards/hate-speech/> accessed 1 September 2022.

16 Twitter, 'Rules enforcement' (*Twitter*, 2022) <https://transparency.twitter.com/en/reports/rules-enforcement.html#2020-jan-jun> accessed 1 September 2022. Note: Twitter defines hateful content as 'violence against or directly attack or threaten other people on the basis of race, ethnicity, national origin, caste, sexual orientation, gender, gender identity, religious affiliation, age, disability, or serious disease'. See, Twitter, 'Hateful conduct policy' (*Twitter*, 2022) <https://help.twitter.com/en/rules-and-policies/hateful-conduct-policy> accessed 1 September 2022.

17 Google, 'YouTube community guidelines enforcement' (*Google*, 2022) <https://transparencyreport.google.com/youtube-policy/removals?hl=en&total_channels_removed=period:2021Q1&lu=channels_by_reason&channels_by_reason=period:2021Q4> accessed 1 September 2022. Note: YouTube defines hateful or abusive content as 'violence or hatred against individuals or groups based on any of the following attributes: age, caste, disability, ethnicity, gender identity and expression, nationality, race, immigration status, religion, sex/gender, sexual orientation, victims of a major violent event and their kin [and] Veteran status'. See, YouTube, 'Hate speech policy' (*YouTube*, 2022) <https://support.google.com/youtube/answer/2801939?hl=en-GB> accessed 1 September 2022.

18 TikTok, 'Community guidelines enforcement report' (*TikTok*, 2022) <https://www.tiktok.com/transparency/en/community-guidelines-enforcement-2021-4/> accessed 1 September 2022. Note, TikTok defines hateful behaviour as 'content that attacks, threatens, incites violence against, or otherwise dehumanizes [*sic*] an individual or a group on the basis of the following protected attributes: race, ethnicity, national origin, religion, caste, sexual orientation, sex, gender, gender identity, serious disease, disability [and] immigration status'. See, TikTok, 'Community guidelines: Hateful behaviour' (*TikTok*, 2022) <https://www.tiktok.com/community-guidelines?lang=en#38> accessed 1 September 2022.

19 Home Office (n 9).

19% rise in racially motivated offences compared to the previous year.[20] Although it is impossible to quantify how many of these reported racially motivated offences could be labelled as 'hate speech', studies have shown that racially motivated hate speech is also on the increase, particularly on social media sites.[21] For instance, '[b] etween 2019 and mid-2021, on average there was a new post [online] about race or ethnicity-based hate speech every 1.7 seconds' with a total of 50.1 million racially motivated posts being published during the same data period.[22]

The use of social media platforms to send racist commentary is not a new phenomenon. Indeed, comments made by the then Director of Public Prosecutions, Alison Saunders, in 2017 supported the use of the criminal law to tackle this form of abuse:

> When an ever-greater amount of our time is spent online, it is only right that we [The Crown Prosecution Service] do everything possible to ensure that people are protected from abuse that can now follow them everywhere via the screen of their smartphone or tablet. Whether shouted in their face on the street, daubed on a wall or tweeted into their living room, hateful abuse can have a devastating impact on victims.[23]

Similar arguments were raised again in 2021, following the use of social media sites, such as Twitter and Instagram, to send racist abuse to several footballers following England's defeat in the 2020 Euros.[24] Twitter in the immediate aftermath of the racist abuse removed over 1,000 racist tweets.[25] With many calling for stronger criminal provisions to make such conduct illegal.

4.3 Racism and the Criminal Law

Until the mid-1960s, the UK government was against the specific regulation of racist behaviour, with the Race Relations Act 1965 being the first attempt to regulate such conduct. Since then, numerous provisions have been put in place to combat

20 Ibid.,

21 Baggs (n 13).

22 Bandwatch Academy, 'Uncovered: Online hate speech in the Covid era' (*Bandwatch Academy*, 2022) <https://www.brandwatch.com/reports/online-hate-speech/view/> accessed 1 September 2022.

23 Alison Saunders, 'Hate is hate. Online abusers must be dealt with harshly' *The Guardian* (London, 21 August 2017) <https://www.theguardian.com/commentisfree/2017/aug/20/hate-crimes-online-abusers-prosecutors-serious-crackdown-internet-face-to-face> accessed 26 September 2018.

24 Alastair Jamieson, 'Bukayo Saka, Jadon Sancho and Marcus Rashford racially abused online after England Euro 2020 final defeat' *The Independent* (London, 12 July 2021) <https://www.independent.co.uk/news/uk/home-news/bukayo-saka-racist-england-sancho-rashford-b1882303.html> accessed 28 June 2022.

25 Simon Evans, 'English football faces up to global nature of online hate' (*Reuters*, 26 May 2022) <https://www.reuters.com/lifestyle/sports/english-football-faces-up-global-nature-online-hate-2021-07-13/> accessed 29 June 2022.

racism within society with three approaches being endorsed in the criminal law framework: aggravated offences, enhanced offences, and stirring up racial hatred.

4.3.1 Aggravated Offences: Sentencing Act 2020

S.66 of the SA, previously s.145–146 of the Criminal Justice Act 2003, allows the court to 'uplift' a perpetrators sentence where it is found that the criminal act (and it can be any criminal act, including the sending of unlawful communications online) was aggravated by hostility towards the complainant because of the complainants, whether real or presumed, protected characteristic, including race. In essence, the provision places an obligation on all sentencing judges or magistrates to take into consideration any hostility towards the complainant which was based on the complainant's (whether real or presumed) protected characteristic. If proven, a judge or magistrate is under an obligation to 'treat the fact that the offence is aggravated by hostility of any of those types [protected characteristics] as an aggravating factor and must state in open court that the offence is so aggravated'.[26] Put simply, where it is found that hostility was also present during the commission of a criminal offence, the court has the power to increase a person's punishment.

S.66 of the SA applies to any criminal offence, including, as noted above, communication offences. So, for instance, where a person sends a grossly offensive communication online contrary to s.127(1) of the Communications Act 2003 (CA), as discussed further in Chapter 6, the maximum custodial sentence which can be given is six months. However, where it is deemed an aggravated offence, the maximum custodial sentence is two years, as illustrated in *R v John Nimmo*[27] where the defendant's sentence was increased by 50% for every communication he sent contrary to s.127(1) of the CA, which was found to be motivated by racial hostility.[28] The meaning of hostility and racial group are discussed further in the following section.

4.3.2 Enhanced Offences: Crime and Disorder Act 1988

Unlike s.66 of the SA which allows for sentences to be uplifted for all criminal offences which are motivated or demonstrate hostility towards a person because of their real or presumed protected characteristic, s.31 and 32 of the CDA is only applicable in very defined circumstances.

26 Sentencing Act 2020 s.66(2).

27 *R v John Nimmo*, Newcastle Crown Court, 10 February 2017 (unreported). See also, Sandra Laville, 'Internet troll who sent labour MP antisemitic abused is jailed' *The Guardian* (London, 10 February 2017) <https://www.theguardian.com/uknews/2017/feb/10/internet-troll-who-sent-labour-mp-anti-semitic-messages-is-jailed> accessed 13 January 2020.

28 Note, this case was prior to the enactment of the Sentencing Act 2020 and therefore s.145–146 of the Criminal Justice Act 2003 was applied.

First, it only applies to certain specific criminal offences, including,[29]

1. Public Order Offences (s.31 CDA); and/or
2. Harassment or Stalking (s.32 CDA).

Second, the aggravating factor of the offence is limited to race or religion only.[30] For the purpose of this chapter, only race will be examined. For other types of aggravated offences, or other protected characteristics beyond race and religion, the SA, discussed above, would apply.

In essence, the base offence must be proven first (for instance, the *actus reus* and *mens rea* contained in s.2 of the Protection from Harassment Act 1997 (PfHA)—discussed further in the following chapter) followed by the elements which make up the enhanced offence (motivation or demonstration of hostility—as discussed further below) which will ultimately be for the jury or magistrate to decide. In a social media context, both s.31 and 32 of the CDA can, and have, been used to control online communications. For example, in 2012 Liam Stacey was successfully prosecuted for an offence contrary to s.19 and 4A of the POA,[31] with his sentence being enhanced under s.31 of the CDA. *R v Stacey* is discussed further in Section 4.4.

Under s.31(1) of the CDA:

> a person is guilty of an offence under this section if he commits (a) an offence under section 4 of the Public Order Act 1986 (fear or provocation of violence); (b) an offence under section 4A of that Act (intentional harassment, alarm or distress); or (c) an offence under section 5 of that Act (harassment, alarm or distress), which is racially or religiously aggravated for the purposes of this section.

Likewise, under s.32(1) of the CDA, a person is guilty if they commit an offence under either s.2, 2A, 4, or 4A of the PfHA which was racially or religiously hostile. In essence, for an enhanced sentence under either of these provisions (where the aggravated factor is race) it must be found that the action of the defendant amounts to a 'demonstration' or 'motivation' of 'hostility' to a 'racial group':

> An offence is racially or religiously aggravated [...] if (a) at the time of committing the offence, or immediately before or after doing so, the offender demonstrates towards the victim of the offence hostility based on the victim's membership (or presumed membership) of a racial or religious group; or (b)

29 Note, the Crime and Disorder Act 1988 also applies to a further two offences: assault (s.28) and criminal damage (s.29). However, these have not been included as they are not applicable to social media.

30 These provisions were updated in 2006 to include religion following the implementation of Racial and Religious Hatred Act 2006. And further updated in 2008 to include sexual ordination following the implementation Criminal Justice and Immigration Act 2008.

31 *R v Liam Stacey,* Swansea Crown Court On Appeal From The Magistrates' Court, A20120033.

> the offence is motivated (wholly or partly) by hostility towards members of a racial or religious group based on their membership of that group.[32]

Hostility is the base of the offence, though there is no definition of hostility either within the CDA or other relevant statutes. Instead, it has come to be accepted that hostility takes its everyday meaning and can include 'ill-will, spite, contempt, prejudice, unfriendliness, antagonism, resentment, and dislike'.[33] However, the hostility must be experienced at the time in which the offence took place or immediately prior to or after the event by establishing a connection between the hostility and the offence in question. Where hostility is not proven, it will be concluded that the actions of the defendant were not aggravated.[34] Similarly, a wide definition has been given to the term 'racial group' which is defined in the CDA as a 'group of persons defined by reference to race, colour, nationality (including citizenship), or ethnic or national origins'.[35] This includes, in certain circumstances, Gypsies and travellers, refugees, or asylum seekers, in which the courts have endorsed a flexible approach to the term.[36]

Next, the conduct either needs to demonstrate hostility or be motivated by hostility. Consequently, two limbs of the offence have been created: (1) motivation or (2) demonstration. Due to the difficulties in proving motivation, most cases are brought before the courts under the demonstration limb. To demonstrate hostility, this will usually involve words, though songs may also constitute a demonstration of hostility. This is a purely objective test, for the jury or magistrate to decide. The complainant's perceptions are not considered. Indeed, as is explored in Section 4.5.2 the demonstration of hostility has been heavily criticised as being overly expansive, rendering issues with legality.[37]

Whereas the motivation limb 'requires that the offence be motivated, in whole or in part, by hostility'[38] and requires a subjective analysis of the defendant's motivation. In essence, to be motivated by hostility it must be found that the person harboured some form of ill-will etc., towards the person, based on evidence gathered by the police, which can include social media postings or being part of a particular group. In addition, when it comes to demonstrating hostility, there must be an identifiable complainant—an element not needed under the motivation limb.

32 Crime and Disorder Act 1988 s28(1).
33 The Crown Prosecution Service, 'Hate crime' (*CPS.gov*, 2022) <https://www.cps.gov.uk/crime-info/hate-crime> accessed 24 October 2022.
34 Note, an individual could still be prosecuted for the base offence.
35 Crime and Disorder Act 1998 s28(4).
36 *Rogers* [2007] UKHL 8, [2007] 2 A.C. 62 [12].
37 Law Commission, *Hate Crime Laws: Final Report* (Law Com No 401, 2021) [9.38].
38 Ibid., [2.26].

4.3.3 Public Order Act 1986

The POA, in particular provisions related to 'stirring up' hate,[39] is considered one of the most controversial provisions in combatting hate crime, as it significantly impedes the right to freedom of expression—though considered by many as a legitimate interference. Its use in the criminal law framework is rare, although it has and continues to be used in a social media context, despite, as will be explored in Section 4.5, issues with the principle of legality, particularly given that the stirring up offences discussed in this section, do not explicitly cover internet communications.

The purpose behind the creation of the POA was:

> to abolish the common law offences of riot, rout, unlawful assembly and affray and certain statutory offences relating to public order; to create new offences relating to public order; to control public processions and assemblies; to control the stirring up of racial hatred.[40]

The POA was considered an opportunity to strengthen the law and 'aimed at protecting those in [...] communities who [were] most vulnerable to loutish and abusive behaviour'.[41] It introduced six types of conduct under the provision of 'stirring up racial hatred'.[42] However, the two which will be of focus for the purposes of this chapter are:

1. Using threatening, abusive, or insulting words or behaviour or displaying written material which is threatening, abusive, or insulting—s.18; and
2. Publishing or distributing written material which is threatening, abusive, or insulting—s.19.

Each of these sections will be taken in turn.

4.3.3.1 Section 18

S.18(1) makes it a criminal offence to use or display:

> written material or behaviour which is threatening, abusive or insulting [...] which intends thereby to stir up racial hatred, or having regard to all circumstances racial hatred is likely to be stirred up.

39 The provisions themselves were originally only aimed at stirring up racial hatred but have since been expanded to include religion and most recently, sexual ordination. See, Public Order Act 1986 Part 3A.

40 Public Order Act 1986.

41 HC Deb 13 January 1986, vol 89, col 793.

42 Similar provisions exist for religion and sexual orientation.

Although this does not include words or behaviours used or displayed as part of a programme. For example, those used in a TV drama.[43]

For a prosecution to be brought under this provision, consent of the Attorney General is needed, alongside establishing the *actus reus* and *mens rea* of the offence and disproving any defences raised, though the Crown Prosecution Service (CPS) also maintain:

> In deciding upon the public interest of charging these offences it is essential that prosecutors keep in mind that in a free, democratic, and tolerant society people are able to robustly exchange views, even when these may cause offence.[44]

The following discussion will outline the *actus reus* and *mens rea* of the offence under s.18 of the POA, before turning to examine the defences contained within the provision.

4.3.3.1.1 ACTUS REUS

The *actus reus* of s.18(1) comprises of several elements:

1. To use or display written material or behaviour. Neither display nor behaviour are defined in the POA. Instead, they are given their ordinary English meaning. I.e., their dictionary meaning. Whereas written material is defined as, 'signs or other visual representation',[45] and includes, as noted by the court in *R v Sheppard,*[46] articles sent in electronic form. However, it is important to note that live video broadcasts, which are common on most social media platforms, are not considered written material for the purposes of this section;[47]
2. The material or behaviour needs to be threatening, abusive, or insulting. These words take their 'ordinary English meaning' and are a question based on fact.[48] Though it's important to note, that the conduct does not have to fall under all three categories, one is sufficient. In essence, no specific definition is given in law as to the meaning of threatening, abusive, or insulting—though as discussed in Chapter 2, all could be considered as protected under the right to freedom of expression. Indeed, how terms such as threatening and abusive work in relation to freedom of expression is still not fully understood within

43 Public Order Act 1986 s18(6).

44 The Crown Prosecution Service, 'Racist and religious hate crime – prosecution guidance' (*CPS.gov*, 3 March 2022) <https://www.cps.gov.uk/legal-guidance/racist-and-religious-hate-crime-prosecution-guidance> accessed 24 October 2022.

45 Public Order Act 1986 s.29.

46 *R v Sheppard* [2010] EWCA Crim 65.

47 Law Com No 401 (n 37) [10.387].

48 The Crown Prosecution Service, 'Racist and religious hate crime – prosecution guidance' (*CPS.gov*, 2017) <http://www.cps.gov.uk/legal/p_to_r/racist_and_religious_crime/#a07> accessed 22 October 2017.

the criminal law framework.[49] The issues this renders with legality are discussed in Section 4.5.1.1;

3. The material must or will likely stir up racial hatred. As with the CDA discussed above, racial hatred is considered 'hatred against a group of persons [...] defined by reference to colour, race, nationality (including citizenship) or ethnic or national origins',[50] though the hatred needs to be directed at a group, 'not merely an individual'.[51] In which a literal approach should not be used when it comes to 'race'. Words such as 'African, foreigners, and immigrants' can fall within the definition of race.[52] In *R v Martin Hartshorn*[53] it was held that the use of the word 'Paki' amounted to racial hatred under the provision. The term likely is defined as 'more than merely possible or likely'[54] but does not include 'liable to';[55] and
4. The material or behaviour may be displayed in a public or private setting, however, 'no offence is committed where the words or behaviour are used, or the written material is displayed, by a person inside a dwelling and is not heard or seen except by other persons in that or another dwelling'.[56]

If all the factors above are established the *actus reus* for a s.18(1) offence under the POA can be proven. A failure to establish one or more of the elements discussed above would result in no criminal offence contrary to this provision.

4.3.3.1.2 MENS REA

In addition to establishing the factors discussed above, it must also be found that the accused also had the specific *mens rea* to commit an offence under s.18(1) of the POA. Two *mens rea* elements exist under this provision: (1) intent or (2) awareness. Intent under this provision can be summarised as to 'intentionally denigrate or demean those against whom the words are directed'.[57] Here intent is judged wholly objectively. Whereas to prove the *mens rea* of 'awareness' it must be found that the defendant 'intended his conduct to be, or was aware that it might be, "threatening,

49 Law Com No 401 (n 37) [10.96].

50 Public Order Act 1986 Part 3 s.17.

51 Law Com No 401 (n 37) [2.134].

52 The Crown Prosecution Service, 'Violent extremism and related criminal offences' (*CPS.gov*, 2017) <https://www.cps.gov.uk/publications/prosecution/cases_of_inciting_racial_and_religious_hatred_and_hatred_based_upon_sexual_orientation.html> accessed 22 October 2017.

53 *R v Martin Hartshorn*, Grimsby Crown Court, 4 November 2011 (unreported). See also, Dave Higgens, 'Man jailed for riot race-hate posts' *The Independent* (London, 4 November 2011) <http://www.independent.co.uk/news/uk/crime/man-jailed-for-riot-race-hate-posts-6257282.html> accessed 22 October 2017.

54 Violent Extremism and Related Criminal Offences (n 52).

55 *Parkin v Norman* [1983] QB 92, 100.

56 Public Order Act 1986 s.18(4).

57 David Ormerod and Karl Laird, *Smith, Hogan and Ormerod's Criminal Law* (16 edn, Oxford University Press 2021) [31.10.1.2].

abusive, or insulting" and that having regard to all the circumstances, racial hatred was likely to be stirred up thereby'.[58]

4.3.3.1.3 DEFENCES

Two specific defences are contained in s.18. First, it is a

> defence for the accused to prove that he was inside a dwelling and had no reason to believe that the words or behaviour used, or the written material displayed, would be heard or seen by a person outside that or any other dwelling.[59]

Second,

> A person who is not shown to have intended to stir up racial hatred is not guilty of an offence under this section if he did not intend his words or behaviour, or the written material, to be, and was not aware that it might be, threatening, abusive or insulting.[60]

If either of these defences can be proven, no offence has taken place contrary to s.18(1) of the POA. However, the defence itself does not apply to material published on the internet, even if such a communication was sent from a private dwelling, i.e., a person sending a message on X in the comfort of their own home.[61] In addition, the law has extended to note that this defence does not apply to all private conversations, where in *BC v Chief Constable of Scotland* it was held that the sending of messages on WhatsApp which were deemed as sexist, racist, antisemitic, homophobic, and disablist between a group of police officers, was not inherently private.[62]

4.3.3.2 Section 19

Whereas s.18(1) of the POA makes it an offence to display certain material, s.19(1) makes it a criminal offence to publish:

> written material which is threatening, abusive, or insulting [...] which intends thereby to stir up racial hatred, or having regard to all circumstances racial hatred is likely to be stirred up.

Like previous sections, the following discussion will outline the *actus reus* and *mens rea* of the offence under s.19(1) of the POA. Before turning to outline the defence contained within this provision.

58 Ibid., [31.10.1.3].
59 Public Order Act 1986 s.18(4).
60 Ibid., s.18(5).
61 *Sheppard* (n 46).
62 Law Com No 401 (n 37) [10.293].

4.3.3.2.1 ACTUS REUS

The *actus reus* under s.19(1) comprises of three elements:

1. The distribution or publication of written material. Here, it must be found that written material, which includes 'signs or other visual representation' is published or distributed to the 'public or a section of the public'.[63] As noted above, this would include material published on the internet, though would not necessarily cover emojis, memes, or gifs;[64]
2. The material published needs to be threatening, abusive, or insulting. As previously discussed, these words will take their 'ordinary English meaning' and are a question based on fact;[65] and
3. The material must or will likely stir up racial hatred. Again, the same meaning is given to this element of the offence as with s.18 of the POA discussed in Section 4.3.3.1.1.

If all three elements are established the *actus reus* of a s.19(1) public order offence can be proven. A failure to establish one or more of the elements discussed above would result in no criminal offence contrary to s.19(1) of the POA.

4.3.3.2.2 MENS REA

The *mens rea* under s.19(1) of the POA is the same as s.18(1)—done with intent or an awareness that a person's actions were likely to stir up racial hatred.

4.3.3.2.3 DEFENCE

Whereas s.18 of the POA has several defences, s.19 contains one very specific defence:

> In proceedings for an offence under this section it is a defence for an accused who is not shown to have intended to stir up racial hatred to prove that he was not aware of the content of the material and did not suspect, and had no reason to suspect, that it was threatening, abusive or insulting.[66]

If such can be proven, no offence will be deemed to have taken place contrary to s.19(1) of the POA.

63 Public Order Act 1986 s.29.
64 Law Com No 401 (n 37) [10.323].
65 Racist and Religious Hate Crime – Prosecution Guidance (n 48).
66 Public Order Act 1986 s.19(2).

4.3.4 Summary

It is clear that the provisions discussed above all have one recurring theme: they are all embedded in vague terminology. Concerns can be raised with the lack of understanding as to what is meant by the terms threatening, abusive, or insulting. Indeed, as outlined in Section 4.5.1.1, each of these types of communications could fall within the right to freedom of expression. For the Law Commission, during their consultation into hate crime laws:

> [w]here the law affects a right like freedom of expression, uncertainty, and misunderstandings of the law can create a 'chilling effect' on the exercise of that right, even if that interference itself is permissible, proportionate, and justified.[67]

Further, as illustrated in Section 4.5.2, issues can also be raised with proving the 'demonstration of hostility'. Issues, which undermine the principle of legality, especially when examining the use of the POA in a social media context.

4.4 Social Media, Racism, and the Criminal Law

As social media usage has increased, and in turn, we have seen a rise in the use of such platforms to send racist communications, we have witnessed the use of all the provisions discussed above, being used to arrest, prosecute, and/or convict individuals for their online conduct. In particular, the use of s.18 and 19 of the POA. For instance, these provisions were used to arrest several individuals in the wake of England's defeat in the 2020 Euros.

Following the defeat, some individuals took to social media platforms to vent their frustrations, and in some cases, grounding these frustrations in racist commentary. For example, in the aftermath of the defeat, three individuals were arrested on suspicion of committing an offence contrary to either s.18 or 19 of the POA—though none were actually convicted of a POA offence.[68]

In *R v Paul Bradbury*,[69] the defendant was originally arrested on suspicion of displaying written material which was threatening, abusive, or insulting which was likely to stir up racial hatred contrary to s.18(1) of the POA after posting the following message: 'Whites only in future'. Similarly, in *R v Hugh Laidlaw* the defendant was originally arrested under s.18 of the POA for allegedly posting images and comments containing racist material on Facebook. Whereas in *R v*

67 Law Com No 401 (n 37) [10.10].

68 National Police Chiefs' Council, 'Hate crime investigation following Euro 2020 final leads to 11 arrests' (*NPCC*, 5 August 2021) <https://news.npcc.police.uk/releases/hate-crime-investigation-following-euro-2020-final-leads-to-11-arrests> accessed 24 October 2022.

69 *R v Paul Bradbury*, Telford Magistrates' Court, 4 March 2022 (unreported). See also, The Crown Prosecution Service, 'Former councillor pleads guilty to posting racist comments about England football players' (*CPS.gov*, 4 March 2022) <https://www.cps.gov.uk/west-midlands/news/former-councillor-pleads-guilty-posting-racist-comments-about-england> accessed 24 October 2022.

Scott McCluskey,[70] the defendant was arrested under suspicion of displaying threatening, abusive, or insulting written material that was likely to stir up racial hatred contrary to s.19(1) of the POA, for using Facebook to make several racist remarks.

However, in all the cases outlined above, each defendant was later charged and pleaded guilty to sending a grossly offensive message contrary to s.127(1) of the CA as opposed to a public order offence. Similarly, in *DPP v Bussetti*,[71] the defendant was originally arrested contrary to an offence under the POA. He was later charged and convicted of committing an offence contrary to s.127(1) of the CA, after sharing a video on WhatsApp of a bonfire party, mocking the deaths of those who died in a tower block fire in London, in 2017.

There have however been some successful prosecutions in a social media context under the 'stirring up' offences contained in the POA.[72] For example, s.19(1) of the POA was successfully utilised in *R v Liam Stacey*, who in 2012, was convicted and sentenced to 56 days in jail for sending racist and obscene tweets, following the collapse of Bolton Wanderers star Fabrice Muamba during a football match.[73] Fabrice Muamba went into cardiac arrest live on television. For six minutes medical staff helped to resuscitate him on the pitch.[74] Following the incident, Stacey took to his Twitter page to make several racist comments about the footballer including: 'LOL [Laughing out Loud]. Fuck Muamba he's dead [*sic*]!!! #Haha' and 'Go suck a nigger [*sic*] dick you fucking aids-ridden cunt'. Stacey made numerous tweets of this nature not only aimed at Fabrice Muamba but also other individuals who attempted to defend the footballer.[75]

Despite some successful prosecutions, it is not always clear why the POA is used in some cases, but not in others, as highlighted in Section 4.5.3 below. This creates inconsistencies within the law. The issues this presents with the principle of legality, alongside the vagueness inherent in the provisions outlined thus far, are discussed in the final parts of this chapter.

70 *R v Scott McCluskey,* Warrington Magistrates' Court, 8 September 2021 (unreported). See also, The Crown Prosecution Service, 'Cheshire man sentenced for racist abuse of England players' (*CPS .gov*, 8 September 2021) <https://www.cps.gov.uk/mersey-cheshire/news/cheshire-man-sentenced-racist-abuse-england-players> accessed 24 October 2022.

71 *DPP v Kingsley Anthony Smith* [2017] EWHC 359 (Admin).

72 Another 'successful' case includes *R v Stuart Sutton,* Bolton Crown Court, 21 December 2022 (unreported). See, Greater Manchester Police, 'Wigan man jailed for posting racist and anti-Semitic material' (*GMP*, 22 December 2022) <https://www.gmp.police.uk/news/greater-manchester/news/news/2022/december/wigan-man-jailed-for-posting-racist-and-anti-semitic-material/> accessed 1 Feb 2023.

73 *Stacey* (n 31).

74 BBC Sport, 'Bolton's Fabrice Muamba collapses during Spurs-Bolton match' *The BBC* (London, 17 March 2012) <http://www.bbc.co.uk/sport/football/17417973> accessed 10 January 2018.

75 Steven Morris, 'Student jailed for racist Fabrice Muamba tweets' *The Guardian* (London, 27 March 2012) <https://www.theguardian.com/uk/2012/mar/27/student-jailed-fabrice-muamba-tweets> accessed 10 January 2018.

4.5 Hate Crime, Legality, and the Criminal Law

It is important that the law, in particular the criminal law, is not used to send social signals as to what is or is not socially acceptable; or to impose unjust moral standpoints on freedom of expression. Though the effect of hate speech, in particular, racist speech online should not, and cannot, be downplayed, the use of such words is a systematic societal issue—not an issue that is unique to the digital world. And no matter how much criminal law is imposed on the digital world, legal norms will not take effect until societal norms have evolved.

Yet there continues to be a strong emphasis on using the criminal law to tackle such comments being made on social media sites despite, as will be outlined below, issues with the principle of legality in the legal provisions discussed above and their application to social media. Indeed, as will be shown, some of these provisions are being stretched well beyond their original purpose and in turn, threatening freedom of expression. The discussion below argues that such use of the criminal law, in the context of social media, is not prospective or clear. As a result, inconsistent application of the law, across the criminal justice system, is leading to unfair enforcement of the law—all of which undermines the principle of legality.

4.5.1 The Issue of Language

As was touched upon in Section 4.3, all the provisions discussed in this chapter are grounded in vague terminology. In particular, issues can be raised with the use of the terms insulting, abusive, and hostile—all of which are deemed to take their ordinary English meaning, rendering issues with the principle of legality and the right to freedom of expression. Each of these terms will be taken in turn and examined against the principle of legality in the following discussion.

In addition, the use of the term threatening, as found in both s.18(1) and 19(1) of the POA, renders issues with clarity in the criminal law. However, the issues the term threatening posses with legality and the right to freedom of expression will not be discussed here. Instead, the issue of quantifying what a threatening communication is, will be discussed in Chapters 6 and 7, where a similar term, threat, was used in s.1 of the Malicious Communications Act 1988 and now contained in s.181 of the OSA, alongside 'menacing' in s.127(1) of the CA.

4.5.1.1 The Meaning of Abusive and Insulting

Both s.18(1) and 19(1) of the POA prohibit either the use or display (s.18) or the publishing or distributing (s.19) of material which can be considered either abusive or insulting and has the possibility of stirring up racial hatred. Yet neither of these terms, abusive or insulting, are defined within the POA, nor are defined elsewhere in the criminal law framework. Consequently, both abusive and insulting are deemed to take their ordinary English meaning. I.e., insulting can be defined, with reference to the Cambridge English Dictionary, as 'rude or offensive';[76] abusive can be defined as 'using rude and offensive words'.[77]

The lack of a definition as to the meaning of abusive and insulting has surprisingly been supported by those working in the judicial system. For instance, in *Brutus v Cozens*,[78] the House of Lords, who in the context of s.5 of the Public Order Act 1936[79] supported their inherent vagueness:

> We were referred to a number of dictionary meanings of 'insult' such as treating with insolence or contempt or indignity or derision or dishonour or offensive disrespect. Many things otherwise unobjectionable may be said or done in an insulting way. There can be no definition. But an ordinary sensible man knows an insult when he sees or hears it [...] vigorous and it may be distasteful or unmannerly speech or behaviour is permitted so long as it does not go beyond any one of three limits. It must not be threatening. It must not be abusive. It must not be insulting. I see no reason why any of these should be construed as having a specially wide or a specially narrow meaning. They are all limits easily recognisable by the ordinary man. [80]

Indeed, the House of Lords even went as far as suggesting that prohibiting such behaviour did not restrict the right to freedom of speech.[81]

However, it is important to note that the Public Order Act 1936, to which the House of Lords was referring to in *Brutus* predates the European Convention on Human Rights (ECHR) and therefore such terminology may not be complicit with human rights today. This is especially true given that the European Court of Human Rights (ECtHR), as discussed in detail in Chapter 2, has acknowledged that free speech includes the right to be offensive.[82] And most recently, the UK Divisional Court suggested that free speech encompasses the right to be abusive.[83] This has been further supported by the Law Commission which noted, in their recent review on hate crimes that prohibiting insulting material, is not necessarily compatible with Article 10 of the ECHR[84] and indeed, raised concerns about the lack of understanding as to when certain conduct will invoke s.18 or 19 of the POA:

76 Cambridge Dictionary, 'Insult' (*Cambridge Dictionary*, 2023) <https://dictionary.cambridge.org/dictionary/english/insult> accessed 8 February 2023.

77 Cambridge Dictionary, 'Abusive' (*Cambridge Dictionary*, 2023) <https://dictionary.cambridge.org/dictionary/english/abusive> accessed 8 February 2023.

78 *Brutus v Cozens* [1973] A.C. 854.

79 Which prohibited an individual in a public place or at any public meeting from using 'threatening, abusive or insulting words or behaviour with intent to provoke a breach of the peace'.

80 *Brutus* (n 78) per Lord Reid at 862.

81 Ibid.,

82 *Handyside v The United Kingdom* (1976)1 EHRR 737 [49].

83 *Katherine Elizabeth Scottow v Crown Prosecution Service* [2020] EWHC 3421 (Admin) per Justice Warby [43].

84 Law Com No 401 (n 37) [10.305].

> We believe that insofar as the law itself may be giving rise to ill-founded complaints that interfere with the right to freedom of expression, the correct way to address this is by clearly defining the limits of the stirring up offences [...] It is possible that in making clear that the law does not criminalise—for instance—discussion of controversial topics, our recommendations will enable law enforcement officials to deal robustly in dismissing complaints that do not amount to a criminal offence.[85]

Yet, as it currently stands, s.18 and 19 of the POA continues to be used to prohibit online communications.

With such a reliance on the 'ordinary meaning' of the terms insulting and abusive it is difficult to see how consistency can be maintained in the law, particularly when it comes to social media posts, where in the online world, it is expected that there should be a little bit of give-and-take. What one police force or Crown Prosecutor might consider to be insulting or abusive another may not, and the boundary between protected speech and non-protected speech is not easily identifiable. To set the bar so low, in this instance, abusive or insulting, when it comes to speech, is to risk the overcriminalisation of free speech. As potently put by the Law Commission:

> We are wary of attempts to use the criminal law merely to send a social signal, whether that is towards making the expression of certain views unacceptable, or, conversely, to encourage social acceptance of a broader range of views.[86]

The issues of consistency and clarity are further reflected in the notion of what constitutes hostility.

4.5.1.2 The Meaning of Hostility

Hostility is 'central to [...] hate crime provisions in England and Wales'.[87] Yet, there is no definition in law as to the meaning of hostility, 'nor is there any standard direction on what types of conduct it might encompass'.[88] This is despite hostility being central to all the provisions discussed above. With a lack of a statutory definition, alongside a failure of the courts to establish the boundaries of what constitutes hostility, the term has been given its ordinary dictionary meaning:

85 Ibid., [10.38].

86 Ibid., [10.34].

87 Mark Austin Walters, 'Conceptualizing Hostility for Hate Crime Law: Minding the Minutiae When Interpreting s.28(1)(a) of the Crime and Disorder Act 1998' (2014) 34 (1) Oxf. J. Leg. Stud 47, 48.

88 Ibid.,

> Hostility is not defined in the legislation. Consideration should be given to ordinary dictionary definitions, which include ill-will, ill-feeling, spite, prejudice, unfriendliness, antagonism, resentment, and dislike.[89]

This is a particularly wide net to set, with Walters stating: '[i]t is likely that many fact finders will simply turn to colloquial understandings of what they think hostility means when determining an offender's guilt'.[90] In turn, it cannot be said that consistency is being maintained in the criminal law. What one 'fact finder' may consider 'ill-will, ill-feeling, spite, prejudice, unfriendliness, antagonism, resentment, and dislike' and therefore hostile, another may not—a reoccurring theme throughout this monograph. This becomes more complex when the provisions discussed above are applied to communications sent *via* social media. Here messages can be exchanged in an instant, but the context behind such messages can be lost, and not fully understood to those on the outside looking in.

Indeed, the ordinary dictionary meaning given to hostility includes many natural human emotions or behaviours, which all fall within the boundaries of freedom of expression, such as 'unfriendliness' and 'dislike'. Such reliance on a term, without a clear understanding of its meaning, can result in broad interpretations and at its very basic, for the law to be compatible with the principle of legality, provisions need to be clear and prospective. How can digital citizens guide their online behaviour in accordance with the law, if the law itself casts such a wide net over what might be considered hostile?

What might be considered as 'dislike' or 'contempt' to one, and therefore hostile, to another might be considered political debate to others. As noted at the start of this chapter, for Murray, 'sometimes there is a fine line between political speech and hate speech'.[91] Therefore to centralise criminal provisions around hostility, without clearly defining the boundaries of the term, is to risk unfair enforcement of the law.

4.5.1.3 Summary

It is evidently clear, from discussions above, that the provisions used to tackle racist comments online are embedded in significantly vague terminology, creating inconsistencies in their application to complaints of social media (mis)usage. This, in turn, renders issues with the principle of legality. For legality to be maintained in the criminal law, criminal provisions should not be so overly vague. Yet, the use of the terms insulting, abusive or hostile have no true definition in law. Consequently, the law, as it currently stands, does not allow individuals to reasonably understand when their behaviour may fall foul of the law. Again, concerns which have not gone unnoticed with the Law Commission previously noting:

89 Hate Crime (n 33).
90 Walters (n 87).
91 Murray (n 6).

> [we] are deeply concerned that misrepresentation as to the sort of conduct which are caught by the stirring up offences may lead people to avoid saying things that they are perfectly entitled to express.[92]

This is even more concerning given, as illustrated above, the dictionary definitions of these terms, insulting, abusive, or hostile could all fall within the right to freedom of expression. Democracy depends on people being free to express, debate, and criticise opposing viewpoints and social media is an important aspect of this, where political debate or contentious issues are often discussed. And it is only through having these discussions that we can attempt to seek 'truth'.[93] Indeed, the ECtHR in *Jersild v Denmark* maintains speech that is intended to inform rather than offend attracts greater protection, even if it could be construed as racist.[94]

In turn, when complaints are made to police forces, Crown Prosecutors, etc., without a clear understanding as to when a communication crosses the threshold to be considered so insulting, abusive, or hostile to invoke the criminal law, results in consistency being lost. Consistency is needed, to ensure public faith in the criminal justice system is maintained. Similar arguments are raised in Chapters 6 and 7. These concerns are further amplified when considering what is meant by demonstrating hostility under the CDA and the SA.

4.5.2 Demonstrating Hostility

The demonstration of hostility is central to both s.66 of the SA and s.31 and 32 of the CDA. Yet it has been heavily criticised in the literature for being overly broad and in turn, overly expansive:

> What constitutes the 'hostility' needed to prove 'racial aggravation', for example, is a source of contention for legal practitioners. In some local magistrates' courts, for example, there is: 'a current of opinion, most often expressed by stipendiary magistrates and defence solicitors, that the law came down rather hard on people who, in the course of "normal working class mayhem" as one person put it, uttered words which were part of their natural vocabulary'.[95]

Consequently, there is growing evidence that 'any reference to the victim's ethnicity in connection with an offence' proves 'the necessary element of racial

92 Law Com No 401 (n 37) [10.12].

93 John Stuart Mill, *On Liberty* (first published 1859, Enhanced Media 2016) 40.

94 *Jersild v Denmark* (1994) (Application no. 15890/89).

95 David Gadd, 'Aggravating Racism and Elusive Motivation' (2009) 49 Brit. J. Criminol 755, 758. Quote found in Elizabeth Burney and Gerry Rose, *Racist Offences: How Is the Law Working?; the Implementation of the Legislation on Racially Aggravated Offences in the Crime and Disorder Act 1998* (Home Office Research Study, 2002) 20.

aggravation' due to the purely objective test used to determine what constitutes the demonstration of hostility.[96]

By assessing the demonstration of hostility objectively, it has resulted in conflicting opinions:

> those who adopt a free-speech outlook are likely to view a (potentially) hateful act as non-hostile whereas those who adopt a critical race theory perspective may view it as definitely hostile and hateful. These differing positions are often irreconcilable.[97]

This is even more glaringly apparent in a social media situation where, as noted previously and will be echoed throughout this monograph, context is often lost and opposing viewpoints are easy to come by—whether a person is actively looking for it or not. Indeed, many social media platforms use algorithms to bring content to a user's attention, without the user actively searching for such content. The role social media platforms play in spreading such content is discussed further in Chapter 8.

Consequently, the broad understanding as to what is considered the demonstration of hostility gives actors working in the criminal justice system significant discretion as to what constitutes not only the meaning of 'hostility', but also the demonstration requirement. In turn, this poses significant issues with the principle of legality. As discussed at length in Chapter 3: 'legality requires that judges and other officials apply statutory law, not according to their fancy or with crabbed literalness, but in accordance with principles of interpretation'.[98] Yet, growing research suggests that 'crabbed literalness' is being applied to such offences.[99]

For The Alan Turing Institute, if the bar is not set high enough in determining what is considered as demonstrating hostility, there is the real possibility of the overcriminalisation of speech.[100] When it comes to social media, something said in the heat of the moment, to hostile and hateful behaviour, is not easily identifiable and embedding legal provisions in broad concepts, such as 'demonstrating hostility' undermines the action-guiding nature of the law. In turn, due process is at risk, alongside the coercive nature of the law being abused. Anecdotally it has been suggested that

> defendants have tended to contest this inference, often proving willing to admit to the basic (non-racially aggravated) charges, but unwilling to plead guilty to their racially aggravated equivalents.[101]

96 Ibid.,
97 Law Com No 401 (n 37) [9.51].
98 Lon L Fuller, *The morality of law* (Yale University Press 1964) 82.
99 Walters (n 87).
100 Law Com No 401 (n 37) [9.51].
101 Gadd (n 95).

4.5.3 Going Beyond Parliament's Intent: The Purpose of the POA

The purpose and rationale behind the creation of the POA was, and still preserves to be, to maintain public order, with Moses J in *Dehal v CPS* when referring to the POA stating:

> the criminal law should not be invoked unless and until it is established that the conduct which is the subject of the charge amounts to such a threat to public order as to require the invocation of the criminal as opposed to the civil law.[102]

Indeed, for Dorfman, the POA should not be used in the context of social media, especially when there is no element of violence present. Using *R v Stacey*, discussed above, Dorfman argues that:

> [U]sing the Public Order Act for a few nasty Twitter comments which never advocated violence or hatred against specific people is a downright abuse of the law; at no time was 'public order' ever threatened in any reasonable conception of the term.[103]

For Dorfman, the conduct of Stacey lacked the relevant criteria needed to prosecute an individual under the POA, despite Stacey's successful conviction. Though his behaviour was abusive and had a racial element, his actions did not stir up racial hatred nor could it be said that it was likely to cause racial hatred and consequently, criminal proceedings under the POA was an abuse of the law. Similar arguments were raised by Walters:

> Though this author is in agreement with the outpouring of social disapproval and the prosecution of offenders who commit public order offences aggravated by racism, it is felt that the sentence in this case [*Stacey*] was grossly disproportionate to the seriousness of the offence [...] it is worth highlighting a couple of points about the punishment of hate crime offenders. First, it cannot be denied that without effective punishments the criminalization [*sic*] of hate would become almost meaningless, and as such those who transgress hate crime laws must face some form of punishment. Still, some judicial restraint is required if hate crime laws are not to become simply another means through which we add to an ever growing prison population.[104]

Indeed, the CPS guidelines on social media related offences from 2016 stated:

102 *Dehal v Crown Prosecution Service* [2005] EWHC 2154 per Moses J [5].

103 Rosalee Dorfman, 'Can you say "social media prosecutions" with a straight face? The Crown Prosecution Service can' (2013) LSLCJR <http://criminology.leeds.ac.uk/2013/09/05/social-media-prosecutions/> accessed 20 October 2016.

104 Walters (n 87) 57.

> [P]articular care should be taken in dealing with social media cases in this way because public order legislation is primarily concerned with words spoken or actions carried out in the presence or hearing of the person being targeted (i.e. where there is physical proximity between the speaker and the listener).[105]

Yet in December 2022, Stuart Sutton was convicted under s.19(1) of the POA for sending racist and antisemitic material on social media, despite no complaint being made and his posts only coming to the attention of the police following the gathering of intelligence in another matter. He received a 16 month custodial sentence.[106]

The CPS maintain that the POA should only be used in limited circumstances, but it is not clear from the guidelines what constitutes these conditions. The guidelines mention the difference between 'irritating, contentious, unwelcome, and provocative' conduct and behaviour that provokes violence, though no clarity is given beyond this.[107] Although the Law Commission notes:

> [t]he offences [stirring up hate] do not criminalise conduct expressing or inciting hostility or hatred towards specific individuals. Rather, they address conduct intended or likely to cause others to hate entire national or ethnic groups.[108]

Further, the POA was used on several occasions in 2021 to arrest several individuals for sending racist abuse online aimed at three English footballer's, as mentioned in Section 4.4 above. The National Police Chief's Council confirmed in the aftermath of England's defeat in the 2020 Euros, 11 arrests, of which three individuals were originally arrested under provisions contained in the POA, yet later convicted under s.127(1) of the CA, as shown in Table 4.1. The use of the POA in some circumstances, and not in others, evidently leaves open, once again, questions on consistency within this area of the criminal law. For instance, the POA was applied in *Stacey* but not in the matter of *R v Alison Chabloz*.[109]

Chabloz, who defines herself as a holocaust revolutionist, as discussed further in Chapter 6, uploaded several YouTube videos online mocking Holocaust victims and survivors, including Anne Frank. In these videos, she also made 'expressions of anti-Semitic hatred',[110] in which it was put before the court that her actions were

105 The Crown Prosecution Service, 'Guidelines on prosecuting cases involving communications sent via social media' (*CPS.gov*, 2016) <https://www.cps.gov.uk/legal-guidance/guidelines-prosecuting-cases-involving-communications-sent-social-media> accessed 10 January 2018. Note, this is no longer included in the most updated version of the guidelines.

106 *Sutton* (n 72).

107 Racist and Religious Hate Crime – Prosecution Guidance (n 48).

108 Law Com No 401 (n 37) [2.126].

109 *R v Alison Chabloz,* Westminster Magistrates' Court, 11 January 2018 (unreported).

110 ITV News, 'Blogger "mocked Anne Frank and Holocaust survivors" court told' *ITV News* (London, 11 January 2018) <http://www.itv.com/news/2018-01-11/blogger-mocked-anne-frank-and-holocaust-survivors-court-told/> accessed 11 January 2018.

Table 4.1 Arrests and outcomes following the abuse of three England footballer's in the aftermath of the Euros 2020

Details	*Arrest*	*Outcome*
Scott McCluskey arrested for posting racist and insulting comments on Facebook.	Arrested on suspicion of displaying threatening, abusive, or insulting written material that is likely to stir up racial hatred contrary to s.19(1) of the POA.	Convicted of a s.127(1) offence, in which s.66 of the SA was applied to 'uplift the punishment'.
Paul Bradbury arrested for posting 'whites only in the future'.	Arrested on suspicion of committing an offence contrary to s.18(1) of the POA.	Convicted of a s.127(1) offence.
Hugh Laidlaw arrested for posting comments and images online of a racist nature.	Arrested on suspicion of committing an offence contrary to s.18(1) of the POA.	Convicted of a s.127(1) offence.

'designed to provoke maximum upset and discomfort'.[111] Despite this, she was convicted for sending grossly offensive material *via* a communications network contrary to s.127(1) of the CA, even though her actions, by applying the case of *Stacey,* could be *akin* to an offence under the POA.

Both Stacey's and Chabloz's conduct can be considered abusive, at the very least, and arguably demonstrated racial hatred. Stacey used the phrase, 'go suck a nigger [*sic*] dick you fucking aids-ridden cunt'. Chabloz used several antisemitic terms, including comparing Auschwitz concentration camp to 'a theme park just for fools'. The main issue falls on whether the behaviour of both defendants was likely to stir up racial hatred. In *Stacey,* the CPS concluded that this was the case, though this is not fully accepted in the academic literature.[112] Whereas in *Chabloz* it is unclear if this was considered by the CPS as charges were brought under a different Act of Parliament. If the rationale of *Stacey* is applied, it is hard to distinguish why Chabloz was not prosecuted for a breach of s.19(1) of the POA. This is even more apparent as during the hearing held at Westminsters' Magistrates' Court, one of Chabloz's videos was played to the court, which was met with a round-of-applause by supporters in the public gallery.[113] Arguably, the POA fails to uphold the key principles of legality, as it is uncertain when this Act will be used in a social media context, as there is a lack of consistency as to when the CPS will press charges under the POA for social media related offences.

It could be said that the law has adapted to the changing nature of society, by using the POA to criminalise conduct carried out online. The adaptation of the law to fit the changing circumstances of a given society conforms to the principle of

111 Ibid.,
112 Dorfman (n 103).
113 ITV News (n 110).

legality as affirmed in *SW and CR v The United Kingdom*,[114] so long as the change is foreseeable. However, under the POA the prohibited conduct must incite public disorder as public order is considered a 'fundamental social good'.[115] Whereas public disorder affects the social wellbeing of a society, this was reflected in the tough stance taken by Parliament during the implementation of the POA:

> The 1986 Act like its predecessor is very much a pragmatic reaction to recent events. It was passed against the background of inner-city disturbances, soccer hooliganism, racist marches, and racist attacks on members of the ethnic minorities, mass industrial picketing and the resurgence of major public demonstrations. The Act is not founded on well articulated premises addressing the scope and ambit of the criminal law in the area of public order.[116]

The purpose of the POA was to regulate public disorder in particular, riots, football hooliganism, and protests which were very much apparent during the early 1980s, an element missing in the matter of *Stacey*. Yet the Act has been used to cover social media related offences, despite the POA being enacted at least 20 years before the likes of X, Facebook, Snapchat, TikTok, etc. For Haralambous and Geach this is a clear breach of the rule of law, and consequently undermines the principle of legality in the criminal law,[117] as the law, at the very least should 'be accessible and so far, as possible intelligible, clear, and predictable',[118] arguably areas missing regarding the use of the POA in a social media context, in turn, creating retrospective criminal law.

4.6 Chapter Summary

As eloquently put by the Law Commission,

> [w]hile there is a role for legislation in underpinning this and criminalising the most serious forms of hate speech, we consider that the most important driver of this change must be social change.[119]

Yet, there continues to be significant emphasis being placed on the criminal law to tackle racist commentary online. This could be partly because the underlying message behind hate crime legislation is:

> [t]o deal with this uniquely expressive form of offending, society needs to send an equally forceful and unambiguous message in reply and, for

114 *SW v The United Kingdom, CR v The United Kingdom* App no. 20166/92 (ECtHR, 22 November 1995).

115 HC Deb 13 January 1986, vol 89, cols 793.

116 Jim Driscoll, 'Protest and Public Order: The Public Order Act 1986' (1987) Sep J.S.W.L. 280.

117 Nicola Haralambous and Neal Geach, 'Online Harassment and Public *Dis*-order' (2010) 174 CL&J 409, 411.

118 Lord Bingham, 'The Rule of Law' (2007) 66(1) CLJ 67, 69-70.

119 Law Com No 401 (n 37) [10.40].

advocates of hate crime legislation, the criminal law is an important, if not the only, suitable means of communication.[120]

But the criminal law cannot always be the answer. We need to ensure that due process is being maintained.

This is a key element missing in the current use of applying the provisions discussed in this chapter to conduct carried out online. This chapter has demonstrated key issues with the principle of legality. In particular,

- The vagueness inherent in the language used in all three provisions. Of note, is the lack of understanding as to what is deemed insulting, abusive, or hostile. The definitions that have been given to these terms by the jurisprudence of the courts, through the application of their ordinary English meaning, can all fall within the right to freedom of expression;
- The demonstration of hostility as contained in s.66 of the SA and s.31 and 32 of the CDA. This poses significant issues with the principle of legality as there is a lack of understanding as to what constitutes the demonstration limb of the offence. What one police force might consider the demonstration of hostility, another may not, leading to inconsistent application of the law; and
- The application of stirring up offences going beyond Parliament's original intent, creating retrospective criminal law.

Many of the issues highlighted in this chapter are also applicable to other areas of the criminal law and its application to social media abuse.

Reference List

Baggs M, 'Online hate speech rose 20% during pandemic: "We've normalised it"' *The BBC* (London, 15 November 2021) https://www.bbc.co.uk/news/newsbeat-59292509

Bandwatch Academy, 'Uncovered: Online Hate Speech in the Covid Era' (*Bandwatch Academy*, 2022) https://www.brandwatch.com/reports/online-hate-speech/view/

BBC Sport, 'Bolton's Fabrice Muamba collapses during Spurs-Bolton match' *The BBC* (London, 17 March 2012) http://www.bbc.co.uk/sport/football/17417973

Bell, M, 'John Stuart Mill's Harm Principle and Free Speech: Expanding the Notion of Harm' (2021) 33(2) Utilitas 162

Bingham B, *The Rule of Law* (Penguin 2011)

Bleich E, 'The Rise of Hate Speech and Hate Crime Laws in Liberal Democracies' (2011) 37(6) J Ethn Migr Stud 917

Burney E & Rose G, *Racist Offences: How Is the Law Working?; the Implementation of the Legislation on Racially Aggravated Offences in the Crime and Disorder Act 1998* (Home Office Research Study, 2002)

Cambridge Dictionary, 'Abusive' (*Cambridge Dictionary*, 2023) https://dictionary.cambridge.org/dictionary/english/abusive

120 Bill Dixon and David Gadd, 'Getting the Message? "New" Labour and the Criminalization of "Hate"' (2006) 6(3) CCJ 309, 310.

Cambridge Dictionary, 'Insult' (*Cambridge Dictionary*, 2023) https://dictionary.cambridge.org/dictionary/english/insult

de Varennes F, 'Recommendations Made by the Forum on Minority Issues at Its thirteenth Session on the Theme "Hate Speech, Social Media and Minorities"' (*United Nations*, 26 January 2021) https://documents-dds-ny.un.org/doc/UNDOC/GEN/G21/017/29/PDF/G2101729.pdf?OpenElement

Discourse and Barring Service, 'About Us' (*Gov.uk*, 2022) https://www.gov.uk/government/organisations/disclosure-and-barring-service/about

Dixon B & Gadd D, 'Getting the Message? "New" Labour and the criminalization of "Hate"' (2006) 6(3) CCJ 309

Dorfman R, 'Can You Say "Social Media Prosecutions" with a Straight Face? The Crown Prosecution Service Can' (2013) LSLCJR http://criminology.leeds.ac.uk/2013/09/05/social-media-prosecutions/

Driscoll J, 'Protest and Public Order: The Public Order Act 1986' (1987) Sep JSWL 280

Evans S, 'English Football Faces up to Global Nature of Online Hate' (*Reuters*, 26 May 2022) https://www.reuters.com/lifestyle/sports/english-football-faces-up-global-nature-online-hate-2021-07-13/

Fuller L L, *The Morality of Law* (Yale University Press 1964)

Gadd D, 'Aggravating Racism and Elusive Motivation' (2009) 49 Brit J Criminol 755

Google, 'YouTube Community Guidelines Enforcement' (*Google*, 2022) https://transparencyreport.google.com/youtube-policy/removals?hl=en&total_channels_removed=period:2021Q1&lu=channels_by_reason&channels_by_reason=period:2021Q4

Greater Manchester Police, 'Wigan Man Jailed for Posting Racist and Anti-Semitic Material' (*GMP*, 22 December 2022) https://www.gmp.police.uk/news/greater-manchester/news/news/2022/december/wigan-man-jailed-for-posting-racist-and-anti-semitic-material/

Haralambous N, & Geach N, 'Online Harassment and Public *Dis*-order' (2010) 174 CL&JW 409

HC Deb 13 January 1986, vol 89, col 793

Heard C, 'Hate Crime Law: More Incrementalism or Time for Reform?' (2014) (7) Arch Rev 4

Higgens D, 'Man jailed for riot race-hate posts' *The Independent* (London, 4 November 2011) http://www.independent.co.uk/news/uk/crime/man-jailed-for-riot-race-hate-posts-6257282.html

Home Office, 'Hate Crime, England and Wales, 2021 to 2022' (*Gov.uk*, 6 October 2022) <https://www.gov.uk/government/statistics/hate-crime-england-and-wales-2021-to-2022/hate-crime-england-and-wales-2021-to-2022>

ITV News, 'Blogger "mocked Anne Frank and Holocaust survivors" court told' *ITV News* (London, 11 January 2018) http://www.itv.com/news/2018-01-11/blogger-mocked-anne-frank-and-holocaust-survivors-court-told/

Jamieson A, 'Bukayo Saka, Jadon Sancho and Marcus Rashford racially abused online after England Euro 2020 final defeat' *The Independent* (London, 12 July 2021) https://www.independent.co.uk/news/uk/home-news/bukayo-saka-racist-england-sancho-rashford-b1882303.html

Laville S, 'Internet troll who sent labour MP antisemitic abused is jailed' *The Guardian* (London, 10 February 2017) https://www.theguardian.com/uknews/2017/feb/10/internet-troll-who-sent-labour-mp-antisemitic-messages-is-jailed

Law Commission, *Hate Crime Laws: Final Report* (Law Com No 401, 2021)

Lord Bingham, 'The Rule of Law' (2007) 66(1) CLR 67

Meta, 'Hate Speech' (*Meta*, 2022) https://transparency.fb.com/en-gb/policies/community-standards/hate-speech/

Mill J S, *On Liberty* (first published 1859, Enhanced Media 2016)

Morris S, 'Student jailed for racist Fabrice Muamba tweets' *The Guardian* (London, 27 March 2012) https://www.theguardian.com/uk/2012/mar/27/student-jailed-fabrice-muamba-tweets

Murray A, *Information Technology Law: The Law and Society* (5th edn, Oxford University Press 2023)

National Police Chiefs' Council, 'Hate Crime Investigation Following Euro 2020 Final Leads to 11 Arrests' (*NPCC*, 5 August 2021) https://news.npcc.police.uk/releases/hate-crime-investigation-following-euro-2020-final-leads-to-11-arrests

Newman S L, 'Finding the Harm in Hate Speech: An Argument against Censorship' (2017) 50(3) CJPS 679

Ormerod D & Laird K, *Smith, Hogan and Ormerod's Criminal Law* (16 edn, Oxford University Press 2021)

Saunders A, 'Hate is hate. Online abusers must be dealt with harshly' *The Guardian* (London, 21 August 2017) https://www.theguardian.com/commentisfree/2017/aug/20/hate-crimes-online-abusers-prosecutors-serious-crackdown-internet-face-to-face

Statista, 'Global number of hate speech-containing content removed by Facebook from 4th quarter 2017 to 1st quarter 2022' (*Statista*, 1 June 2022) https://www.statista.com/statistics/1013804/facebook-hate-speech-content-deletion-quarter/

Stephens H, 'Facebook: Who Bears Responsibility for Them?' (*The International Forum for Responsible Media Blog*, 25 November 2021) https://inforrm.org/2021/11/25/facebook-who-bears-responsibility-for-them-hugh-stephens/

The Crown Prosecution Service: 'Former Councillor Pleads Guilty to Posting Racist Comments about England Football Players' (*CPS.gov*, 4 March 2022) https://www.cps.gov.uk/west-midlands/news/former-councillor-pleads-guilty-posting-racist-comments-about-england

The Crown Prosecution Service, 'Racist and Religious Hate Crime - Prosecution Guidance' (*CPS.gov*, 3 March 2022) https://www.cps.gov.uk/legal-guidance/racist-and-religious-hate-crime-prosecution-guidance

The Crown Prosecution Service, 'Hate Crime' (*CPS.gov*, 2022) https://www.cps.gov.uk/crime-info/hate-crime

The Crown Prosecution Service: 'Cheshire Man Sentenced for Racist Abuse of England Players' (*CPS.gov*, 8 September 2021) https://www.cps.gov.uk/mersey-cheshire/news/cheshire-man-sentenced-racist-abuse-england-players

The Crown Prosecution Service, 'Hate Crime' (*CPS.gov*, 2018) https://www.cps.gov.uk/hate-crime

The Crown Prosecution Service: 'Racist and Religious Hate Crime - Prosecution Guidance' (*CPS.gov*, 2017) http://www.cps.gov.uk/legal/p_to_r/racist_and_religious_crime/#a07

The Crown Prosecution Service: 'Violent Extremism and Related Criminal Offences' (*CPS.gov*, 2017) https://www.cps.gov.uk/publications/prosecution/cases_of_inciting_racial_and_religious_hatred_and_hatred_based_upon_sexual_orientation.html

The Crown Prosecution Service: 'Guidelines on Prosecuting Cases Involving Communications Sent Via Social Media' (*CPS.gov*, 2016) https://www.cps.gov.uk/legal-guidance/guidelines-prosecuting-cases-involving-communications-sent-social-media

TikTok, 'Community Guidelines Enforcement Report' (*TikTok*, 2022) https://www.tiktok.com/transparency/en/community-guidelines-enforcement-2021-4/

TikTok, 'Community Guidelines: Hateful Behaviour' (*TikTok*, 2022) https://www.tiktok.com/community-guidelines?lang=en#38

Twitter, 'Hateful Conduct Policy' (*Twitter*, 2022) https://help.twitter.com/en/rules-and-policies/hateful-conduct-policy

Twitter, 'Rules Enforcement' (*Twitter*, 2022) https://transparency.twitter.com/en/reports/rules-enforcement.html#2020-jan-jun

Walters M A, 'Conceptualizing Hostility for Hate Crime Law: Minding the Minutiae When Interpreting Section 28(1)(a) of the Crime and Disorder Act 1998' (2014) 34 (1) Oxf J Leg Stud 47

Weale S, 'Children coming across far-right material when researching, teachers say' *The Guardian* (London, 18 April 2022) https://www.theguardian.com/politics/2022/apr/18/children-coming-across-far-right-material-when-researching-teachers-say

YouTube, 'Hate Speech Policy' (*YouTube*, 2022) https://support.google.com/youtube/answer/2801939?hl=en-GB

5 Harassment and Stalking Online

5.1 Introduction

As the world becomes more digital, behaviours which were once traditionally linked to the physical world have now emerged online. Nothing has demonstrated this more than harassment and stalking, where social media has become a relatively new way to harass or stalk another.[1] Both these behaviours have become interchangeable in recent years, and as will be discussed in later parts of this chapter, confusion between the two has caused problems across the criminal justice system, particularly where these behaviours are conducted online. Indeed, for the Law Commission, harassment and stalking are difficult to define and in turn, create significant issues in determining when someone's behaviour constitutes harassment or stalking.[2] Issues which become even more glaringly apparent in the context of social media.

Though not universally defined, harassment has come to be considered as 'repeated attempts to impose unwanted communications and contact upon a victim in a manner that could be expected to cause distress or fear in any reasonable person'.[3] Whereas stalking can be considered as 'a constellation of behaviours in which one individual inflicts on another repeated unwanted intrusions and communications'.[4] Behaviours can include, to name but a few, 'following a person [...] monitoring the use by a person of the internet, email or any other form of electronic communication [... and] watching or spying on a person'.[5] With the aid of social media, both these behaviours can now occur around the clock. Stalking and harassment are therefore not only mirrored online but arguably are more intense.[6] In the online context, these behaviours have been coined as cyberharassment and

1 Azy Barak, 'Sexual Harassment on the Internet' (2005) 23(1) Soc. Sci. Comput. Rev 77.

2 Law Commission, *Abusive and Offensive Online Communications: A Scoping Report* (Law Com No 381, 2018) [8.9].

3 The Crown Prosecution Service, 'Stalking and harassment' (*CPS.gov*, 23 May 2018) <https://www.cps.gov.uk/legal-guidance/stalking-and-harassment> accessed 2 December 2022.

4 Michele Pathé and Paul Mullen, 'The Impact of Stalkers on their Victims' (1997) 170(1) BJPsych 12.

5 Protection from Harassment Act 1997 s.2A(3).

6 Subhajit Basu and Richard Jones, 'Regulating Cyberstalking' 2007 7(2) JILT <https://warwick.ac.uk/fac/soc/law/elj/jilt/2007_2/basu_jones/> accessed 2 December 2022.

DOI: 10.4324/9781003303688-7

cyberstalking—though like that of harassment and stalking, both terms are inherently difficult to define.

How the law has attempted to regulate cyberharassment and cyberstalking will be explored in the following chapter. First, the rise in these types of behaviours will be outlined. Next, the Protection from Harassment Act 1997 (PfHA) which criminalises the conduct of harassment and stalking, both online and offline, will be discussed. Taking each of these behaviours in turn, with specific reference to s.2, 2A, 4, and 4A of the Act, the law will be outlined with case examples, before then turning to highlight the issues of applying the PfHA to the online world and the principle of legality. Like that of previous chapter, it will be argued that imposing such provisions, without adhering to the principle of legality, poses significant issues with freedom of expression.

5.2 The Rise in Cyberharassment and Cyberstalking

Though difficult to define, research suggests that the prevalence of cyberharassment and cyberstalking is high, with stalking by an unknown person being more common online than in the offline world.[7] Both cyberharassment and cyberstalking encompass a range of behaviours online, including, though not limited to: repeated unwanted communications, false profiles, the publication of false information, unauthorised access to personal information, and covert surveillance.[8] The difficulty in defining the two behaviours means that much of the research into cyberharassment and cyberstalking is grouped together. Indeed, as discussed in later parts of this chapter, law enforcement often use these terms interchangeably. Even before the likes of Facebook and X, which are still to-date, two of the biggest social media platforms in the world, both cyberstalking and cyberharassment were causing growing concerns at the turn of the millennium.[9]

In 2003, Bocij conducted a survey examining the extent of cyberstalking online.[10] Bocij, using an email snowballing sample,[11] surveyed 169 participants aged between 16 and 84 years old.[12] Bocji asked several questions related to certain types of conduct associated with stalking online, to determine if a person had been cyberstalked. For example, the receiving of threatening or abusive emails and the spread of false information. Using this approach Bocji was able to conclude that

7 Law Com No 381 (n 2).

8 Ibid., [8.13].

9 For a brief discussion on the history and development of the internet see Chapter 1.

10 Paul Bocij, 'Victims of Cyberstalking: An Exploratory Study of Harassment Perpetrated via the Internet' (2003) 8(10) First Monday <http://firstmonday.org/ojs/index.php/fm/article/view/1086> accessed 30 October 2016.

11 In a snowballing sample the researcher recruits a few participants, who in turn recommends others to take part in the study. See, Earl Babbie, *The Basics of Social Research* (Cengage Learning 2007) 205.

12 Bocij (n 10).

21.9% of his participants had been subjected to what he deemed cyberstalking.[13] Interestingly, although social media existed at the time in which Bocji conducted his research, its use and prevalence were nothing compared to today.

The expansion of both social media platforms and users, has revolutionised how cyberstalking and cyberharassment can be conducted. Research undertaken on behalf of Bedfordshire University by Brown, Maple and Short in 2011, found that of the 353 participants who took part in their survey, 92% had been subjected to some form of cyberstalking or cyberharassment, with social media playing a pivotal role.[14] As social media usage has increased, evidence suggests so has cyberharassment and cyberstalking, with research conducted by the Pew Research Centre in 2022 concluding that 41% of Americans had experienced cyberharassment or cyberstalking. Although the Pew Research Centre accepted that this figure was the same as 2017, their study suggests that such behaviours have intensified.[15] Of those who took part in the study conducted by the Pew Research Centre, 75% had experienced such behaviours on some form of social media.[16]

Even in the United Kingdom, there is growing evidence that cyberharassment and cyberstalking are prevalent on social media platforms, with the Criminal Justice Inspectorates and HM Crown Prosecution Service Inspectorate (HMCPSI) finding that of the 112 cases they reviewed as part of a larger investigation into the criminal justice systems response to harassment and stalking, 82 cases (73%) had a social media element.[17] The HMCPSI concluded that harassment and stalking are increasingly likely to involve some form of digital media.[18] Indeed, during the COVID-19 pandemic, social media was one of the main methods utilised to stalk and harass others.[19] As shown in Figure 5.1, cyberharassment is considered the second most common form of online abuse experienced by complainants in the United Kingdom, following research conducted by the Victims Commissioner.

Despite a growing perception that cyberharassment and cyberstalking are on the increase, which in turn has placed growing pressure on the criminal justice system

13 Ibid.,

14 Antony Brown, Carsten Maple and Emma Short, 'Cyberstalking in the United Kingdom: An Analysis of the ECHO Pilot Survey' (*University of Bedfordshire National Centre for Cyberstalking Research*, 2011) 9 <https://www.beds.ac.uk/__data/assets/pdf_file/0003/83109/ECHO_Pilot_Final.pdf> accessed 25 October 2016.

15 Emily A. Vogels, 'The State of Online Harassment' (*Pew Research Centre*, 13 January 2021) <https://www.pewresearch.org/internet/2021/01/13/the-state-of-online-harassment/> accessed 2 December 2022. To conduct this research, the centre surveyed 10,093 adults in the United States, over a period of three days. Participants were representative of the demographic of the United States.

16 Ibid.,

17 Criminal Justice Inspectorates and HM Crown Prosecution Service Inspectorate, 'Living in fear – the police and CPS response to harassment and stalking' (*justiceinspectorates.gov*, July 2017) 27 <http://www.justiceinspectorates.gov.uk/hmicfrs/wp-content/uploads/living-in-fear-the-police-and-cps-response-to-harassment-and-stalking.pdf> accessed 29 November 2017.

18 Ibid., 28

19 Suzy Lamplugh Trust, 'Unmasking Stalking: A Changing Landscape' (*Suzy Lamplugh Trust*, April 2021) <https://www.suzylamplugh.org/Handlers/Download.ashx?IDMF=fcfb781a-f614-48c8-adcf-4cfa830c16a7> accessed 1 December 2023.

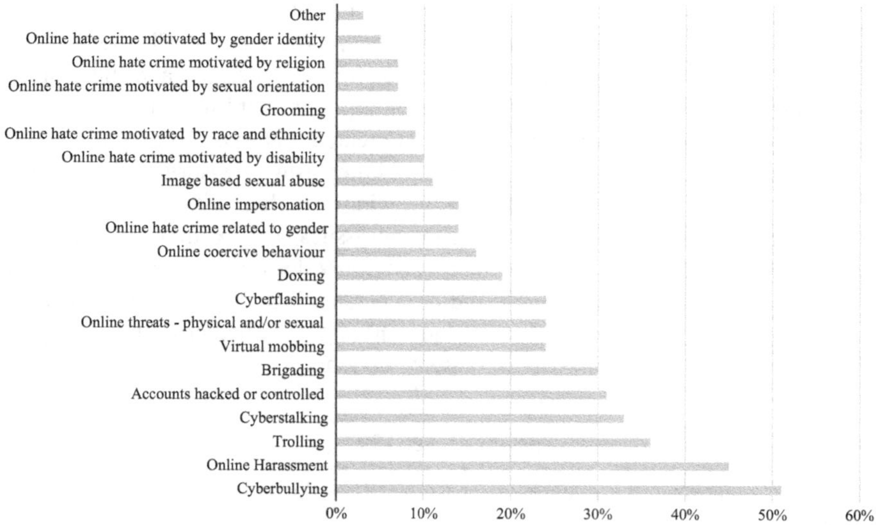

Figure 5.1 Types of online abuse experienced by victims in the United Kingdom as of February 2022.

Note: Madeline Storry & Sarah Poppleton, 'The Impact of Online Abuse: Hearing the Victims Voice' (*Victims Commissioner*, 1 June 2022) <https://s3-eu-west-2.amazonaws.com/jotwpublic-prod-storage-1cxo1dnrmkg14/uploads/sites/6/2022/05/Hearing-the-Victims-Voice.pdf> accessed 2 December 2022. This data was collected from 534 surveys.

and the government to do more to tackle this 'harm' associated with the online world, studies report varying levels. As noted by Davidson *et al*, these levels can fluctuate from 9% to 46.7%, dependent entirely on the definition given to these behaviours.[20] For instance, Brown *et al*, as discussed above, defined cyberharassment as 'the intimidation, repeated or otherwise, of one individual by another or a group perpetrated through or utilising electronic means'.[21] Whilst defining cyberstalking as 'a course of action that involves more than one incident perpetrated through or utilising electronic means, that causes distress, fear, or alarm'.[22] Whereas the Pew Research Centre did not specifically define cyberharassment, and instead encompassed a list of six behaviours they associated with cyberharassment: (1) offensive name-calling; (2) purposeful embarrassment; (3) stalking; (4) physical threats; (5) harassment over a sustained period of time and; (6) sexual harassment.

20 Julia Davidson, Sonia Livingtone, Sam Jenkins, Anna Gekoki, Clare Choak, Tarela Ike and Kirsty Phillips, 'Adult Online Hate, Harassment & Abuse: A Rapid Evidence Assessment' (*Gov.uk*, June 2019) 4 <https://assets.publishing.service.gov.uk/government/uploads/system/uploads/attachment_data/file/811450/Adult_Online_Harms_Report_2019.pdf> accessed 2 December 2022.

21 Brown, Maple and Short (n 14) 4.

22 Ibid.,

Each of these definitions used in the research examining the extent and effect of cyberharassment and cyberstalking has issues. As discussed in Chapter 2, being offensive falls within a person's right to freedom of expression and therefore to define cyberharassment as 'offensive name calling' does not truly reflect the reality of cyberharassment. In turn, a perception is created that cyberharassment and/or cyberstalking are significant issues, and places increasing pressure on the criminal justice system to do more to tackle this 'growing' problem within society, which might not necessarily be true, posing significant issues with freedom of expression. Yet, the issue with how we define such behaviours does not relate solely to academic research on cyberharassment and/or cyberstalking. The PfHA, which criminalises harassment and stalking in England and Wales, whether online or offline, also fails to grasp the complexity of these behaviours.

5.3 The Protection from Harassment Act 1997

Before the creation and implementation of the PfHA the behaviours associated with stalking and harassment were considered by some as already prohibited under the criminal law of England and Wales. For instance, during a parliamentary debate, MPs argued that the conduct of harassment and stalking was criminalised contrary to, the Malicious Communications Act 1988, the Telecommunications Act 1984 (both discussed further in the following chapter), and the Public Order Act 1986 (as discussed in the previous chapter), to name but a few.[23] In addition, the House of Lords expanded the scope of the law to prohibit harassment and/or stalking under the Offences against the Person Act 1861 (OAPA),[24] in *R v Ireland*.[25]

Despite some consensus prior to the implementation of the PfHA that the conduct of stalking and harassment was already contrary to law,[26] during a Home Office consultation committee, it was found that the criminal law was, in fact, inadequate in protecting individuals from this form of abuse:

> Though the offences under the Public Order Act may provide a sanction against stalkers in some instances, offences under the provisions of sections 4 and 4A would be committed only if the stalker intended his behaviour to cause the victim to believe that immediate violence would be used (section 4) or if harassment, alarm or distress is caused (section 4A). There are problems also in applying other aspects of the criminal law against stalkers. The Malicious Communications Act 1988 requires that the article sent must be indecent or grossly offensive. It must also be proved that the sender's purpose was to cause distress or anxiety. In the situations where stalkers continually

23 Home Office, *Stalking A Consultation Paper* (11 July 1996).

24 Mary Baber and Helena Jeffs, 'Stalking, Harassment and Intimidation and the Protection from Harassment Bill' (Research Paper 96/115, 13 December 1996) 5–6.

25 *R v Ireland* [1998] A.C. 147.

26 Home Office (n 23).

send greetings cards, flowers or other unsolicited gifts, such intent cannot be proven.[27]

Further, the *ad-hoc* nature of attempting to apply criminal provisions to stalking and harassment resulted in failures by the criminal justice system to adequately protect individuals from this type of conduct—issues the PfHA sought to amend.

5.3.1 Creation and Purpose

The anti-stalking Bill, as it was first known, was introduced into the House of Commons on 5 December 1996, a year before the first form of social media, as we know it today, was made available to the public—sixdegrees.com.[28] The Bill itself, which was to become the PfHA, was rushed through Parliament by the then conservative government, in a bid to prove to voters that the government was being tough on crime.[29] The PfHA received Royal Assent in March 1997 with an overall objective of protecting 'victims of harassment [... including from ...] so-called stalking behaviour, racial harassment, or anti-social behaviour by neighbours'.[30]

The Act itself consists of several provisions and imposes both criminal and civil law repercussions, with the remainder of this chapter focussing on the criminal provisions contained within the Act.[31] It is also important to note that the Act, in its original format, was not without fault. In particular, the Act treated stalking and harassment as the same offence—despite concerns being raised at the time that both conducts were inherently different. This was amended in 2012 under the Protection of Freedoms Act s.111(1) (PFA). However, as will be explored below, the difference between the two, harassment and stalking, by law, is not easily identifiable as they are heavily interlinked. In fact, as the law currently stands, to prosecute an individual for stalking, harassment first needs to be proven. Consequently, this has led to confusion across the criminal justice system—and even more confusion has been created, where such behaviours are conducted on the likes of social media.[32]

5.3.2 Harassment

S.1(1) of the PfHA prohibits 'a course of conduct which amounts to harassment of another, and which he knows or ought to know amounts to harassment of the other'. The provision covers both harassment from a single person and harassment

27 Ibid., [3.4–3.6].

28 Laura Scaife, *Handbook of Social Media and the Law* (Routledge 2015) 4.

29 Judith Gowland, 'Protection from Harassment Act 1997: The "new" Stalking Offences' (2013) 77(5) J. Crim. Law 387.

30 HL Deb 24 January 1997, vol 1, col 917.

31 Where such as offence demonstrates hostility because of a persons, whether real or presumed characteristic, a person may be charged under s.32 of the Crime and Disorder Act 1988 (as discussed in Chapter 4).

32 Criminal Justice Inspectorates and HM Crown Prosecution Service Inspectorate (n 17).

by a group,[33] which has come to be known in the online world as 'dog-piling'. S.2(1) of the Act makes it a specific criminal offence to subject another to this behaviour, with a maximum custodial sentence of six months. However, if the behaviour can be regarded as a hate crime, as discussed in the previous chapter, a higher sentence can be imposed.[34]

The following discussion, taking a similar format to Chapter 4, will outline the *actus reus* and *mens rea* of the offence of harassment, before turning to examine the defences contained within the provision. Later sections of this chapter will expose significant issues with the language contained in the PfHA.

5.3.2.1 Actus Reus

The *actus reus* contained in s.1(1) of the PfHA consists of two elements: a course of conduct and harassment. A course of conduct is defined in s.7(3) of the Act: 'a "course of conduct" must involve—(a) in the case of conduct in relation to a single person [...] conduct on at least two occasions in relation to that person'.[35] The Crown Prosecution Service (CPS) have further confirmed that a course of conduct can include speech.[36] In essence, 'each separate complained about behaviour must directly link back to the accused'.[37]

A minimum requirement has therefore been set by Parliament as to when certain behaviours may invoke the PfHA, though in reality, for a course of conduct to be found in relation to a single individual, it is likely that more than two incidents would need to be proven:

> I fully accept that the incidents which need to be proved in relation to harassment need not exceed two incidents, but, as it seems to me, the fewer the occasions and the wider they are spread the less likely it would be that a finding of harassment can reasonably be made.[38]

In most circumstances, for the courts to be satisfied that a course of conduct is present, contact must occur on more than two occasions, as acknowledged further by Agate and Ledward.[39]

33 Which was substituted into the Act by the Serious Crime and Police Act 2005.

34 This would be under either s.66 of the Sentencing Act 2020 or s.32 of the Crime and Disorder Act 1988. See Chapter 4.

35 Protection from Harassment Act 1999 s.7(3). This was substituted into the Act by the Serious Organised Crime and Police Act 2005.

36 Stalking and Harassment (n 3).

37 Laura Bliss, 'The Protection from Harassment Act 1997: Failures by the Criminal Justice System in a Social Media Age' 83(3) J. Crim. Law 217.

38 *Lau v DPP* [2000] 1 F.L.R 799 (DC) per Mr Justice Schiemann [15].

39 Jennifer Agate and Jocelyn Ledward, 'Social Media: How the Net is Closing in on Cyber Bullies' (2013) 24(8) ELR 263.

In *Pratt v DPP*,[40] it was found that two incidents which occurred almost three months apart were 'close to the line' but did not cross the threshold to establish a course of conduct. Whereas in *Kelly v DPP*,[41] three phone calls in the space of five minutes, constituted a course of conduct. This leaves many questions unanswered when it comes to prosecuting harassment conducted online. For example, could it be said that contact once a month over the course of a year can amount to harassment, or would it need to be more contact over a shorter period of time? What if the person being targeted online did not know about the messages sent until months after the event? Indeed, in *Wass v DPP* the Divisional Court considered two incidents that occurred within minutes of each other as a course of conduct.[42]

The second part of the *actus reus* is harassment. Under the PfHA harassment is defined as 'alarming' a person or causing them 'distress'.[43] No further information is given within the Act itself as to the meaning of these terms and will simply be based on the evidence, in which the behaviour needs to be oppressive or unreasonable:

> Harassment is a persistent and deliberate course of unreasonable and oppressive conduct, targeted at another person, which is calculated to and does cause that person alarm, fear or distress.[44]

Simply put, there must be evidence that the course of conduct was calculated to cause alarm or distress, which was oppressive or unreasonable—here it must be found that the reasonable person in the same position as the complainant would find that harassment had taken place. Further, there must be proof of distress. If from the evidence provided it can be established that the complained about behaviour amounts to alarming or distressing a person, the condition of harassment will be satisfied. Though

> [w]here the quality of the conduct said to constitute harassment is being examined, courts will have in mind that irritations, annoyances, even a measure of upset, arise at times in everybody's day-to-day dealings with other people. Courts are well able to recognise the boundary between conduct which is unattractive, even unreasonable, and conduct which is oppressive and unacceptable. To cross the boundary from the regrettable to the unacceptable the gravity of the misconduct must be of an order which would sustain criminal liability.[45]

40 *Pratt v DPP* [2001] EWHC 483.
41 *Kelly v DPP* [2002] EWHC 1428.
42 *Wass v DPP* (QBD, 11 May 2000).
43 Protection from Harassment Act 1997 s.7(2).
44 *Hayes v Willoughby* [2013] UKSC 17.
45 *Majrowski v Guy's and St Thomas's NHS Trust* [2006] UKHL 34, [2007] 1 A.C. 224 per Lord Nicolls of Birkenhead [30].

This has created issues when it comes to cyberharassment. In many cases of online harassment, the conduct is 'disturbing, unpleasant, and may transgress the norms of socially acceptable' behaviour but *should not* cross the harassment threshold to warrant criminal law intervention. But as discussed in Section 5.2 above, it is often found that those who experience 'disturbing' or 'unpleasant' conduct online, consider this to be harassment.[46] And it is studies like these which are often used as evidence to support stronger criminal legal provisions to tackle the 'harms' associated with the online world.

5.3.2.2 Mens Rea

The *mens rea* of harassment is based on the construction of knowledge. Under the PfHA in order to bring a successful prosecution for harassment it must be proven that the defendant, 'knows or ought to know that the[ir] behaviour would amount to [the] harassment of another'.[47] The concept of 'knowledge' is based on the reasonable person test.[48] Essentially, it must be established that the average sober person in the same position as the defendant would come to the knowledge *or should have* come to the knowledge, that their conduct would amount to the harassment of another individual.

This is a purely objective test, where the feelings or perceptions of the accused are not taken into consideration. As noted by Herring:

> [i]t means that it is no defence for a defendant to claim, "I thought I was expressing my love for the victim; I did not realize [*sic*] she would find this distressing" if it would have been obvious to a reasonable person that the conduct was harassing.[49]

The Court of Appeal confirmed in *R v Colohan*,[50] that the characteristics of the accused, in this case, their mental health, could not be taken into consideration.

If both the *actus reus* and *mens rea* of the offence can be found, then the defendant is liable for a breach of s.1(1) of the PfHA, which as noted above is made a criminal offence under s.2(1) of the Act: 'a person who pursues a course of conduct in breach of [s.1(1) or (1A)] is guilty of an offence'—provided the defences discussed below do not apply. However, if the behaviour can be considered as putting someone in fear of violence, this may constitute a more serious offence under s.4(1) of the PfHA, as discussed further in Section 5.3.4.1.

46 For example, in the research conducted by the Pew Research Centre as discussed in Section 5.2, the definition given to harassment included offensive name calling.

47 Protection from Harassment Act 1997 s.1(1)(b).

48 For a discussion on the reasonable person see, Reid Griffith Fontaine, *The Mind of the Criminal: The Role of Developmental Social Cognition in Criminal Defense Law* (Cambridge University Press 2012) 13.

49 Jonathan Herring, *Criminal Law: Text, Cases and Materials* (10th edn, Oxford University Press 2022) 348.

50 *R v Colohan* [2001] EWCA Crim 1251.

5.3.2.3 Defences

It is important to note that s.1(3) of the PfHA specifically outlines three situations in which it will be found that there was no course of conduct present, and therefore no offence:

1. Where the course of conduct is done for the purpose of preventing or detecting a crime. For example, police officers investigating a criminal act would be able to rely upon this defence. Although it could, in some circumstances, be raised by journalists or neighbourhood watch bodies as a defence, although it would need to be proven that a person acted rationally in the circumstances;[51] or
2. Where the course of conduct is 'pursued under any enactment or rule of law or to comply with any condition or requirement imposed by any person under any enactment'.[52] For example, a company acting within their legal boundaries; or
3. Where the course of conduct can be considered reasonable—with reasonability being assessed by the courts.

It is under the reasonability defence element, where consideration should be given by actors within the criminal justice system to Articles 10 and 8 of the European Convention on Human Rights (ECHR), as confirmed by the European Court of Human Rights (ECtHR) in *Pal v The United Kingdom*[53]—a case discussed at length in Section 5.4. Indeed, journalistic speech will fall within the defence of reasonableness, provided such behaviour is not so unreasonable.[54] If any of the defences above are found, it will be concluded that a course of conduct cannot be established, and consequently, no offence has taken place under this Act.

5.3.3 Stalking

As previously noted, before 2012 stalking and harassment were treated as the same offence, and both governed under s.1(1) of the PfHA and criminalised under s.2(1). Although there is evidence that stalking offences were successfully prosecuted under s.2(1), many of those subjected to such behaviour felt that they were not taken seriously by those working in the criminal justice system.[55] In 2012, the conduct of stalking was implemented into the Act under s.111(1) of the PFA, following concerns that the PfHA did not cover stalking sufficiently.[56]

The provision came into force in November 2012, with a maximum custodial sentence of six months and like that of harassment, a higher sentence can

51 *Hayes* (n 44).

52 Protection from Harassment Act 1997 s.1(3)b.

53 *Pal v The United Kingdom* (44261/19) [2021] 11 WLUK 603 Times, 9 February 2022 (ECHR).

54 *Carina Trimingham v Associated Newspapers Limited* [2012] EWHC 1296 (QB).

55 Stalking and Harassment (n 3).

56 Neil MacEwan, 'The New Stalking Offences in English law: Will They Provide Effective Protection from Cyberstalking?' (2012) 10 Crim.L.R. 767.

be imposed if it falls within the definition of a hate crime.[57] Although there were calls for cyberstalking to be included as a separate offence under the PfHA, this was rejected at the time of amendment, with MacEwan noting that it was 'naïve, to view it simply as "old behaviour using new technologies"'.[58] Below, the *actus reus* and *mens rea* of the offence is set out, before turning to outline the defences available under this provision. As will be shown in later sections, the interchangeable nature of harassment and stalking poses significant issues with the principle of legality.

5.3.3.1 Actus Reus

S.2A(1) of the PfHA takes a very similar format to that of s.1(1). However, the *actus reus* consists of three elements in total:

1. A course of conduct—what is considered a course of conduct under this section of the Act has the same meaning as s.1(1) discussed above—where one single person is the perpetrator, there must be at least two incidents which are close in time;
2. The course of conduct must amount to harassment—again, the same meaning is given to harassment as with s.1(1), as discussed in Section 5.3.2.1; and
3. The behaviour must amount to stalking.

There is no definition of stalking contained in the Act, instead, a non-exhaustive list of behaviours is included:

> (a) following a person; (b) contacting, or attempting to contact, a person by any means; (c) publishing any statement or other material—(i) relating or purporting to relate to a person, or (ii) purporting to originate from a person; (d) monitoring the use by a person of the internet, email, or any other form of electronic communication; (e) loitering in any place (whether public or private); (f) interfering with any property in the possession of a person; [and] (g) watching or spying on a person.[59]

Consequently, 'as "stalking" lacks an overarching definition, it is not always clear when harassing conduct has crossed the threshold into stalking'.[60] This confusion is an inevitable consequence as upon the drafting s.2A of the PfHA, as noted above, a person cannot be stalked if harassment is not present. Indeed, it becomes further complicated in a social media context, where the 'monitoring of social media is

57 Where such as offence demonstrates hostility because of a persons, whether real or presumed characteristic, a person may be charged under s.32 of the Crime and Disorder Act 1988 (as discussed in Chapter 4).

58 MacEwan (n 56) 768.

59 Protection from Harassment Act 1997 s.2A(3).

60 Law Com No 381 (n 2) [8.171].

typically expected and consented to within social media environments'.[61] The issue with what constitutes stalking by law, is discussed further in Section 5.5.1.3.

5.3.3.2 Mens Rea

Like that of harassment, as discussed above, the *mens rea* for the offence of stalking is based on the construction of knowledge. Here, it must be found that the perpetrator 'knows or ought to know that the[ir] behaviour would amount to [the] harassment of another'.[62] Like that of harassment, if the behaviour can be considered as putting someone in serious fear of violence or serious alarm or distress, this may constitute a more serious offence under s.4A of the PfHA, as discussed further in Section 5.3.4.2.

5.3.3.3 Defences

As with harassment, it is a defence to stalk another where the course of conduct is done for the purpose of preventing or detecting a crime; or is 'pursued under any enactment or rule of law or to comply with any condition or requirement imposed by any person under any enactment';[63] or where it can be considered reasonable in the circumstances to pursue a course of conduct.

5.3.4 Putting Someone in Fear of Violence and/or Serious Alarm or Distress

A more serious offence of both harassment and stalking are contained in the PfHA: putting someone in fear of serious violence as outlined in s.4 (harassment) or putting someone in fear of serious violence or alarm or distress as prohibited under s.4A (stalking) of the Act. Both provisions carry a custodial sentence of up to ten years.[64]

5.3.4.1 Section 4: Putting Someone in Fear of Violence (Harassment)

For an offence to be established under s.4(1) of the PfHA—the harassment of another which puts someone in fear of violence—first the *actus reus* for harassment, as discussed above in Section 5.3.2.1, must be present (a course of conduct that amounts to harassment). In addition to the above, it must also be found that the defendant:

61 Ibid., [8.174].

62 Protection from Harassment Act 1997 s.2A 2(c).

63 Ibid., s.1(3)b.

64 Until 2017, the maximum custodial sentence under s.4 or s.4A of the Protection from Harassment Act 1997 was five years. This was changed under s.175(1)a & s.175(1)b of the Policing and Crime Act 2017.

> ought to know that his course of conduct will cause another to fear that violence will be used against them if a reasonable person in possession of the same information would think that the course of conduct would cause the other so to fear on that occasion.

Put simply, 'it has to be shown that the accused has undertaken a course of conduct which on at least two occasions led the victim to fear that violence would be used against them'.[65] With the court confirming in *Henley* that the conduct needs to be more than merely frightening, it must put the complainant in fear of violence.[66] Further, it must be directed at an individual. So, for example, in a social media context, an offence would not be committed under this provision, if the message was not directly aimed at another.

To determine if a course of conduct, which amounts to harassment can be considered as putting a person in fear of violence, the reasonable person test is used. Here, it must be found that the reasonable sober person in the same position as the complainant would have feared that violence might be used against them. Like that of the reasonable person test contained in s.1(1) and 2A(1), the perpetrator's perceptions are not taken into consideration, nor their personal characteristics, such as their mental health.

5.3.4.2 Section 4A: Putting Someone in Fear or Serious Alarm or Distress (Stalking)

Like that of s.4(1), for an offence to be established under s.4A(1), it must first be found that an offence contrary to s.2A(1) of the PfHA (a course of conduct, that amounts to harassment and can be considered as stalking) is present. However, whereas s.4(1) is only applicable to situations which cause a person fear of violence, s.4A(1) also covers the situation whereby a person fears 'serious alarm or distress'. Put simply, an offence under s.4A(1) can be conducted in one of two ways (provided an offence under s.2A(1) is also present):

1. It causes another to fear, on at least two occasions, that violence will be used against them; or
2. It causes another serious alarm or distress which has a substantial adverse effect on his or her usual day-to-day activities.

The first way of committing the offence, similar to s.4(1), is based on the reasonable person in the same position as the complainant, though personal characteristics are not taken into account. The second is more complex, and 'recognises the overall

65 Herring (n 49) 350.
66 *Henley* [2000] Crim LR 582.

emotional and psychological harm that stalking may cause to victims, even where an explicit fear of violence is not created by each incident of stalking behaviour'.[67]

To cause serious alarm or distress it must be found that the conduct had a 'substantial adverse effect on his or her usual day-to-day activities' with no further information contained within the Act. Indeed, neither 'alarm' nor 'distress' are appropriately defined. However, guidelines issued by the Home Office, have attempted to bring some clarity to the phrase by suggesting that such behaviour may include:

> (a) the victim changing their routes to work, work patterns, or employment; (b) the victim arranging for friends or family to pick up children from school (to avoid contact with the stalker); (c) the victim putting in place additional security measures in their home; (d) the victim moving home; (e) physical or mental ill-health; (f) the deterioration in the victim's performance at work due to stress; (g) the victim stopping/or changing the way they socialise.[68]

It is important to note this list is non-exhaustive and could perhaps include removing oneself from a social media platform. Though it must be proven that the accused knows or ought to know that the course of conduct will cause another alarm or distress and again, is based on the reasonable person, with the court clarifying in *Pendlebury v DPP:*

> it is not enough to establish that conditions existed which might reasonably have engendered a fear of violence: that will be so in many stalking cases. The matter is one of fact. The Bench must be sure that such a fear was actually engendered.[69]

5.3.4.3 Section 4 and 4A: Defences

Both provisions also carry a defence element:

> It is a defence for a person charged with an offence under this section (4 and 4A) to show that—(a) his course of conduct was pursued for the purpose of preventing or detecting crime, (b) his course of conduct was pursued under any enactment or rule of law or to comply with any condition or requirement imposed by any person under any enactment, or (c) the pursuit of his course of conduct was reasonable for the protection of himself or another or for the protection of his or another's property.[70]

67 Stalking and Harassment (n 3).

68 Home Office, 'Circular: a change to the Protection from Harassment Act 1997' (*Gov.uk*, 16 October 2012) <https://www.gov.uk/government/publications/a-change-to-the-protection-from-harassment-act-1997-introduction-of-two-new-specific-offences-of-stalking> accessed 4 December 2023.

69 *Pendlebury v DPP* [2018] EWHC 3567 (Admin) per Lord Justice Irwin [29].

70 Protection from Harassment Act 1997 s.4(3) & 4A(4).

If any of the defences above can be established, no offence has taken place.

5.3.5 Summary

Though s.2 and 2A of the PfHA are intended to cover different types of behaviours, it is clear that both overlap, and the distinction between harassment and stalking is not easily identifiable. Both provisions, however, have been used in a social media context, though a recent case before the ECtHR has confirmed that even when it comes to harassment or stalking, freedom of expression may well constitute reasonability to pursue a course of conduct against another, particularly when it comes to comments made on social media against individuals in the public domain.[71] Discussed further in the following section.

5.4 The Protection from Harassment Act 1997 and Social Media

There is growing evidence of all the provisions discussed above being used in the context of social media. For instance, a successful prosecution for an offence contrary to s.2 of the PfHA, involving social media and new technologies, can be seen in *R v Danevska*,[72] where it was held that exceptional as a restraining order was (including prohibiting the defendant from publishing any information about the complainant and other interested persons) it was justified.

What is believed to be the first successful prosecution of an individual under s.2 of PfHA for cyberharassment occurred in 2009, where Kelly Houghton was jailed for three months for sending death threats *via* Facebook.[73] Following the implementation of stalking into the PfHA in 2012, the first successful conviction for cyberstalking under s.4A occurred in 2014, following an individual using computer software to spy on women in their own homes.[74]

Since then, there have been numerous successful convictions under s.4A of the PfHA, including *R v Gomes*,[75] where a conviction contrary to s.4A was upheld by the court following the defendant bombarding the complainant with emails, telephone calls, and other online communications. Similarly, in *R v Patterson*[76] the court upheld the conviction of the defendant under s.4A of the PfHA, where the defendant made unwanted contact on social media with the complainant over several years, expressing his love for her:

71 *Pal* (n 53).

72 *R v Danevska* [2017] EWCA Crim 1084.

73 Helen Carter, 'Teenage girl is first to be jailed for bullying on Facebook' *The Guardian* (London, 21 August 2009) <https://www.theguardian.com/uk/2009/aug/21/facebook-bullying-sentence-teenage-girl> accessed 7 February 2023.

74 *R v Andrew Meldrum*, Woolwich Crown Court, 30 May 2014 (unreported). See also, Nicola Fifield, 'Cyber stalker bugged women's computers to spy on them in their bedrooms' *The Telegraph* (London, 30 May 2014) <http://www.telegraph.co.uk/news/uknews/crime/10866262/Cyber-stalker-bugged-womens-computers-to-spy-on-them-in-their-bedrooms.html> accessed 25 October 2016.

75 *R v Gomes* [2022] EWCA Crim 1395.

76 *R v Patterson* [2021] EWCA Crim 1475.

> She [the complainant] has frequently had panic attacks and had to undergo intensive group therapy. The repeated contacts with the victim and family members—even those living in other countries—has caused embarrassment and shame. The appellant's conduct has caused Miss Neilson [the complainant] to become isolated from friends and has harmed romantic relationships. Her work as an artist requires a public presence and reliance on social media as well as galleries. The appellant's behaviour has interfered with her ability to use Facebook and Instagram to promote her work online—an essential tool.[77]

Arguably, these cases warranted criminalisation under the PfHA. However, issues arise in the context of messages sent on social media sites, where a course of conduct maybe apparent, but that course of conduct is reasonable. For example, sending multiple messages which might not be offensive or even abusive but might cause another distress—an issue the ECtHR had to consider in *Pal v The United Kingdom*.[78]

Pal concerned a dispute between a journalist and a barrister (who was also considered a part-time journalist), with several comments being exchanged between the two on Twitter around transgender rights. Several of these disputes had been republished in the national press. However, at no point could it be said that the comments made between the two were either abusive or relentless. Despite this, the initial complainant, known only as AB, reported the tweets and an article written by Pal on the dispute to the Metropolitan Police (MET). Pal was later arrested and charged under s.2 of the PfHA. The charge was however eventually dropped by the CPS after they concluded, upon review of the case, that the article published was 'an informative piece' and the tweets complained about, could not amount to harassment. Despite no further action being taken by the CPS, Pal and their legal team issued legal proceedings before the Courts against the MET for various procedural breaches, including a breach of Article 10 of the ECHR. The grounds for review were rejected by both the County Court and the High Court, with an appeal to the Court of Appeal and the Supreme Court being disallowed. Pal and their legal team were later granted permission to have their case heard before ECtHR.

The ECtHR concluded that there had been a breach of Article 10, in which the domestic courts of the United Kingdom, when coming to their decision on the previous appeals, had not taken Article 10 into account: '[n]o consideration appears to have been given to the subject matter of the applicant's article or tweets, and whether they could be said to have contributed to a debate of general interest'.[79] The ECtHR distinguished between the public and private nature of the complained about conduct. When a person can be considered as a public person, such as a

77 Ibid., per Justice Holgate [6].
78 *Pal* (n 53).
79 Ibid., [59].

journalist, 'they could be subject to wider limits of acceptable criticism than the ordinary person'.[80]

In light of the finding of the ECtHR in *Pal* and on further reflection of *Magyar Helsinki Bizottsag v Hungary*,[81] it could be argued that in certain circumstances, posts on social media platforms, or tweets/Xs, could be considered as journalistic material. However, it is important to note that in disputes of a private nature involving words or actions 'the courts are unlikely to side with free speech once they are satisfied that there is a strong *prima facie* claim for harassment'.[82] But

> [w]hat the judgment in *Pal* has done, however, is to concentrate the minds of the police and the courts, at first instance and on appeal and review, on the importance of human rights in the interpretation and application of domestic law, both generally and in the area of free speech, in our case specifically the law of harassment.[83]

In essence, the PfHA should only be used, particularly in cases related to public communications, where the rights of the complainant have been disproportionally affected and consideration must always be given to tolerance and open debate. Failure to do so may render a decision incompatible with human rights.

5.5 The Protection from Harassment Act, Social Media, and Legality

Like that of hate speech, the effects of cyberharassment and/or cyberstalking cannot be downplayed, with its effects well documented within the literature.[84] However, the PfHA was never created with the digital world in mind, and many of the justifications for the use of vague terminology, surrounds the stalking or harassment of another in the physical world. Although it is accepted that some form of vagueness is inherent within the criminal law when it comes to offences such as harassment and/or stalking, particularly in the context of social media, which is not as clear cut, to use Bingham's example, as offences such as robbery,[85] it is vitally important that we strive for the 'maximum clarity which the imperfect medium of language can attain'.[86]

The discussion below will outline two key issues with the PfHA and its application in a social media context, against the principle of legality:

1) Terminology issues; and
2) The reasonable person test.

80 Ibid.,
81 *Magyar Helsinki Bizottsag v Hungary* (2020)71 E.H.R.R. 2.
82 Steve Foster, 'The Right to Criticise and the Determination of Permissible Expression in Harassment Cases: The Decision in Pal v United Kingdom' (2022) 6 E.H.L.R 571, 580.
83 Ibid., 586.
84 See for example, Law Com No 381 (n 2) Chapter 8.
85 Tom Bingham, *The Rule of Law* (Penguin 2011) 37.
86 Law Commission, *Report on Conspiracy and Criminal Law Reform* (1976), Law Com No. 76 [1.8].

Though arguably when viewed on their own, these factors might not be considered significant enough to breach the principle of legality, when looked at in the round, with social media in mind, legality is not being maintained.

5.5.1 Terminology Issues

As noted in earlier parts of this chapter, the PfHA contains several ambiguous terms, in particular, a course of conduct, harassment, and stalking. This is significant, considering the purpose behind the PfHA is to protect 'victims of harassment [... including from ...] so-called stalking behaviour'.[87] Neither behaviour can be present if there is no course of conduct. Yet the meaning of these terms, course of conduct, harassment and stalking are not clearly defined, nor is it clear what the difference is between harassment and stalking—an issue that becomes relevant in a social media context, where, as noted earlier, 'the general monitoring of a person's social media page, is expected, and somewhat consented to'.[88]

For the law to adhere to the principle of legality, and in turn, protect freedom of expression online, citizens need to be able to guide their behaviour in accordance with clear and understandable legal provisions—this is a fundamental aspect of legality—and something the PfHA lacks.

5.5.1.1 A Course of Conduct

As outlined above, to establish a course of conduct, it must be found that there is a connection between at least two incidents, which causes another harassment. Although, in reality, it is likely that there needs to be more than two incidents.[89] In addition, these incidents need to be close in time—though each event does not need to amount to a crime in itself.[90] And like that of harassment, discussed in Section 5.5.1.2 below, what constitutes a course of conduct, has been decided in an ad-hoc manner, with no clear meaning as to what is meant by a course of conduct, despite it being accepted that we should not rely on a 'case by case' account of insight into how the law should develop.[91]

In *Hills*,[92] the court concluded that two violent incidents between a couple over the course of six months, could not constitute a course of conduct, as the couple had separated and later reconciled. Similarly, in *Lau v DPP*,[93] a slap, followed by a threat four months later, was not considered a course of conduct. Interestingly in *Lau*, it was not just that the two incidents were not close in time, but consideration

87 HL Deb (n 30).
88 Law Com No 381 (n 2) [8.174].
89 *Lau* (n 38) [15].
90 *Jones v DPP* [2010] EWHC 523 (Admin), [2011] 1 W.L.R. 833 at [27].
91 Lon L Fuller, *The Morality of Law* (Yale University Press 1964) 46.
92 *Hills* [2001] Crim LR 318.
93 *Lau* (n 38).

was also given to the different nature of the events in question by the court.[94] However, the court did maintain that an incident once a year could, in certain circumstances, constitute a course of conduct.[95] For example, a threat once a year on a person's birthday.

Much of the case law relating to a course of conduct stems from contact that has occurred in the physical world, as opposed to the virtual. There are some cases, where 'modern' communications are at play, such as in *Kelly v DPP*,[96] where it was held that three voicemail messages which were left in the space of five minutes and listened to consecutively, did amount to a course of conduct. However, the finding of the court in *Kelly,* leaves open several questions in the context of communications aided by social media. For example:

1. Would, hypothetically, five messages sent over the course of a few months, which are all read by a person on the same day, constitute a course of conduct, if it caused another harassment? In the social media world, it is common for individuals to have hundreds, if not millions of followers online, and it might be that some communications are not always seen at the point in which they were sent;
2. In the context of X, where communications are limited to a maximum of 240 characters,[97] would several Xs linked together, commonly referred to as a 'thread' constitute a course of conduct? Or could they be perceived as one incident?
3. In the context of Instagram, where video content has a specified time limit, would two videos continuing a conversation be enough to constitute a course of conduct?

To prove a course of conduct in the physical world seems significantly easier, compared to that of the online world. In the online world consideration must be given to the innerworkings of the platform, the limits placed on users by platform creators, such as character limitations or time constraints, and the need to ensure consistency across the criminal justice system. Here, as discussed at length in Chapter 3, we need to ensure that terms such as course of conduct are not so generously overly interpreted that they would, in theory, create retrospective criminal law.

As noted by Murray and Reed 'obedience of the law depends on humans understanding the law'.[98] As echoed earlier, on its own, the lack of understanding as to what is meant by a course of conduct might not be so vague to render the PfHA incompatible with legality, but when examined in light of the other vague terminology used in the Act, issues with legality become obviously apparent.

94 Ibid., [16].
95 Ibid., [15].
96 *Kelly* (n 41).
97 Note, there are some exceptions to the 240 character rule.
98 Chris Reed and Andrew Murray, *Rethinking the Jurisprudence of Cyberspace* (Elgar 2018) 85.

5.5.1.2 The Meaning of Harassment

Like that of a course of conduct, harassment has no specific meaning in law, despite its importance within the legal provision, because without it, no offence will be committed under any of the provisions discussed in earlier parts of this chapter. Instead, the Act considers harassment to be conduct that causes another alarm or distress. There has been some attempt to clarify the meaning of alarm and distress, with the court in *Majrowski v Guy's and St Thomas's NHS Trust* suggesting that anxiety is considered something just short of a recognised psychiatric illness.[99] Whilst defining distress as 'oppressive and unreasonable behaviour'.[100]

There is, therefore, a degree of subjectivity in the law when it comes to harassment—which is not necessarily a breach of the principle of legality because, as noted by Lord Morris 'those who skate on thin ice can hardly expect to find a sign which will denote the precise spot where he […] will fall in'.[101] Horder interprets the 'thin ice' principle to mean, that where a person's behaviour is on the borders of criminal liability, they risk criminalisation because

> [u]nless the criminal law occasionally resorts to such open-ended terms […], it would have to rely on immensely detailed and lengthy definitions which might be so complicated as to restrict the intelligibility of the law.[102]

Indeed, for Foster, the vagueness of the term harassment does not warrant issues with legality due to extensive case law.[103]

For the Court of Appeal in *Thomas v News Group Newspapers*

> "Harassment" is […] a word which has a meaning which is generally understood. It describes conduct targeted at an individual which is calculated to produce the consequences […] which is oppressive and unreasonable.[104]

But even so, difficulties have emerged—which in turn, creates issues with legality. For Fuller, for the law to adhere to the principle of legality, the criminal justice system must refrain from deciding cases in an ad-hoc manner. As argued above, we should not decide legal disputes case-by-case—there needs to be some consistency in law and in turn this will ensure that fair enforcement of the law is being upheld—maintaining due process. For this to happen, and to avoid a case-by-case approach of enlightenment, we need clarity. However, the difficulty in establishing the meaning of harassment, particularly in the context of social media, means that

99 *Majrowski* (n 45) per Auld LJ [45].

100 Ibid., per Auld LJ May LJ [82].

101 *Knuller (Publishing, Printing and Promotions) Ltd. and Others v DPP* [1972] 3 W.L.R. 143, [1973] A.C. 435 per Lord Morris 463.

102 Jeremy Horder, *Ashworth's Principles of Criminal Law* (8th edn, Oxford University Press 2016) 27.

103 Foster (n 82) 573.

104 *Thomas v News Group Newspapers Ltd* [2001] EWCA Civ 1233 [30]. This definition was further endorsed by the Supreme Court in *Hayes* (n 44).

not only are cases being decided in an *ad-hoc* manner, but also legal provisions are being applied inconsistently—a similar argument raised in the previous chapter. Demonstrated further in *R v Peter Nunn.*[105]

In 2013, Nunn was arrested and convicted under s.127(1) of the Communications Act 2003 (CA)—an Act discussed further in Chapter 6—for sending grossly offensive messages, including threats of rape, to Caroline Criado-Perez, an active feminist campaigner. Caroline Criado-Perez had launched a public campaign to get the author, Jane Austin, printed on banknotes in England and Wales. Following this public campaign, she was subjected to a crusade of abuse online, in particular, from Peter Nunn:

> He dug up my work history. He dug up my relationship and family history. He dug up my family's work history—including publishing home addresses. He wrote reams of blogs about me and my every public move. He made numerous videos about me. He set up numerous [T]witter accounts all of which spoke almost exclusively about me. In these same [T]witter accounts he detailed the best way to rape and drown a witch, alongside repeatedly naming me as the head of the 'witches' coven'. He also boasted on [T]witter in the same account about having bought a gun, and wondered 'how much death' this gun could buy him.[106]

Despite a clear course of conduct being present, which arguably amounted to harassment and caused Caroline Criado-Perez distress, Nunn was prosecuted and found guilty of sending grossly offensive communications contrary to s.127(1) of the CA, receiving a six week custodial sentence.[107]

It's difficult, by applying the language of the PfHA, to determine why Nunn was pursued under a communication offence, as opposed to the PfHA, a decision Caroline Criado-Perez has been heavily critical of:

> This man [Peter Nunn] made me fear for my life as no-one ever has before. I felt he was a clear and present threat to me. He made me scared to go outside, to appear in public. He stopped me being able to sleep; being able to work. He seemed obsessed enough to carry out his threats. I am glad he has been found guilty. I am glad he cannot contact me again. I hope he has learnt from this. But I think the CPS got the charge wrong. I don't feel they understood what happened to me.[108]

As noted in Chapter 3, unfair enforcement of the law creates criticism in the community, which is evidently clear here. In turn, consistency is lost. All issues which

105 *R v Peter Nunn,* The City of London Magistrates' Court, 29 September 2014 (unreported).

106 Caroline Criado-Perez, 'A brief comment on Peter Nunn, sentenced today For Twitter abuse' (*Week Women*, 2014) <https://weekwoman.wordpress.com/2014/09/29/a-brief-comment-on-peter-nunn/> accessed 29 October 2016.

107 *Peter Nunn* (n 105).

108 Criado-Perez (n 106).

undermine the principle of legality. The lack of understanding as to what constitutes harassment is even more apparent when attempting to differentiate between stalking and harassment.

5.5.1.3 The Meaning of Stalking

Like that of harassment, there is no specific meaning given to stalking. Instead, as outlined in Section 5.3.3.1, the PfHA gives a non-exhaustive list of behaviours which may constitute stalking, many of which are applicable to cyberstalking. However, to prove a person's behaviour crosses the line into stalking, due to the construct of s.2A of the PfHA, first harassment needs to be proven. Consequently, harassment and stalking are inherently interlinked, as legally you cannot be stalked, if harassment is not present. As a result, the difference between harassment and stalking is not easily identifiable.

The lack of understanding between these two behaviours was exposed in a HMCPSI report, as previously mentioned, into the PfHA in July 2017, where it was found that there was a serious lack of understanding between police forces as to what constitutes harassment or stalking, specifically the difference between the two behaviours. From a study of 112 police reports, across six forces, it was found that the police had failed to deal with any of these cases correctly and in many cases, misunderstood the severity of the behaviour being reported:

> [L]egislation does not exhaustively define stalking or the particular circumstances that make stalking different from those of harassment. Therefore, without any additional clarification, what differentiates harassment and stalking can be open to interpretation and result in confusion.[109]

Consequently, a recommendation was put forward in the report for a more definitive definition of stalking to try and combat this issue. However, the law is still yet to change, meaning that both behaviours are often misunderstood, and when it comes to social media, the difference between the two is often important to ensure faith in the criminal justice system is maintained.

As discussed in Chapter 3:

> The most subtle element in the task of maintaining congruence between law and official actions lies, of course, in the problem of interpretation. Legality requires that judges and other officials apply statutory law, not according to their fancy or with crabbed literalness, but in accordance with principles of interpretation.[110]

However, where two elements of an offence, such as harassment and stalking are so inherently interlinked, a clear understanding of the boundaries between the two

109 Criminal Justice Inspectorates and HM Crown Prosecution Service Inspectorate (n 17) 24.
110 Fuller (n 91) 82.

becomes significantly difficult to articulate. In turn, the action-guiding nature of the law, which is an important aspect of legality, is heavily affected. At its very basic, citizens should be able to guide their behaviour in accordance with clear and distinct rules. Without further clarity on the difference between stalking and harassment, particularly considering the ease with which both behaviours can now be conducted, renders significant issues with the principle of legality and in turn, poses a threat to freedom of expression.

5.5.1.4 Summary

As echoed earlier, taking each element of the offence discussed above on its own, might not necessarily render the PfHA incompatible with legality, but when considered together, the ambiguity present does not maintain the action-guiding nature of the law:

> [i]f the legitimacy of the law's claim to authority is conferred on it by the collective acceptance of those to whom it is addressed, it must follow that structuring or wording the law in a way which makes it inaccessible to those addresses will reduce the likelihood of acceptance. Achieving legitimacy requires attention to style as well as substance.[111]

By not being able to clearly differentiate between harassment and stalking, this creates issues for those working in the criminal justice system. This is heighten further given the lack of understanding as to what constitutes harassment, stalking, or indeed, a course of conduct, risking the overcriminalisation of speech. We need legality to ensure due process. We need legality to ensure the protection of freedom of expression, particularly where an offence is grounded in the reasonable person.

5.5.2 The Reasonable Person

As noted in Chapter 3, for Fuller, comparing a person's actions against that of the reasonable person, may in some circumstances be asking the impossible, as his education or even personal characteristics may not meet such a requirement. Yet imposing the 'reasonable man with the same characteristics as the defendant' as the boundary for criminal liability risks objectivity being lost.[112] There is clearly a balance that needs to be struck.

In cases of harassment and/or stalking, whether online or offline, the reasonable person test is used to determine the *mens rea* element of the offence: 'knows or should have known'. This is a purely objective test, in which the characteristics of the accused are not taken into consideration, such as a persons mental health. This objective approach to determining the *mens rea* of harassment and/or stalking has been supported and justified by the courts:

111 Reed and Murray (n 98) 183.
112 Fuller (n 91) 71–72.

> The conduct at which the Act [PfHA] is aimed, and from which it seeks to provide protection, is particularly likely to be conduct pursued by those of obsessive or otherwise unusual psychological make-up and very frequently by those suffering from an identifiable mental illness. Schizophrenia is only one such condition which is obviously very likely to give rise to conduct of this sort. We are satisfied that to give the Act the construction for which Mr. Butterfield contends [a subjective test] would be to remove from its protection a very large number of victims and indeed to run the risk of significantly thwarting the purpose of the Act.[113]

However, in the context of social media, the reasonable person test may well be flawed, particularly where the elements which make up a certain offence, are inherently vague, as with the PfHA. Indeed, to ensure legality is maintained, not only should we perhaps re-examine what constitutes harassment, a course of conduct and stalking, in a social media context, but we should also rethink what we consider to be the reasonable person. Here, the offence of cyberharassment or cyberstalking should not be judged solely on the reasonable person, but instead should be based on the *reasonable social media user*—to ensure the law is not asking the impossible. This was an approach endorsed by the Supreme Court in *Stoker v Stoker*[114] when determining if comments made on Facebook, amounted to defamation.

Mrs Stoker, in a series of posts on Facebook about her ex-husband's new partner, used the phrase 'he tried to strangle me', which Mr Stoker took to mean, he tried to kill her. He issued proceedings for defamation. The issue before the court turned on the meaning of strangle, with the case eventually making its way to the Supreme Court. The Justices of the Supreme Court, in determining the meaning of strangle, confirmed that the proper approach to determining its meaning, was not with reference to a dictionary, as was done by the judge at first instance, but to consider how it would be understood by the ordinary reasonable reader, taking into account context as 'a factor of considerable importance'.[115] And for the Supreme Court Justices, this meant taking into account social media where communications are considered a casual medium, 'in the nature of conversation rather than carefully chosen expression'.[116] Indeed, a person's reaction to a communication online is 'impressionistic and fleeting'.[117] Consequently, the reasonable person, in the context of *Stoker* was considered by the court to be the reasonable social media user:

> The touchstone remains what would the ordinary reasonable reader consider the words to mean [...] All of this, of course, emphasises that the primary role of the court is to focus on how the ordinary reasonable reader would construe the words. And this highlights the court's duty to step aside from a

113 *Colohan* (n 50) per Justice Hughes [18–19].
114 *Stoker v Stoker* [2020] A.C. 593.
115 Ibid., [40].
116 Ibid., [43].
117 Ibid., [44].

> lawyerly analysis and to inhabit the world of the typical reader of a Facebook post. To fulfil that obligation, the court should be particularly conscious of the context in which the statement was made.[118]

When it comes to complaints of harassment involving written words, 'there are two relevant persons: the writer and the subject of what is written'.[119] When it comes to complaints of cyberharassment and/or cyberstalking, this is even more complex as the context of social media involves 'tactics employed by [...] parties [which] can be belligerent and robust'.[120]

Embedding the concept of the reasonable person, into the reasonable social media user, will allow the court to be more considerate of the nature of social media and how it's different from the physical world. In turn, it will allow the court to also ensure that the definition of harassment is not 'given an interpretation which restricts the right of freedom of expression, save in so far as this is necessary in order to achieve a legitimate aim'.[121] Particularly given that:

> there may be some concern that the permissible limits of free speech—including the right to shock and offend, particularly in the context of public interest speech—might be given less credence in harassment cases.[122]

5.6 Chapter Summary

There is no doubt that the increase in new technology has revolutionised the ways in which harassment and stalking can occur. Its effects on those subjected to such behaviour are well documented. Although, as noted in earlier parts of this chapter, there are legitimate concerns over the definitions used in the research into this area of online abuse—something we need to consider given that it is often studies such as those discussed in Section 5.2 above, which are used to justify the increased usage of the criminal law to tackle cyberharassment and cyberstalking.

The effects of those subjected to intense cyberharassment or cyberstalking cannot, and should not be downplayed, but as highlighted throughout this chapter, and echoed throughout this monograph, we need to be careful in applying the coercive nature of the criminal law to such conduct. Broadly speaking, the discussions above have highlighted two wider points of concern:

1. The use of vague terminology throughout the PfHA. Of particular concern, is the use of the terms course of conduct, harassment, and stalking. What constitutes a course of conduct has been debated at length in cases before the judicial system, but as discussed in Section 5.5.1.1, there is little discussion

118 Ibid., [38].
119 *Carina Trimingham* (n 54) per Justice Tugendhat [57].
120 Foster (n 82) 572.
121 *Thomas* (n 104).
122 Foster (n 82) 572.

of how a course of conduct is established in the virtual world. For example, as noted above, '[i]n the context of X, where communications are limited to a maximum of 240 characters, would several Xs linked together, commonly referred to as a "thread" constitute a course of conduct? Or could they be perceived as one incident?'. Further issues were also highlighted with the term's harassment and stalking. Indeed, as illustrated above stalking and harassment are two different types of behaviours, but the law is struggling to articulate the difference between the two. And it's important that those working in the criminal justice system can articulate the differences between these two behaviours, to ensure trust is maintained in a given society and to uphold the principle of legality; and

2. The reasonable person test. Though a longstanding provision in the criminal law, the use of the reasonable person test, as discussed in Section 5.5.2, when applied in a social media context presents significant issues. This is particularly acute in the digital world, where context is everything but is often lost. To better protect the right to freedom of expression and adhere to the principle of legality, it has been suggested that we should, when considering online behaviours, ground the reasonable person test into that of the reasonable social media user—to better protect not only the right to freedom of expression but also to help maintain the principle of legality.

The concerns raised above, mirror many of the previous concerns highlighted in Chapter 4 and are further reflected in Chapters 6 and 7 in the application of communication offences to the online world.

Reference list

Agate J & Ledward J, 'Social Media: How the Net Is Closing in on Cyber Bullies' (2013) 24(8) ELR 263

Babbie E, *The Basics of Social Research* (Cengage Learning 2007)

Baber M & Jeffs H, Stalking, *harassment and Intimidation and the Protection from Harassment Bill* (Research Paper 96/115, 13 December 1996)

Barak A, 'Sexual Harassment on the Internet' (2005) 23(1) Soc Sci Comput Rev 77

Basu S & Jones R, 'Regulating Cyberstalking' (2007) 7(2) JILT https://warwick.ac.uk/fac/soc/law/elj/jilt/2007_2/basu_jones/

Bingham T, *The Rule of Law* (Penguin 2011)

Bliss L, 'The Protection from Harassment Act 1997: Failures by the Criminal Justice System in a Social Media Age' (2019) 83(3) J Crim Law 217

Bocij P, 'Victims of Cyberstalking: An Exploratory Study of Harassment Perpetrated via the Internet' (2003) 8(10) First Monday http://firstmonday.org/ojs/index.php/fm/article/view/1086

Brown A, Maple C & Short E, 'Cyberstalking in the United Kingdom: An Analysis of the ECHO Pilot Survey' (*University of Bedfordshire National Centre for Cyberstalking Research*, 2011) https://www.beds.ac.uk/__data/assets/pdf_file/0003/83109/ECHO_Pilot_Final.pdf

Carter H, 'Teenage girl is first to be jailed for bullying on Facebook' *The Guardian* (London, 21 August 2009) https://www.theguardian.com/uk/2009/aug/21/facebook-bullying-sentence-teenage-girl

Criado-Perez C, 'A Brief Comment on Peter Nunn, Sentenced Today for Twitter Abuse' (*Week Women*, 2014) https://weekwoman.wordpress.com/2014/09/29/a-brief-comment-on-peter-nunn/

Criminal Justice Inspectorates & HM Crown Prosecution Service Inspectorate, 'Living in Fear – the Police and CPS Response to Harassment and Stalking' (*justiceinspectorates.gov*, July 2017) http://www.justiceinspectorates.gov.uk/hmicfrs/wp-content/uploads/living-in-fear-the-police-and-cps-response-to-harassment-and-stalking.pdf

Davidson J, Livingtone S, Jenkins S, Gekoki A, Choak C, Ike T & Phillips K, 'Adult Online Hate, Harassment & Abuse: A Rapid Evidence Assessment' (June 2019) https://assets.publishing.service.gov.uk/government/uploads/system/uploads/attachment_data/file/811450/Adult_Online_Harms_Report_2019.pdf

Fontaine R G, *The Mind of the Criminal: The Role of Developmental Social Cognition in Criminal Defense Law* (Cambridge University Press 2012)

Foster S, 'The Right to Criticise and the Determination of Permissible Expression in Harassment Cases: The Decision in Pal v United Kingdom' (2022) 6 EHLR 571

Fuller L L, *The Morality of Law* (Yale University Press 1964)

Gowland J, 'Protection from Harassment Act 1997: The "New" Stalking Offences' (2013) 77(5) J Crim Law 387

Herring J, *Criminal Law: Text, Cases and Materials* (10th edn, Oxford University Press 2022)

HL Deb 24 January 1997, vol 1, col 917

Home Office, 'Circular: A Change to the Protection from Harassment Act 1997' (*Gov.uk*, 16 October 2012) https://www.gov.uk/government/publications/a-change-to-the-protection-from-harassment-act-1997-introduction-of-two-new-specific-offences-of-stalking

Home Office. *Stalking A Consultation Paper* (11 July 1996)

Horder J, *Ashworth's Principles of Criminal Law* (8th edn, Oxford University Press 2016)

Law Commission, *Abusive and Offensive Online Communications: A Scoping Report* (Law Com No 381, 2018)

Law Commission, *Report on Conspiracy and Criminal Law Reform* (Law Com No. 76, 1976)

MacEwan N, 'The New Stalking Offences in English Law: Will They Provide Effective Protection from Cyberstalking?' (2012) 10 Crim L R 767

Pathé M & Mullen P, 'The Impact of Stalkers on Their Victims' (1997) 170(1) B J Psych 12

Reed C & Murray A, *Rethinking the Jurisprudence of Cyberspace* (Elgar 2018)

Scaife L, *Handbook of Social Media and the Law* (Routledge 2015)

Storry M & Poppleton S, 'The Impact of Online Abuse: Hearing the Victims Voice' (*Victims Commissioner*, 1 June 2022) https://s3-eu-west-2.amazonaws.com/jotwpublic-prod-storage-1cxo1dnrmkg14/uploads/sites/6/2022/05/Hearing-the-Victims-Voice.pdf

Suzy Lamplugh Trust, 'Unmasking Stalking: A Changing Landscape' (*Suzy Lamplugh Trust*, April 2021) https://www.suzylamplugh.org/Handlers/Download.ashx?IDMF=fcfb781a-f614-48c8-adcf-4cfa830c16a7

The Crown Prosecution Service, 'Stalking and Harassment' (*CPS.gov*, 23 May 2018) https://www.cps.gov.uk/legal-guidance/stalking-and-harassment

Vogels E A, 'The State of Online Harassment' (*Pew Research Centre*, 13 January 2021) https://www.pewresearch.org/internet/2021/01/13/the-state-of-online-harassment/

6 Abusive Communications Online

The Development of Communication Law

6.1 Introduction

The regulation of communications between private individuals is not a new phenomenon. As outlined in Chapter 2, since as early as 1884 the criminal law has been used to regulate private communications following the enactment of the Post Office Protection Act, which criminalised the sending of grossly offensive material *via* the postal system.[1] Since then, following a rise in new technologies, the law has developed to expand beyond just the postal system, to fax machines, to telephone calls and in 2001, expanded to cover all forms of electronic communications. In England and Wales, until 2024, only two communication offences existed: the Malicious Communications Act 1988 (MCA) and s.127(1) and (2) of the Communications Act 2003 (CA). As will be outlined in later parts of this chapter, both provisions are very similar, though there are some subtle, but important, differences between the two. However, through the creation and implementation of the Online Safety Act 2023 (OSA), this has since expanded. Some of these 'new' communication offences, will be outlined in Chapter 7. In addition, on 31 January 2024, several changes were made to the MCA and s.127(2) of the CA, as will be outlined in the discussions below.

As discussed in Chapter 1, the rise and dominance of the internet has placed unprecedented pressure on governments, law enforcement, and society to do more to tackle the growing concerns related to the use of the internet, in particular, social media sites to send abusive communications to another. Since, we have witnessed a significant rise in the use of communication offences to prosecute and criminalise comments made online, with, as noted by Gibbon, these provisions often being associated with offensive language that generally only becomes a problem when it is imposed on a person who finds it objectionable.[2] In recent years there have been several calls for the repeal and replacement of both the MCA and s.127 of the CA.[3]

1 Post Office Protection Act 1884 s.4(1)c.

2 Thomas Gibbon, 'Case Comment: Grossly Offensive Communications' (2006) 11(4) Comms L 136, 137 (note).

3 The Law Commission in 2021 recommended their repeal and replaced with a new 'harms' offence. This is discussed in length in Chapter 7.

DOI: 10.4324/9781003303688-8

The discussion below will provide a brief history of communication offences, before turning to outline the continued usage of social media platforms to send inappropriate communications to another, often referred to as online abuse. Following on from this, the offences which were originally prohibited under the MCA and s.127(1) and (2) of the CA, until very recently, will be discussed, with particular reference to the language contained within these two provisions—highlighting issues with legality. Therefore allowing, in Chapter 7, direct comparisons between the 'new' communication offences and the 'old' offences.

6.2 A Brief History of Communication Law

As noted above, the regulation of communications is not new with discussions predating many forms of technology we know today. For example, as previously discussed in Chapter 2, in 1857 an individual was given a 21 month custodial sentence for writing offensive words relating to Christianity on a gate, under the Common Law.[4] Since, criminal law provisions have continued to be created and utilised in an attempt to regulate communications, including speech, articles sent through the postal system and the prohibition of certain conduct or the display of certain material(s), including such material(s) online.

What is believed to be the first parliamentary attempt to use the criminal law to limit communications can be traced back to 1884 with the enactment of the Post Office Protection Act which made it an offence to send 'any words, marks, or designs of an indecent, obscene, or grossly offensive character'.[5] Yet, even in 1884, concerns were raised that prohibiting the sending of material which could be defined as 'indecent, obscene, or grossly offensive' was so significantly vague, that it would render issues with consistency across the criminal justice system:

> 'grossly offensive' might be taken to mean something very different to indecent or obscene [...] it might happen that one man would use words—for instance, he might write 'swindler' or 'liar' upon the outside of a letter—which were not really indecent or obscene, only what they would call vulgar [...] the words 'grossly offensive' might be taken to mean something that was extremely offensive to the person who received it, although it did nothing more than lacerate the feelings of the person receiving it.[6]

Concerns, which later became a reality.[7]

Yet the use of these terms, indecent, obscene or grossly offensive, have continued to be utilised to control communications—both verbal and written. Indeed,

4 John Stuart Mill, *On Liberty* (first published 1859, Enhanced Media 2016) 25.

5 Post Office Protection Act 1884 s.4(1)c.

6 HC Deb, 09 August 1884, vol 292, col 371.

7 Graham Smith, 'From telegram to tweet: Section 127 and all that' (*Cyberlegal*, 22 February 2015) <https://www.cyberleagle.com/2015/02/from-telegram-to-tweet-section-127-and.html> accessed 5 July 2022.

not only did the law expand to prohibit the types of materials which could be sent, but it also extended beyond just the postal system to include new forms of technology. For instance, the Post Office Amendment Act 1935 made it an offence for any person to send:

> (1) any message by telephone which is grossly offensive or of an indecent, obscene, or menacing character; or (2) sends any message by telephone, or any telegram, which he knows to be false, for the purpose of causing annoyance, inconvenience, or needless anxiety to any other person; or (3) persistently makes telephone calls without reasonable cause and for any such purpose as aforesaid.[8]

Similar provisions were contained in the Telecommunications Act 1984 (TCA) which prohibited a person from sending:

> (a) by means of a public telecommunication system, a message or other matter that is grossly offensive or of an indecent, obscene, or menacing character; or (b) sends by those means, for the purpose of causing annoyance, inconvenience, or needless anxiety to another, a message that he knows to be false or persistently makes use for that purpose of a public telecommunication system.[9]

The only element that has altered since 1884, is the mode of communication, with the content of such communications which are prohibited by law remaining, until recently, relatively consistent—the prohibition of sending material which can be defined as:

- Grossly offensive;
- Indecent;
- Obscene;
- Threatening;
- Menacing; or
- False.

Until 31 January 2024, such content continued to be prohibited under both the MCA and s.127(1) and (2) of the CA—two provisions which became prominent in attempting to tackle the 'harms' associated with the online world.

6.3 The Rise in Online Abuse

There does not seem to be a day in the United Kingdom where a story does not emerge concerning the rise in the use of social media platforms to send abusive

8 Post Office Amendment Act 1935 s.10(2).
9 Telecommunication Act 1984 s.34(1)a & s.34(1)b.

communications to another. Put simply, the rise in online abuse is well documented with ex-police Chief Constable for Essex, Stephen Kavanagh, suggesting that the current research into online abuse is only 'the tip of the iceberg', with police forces unable to cope with the scale of abuse that is currently taking place online.[10]

In October 2017 the BBC released a Freedom of Information request exposing the number of police reports made between 2015 and 2016, where malicious communications were the main element of the crime being complained about.[11] 38 out of 42 police forces responded to the request. The BBC uncovered that between 2015 and 2016, there had been an increase of 36,462 police reports involving malicious communications. Similarly, in 2017 Amnesty International, a human rights organisation, conducted an IPSOS[12] poll examining the extent to which women are abused *via* social media.[13] The poll was conducted across eight states looking at the online experiences of women aged between 18 and 55. 23% of those surveyed stated that they had, on at least one occasion, experienced online abuse. A significant proportion of this abuse was sent *via* Facebook. Findings which were further mirrored in research by Amnesty International following the 2017 General Election in the United Kingdom.[14]

The growing trend in the use of the internet to send abusive communications to others is further highlighted throughout research studies exploring online abuse. For instance, in 2018 OFCOM conducted a representative sample of 1,882 UK adults on their experiences of seeing abusive content online, finding that 53% of internet users had viewed hateful content, a rise of 6% on the previous year.[15] Further research conducted on behalf of OFCOM in 2020 revealed that 63% of adults had experienced at least one harmful incident in the previous 12 months.[16] Outside of the United Kingdom, studies further support the concept that online abuse is prevalent. For example, in 2018 Pacheco and Melhuish conducted a representative sample of 1,001 adults in New Zealand (weighted to ensure representation of minorities) on their experience of seeing or encountering online abuse.

10 The BBC, 'Teenager's life "ruined" by Live.me and Twitter "trolls"' *The BBC* (London, 24 October 2017) <http://www.bbc.co.uk/news/uk-england-41693437> accessed 30 January 2018.

11 Ibid.,

12 IPSOS is a global market research firm.

13 Amnesty International, 'Amnesty reveals alarming impact of online abuse against women' (*Amnesty International*, 20 November 2017) <https://www.amnesty.org/en/latest/news/2017/11/amnesty-reveals-alarming-impact-of-online-abuse-against-women/> accessed 9 December 2018.

14 Amnesty International UK, 'Black and Asian women MPs abused more online' (*Amnesty International*, 2017) <https://www.amnesty.org.uk/online-violence-women-mps> accessed 9 December 2018. See also, Laura Bliss, 'Abuse of women MPs is not just a scandal – it's a threat to democracy' *The Conversation* (London, 17 July 2017) <https://theconversation.com/abuse-of-women-mps-is-not-just-a-scandal-its-a-threat-to-democracy-80781> accessed 9 December 2018.

15 OFCOM, '"Adults"' media use and attitudes report' (*OFCOM*, 25 April 2018) <https://www.ofcom.org.uk/__data/assets/pdf_file/0011/113222/Adults-Media-Use-and-Attitudes-Report-2018.pdf> accessed 1 May 2023.

16 OFCOM, '"Adults"' media use and attitudes report 2020/21' (*OFCOM*, 28 April 2021) <https://www.ofcom.org.uk/__data/assets/pdf_file/0025/217834/adults-media-use-and-attitudes-report-2020> accessed 1 May 2023.

28% of participants in Pacheco and Melhuish's study had seen or encountered online abuse.[17] Similarly, in Australia, in 2022, 40% of adults, rising to 50% for the LGBTQIA+ and the CALD (culturally and linguistically diverse) community, had experienced an online harm in the prior 12 months.[18]

It is figures such as these, that are often used to justify stronger criminal provisions in tackling the use of the internet, in particular social media, to send abusive communications. However,

> [p]art of the challenge is that, at present, the data, tools, processes and systems needed to effectively and accurately monitor online abuse are not fully available and the field is beset with terminological, methodological, legal and theoretical challenges.[19]

Consequently, the evidence that is often used to demonstrate the rise in the use of the internet to send abusive communications is 'incomplete and inadequate'.[20] The Alan Turing Institute estimates that the prevalence of abusive communications on online platforms, which is serious enough to warrant intervention, is extremely low, giving an estimate of 0.001% to 1%.[21] Given that the required proof of wrongdoing by platforms to justify the removal of such content compared to that of the criminal law is significantly lower, this is concerning.

Reviewing several academic and thinktanks studies into online abuse, including some of those discussed above, The Alan Turing Institute were able to conclude that 0.001% to 1% of content on mainstream platforms, such as Facebook, Twitter, etc., could be labelled as abusive. Though do acknowledge that 'some users and events generate far more abuse, such as prominent figures (e.g., MPs) and terror attacks'.[22] Consequently, as noted in the report:

> [t]he available evidence is fragmented, incomplete and inadequate for understanding the prevalence of online abuse. Appropriate statistics are difficult

17 Pacheco Edgar and Neil Melhuish, 'NetSafe online hate speech: A survey on personal experiences and exposure among adult New Zealanders' (*Netsafe*, 12 December 2018) <https://netsafe.org.nz/wp-content/uploads/2016/12/Netsafe-insights-into-New-Zealands-experience-of-online-hate-speech.pdf> accessed 1 May 2023.

18 Michelle Rowland, 'Release of the 2022 National Online Safety Survey' (*Ministers for Infrastructure, Transport, Regional Development, Communications and the Arts*, 14 November 2022) <https://minister.infrastructure.gov.au/rowland/media-release/release-2022-national-online-safety-survey> accessed 11 May 2023.

19 Bertie Vidgen, Helen Margetts and Alex Harris, 'How Much Online Abuse Is There? A Systematic Review of Evidence for the UK. Policy Briefing – Full Report' (*The Alan Turing Institute*, 2020) 3 <https://www.turing.ac.uk/sites/default/files/2019-11/online_abuse_prevalence_full_24.11.2019_-_formatted_0.pdf> accessed 3 May 2023.

20 Ibid., 4.

21 Ibid.,

22 Ibid., 28.

> to find and, in many cases, are not provided with the necessary contextual information to fully interpret them.[23]

Put simply, 'in the absence of a mature and rigorous evidence base, it is hard to see how [...] the broad ambitions to regulate [are justified]'.[24] Nothing demonstrated this more than the MCA and s.127(1) and (2) of the CA. Both provisions contained, and still do, despite recent changes, overly broad language, creating significant issues with the principle of legality and in turn, threatens the right to freedom of speech.

6.4 The Malicious Communications Act 1988

One of the most significant changes to communication law came in 1988 with the enactment of the MCA following growing concerns relating to the rise in the use of the postal system to send poison pen letters or articles to another.[25] Many of these communications, though distressing upon the receiver, fell outside the realms of criminal law intervention. For instance, the case of a coffin being sent through the postal system, though distressing upon the recipient, was not unlawful.[26] This small but significant void in the law paved the way for the creation and enactment of the MCA.

The MCA is a prime example of Parliament's attempt to keep pace with how individuals communicate with each other. Though was never intended, in its original form, to cover electronic communications, as during the Law Commission's consultation into poison-pen letters, an informed decision was made not to include electronic communications within the scope of the proposed offence.[27] This was amended under s.43 of the Criminal Justice and Police Act 2001, in which 'electronic communications' was substituted into the Act.

As technology has evolved and how we communicate with others has changed, the MCA has undergone several alterations in an attempt to keep pace with changing technology. Before 2015, the MCA was a summary only offence, carrying a maximum custodial sentence and a limitation period of six months.[28] This was,

23 Ibid., 4.

24 Victoria Nash, 'Revise and Resubmit? Reviewing the 2019 Online Harms White Paper' 2019 11(1) J. Media Law 18, 24.

25 Poison pen letters and articles are considered 'a communication, written or otherwise, which is grossly offensive, or of an indecent, shocking, or menacing character, [which is sent] for the purpose of causing needless anxiety or distress [to the recipient] or any other person'. See, Law Commission, *Report on Poison-Pen Letters* (Law Com No 147 1985) [2.1].

26 HC Deb 12 February 1988, vol 127, col 620.

27 During the Law Commission's consultation into poison-pen letters, a decision was made not to include electronic communications within the scope of their proposed bill. See, Law Com No 147 (n 25) [2.11]. This was amended under s.43 of the Criminal Justice and Police Act 2001.

28 Limitation periods are 'the time limit within which the state may prosecute a particular crime'. See, George P. Fletcher, *Basic Concepts of Criminal Law* (Oxford University Press 1998) 10.

however, later raised as an issue before Parliament by former MP Angie Bray,[29] with the MCA now an either-way offence as per s.15 of the Criminal Justice and Courts Act 2015. Increasing the maximum custodial sentence under the MCA from six months to two years.

Until 31 January 2024, the MCA made it an offence:

> to send to another (a) a letter, electronic communication or article of any description which conveys—(i) a message which is indecent or grossly offensive; (ii) a threat; or (iii) information which is false and known or believed to be false by the sender; or (b) any article of electronic communication which is, in whole or part, of an indecent or grossly offensive nature.[30]

Today, by way of the OSA, the MCA only covers indecent or grossly offensive communications. Threatening and false communications are now prohibited under s.181(1) and 179(1) of the OSA—discussed further in Chapter 7. However, as highlighted above, for the purposes of this chapter, the MCA in its original format will be examined, to highlight why it was thought necessary to amend and allow for further discussions to take place in the following chapter directly comparing the 'old' offences to the 'new' offences.

6.4.1 Actus Reus

The *actus reus* of the MCA consists of two elements. First, the message must be sent in the form of a letter, electronic communication, or an article. What is a letter is self-explanatory, whereas what constitutes an 'electronic communication' or indeed an 'article', is a little more complex. S.2A of the MCA defines an electronic communication as: '(a) any oral or other communication by means of an electronic communications network; and (b) any communication (however sent) that is in electronic form'. Therefore, messages sent on social media platforms would constitute an electronic communication under the MCA. Whereas 'article' takes a very broad meaning and is defined under the Obscene Publications Act 1959 and 1964 (OPA) as anything 'containing or embodying matter to be read or looked at or both, any sound record, and any film or other record of a picture or pictures'.[31]

29 Ministry of Justice, 'Impact assessment: Making the offence in s.1 of the Malicious Communications Act 1988 a triable either-way offence' (*Gov.uk*, 30 May 2014) <https://assets.publishing.service.gov.uk/government/uploads/system/uploads/attachment_data/file/321285/malicious-communicationss-impact-assessment.pdf > accessed 11 July 2021. In her constituency, the police had attempted to prosecute an individual under s.15 of the Sexual Offences Act 2003, following an adult male sending sexually explicit text messages to a young female. Yet the prosecution failed because a meeting had not taken place, and therefore no offence had occurred under the Sexual Offences Act 2003. No further action could be taken against the individual as the six month limitation period under the Malicious Communications Act 1988 had surpassed.

30 Malicious Communications Act 1988 s.1(1).

31 Obscene Publications Act 1959 and 1964 s.1(2).

It could therefore include, and has included, the sending of an image showing an aborted foetus.[32]

Further, to fulfil the first part of the *actus reus*, the message *must be sent to another*, meaning in theory a public message sent on X, would not be covered under this Act of Parliament. In essence, the MCA *should* only cover communications sent privately. However, there are examples in which the MCA has been applied incorrectly, such as the matter of an anonymous blogger, who in July 2011 received a caution under the MCA for sending false information *via* a communications network.[33] The anonymous blogger had made allegations that a contestant on the television show 'Britain's Got Talent' had been groomed for the show by key organisers. The allegations were later proven to be false. Nevertheless, on a literal interpretation of the MCA, the matter was indeed pursued under the wrong Act of Parliament—the communication was never sent to another.[34] A similar case was brought before the courts in 2018, where Michael John Paley had his conviction quashed for sending a false communication under the MCA after it was concluded that the *actus reus* of the MCA had not been met, as the message had not been sent to another.[35]

Second, for the *actus reus* of the MCA to be fulfilled, it must have been found, in its original format, that the message sent was either indecent, grossly offensive, threatening, or false. As noted above, today the message would need to be considered either indecent or grossly offensive to fulfil this part of the *actus reus*.

As highlighted in the Act itself—'whole or in part'—it is sufficient if only part of the message falls into one of these categories. For example, it does not need to be found that the whole communication was grossly offensive to breach the MCA. How these terms are defined will be critically examined in later parts of this chapter. However, it is important to note that the actual criminal offence is in the physical sending of a letter, electronic communication, or an article which conveys a prohibited message. Consequently, there is no need for the intended message to be received by the recipient. This allows the law to intervene even if the communication is intercepted by a third party or the recipient does not receive the intended communication.[36]

6.4.2 Mens Rea

For the *mens rea* to be established it must be concluded that the *purpose* on behalf of the sender was to cause anxiety or distress upon the intended recipient,

32 *Connolly v DPP* [2007] EWHC 237 (Admin), [2008] 1 W.L.R. 276 (DC). Discussed further in Section 6.4.2.

33 Press Association, 'Britain's Got Talent blogger cautioned by police' *The Guardian* (London, 3 July 2011) <https://www.theguardian.com/tv-and-radio/2011/jul/03/britains-got-talent-blogger-cautioned> accessed 1 May 2018.

34 Laura Scaife, *Handbook of Social Media and the Law* (Routledge 2015) 165–166.

35 *R v Michael John Paley*, Preston Crown Court, 26 April 2018 (unreported).

36 Law Com No 147 (n 25) [4.4].

the recipient does not need to demonstrate they experienced anxiety or distress.[37] Though the MCA contains no definition of anxiety or distress, previous cases of harassment have shed some light on the meaning given to these terms by the courts. As affirmed in *Majrowski v Guy's and St Thomas's NHS Trust*,[38] anxiety is considered something just short of a recognised psychiatric illness. Whereas distress can be defined as 'oppressive and unreasonable behaviour'.[39] If a person sends a communication for another purpose, for instance in the form of a lawful protest, no offence would have occurred under the MCA; an issue the High Court considered in *Connolly v DPP*.[40]

Connolly, a Roman Catholic pro-life campaigner, sent several pictures to pharmacies of aborted foetuses clearly depicting the limbs and faces of the foetus, as a form of protest against the issuing of the morning after-pill by the pharmacies. One image sent by Connolly included a photograph of a deceased 21-week-old foetus with the face and limbs visible to the person viewing the image. The court concluded that the images were indecent and grossly offensive and therefore the *actus reus* of the MCA was present. However, the matter turned on whether the images were sent for the purpose of causing anxiety or distress, and therefore unlawful under the MCA. Or, were in fact, sent as a form of lawful protest:

> A person who sends an indecent or grossly offensive communication for a political or educational purpose will not be guilty of the offence unless it is proved that his purpose was also to cause distress or anxiety.[41]

For the High Court, a balance had to be struck between Connolly's right to freedom of expression and freedom of thought, conscience and religion as protected under Articles 10 and 9 of the European Convention on Human Rights (ECHR) respectively, alongside the 'rights of others', which would allow the court to legitimately infringe upon these Article rights.[42] On balance, the High Court upheld the decision of Coventry Crown Court and came to the judgment that the images sent were sent for the purpose of causing anxiety or distress contrary to the MCA:

> We have seen the photographs. They are close-up colour photographs of dead 21-week-old foetuses. The face and limbs are clearly visible. One of them is a close-up showing an abortion taking place. They are shocking and disturbing. That is why Mrs Connolly sent them to the pharmacists.[43]

37 Malicious Communications Act 1988 s.1(1).

38 *Majrowski v Guy's and St Thomas's NHS Trust* [2005] EWCA Civ 251, [2005] Q.B 848 per Auld LJ [45].

39 Ibid., per May LJ [82].

40 *Connolly* (n 32).

41 Ibid., per Dyson LJ [9].

42 See Chapter 2 for an in-depth discussion of when a person's right to freedom of expression can be restricted.

43 *Connolly* (n 32) [11].

Put simply, if the sending of such material is not sent for the purpose of causing anxiety or distress, no offence has taken place contrary to the MCA.

6.4.3 Summary

The scope of the MCA has shifted dramatically since its conception by the Law Commission in the early 1980s. We have moved away from covering communications sent *via* the postal system only, to electronic communications, including communications sent *via* social media. However, as will be discussed in later parts of this chapter, significant issues with legality were, and continue to be raised against the MCA, particularly the prohibited conduct under the Act. Issues which are also directly applicable to s.127(1) and (2) of the CA.

6.5 The Communications Act 2003: S.127 (1) and (2)

Following the turn of the new millennium, the use of technology, the internet and electronic communications increased dramatically across the globe; a trend that continues to occur even to this day. Like the reasoning behind the creation of the MCA, concerns were raised that the law was struggling to keep pace with the advancement of new technology, in particular, how individuals communicated:

> We are living at a time of revolution in the ways in which we communicate. The worlds of telephone, broadcasting, mobile communications, and the internet are changing and converging with astonishing speed. Meanwhile, our current regulatory framework was designed for a different age. We need to update the framework of regulation, and put in place a system that recognises the current fast-changing picture and can cope with the inevitability of change in years to come.[44]

In 2003 Parliament enacted s.127(1) and (2) of the CA to address the issues raised above.[45]

The CA had several aims. The Act created The Office of Communications commonly referred to as OFCOM, paved the way for the switch from analogue to digital television broadcasting and ensured universal internet access. In addition, it repealed and replaced s.43 of the TCA, discussed in Section 6.2, with s.127 (1) and (2) of the CA.

Under s.127(1) of the CA, it is a criminal offence to send:

> (a) by means of a public electronic communications network a message or other matter that is grossly offensive or of an indecent, obscene or menacing character; or (b) causes any such message or matter to be so sent.

44 HC Deb 12 December 2000, vol 359, col 481.
45 HC Deb 12 December 2000, vol 359, col 483.

Whereas under s.127(2), initially it was an offence to send, 'for the purpose of causing annoyance, inconvenience, or needless anxiety to another [...] by means of a public electronic communications network' a knowingly false message; or caused 'such a message to be sent; or persistently made use of a public electronic communications network'. However, s.127(2)a and 127(2)b have since been repealed.[46] False communications are now criminalised under s.179(1) of the OSA, discussed in Chapter 7. Below, the *actus reus* and *mens rea* of s.127(1) of the CA will be examined, alongside s.127(2) of the CA (as originally enacted).

6.5.1 Actus Reus

The *actus reus* of the offences prohibited under s.127 of the CA constitutes two elements. First, a message must be sent *via* a public electronic communications network. Like that of the MCA the offence is in the sending of the message (provided all other elements of the offence are present). There is no need for the message to be received. The term 'message' is given a wide definition in law, and includes text, images, or videos. However, the message *must be* sent *via* a public electronic communications network, defined under s.32 of the CA as:

> (a) a transmission system for the conveyance, by the use of electrical, magnetic or electro-magnetic energy, of signals of any description; and (b) such of the following as are used, by the person providing the system and in association with it, for the conveyance of the signals: (i) apparatus comprised in the system; (ii) apparatus used for the switching or routing of the signals; (iii) software and stored data.

A public electronic communications network therefore includes the internet and social media. However, a public electronic communications network does not include the sending of material *via* Bluetooth or Apple Airdrop.

Secondly, to prove the *actus reus* of an offence under s.127(1) of the CA, the content of such messages sent must be either grossly offensive or of an indecent, obscene or menacing character. Under s.127(2), as originally enacted, the message must have been false—terminology which will be defined and examined further in Section 6.6.2.

6.5.2 Mens Rea

Under s.127(1) of the CA as enacted by Parliament, no *mens rea* was present. Traditionally speaking, criminal acts which lack a definitive *mens rea* are considered strict liability offences.[47] However, using the principles laid out in *Sweet v*

46 S.127(2)c of the Communications Act 2003 remains but has been amended to cover hoax phone calls.

47 Strict liability offences are not dependent on actual negligence or intent to harm.

Parsley,[48] the House of Lords substituted a *mens rea* element into s.127(1) of the CA, arguing that it would be illogical for there to be no *mens rea* present:

> Parliament cannot have intended to criminalise the conduct of a person using language which is, for reasons unknown to him, grossly offensive to those to whom it relates, or which may even be thought, however wrongly, to represent a polite or acceptable usage. On the other hand, a culpable state of mind will ordinarily be found where a message is couched in terms showing an intention to insult those to whom the message relates or giving rise to the inference that a risk of doing so must have been recognised by the sender.[49]

Therefore, for an individual to be held liable for a breach of s.127(1) of the CA, it must be found that a grossly offensive, menacing, indecent, obscene message was sent to another recklessly or with intent.

The *mens rea* element of s.127(1) of the CA has recently been reaffirmed by the Divisional Court in *DPP v Kingsley Anthony Smith*[50] and *DPP v Bussetti*.[51] Although both *Kingsley* and *Bussetti* concerned the sending of grossly offensive communications, it has been confirmed by the Crown Prosecution Service (CPS), in their 2023 social media prosecution guidelines (and discussed further in later parts of this chapter) that messages which can be defined as 'indecent, obscene, or of a menacing character' contain the same *mens rea* element—intention or recklessness.[52]

Whereas for an offence to have occurred under s.127(2) of the CA, prior to the passing of the OSA, the defendant's purpose must have been to cause annoyance, inconvenience, or needless anxiety to another. As with the MCA, anxiety was considered as something just short of a recognised psychiatric illness, with the court noting in *Scottow v CPS*:

> what Parliament intended was to proscribe a course of persistent conduct the sole purpose of which is to cause annoyance, anxiety, or inconvenience by virtue of its persistence, rather than its informational content.[53]

Indicating that annoyance or inconvenience was met when a false message was persistently sent.

48 *Sweet v Parsley* [1969] 2 W.L.R. 470, [1970] A.C. 132. The principles created by the House of Lords in this case allow the court to substitute a *mens rea* into an offence where the criminal act is considered a true crime as opposed to a regulatory offence.

49 *DPP v Collins* [2006] UKHL 40, [2006] 1 W.L.R. 2223 per Lord Bingham of Cornhill [11].

50 *DPP v Kingsley Anthony Smith* [2017] EWHC 359 (Admin).

51 *DPP v Busetti* [2021] EWHC 2140 (Admin).

52 The Crown Prosecution Service, 'Social media and other electronic communications (*CPS.gov*, 9 January 2023) <https://www.cps.gov.uk/legal-guidance/social-media-and-other-electronic-communications> accessed 1 May 2023.

53 *Scottow v CPS* [2020] EWHC 3421 per Mr Justice Warby [32].

6.5.3 Summary

Both the MCA and s.127(1) and (2) of the CA, in their original format, covered very similar behaviours. Put simply, under the MCA it was an offence to send to another a message which could be labelled as:

- Threatening;
- False;
- Indecent; or
- Grossly offensive.

The following were prohibited under s.127(1) and (2) of the CA:

- Grossly offensive;
- Indecent;
- Obscene;
- Menacing; or
- False communications.

The behaviours prohibited under each provision above, caused difficulties for those working in the criminal justice system, with Scaife going as far as arguing that both provisions had become 'interchangeable in recent years'.[54] And even with the modest changes made to both provisions under the OSA, issues remain, particularly with the prohibited behaviours under both provisions and the principle of legality.

6.6 Communication Offences, Social Media, and Legality

Under the principle of legality, as discussed in Chapter 3, legal provisions need to be constructed in a clear and precise manner, for an individual to be liable for a criminal offence. In *Kafkaris v Cyprus*[55] the European Court of Human Rights (ECtHR) noted that

> [a]n individual must know from the wording of the relevant provision and, if need be, with the assistance of the courts' interpretation of it, what acts and omissions will make him criminally liable and what penalty will be imposed.[56]

As will be demonstrated below, the above is not being adhered to in the application of communication offences to complaints of social media abuse. In summary, issues will be exposed with the principle of legality, in particular, the interchangeable nature of the MCA and s.127 of the CA and the meaning of the prohibited

54 Scaife (n 34) 166.

55 *Kafkaris v Cyprus* App no. 21906/04 (ECtHR, 12 February 2008).

56 Ibid., [140].

conduct under each provision, despite the creation and implementation of social media prosecution guidelines in an attempt to bring some form of clarity to this area of the law. Indeed, as will be highlighted further in Chapter 7, many of these issues remain despite changes made by the OSA.

6.6.1 Malicious Communications Act v Communications Act

There are clearly some parallels between both the MCA and s.127 of the CA. Which, as alluded to in earlier parts of this chapter, has caused issues for actors working in the criminal justice system. In essence, both provisions have become interchangeable.[57] And even with the removal of false and threatening communications, overlaps remain. Yet, it is vital that a distinction is made between the two, as they both carry different sentencing tariffs.[58]

One justification for the overlap between the two offences is that the MCA was never intended to cover electronic communications, with little attention being given to other offences at the time of amendment (mainly, s.43 of the TCA) which already prohibited such conduct. However, there are some subtle, but significant, differences between the two. The biggest being the type of communications covered under each provision. The MCA covers all forms of communication, including the postal system. Whereas s.127(1) and (2) of the CA only covers public electronic communications. In essence, a message sent through the postal system which, as an example, is grossly offensive, is only prohibited under the MCA. Further, as noted previously, the MCA should only be used to cover private communications, yet this has clearly not always been the case, with the Law Commission warning that interpretive challenges are likely to remain without amendments to these provisions.[59] And this becomes even more significant given that the passing of the OSA has complicated this further, as discussed at length in Chapter 7.

In an attempt to bring some clarity to this area of the law the CPS created and implemented social media prosecution guidelines in 2013, following cases such as *Chambers v DPP*[60] and *R v Woods*[61]—cases discussed further below. The guidelines were later updated in 2016, 2018, January of 2023 and most recently, in early 2024 following the enactment of the OSA.[62] The purpose of the guidelines was to

57 Scaife (n 34).

58 The maximum custodial sentence which can be imposed on a person under either s.127(1) or (2) of the Communications Act 2003 is six months. Under s.1 of the Malicious Communications Act 1988, the maximum custodial sentence is two years.

59 Law Commission, *Abusive and Offensive Online Communications: A Scoping Report* (Law Com No 381, 2018) [4.30].

60 *Chambers v DPP* [2012] EWHC 2157 (Admin), [2013] 1 W.L.R. 183.

61 *R v Matthew Woods*, Chorley Magistrates' Court, 8 October 2012 (unreported).

62 The Crown Prosecution Service, 'Communication offences' (*CPS.gov,* 2024) <https://www.cps.gov.uk/legal-guidance/communications-offences#:~:text=the%20summary%20offences%20under%20section,of%20a%20public%20communications%20network.> accessed 11 March 2024.

bring consistency to this area of the law but as will be demonstrated below, this has not necessarily been the case.

In their updated social media guidelines in 2018, the CPS attempted to highlight the key differences between both the MCA and s.127 of the CA, in particular the difference between the mental elements of the crime.[63] Yet, the Law Commission in their scoping report, found examples of the two provisions continuing to be applied incorrectly, concluding that there is considerable overlap between the 'two offences in the online context and the purpose of this has not been convincingly demonstrated or explained'.[64] This renders issues with the principle of legality, as consistency and clarity are lost because

> if you and I are liable to be prosecuted, fined or perhaps imprisoned for doing or failing to do something, we ought to be able, without undue difficulty, to find out what we must or must not do.[65]

If actors in the criminal justice system are struggling to comprehend the differences between both the MCA and s.127 of the CA, and now also the OSA, it is difficult to see how communication offences under any of these provisions can be considered action-guiding — as noted further in Chapter 7. This is even more important because, as noted above, there are differences in the sentencing tariffs contained in each provision. Indeed, for Bakalis, both the MCA and s.127 of the CA have become fragmented and outdated.[66]

Significant weight is therefore given to prosecutorial discretion in determining the best course of action when it comes to complaints regarding behaviours carried out on social media platforms—all of which undermine the principle of legality. The confusion between the MCA and s.127 of the CA, and their place within the wider criminal law framework, is further amplified by the ambiguous terminology contained in each provision—in both their original enactment and their current format.

6.6.2 Terminology

Under the MCA, it was an offence to send a message which could be categorised as indecent or grossly offensive, a threat, or a message which could be deemed to be false. S.127(1) and (2) of the CA prohibited the sending of a message which was false, grossly offensive, indecent, obscene, or of a menacing character. For the Law Commission, prior to the OSA, we had 'a set of offences that [were]

63 The Crown Prosecution Service, 'Guidelines on prosecuting cases involving communications sent via social media' (*CPS.gov*, 21 August 2018) <https://www.cps.gov.uk/legal-guidance/social-media-guidelines-prosecuting-cases-involving-communications-sent-social-media> accessed 11 October 2018.

64 Law Com No 381 (n 59) [4.148].

65 Tom Bingham, *The Rule of Law* (Penguin 2011) 37.

66 Chara Bakalis, 'Rethinking Cyberhate Laws' (2017) 27(1) Inf. Commun. Technol. Law 86.

remarkably broad' where such speech was criminalised online, but not necessarily in the 'offline' world.[67] For instance, a person who writes a grossly offensive communication which they save to 'the cloud' could be liable for a s.127(1) offence. However, if the same communication was typed and then printed, being stored in a draw, no offence would have been committed. In addition, the vague terminology contained in both provisions, as outlined below, placed significant weight on prosecutorial discretion and court cases to clarify the meaning of these terms—all of which undermined the principle of legality. Indeed,

> The breadth of the offence[s] and its potential for infringing freedom of expression, can also be seen in the fact that what is outlawed is communications that are 'grossly offensive', 'indecent', or 'obscene'. It is difficult to see how proscribing such words would come within the Art 10(2) exceptions, as it is unlikely to be seen as 'necessary in a democratic society' to outlaw communications simply based on their gross offensiveness, indecency, or obscenity.[68]

Issues that remain, despite the modest changes made by the passing of the OSA as the behaviours in the quote above, are still prohibited between both the MCA and s.127(1) of the CA.

6.6.2.1 Indecent

The conduct of sending an indecent communication is criminalised under both the MCA and s.127(1) of the CA. Neither Act defines the term indecent, and its meaning is unclear. Though it could include conversations between individuals online or the sharing of materials. Indecent is also considered as being less serious than obscene but more serious than grossly offensive.[69] In *Collins*, indecency was understood to be 'in the eye of the beholder; but the law has generally treated them as a matter of objective fact to be determined by contemporary standards of decency'.[70] The CPS prosecuting guidelines on social media offences also continues to fail to fully articulate the meaning of this term, with the courts arguing that the term indecent takes its ordinary meaning in a given society and will be subjective depending on the context of a case.[71]

Under the principle of legality, as discussed in Chapter 3, legal provisions must be clear and certain so citizens can abide by the law. The idea that the term indecent will be subjective depending on the case before the courts creates uncertainty within the law. Indeed, for the Law Commission, the failure of legislation to define the term indecent and subsequently the failure of the courts to bring clarity to this

67 Law Com No 381 (n 59) [4.63].

68 Bakalis (n 66) 107.

69 The meaning of 'grossly offensive' is discussed further in Section 6.6.2.6.

70 *Collins* (n 49) per Sedley LJ [10].

71 Ibid.,

area of the law, creates interpretative challenges for all.[72] In particular, the difference between obscene, indecent and grossly offensive—there is a threshold between these behaviours, but that threshold is difficult to articulate. Further, by simply stating that indecent takes its ordinary dictionary meaning, here under the Oxford English Dictionary the term would be defined as 'morally offensive', little clarity is brought to this area of the law. Indeed, should something that is morally offensive, be criminal? For instance, Gillespie argues that indecency could include the sharing of naked images of adults, even where both adults consent to the sending of these images, commonly referred to as sexting:

> The meaning of indecent must mean that virtually any sexualised conversation could be captured by this offence, even that between consenting adults—something that would seem on the face of it extraordinary.[73]

This is especially true in matters concerning social media, as what one person may find indecent another may not. Arguably, the sending of an image online of a female without a burqa on could be considered as indecent by some.[74]

6.6.2.2 Obscene

Like that of indecent, there is no definition of obscene contained in s.127(1) of the CA, which prohibits the sending of such material. However, obscene is defined elsewhere within the criminal law framework of England and Wales, in particular under s.1(1) of the OPA which defines obscene as

> an article [which …] tend[s] to deprave and corrupt persons who are likely, having regard to all relevant circumstances, to read, see or hear the matter contained or embodied in it.[75]

Indeed, in most cases where a communication can be labelled as obscene, it is likely to be pursued under s.1(1) of the OPA as opposed to s.127(1) of the CA, as illustrated in *R v Smith (Gavin)*.[76]

Put simply, a matter will be obscene if the content goes beyond what is acceptable in a multicultural society and has the possibility of corrupting public morality.[77] In essence, it is a context-dependant crime, in which the matter is left to the judge, magistrates or jury to decide if such material is obscene. Though the term, obscene lacks a clear definition, the concept that obscene material is based on acceptability in a multicultural society, as opposed to the context of the case, like that of the term

72 Law Com No 381 (n 59) [6.84].

73 Alasdair A. Gillespie, 'Obscene Conversations, the Internet and the Criminal Law' (2014) 5 Crim. L.R. 350, 359.

74 See, for example, *LCG v OVD* [2023] EWHC 2058 (KB).

75 Obscene Publications Act 1959 and 1964 s.1(1).

76 *R v Smith (Gavin)* [2012] EWCA Crim 398, [2012] 1 W.L.R. 3368.

77 *Handyside v The United Kingdom* (1976)1 EHRR 737.

indecent, allows for the law to adapt to the changing nature of society. As Lord Bingham argues:

> it is accepted that absolute certainty is unattainable, and might entail excessive rigidity since the law must be able to keep pace with changing circumstances, some degree of vagueness is inevitable and development of the law is a recognised feature of common law courts.[78]

Indeed, what may have been classified as obscene 30 years ago, may not be today. But this creates issues when it comes to the publication of obscene material online, whereby anyone could read or see the material. This could mean, in the case of a communication sent on a social media site, obscene could be judged as corrupting the morality of those aged 13 or above.[79] In turn, this poses a significant issue with the right to freedom of expression.

6.6.2.3 False

Both the MCA and s.127(2) of the CA prohibited the sending of a message which could be categorised as false, in which it would have been for the judge, magistrate, or jury to determine if such a message could be considered as false. Such as, Stephen Dure, who in 2018, received a 15 week custodial sentence for making false claims on a social media platform that another person was engaging in paedophilic activities contrary to s.127(2) of the CA.[80]

The use of social media platforms to send false communications has created, and still creates significant debate in the United Kingdom. In particular, concerns have been raised around the use of social media sites to distribute mis/disinformation, commonly referred to as fake news and the use of fake social media accounts to send abusive communications.[81] Resulting in calls, prior to the OSA, for the meaning of false communications to also cover fake social media accounts and/or mis/disinformation under both the MCA and s.127(2) of the CA.

In 2016 following the CPS updating their prosecuting guidelines on social media offences, emphasis was placed on tackling the growing trend of anonymous online profiles:

78 *R v Rimmington, R v Goldstein* [2005] UKHL 63, [2006] 1 A.C. 459 per Lord Bingham [35].

79 This is because in most cases the minimum age for a person to be on a social media platform is 13.

80 *R v Stephen Dure,* Southampton Magistrates' Court, 3 September 2018 (unreported). See also, *The BBC*, 'Southampton "paedophile hunter" jailed for false claim' *The BBC* (London, 3 September 2018) <https://www.bbc.co.uk/news/uk-england-hampshire-45395607> accessed 16 May 2023.

81 James Titcomb, 'Facebook admits up to 270m users are fake and duplicate accounts' *The Telegraph* (London, 2 November 2017) <https://www.telegraph.co.uk/technology/2017/11/02/facebook-admits-270m-users-fake-duplicate-accounts/> accessed 30 April 2018. In May 2017 Facebook detailed the scale of abuse on its site. Their study found that in one three month period, they had removed 583 million fake accounts. See, Dave Lee, 'Facebook details scale of abuse on its site' *The BBC* (London, 15 May 2018) <http://www.bbc.co.uk/news/technology-44122967> accessed 29 May 2018.

> Online communication is developing at such a fast pace, new ways of targeting and abusing individuals online are constantly emerging [...]. Offenders can mistakenly think that by using false online profiles and creating websites under a false name their offences are untraceable.[82]

This statement given by the CPS during the release of their updated guidelines in 2016, proceeded to give examples of behaviours which were criminalised under both the MCA and s.127(2) of the CA, including the creation of a fake social media profile containing false information.

In August 2018 the guidelines were further updated regarding what could constitute a false communication online:

> The act of setting up a false social networking account or website, or the creation of a false or offensive profile or alias could amount to a criminal offence, depending on the circumstance.[83]

The CPS supported the idea that false communications could encompass fake online profiles 'depending on the circumstance[s]'.[84] But was this a step too far in interpreting the meaning of false under both the MCA and s.127(2) of the CA? Arguably, such a situation could be considered as an arbitrary use of the law.

Though the author does not justify the sending of highly abusive communications on social media platforms through fake profiles, there is a place for anonymity online. For instance, during times of conflict, individuals may be prosecuted for speaking out against their State, here anonymity protects these individuals. Even in more 'stable' societies, anonymity is needed. For example, a person may have to hide their true identity, such as gender or sexuality, from their loved ones for religious or cultural reasons. Indeed, for the Law Commission, prior to the OSA, they noted:

> The offence under section 127(2)(a) and (b) of the CA 2003 is particularly broad, as it may be committed simply where the intention is to cause another person 'inconvenience'. This means that many hoaxes and 'April fools' jokes posted online could technically fall within the offence if the intention is to cause 'inconvenience' to another.[85]

Consequently, the lack of understanding as to what constituted a false message allowed those working in the criminal justice system to stretch its meaning beyond

82 David Barrett, 'Faking social media accounts could lead to criminal charges' *The Telegraph* (London, 3 March 2016) <https://www.telegraph.co.uk/news/uknews/crime/12180782/Faking-social-media-accounts-could-lead-to-criminal-charges.html> accessed 30 April 2018.

83 Guidelines on Prosecuting Cases Involving Communications Sent via Social Media (n 63) [8].

84 Ibid.,

85 Law Com No 381 (n 59) [11.136].

Parliament's original intent, with the ECtHR noting that false communications are actually protected under the ECHR.[86]

Under a strict interpretation of the term false, petty behaviours post break up, could have constituted a criminal offence under the MCA or s.127(2) of the CA. For example, in *R v Alexandra Gregory*[87] the defendant received a four month custodial sentence, suspended for 18 months, after sending hundreds of false messages online to her ex-partner claiming to be pregnant. Although such behaviour cannot be condoned, it is legitimate to ask if the criminal law should have been invoked in this matter. That is not to say the CPS would prosecute in all cases, but significant weight was/is given to prosecutorial discretion.

As previously noted, the sending of false material online is now criminalised under s.179(1) of the OSA in a bid to bring more certainty to this area of the law, and to tackle more directly mis/disinformation. Chapter 7 will highlight that the issues raised above remain even with the changes made to this area of the criminal law.

6.6.2.4 Threatening

The MCA made it a criminal offence to convey a message which was threatening. Like many of the prohibited behaviours previously discussed, there was no legal definition of what constituted a threat. A problem not just unique to communication offences, but also other offences in the criminal law framework of England and Wales.[88]

From case law, and the 2023 CPS prosecuting guidelines on social media offences, it was difficult to articulate what was meant by a threatening message contrary to the MCA. The key issue was whether the communication could have been considered as a credible threat. An issue which is incredibly difficult to determine in an online context where tone is important, but impossible to understand:

> Unlike a face to face communication, there is no accompanying tone, volume or gesture, and no visible reactions from others (such as cowering or hiding). It can be difficult, then, to infer from an online communication whether, for example, a threat is sincere, or whether a person intends to be menacing or grossly offensive, rather than humorous.[89]

Easy access to the online world has also created new forms of threatening behaviour(s). For example, doxing (sharing a person's home address); dogpiling

86 *Salov v Ukraine* (2007) 45 EHRR 51.

87 *R v Alexandra Gregory*, Worcester Magistrates' Court, 2 November 2023 (unreported). See also, Maisie Olah and Alice Cullinane, 'Redditch nurse faked having baby during lockdown' *The BBC* (London, 2 November 2023) <https://www.bbc.co.uk/news/uk-england-hereford-worcester-67264932> accessed 4 December 2023.

88 Peter Alldridge, 'Threats Offences – A Case for Reform' (1994) 8 Crim. LR 176.

89 Law Com No 381 (n 59) [7.83].

(encouraging others to target a specific person online); and sharing of personal intimate images (commonly referred to as revenge porn). Issues like that of false messages which have not gone unnoticed, resulting in the removal of this prohibited behaviour from the MCA and a 'new' offence of sending a threatening message being created under s.181(1) of the OSA which, as discussed in Chapter 7, has attempted to clarify what is meant by the term threat.

6.6.2.5 Menacing

Both the MCA and s.127(1) of the CA prohibit the sending of a communication that can be defined as menacing. Like that of the other prohibited behaviours above, neither provision defines the term. Instead, it has been for the courts to set the boundaries as to what is a menacing message, to ensure that a distinction can be made between a menacing message and a message which can be labelled as a joke or satire humour, even if it is ill-thought-out on behalf of the sender. The leading case on what constitutes a menacing message is *Chambers v DPP*.[90]

Paul Chambers, in January of 2010, took to Twitter to vent his frustration following the closure of Doncaster Robin Hood Airport due to bad weather, tweeting: 'Crap! Robin Hood Airport is closed. You've got week [*sic*] and a bit to get your shit together otherwise I'm blowing the airport sky high'. Quite quickly the tweet, after being brought to the attention of airport officials, was dismissed as a credible threatening communication i.e., it was not a threat of terrorism. Had airport officials considered it a credible threat, the tweet would have been reported to the Ministry of Defence.[91] Foster gives three arguments as to why the threat was deemed non-credible by authorities.[92] First, the communication was posted on Twitter for widespread reading, which would be considered as unusual in the context of threatening to blow an 'airport sky high'. Second, when examining the discourse of the tweet, the language and grammar were inconsistent with the intention of terrorism. Third, it would have been unusual for a person to threaten terrorism in such a way which makes the sender so easily identifiable. Instead, the tweet was reported to the police, with Chambers later being arrested and convicted of sending a menacing message contrary to s.127(1) of the CA.[93]

Chambers and his legal team appealed his conviction in the Crown Court[94] arguing that his message was intended as a joke, and therefore he did not have the relevant *actus reus* needed to commit the offence. This was dismissed by the Crown

90 *Chambers* (n 60).

91 Alisdair A. Gillespie, 'Twitter, Jokes and the Law' (2012) 76(5) J. Crim. Law. 364 (note).

92 Steve Foster, 'Freedom of Expression: Is There a Human Right to Make a Joke?' (2012) 17(2) Cov. L. J. 97, 99.

93 *R v Paul Chambers*, Doncaster Magistrates' Court, 10 May 2010 (unreported).

94 *Chambers v DPP*, Doncaster Crown Court, 3 March 2011 (unreported). For a discussion of the case history see, Gervase de Wilde, 'News: "Twitter joke" case goes to the high court' (*The International Forum for Responsible Media Blog*, 8 February 2012) <https://inforrm.org/2012/02/08/news-twitter-joke-case-goes-to-the-high-court-gervase-de-wilde/> accessed 2 May 2018.

Court who concluded that the tweet sent by Chambers was 'menacing in its content and obviously so. It could not be more clear. Any ordinary person reading this would see it in that way and be alarmed'.[95] He was later permitted to appeal before the High Court.[96]

The original case heard before the High Court was subjected to a second appeal after an agreement was unable to be reached in the first case.[97] Unlike the finding of the Crown Court, the High Court came to the judgment that Chambers' comments, though 'ill-thought-out', were intended as a joke and as a result quashed his conviction in July 2012, concluding that:

> Satirical, or iconoclastic, or rude comment, the expression of unpopular or unfashionable opinion about serious or trivial matters, banter or humour, even if distasteful to some or painful to those subjected to it should and no doubt will continue at their customary level, quite undiminished by this legislation [s.127(1) of the CA].[98]

Put simply, a menacing message means to create a 'sense of apprehension or fear' in another.[99]

The judgment of the High Court has been praised with Foster going as far as arguing that *Chambers* was a 'victory for common sense',[100] after many commentators were heavily critical of the criminal justice system's approach to the matter.[101] Indeed, Gillespie states: 'Paul Chambers should have been told to be careful about his choice of tweets, but prosecution was unnecessary, especially given that nobody took it seriously'.[102] It is estimated that the total cost of this case to the taxpayer was around £18,000.[103]

The vagueness inherent in the term menacing gives actors in the criminal justice system significant discretion, which in turn breaches the principle of legality and threatens freedom of expression. This has however been recognised, to a degree, as an issue, particularly after the finding of the High Court in *Chambers*, resulting in the creation of the CPS social media prosecution guidelines. Yet, there is still a lack of understanding as to the meaning of many of the provisions contained in both

95 Per Judge Jacqueline Davis found in Scaife (n 34) 135.
96 *Chambers* (n 60) per Lord Judge [28].
97 Scaife (n 34) 135.
98 *Chambers* (n 60) per Lord Judge [28].
99 Social Media and other Electronic Communications (n 52).
100 Foster (n 92) 101.
101 Lilian Edwards, 'Section 127 of the Communications Act 2003: Threat or Menace?' (2012) 23(4) Comp. & L. 22.
102 Gillespie (n 91) 368.
103 Nick Cohen, '"Twitter joke" case only went ahead at insistence of DPP' *The Guardian* (London, 28 July 2012) <https://www.theguardian.com/law/2012/jul/29/paul-chambers-twitter-joke-airport> accessed 2 May 2018.

the MCA and s.127(1) of the CA, including that of menacing—as demonstrated in *DPP v Kingsley Anthony Smith.*[104]

In September 2016, Kingsley was acquitted by Luton Magistrates' Court on four counts of sending a menacing message after he had posted several extremist comments on the social media site, YouTube. Including a comment threatening to place an IED on the doorstep of the then Prime Minister, David Cameron. For Luton Magistrates' Court, the comments made were grounded in 'anger and bigotry' but ultimately 'represented empty bombast or ridiculous banter'—which, by applying the outcome of *Chambers*, was not an offence under s.127(1) of the CA. An appeal was sought and granted before the High Court.

The grounds for appeal centred around the assessment in establishing if a communication is menacing, with the High Court concluding that Luton Magistrates' Court had made a mistake:

> the District Judge had first to consider whether the sole element of the *actus reus* that was in dispute on each charge, namely whether the relevant message was of the proscribed character, was proved. To answer that he had to ask himself whether, as a question of fact, taking account of the context and all relevant circumstances, and applying the standards of a reasonable person in an open and just multi-racial (and, I would add, multi-faith) society, it was proved that a particular message [...] was of a menacing character—i.e. would have created a sense of apprehension or fear in a person of reasonable fortitude who received or read it. However, it is clear that the District Judge failed to ask himself that question at all.[105]

Under the principle of legality, the law should be action-guiding, in which citizens should be able to make decisions on their everyday behaviour in accordance with clear and distinct legal provisions. Yet, there are ample examples of the courts struggling to come to a definitive decision on what constitutes a menacing message. Indeed,

> [i]f judicially trained minds can come to diametrically opposite conclusions on the same set of facts it is obvious that expressions such as [...] 'menacing' are so vague that there is no manageable standard by which a person can be said to have committed an offence.[106]

These issues are even more glaringly apparent when trying to qualify the meaning of grossly offensive.

104 *Kingsley Anthony Smith* (n 50).
105 Ibid., per Mr Justice Sweeney [36–37].
106 *Shreya Singhal v Union of India* (2013) 12 S.C.C. 73 [82].

6.6.2.6 Grossly Offensive

The use of the term grossly offensive to label and prohibit certain types of communications, is a significantly controversial term, with concerns being raised that it infringes on the right to freedom of expression: 'Some of us might draw the boundary in one place, whilst others who are particularly concerned about the development of electronic communications might draw it in another'.[107] Though it is important to note, that 'grossly offensive messages do not contribute much to improving our knowledge or participation as citizens in a democracy. Rather, their effect is to distort communications'.[108]

Yet as outlined in Section 6.2 above, its use can be traced back to as early as 1884, where even then, concerns were raised.[109] Yet the term continues to be used in modern communication offences, in which grossly offensive is considered to take its ordinary English meaning.[110] Today, under both the MCA and s.127 (1) of the CA, it is an offence to send a message *via* a (public) electronic communications network[111] that can be labelled as grossly offensive.

For those working in the criminal justice system, it is denoting what is meant by the term grossly offensive, which has caused opposing opinions. For example, in *Collins*, the Magistrates' Court[112] and the High Court[113] would have acquitted Collins for leaving racially aggravated messages on an answering machine, after concluding that the messages did not constitute a grossly offensive communication. Whereas the House of Lords concluded that the messages were of a grossly offensive nature.[114] For Sedley LJ in the High Court, a message could be labelled as grossly offensive when it breached the 'standards of an open and just multiracial society'.[115] Whereas for Lord Bingham in the House of Lords, grossly offensive comments were defined as 'highly abusive, insulting, pejorative, [and of an] offensive character'.[116]

Though *Collins* concerned telephone conversations, the issues relating to what is deemed a grossly offensive message, have become even more apparent following the increased usage of social media. Further complicated by the fact that it can be easy to see why a decision was made in one case, such as that of *R v Woods*,[117] but

107 Law Com No 147 (n 25) [3.6].
108 Gibbon (n 2) 137.
109 HC Deb 09 August 1884, vol 292, col 371.
110 *Connolly* (n 32) per Lord Justice Dyson [10].
111 The Malicious Communications Act 1988 covers electronic communications. S.127 of the Communications Act 2003 covers public electronic communications. Therefore, the Malicious Communications Act 1988 would cover Bluetooth or Apple Airdrop, but s.127 of the Communications Act 2003 would not.
112 *R v Collins*, Leicestershire Magistrates' Court, 4 October 2004 (unreported).
113 *DPP v Collins* [2005] EWHC 1308 (Admin).
114 Ibid., per Sedly LJ [11].
115 *Collins* (n 49) per Lord Bingham of Cornhill [11].
116 Ibid., per Lord Bingham of Cornhill [13].
117 *Matthew Woods* (n 61).

less so in others, such as that of Thomas. Supported further by the Law Commission who found that there is 'controversy over charging and prosecution decisions'.[118] This mirrors similar arguments made in Chapter 4.

On 1 October 2012 a five-year-old child, April Jones, was reported missing by her parents.[119] The case quickly caught the attention of the national press along with her picture being actively shared across social media sites.[120] During the evening of 1 October, Matthew Woods made several remarks on Facebook about the missing schoolchild, before going on to make comments about Madeleine McCann, a child who went missing in Portugal in 2007: 'I woke up this morning in the back of a transit van with two beautiful little girls, I found April in a hopeless place'. 'Could have just started the greatest Facebook argument EVER [*sic*]. April fools, who wants Maddie? I love April Jones'.[121] The next day, 50 people descended on Woods' home, after his address was leaked online, resulting in the police having to arrest him for his safety. He was later rearrested and convicted of sending grossly offensive messages contrary to s.127(1) of the CA.

Whereas a different approach was undertaken in the matter of Daniel Thomas.[122] Thomas took to Twitter following the divers Tom Daley and Peter Waterfield coming fourth during the 2012 London Olympics: 'if there is any consolation for finishing fourth at least [*sic*] daley and waterfield [*sic*] can go bum each other #teamHIV'. Although, unlike in the case of *Woods*, Thomas' message was labelled as 'offensive' as opposed to grossly offensive:

> There is no doubt that the message posted by Mr Thomas was offensive and would be regarded as such by reasonable members of society. But the question for the CPS is not whether it was offensive, but whether it was so grossly offensive that criminal charges should be brought. The distinction is an important one and not easily made.[123]

There is therefore a line between offensive and grossly offensive commentary. However, it is hard to distinguish when a comment crosses the appropriate threshold to warrant criminalisation.[124] For Lilienthal and Ahmad, the distinction simply falls on whether the reasonable person would find the communication grossly

118 Law Com No 381 (n 59) [5.73].

119 Telegraph Reporters, 'What happened to murdered April Jones and who is Mark Bridger?' *The Telegraph* (London, 20 June 2017) <https://www.telegraph.co.uk/news/0/happened-murdered-april-jones-mark-bridger/> accessed 29 April 2018.

120 The following day Mark Bridger was arrested, and later convicted of April's murder.

121 Steven Morris and Dan Sabbagh, 'April Jones: Matthew Woods jailed over explicit Facebook comments' *The Guardian* (London, 8 October 2012) <https://www.theguardian.com/uk/2012/oct/08/april-jones-matthew-woods-jailed> accessed 29 April 2018.

122 The Crown Prosecution News Brief, 'DPP statement on Tom Daley Case and social media prosecutions' (*CPS.gov*, 2012) <http://blog.cps.gov.uk/2012/09/dpp-statement-on-tom-daley-case-and-socialmedia-prosecutions.html> accessed 29 April 2018.

123 Ibid.,

124 Laura Bliss, 'The Crown Prosecution Guidelines and Grossly Offensive Comments: An Analysis' (2017) 9(2) J. Media Law 173, 177.

offensive.[125] However, as argued by Gillespie certain sectors of society will always deem a message more grossly offensive than others, bringing issues in prosecuting abusive comments under these legal provisions.[126] Indeed, for Rowbottom, the current use of grossly offensive in governing online behaviour can be 'overly expansive and catch statements that might not warrant such serious treatment',[127] which in turn has a chilling effect on free speech.[128] There is no distinction as to when a message goes from one being of an offensive nature to one so grossly offensive the criminal law should intervene.

Under the principle of legality:

> no one should be punished under a law unless it is sufficiently clear and certain [...] and no one should be punished for any act which was not clearly and ascertainably punishable when the act was done.[129]

The matters of *Woods* and Thomas highlight the lack of clarity contained in both the MCA and s.127(1) of the CA in terms of what is considered grossly offensive behaviour. Again, issues which have already been recognised, and were a further rationale for the creation and implementation of prosecuting guidelines. Yet, issues remain, even with the guidelines in place. For instance, the case of *R v Alison Chabloz*,[130] a case discussed previously in Chapter 4, illustrates the continued misunderstanding of the term grossly offensive.

Chabloz who defines herself as a Holocaust revolutionist published several videos on the social media site YouTube. These videos contained footage of Chabloz performing songs set to the beat of traditional Jewish folk music, which contained antisemitic hate. 'Campaign Against Antisemitism', a not-for-profit organisation, had made numerous complaints to the police about Chabloz's behaviour online, yet no further action was taken by authorities. In fact, at one point Chabloz herself approached her local police force claiming she was being harassed online by the Jewish community, leading to the police believing she was a victim of online abuse.[131] As a result, 'Campaign Against Antisemitism' chose to pursue a private prosecution against Chabloz, before the CPS eventually took over the handling of the case. Had 'Campaign Against Antisemitism' not pursued the private prosecution, the limitation period under s.127(1) of the CA would have lapsed.[132]

125 Gary Lilienthal and Nehaluddin Ahmad, 'Hate Crime and Social Media in the UK' (2016) 22(7) CTLR 188, 191.

126 Alisdair A. Gillespie, 'Offensive Communications and the Law' (2006) (17)8 ELR 236, 237.

127 Jacob Rowbottom, 'To Rant, Vent and Converse: Protecting Low Level Digital Speech' (2012) 71(2) Cambridge L.J. 355, 375.

128 Ibid., 378.

129 *Rimmington* (n 78) per Lord Bingham [33].

130 *R v Alison Chabloz*, Westminster Magistrates' Court, 11 January 2018 (unreported).

131 Laura Bliss, 'Social Media: "A Theme Park just for Fools"' (2018) 82(4) J. Crim. Law. 301, 303 (note).

132 Under s.127(1) and (2) of the Communications Act 2003 when an incident is reported to the police, the police have six months to act. Failure to act during this time will result in no further criminal proceedings.

Before Westminster Magistrates' Court, Chabloz was found guilty of sending grossly offensive content contrary to s.127(1) of the CA, a decision later upheld by the Crown Court,[133] with the prosecution successfully arguing that:

> [t]he songs, specifically the language used within them, have been carefully considered and composed with the language chosen deliberately [...] They are anti-Semitic, they are targeting the Jewish people as a whole and use both their content and their tone to ensure maximum offence.[134]

Further clarity as to the meaning of grossly offensive was sought in *DPP v Busetti*,[135] where it was concluded that:

> the sender must intend or be aware that the message is not simply offensive but grossly offensive. The fact that the message is in bad taste, even shockingly bad taste, is not enough.[136]

Yet as potently put by Allen:

> in today's new, challenging digital environment, the existing body of legislative instruments, including the Communications Act 2003, do not provide for the degree of harmonisations, clarity nor necessary efficiency to meet the demands which cases such as *Woods* are placing on them.[137]

6.7 Chapter Summary

From the discussion above, a spectrum has been created within the criminal justice system when it comes to inappropriate communications. In essence, there is a hierarchy of unlawful communications as demonstrated in Figure 6.1, but the boundary between them is impossible to quantify. For instance, offensive comments are beyond the scope of the law, but grossly offensive commentary is not. Yet there is no clear distinction in law as to when offensive conduct will be deemed grossly offensive:

> Or, to put the matter more pertinently, if the two cases of *Woods* [the person who sent grossly offensive messages relating to the missing school girl, April Jones] and Thomas [the footballer who sent a homophobic tweet about the divers Tom Daley and Peter Waterfield] are on either side of a line between

133 *R v Alison Chabloz*, Southwark Crown Court, 13 February 2019 (unreported).

134 Bliss (n 131) 302.

135 *Busetti* (n 51).

136 Ibid., per Lord Justice Bean [35].

137 David Allen Green, 'The "Twitter joke trial" returns to the high court' (*NewStatesman*, 22 June 2012) <https://www.newstatesman.com/blogs/david-allen-green/2012/06/twitter-joke-trial-david-allen-green> accessed 30 April 2018.

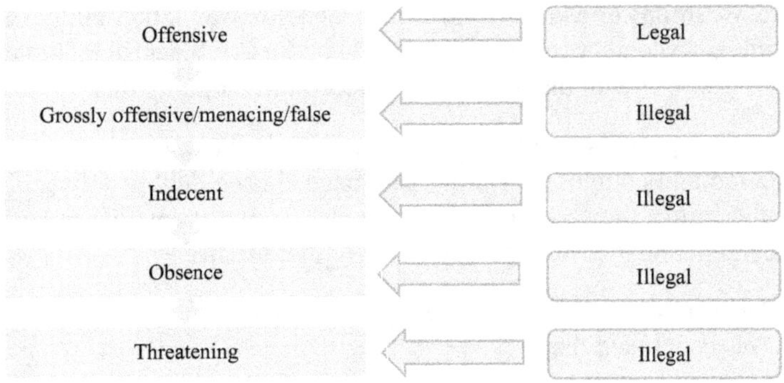

Figure 6.1 The hierarchy of lawful and unlawful communications.

> comments which are merely offensive and those which are grossly so, the question arises as to where that line lies.[138]

This, in turn, has a direct effect on the principle of legality.

As discussed at length in Chapter 3, the law must be certain, clear, and accessible to uphold the principle of legality in the criminal law. Both the MCA and s.127(1) and (2) of the CA in their original format, lacked clarity in terms of what constituted either a threatening, false, indecent, grossly offensive, obscene, or menacing communication, which in turn left both citizens and those working in the criminal justice system at a disadvantage. Indeed,

> [t]he confusion in the case law would seem to demonstrate that emphasising the importance of context in the CPS guidelines may still not be sufficient to guide decisions to charge and prosecute.[139]

For Rowbottom, and noted in Chapter 1,

> [t]he legal responses can, however, seem heavy-handed for what might have been a statement made with little thought while the speaker was sat at a desk at home. Words typed in seconds followed by hitting the enter key can lead to a criminal record or costly civil litigation.[140]

Clearly both the continued use of the MCA and s.127(1) of the CA, even with the minor changes under the OSA, is contentious, for the reasons highlighted throughout this chapter. Significant concern relates mainly to the continued vague language contained in both provisions, concerns which have not gone unnoticed, but have not been addressed in the 'new' communication offences, to which Chapter 7 will turn to examine.

138 Bliss (n 124) 177.
139 Law Com No 381 (n 59) [5.76].
140 Rowbottom (n 127) 356.

Reference list

Alldridge P, 'Threats Offences – A Case for Reform' (1994) 8 Crim LR 176

Amnesty International, 'Amnesty Reveals Alarming Impact of Online Abuse against Women' (*Amnesty International*, 20 November 2017) https://www.amnesty.org/en/latest/news/2017/11/amnesty-reveals-alarming-impact-of-online-abuse-against-women/

Amnesty International UK, 'Black and Asian Women MPs Abused More Online' (*Amnesty International*, 2017) https://www.amnesty.org.uk/online-violence-women-mps

Bakalis C, 'Rethinking Cyberhate Laws' (2017) 27(1) Inf Commun Technol Law 86.

Barrett D, 'Faking Social Media Accounts Could Lead to Criminal Charges' *The Telegraph* (London, 3 March 2016) https://www.telegraph.co.uk/news/uknews/crime/12180782/Faking-social-media-accounts-could-lead-to-criminal-charges.html

Bingham T, *The Rule of Law* (Penguin 2011)

Bliss L, 'Social Media: "A Theme Park Just for Fools"' (2018) 82(4) J Crim Law 301

Bliss L, 'Abuse of women MPs is not just a scandal – it's a threat to democracy' *The Conversation* (London, 17 July 2017) https://theconversation.com/abuse-of-women-mps-is-not-just-a-scandal-its-a-threat-to-democracy-80781

Bliss L, 'The Crown Prosecution Guidelines and Grossly Offensive Comments: An Analysis' (2017) 9(2) J Media Law 173

Cohen N, '"Twitter joke" case only went ahead at insistence of DPP' *The Guardian* (London, 28 July 2012) https://www.theguardian.com/law/2012/jul/29/paul-chambers-twitter-joke-airport

de Wilde G, 'News: "Twitter Joke" Case Goes to the High Court' (*The International Forum for Responsible Media Blog*, 8 February 2012) https://inforrm.org/2012/02/08/news-twitter-joke-case-goes-to-the-high-court-gervase-de-wilde/

Edgar P & Melhuish N, 'NetSafe Online Hate Speech: A Survey on Personal Experiences and Exposure Among Adult New Zealanders' (*Netsafe*, 12 December 2018) https://netsafe.org.nz/wp-content/uploads/2016/12/Netsafe-insights-into-New-Zealands-experience-of-online-hate-speech.pdf

Edwards L, 'Section 127 of the Communications Act 2003: Threat or Menace?' (2012) 23(4) Comp L 22

Fletcher G P, *Basic Concepts of Criminal Law* (Oxford University Press 1998)

Foster S, 'Freedom of Expression: Is There a Human Right to Make a Joke?' (2012) 17(2) Cov L J 97

Geach N & Haralambous N, 'Regulating Harassment: Is the Law Fit for the Social Networking Age?' (2009) 73(3) J Crim Law 241

Gibbon T, 'Case Comment: Grossly Offensive Communications' (2006) 11(4) Comms L 136

Gillespie A A, 'Obscene Conversations, the Internet and the Criminal Law' (2014) 5 Crim LR 350

Gillespie A A, 'Twitter, Jokes and the Law' (2012) 76(5) J Crim Law 364 (note)

Gillespie A A, 'Offensive Communications and the Law' (2006) 17(8) ELR 236, 237

Green D A, 'The "Twitter Joke Trial" Returns to the High Court' (*NewStatesman*, 22 June 2012) https://www.newstatesman.com/blogs/david-allen-green/2012/06/twitter-joke-trial-david-allen-green

HC Deb 09 August 1884, vol 292, col 371

HC Deb 12 December 2000, vol 359, col 481 - 483

HC Deb 12 February 1988, vol 127, col 620

Law Commission, *Abusive and Offensive Online Communications: A Scoping Report* (Law Com No 381, 2018)

Law Commission, *Report on Poison-Pen Letters* (Law Com No 147, 1985)

Lee D, 'Facebook details scale of abuse on its site' *The BBC* (London, 15 May 2018) http://www.bbc.co.uk/news/technology-44122967

Lilienthal G & Ahmad N, 'Hate Crime and Social Media in the UK' (2016) 22(7) CTLR 188
Mill J S, *On Liberty* (first published 1859, Enhanced Media 2016)
Ministry of Justice, 'Impact Assessment: Making the Offence in Section 1 of the Malicious Communications Act 1988 a Triable Either-Way Offence' (*Gov.uk*, 30 May 2014) https://assets.publishing.service.gov.uk/government/uploads/system/uploads/attachment_data/file/321285/malicious-communicationss-impact-assessment.pdf
Morris S & Sabbagh D, 'April Jones: Matthew Woods jailed over explicit Facebook comments' *The Guardian* (London, 8 October 2012) https://www.theguardian.com/uk/2012/oct/08/april-jones-matthew-woods-jailed
Nash V, 'Revise and Resubmit? Reviewing the 2019 Online Harms White Paper' 2019 11(1) J Media Law 18
OFCOM, *"Adults"' Media Use and Attitudes Report 2020/21* (*OFCOM*, 28 April 2021) https://www.ofcom.org.uk/__data/assets/pdf_file/0025/217834/adults-media-use-and-attitudes-report-2020-21.pdf
OFCOM, *"Adults" Media Use and Attitudes Report* (*OFCOM*, 25 April 2018) https://www.ofcom.org.uk/__data/assets/pdf_file/0011/113222/Adults-Media-Use-and-Attitudes-Report-2018.pdf
Olah M & Cullinane A, 'Redditch nurse faked having baby during lockdown' *The BBC* (London, 2 November 2023) https://www.bbc.co.uk/news/uk-england-hereford-worcester-67264932
Press Association, 'Britain's Got Talent blogger cautioned by police' *The Guardian* (London, 3 July 2011) https://www.theguardian.com/tv-and-radio/2011/jul/03/britains-got-talent-blogger-cautioned
Rowbottom J, 'To Rant, Vent and Converse: Protecting Low Level Digital Speech' (2012) 71(2) Cambridge LJ 355
Rowland M, 'Release of the 2022 National Online Safety Survey' (*Ministers for Infrastructure, Transport, Regional Development, Communications and the Arts*, 14 November 2022) https://minister.infrastructure.gov.au/rowland/media-release/release-2022-national-online-safety-survey
Scaife L, *Handbook of Social Media and the Law* (Routledge 2015)
Smith G, 'From Telegram to Tweet: Section 127 and All That' (*Cyberlegal*, 22 February 2015) https://www.cyberleagle.com/2015/02/from-telegram-to-tweet-section-127-and.html
Telegraph Reporters, 'What happened to murdered April Jones and who is Mark Bridger?' *The Telegraph* (London, 20 June 2017) https://www.telegraph.co.uk/news/0/happened-murdered-april-jones-mark-bridger/
The BBC, 'Southampton "paedophile hunter" jailed for false claim' *The BBC* (London, 3 September 2018) https://www.bbc.co.uk/news/uk-england-hampshire-45395607
The BBC, 'Teenager's life "ruined" by Live.me and Twitter "trolls"' *The BBC* (London, 24 October 2017) http://www.bbc.co.uk/news/uk-england-41693437
The Crown Prosecution News Brief, 'DPP Statement on Tom Daley Case and Social Media Prosecutions' (*CPS.gov,* 2012) http://blog.cps.gov.uk/2012/09/dpp-statement-on-tom-daley-case-and-socialmedia-prosecutions.html
The Crown Prosecution Service, 'Communication Offences' (*CPS.gov,* 2024) https://www.cps.gov.uk/legal-guidance/communications-offences#:~:text=the%20summary%20offences%20under%20section,of%20a%20public%20communications%20network
The Crown Prosecution Service, 'Social Media and other Electronic Communications' (*CPS.gov,* 9 January 2023) https://www.cps.gov.uk/legal-guidance/social-media-and-other-electronic-communications
The Crown Prosecution Service, 'Guidelines on Prosecuting Cases Involving Communications Sent via Social Media' (*CPS.gov,* 21 August 2018) https://www

.cps.gov.uk/legal-guidance/social-media-guidelines-prosecuting-cases-involving-communications-sent-social-media

Titcomb J, 'Facebook admits up to 270m users are fake and duplicate accounts' *The Telegraph* (London, 2 November 2017) https://www.telegraph.co.uk/technology/2017/11/02/facebook-admits-270m-users-fake-duplicate-accounts/

Vidgen B, Margetts H & Harris A, 'How Much Online Abuse Is There? A Systematic Review of Evidence for the UK. Policy Briefing – Full Report' (*The Alan Turing Institute*, 2020) https://www.turing.ac.uk/sites/default/files/2019-11/online_abuse_prevalence_full_24.11.2019_-_formatted_0.pdf

Walden I, *Computer Crime and Digital Investigations* (2nd edn, Oxford University Press 2016)

7 The Future of Communication Law

7.1 Introduction

The previous chapter has highlighted significant flaws with the application of communication offences to the digital world. Flaws and concerns which have not gone unnoticed. Following an examination by the Law Commission, starting in 2018 and ending in 2021, into the application of the criminal law to conduct carried out online, in particular social media, the Commission noted several areas of reform. These reforms included the repeal of both the Malicious Communications Act 1988 (MCA) and some aspects of s.127 of the Communications Act 2003 (CA).[1] In addition, several 'new' criminal offences were recommended in the Law Commission's final report into criminalising online conduct. Some of which, were originally included in the first draft of the Online Safety Bill 2022 (OSB) but were eventually removed. Others were included either in the first draft of the Bill or added at a later date, following a lengthy passage through Parliament.[2] However, some of these 'new' offences, are not necessarily new, and as will be shown, in many cases, such offences already existed in the criminal law framework of England and Wales before the passing of the OSB—now the Online Safety Act 2023 (OSA).

Of note, and will be the focus of further discussions below are:

- The original recommendation to create a new harms-based offence to replace both the MCA and s.127(1) of the CA, which has since been rejected;[3]
- Specifically criminalising the sending of threatening communications;[4] and
- Prohibiting the use of a communications device to distribute false information.[5]

1 Note, the Law Commission recommended keeping aspects of s.127(2)c of the Communications Act 2003 to cover hoax communications to the emergency services. See, Law Commission, *Modernising Communications Offences: A final report* (Law Com. No.399, 2021) [3.94].

2 For instance, an offence of encouraging or assisting another to self-harm was added late to the Bill following a House of Lords Amendment.

3 Originally included in the Online Safety Bill 2022 c.150.

4 Online Safety Act 2023 s.179.

5 Ibid., s.181.

DOI: 10.4324/9781003303688-9

Other offences have also been included in the OSA, but will not be examined here, as they are beyond the scope of this monograph.

The majority of the OSA is aimed at search services or user-to-user services, which is discussed at length in the following chapter, as opposed to being aimed at online users. However, the OSA also includes several changes to the criminal law framework, including the offences mentioned above. The following discussion will take each of these offences in turn, and like that of previous chapters, the *actus reus* and *mens rea* of each offence will be outlined. It will expose, as with previous discussions, growing concerns around the use of the criminal law to limit freedom of expression, particularly given the vague terminology used in many of the offences discussed below. In essence, this chapter will demonstrate how the concerns previously raised around communication offences, in both this monograph and by other scholars,[6] including the Law Commission themselves,[7] have not necessarily been addressed by these 'new' criminal offences.

7.2 The Harms Offence

One of the most significant recommendations made by the Law Commission in their final report into communication offences was the recommendation to replace both the MCA and s.127(1) of the CA with a new harms-based offence. As noted in the previous chapter, the Law Commission had found several issues with both the MCA and s.127(1) of the CA,[8] many of which have previously been highlighted. To summarise, the main concerns were:

- The interchangeable nature of the law—the Law Commission noted that both the MCA and s.127 of the CA were often used interchangeably and at times, one was used instead of the other by mistake;
- The vague language in the offences—both offences use vague terminology, which has created confusion for actors in the criminal justice system; and
- Inconsistent prosecutions—the lack of understanding as to the meaning of many of the terms contained in each offence, has led to enforcement by law officials in some cases, but not in others. As a result, discretion is being heavily relied upon and not everyone can be said to be equal before the law.

These concerns, amongst others, led the Law Commission to recommending the repeal of current communication offences in England and Wales, suggesting a new harms-based offence to replace them.

6 See, for example, Laura Higson-Bliss, 'Prosecuting Communication Offences: Interpreting the Harms Model' (2022) 4 CLR 271; Graham Smith, 'Licence to chill' (*Cyberleagle*, 22 November 2021) <https://www.cyberleagle.com/2021/11/licence-to-chill.html> accessed 7 August 2023.

7 Law Commission, *Abusive and Offensive Online Communications: A Scoping Report* (Law Com No 381, 2018) Chapters 4 and 5.

8 Ibid.,

This recommendation was originally accepted by the government at the time and was included in the first draft of the OSB. However, as will be discussed in later sections, significant concerns were raised by politicians, civil liberty organisations, and scholars that the issues previously raised by the Law Commission against current communication offences had not been addressed. In turn, legality was not being maintained, due to vague terminology and as a result freedom of expression was under significant threat. In January 2023, the former conservative government removed this provision, stating:

> The harmful communications offence was one of three new communications offences included in the Bill, alongside the false and threatening communications offences. Since then, stakeholders and members of the public have expressed concerns that the harmful communications offence has the potential to produce unintended consequences on freedom of expression and potentially criminalise legal and legitimate speech on the basis that it has caused someone offence [...] The harmful communications offence has been removed from the Bill.[9]

The MCA and s.127(1) of the CA therefore remain good law, though slightly amended following the passing of the OSA, despite concerns which have been raised against their use to restrict what individuals do or say online. However, it is important to still discuss the recommended offence and its ultimate demise as it illustrates the need to ensure the creation of offences which are grounded in the principle of legality and do not undermine the right to freedom of expression. Further, many of the issues highlighted with this offence, apply to the other 'new' offences contained in the OSA.

The Law Commission recommended, and was accepted initially, the replacement of both the MCA and s.127(1) of the CA with a provision which would have made it a criminal offence to do the following:

> A person commits an offence if—(a) the person sends a message [...] (b) at the time of sending the message—(i) there was a real and substantial risk that it would cause harm to a likely audience, and (ii) the person intended to cause harm to a likely audience, and (c) the person has no reasonable excuse for sending the message.[10]

Below the *actus reus* and *mens rea* of the offence prohibited under the harms offence is outlined. Later parts of this chapter will expose significant issues with the language contained within this recommended criminal law provision, the

9 Department of Digital, Culture, Media and Sport, 'Overview of expected impact of changes to the Online Safety Bill' (*Gov.uk,* 18 Jan 2022) <https://www.gov.uk/government/publications/online-safety-bill-supporting-documents/overview-of-expected-impact-of-changes-to-the-online-safety-bill#:~:text=The%20adult%20safety%20duties%20(%27legal,and%20freedom%20of%20expression%20dutie> accessed 7 August 2023.

10 Online Safety Bill 2022 c.150(1).

principle of legality and the right to freedom of expression, resulting in its removal from the OSB.

7.2.1 Actus Reus

The *actus reus* of the proposed offence consisted of several elements:

1. The sending of a communication;
2. The communication sent must have been likely to cause harm;
3. The likely harm caused must be to a likely audience; and
4. The communication was sent without reasonable excuse.

Under the proposed offence the sending of a message was considered the situation whereby a person:

> (a) causes a communication (including an oral communication) to be sent, transmitted, or published by electronic means, or (b) causes a letter or a thing of any other description to be sent.[11]

Therefore merging the types of communications prohibited between both the MCA and s.127(1) of the CA. Second, for the communication to be considered as likely to cause harm, it must have been found that the communication sent was likely to cause 'psychological harm amounting to at least serious distress'.[12] Therefore, physical, or financial harm, was specifically excluded from the offence. However, as will be highlighted in Section 7.5.1.1, no further information was given as to what would be considered as 'psychological harm amounting to at least serious distress' and instead, serious distress was seen to take its ordinary meaning within the boundaries of the criminal law. This rendered significant issues with the right to freedom of expression and legality.

Third, the likely (undefined) harm had to have the possibility of harming a likely audience, which was defined under the OSB as someone likely to 'encounter' the message.'[13] Which in the context of some social media platforms, could have been anyone in the world. As was noted in the proposed offence itself, the communication sent did not actually need to cause harm, there merely needed to be the possibility that harm might have been inflicted.[14] Last, to fulfil the *actus reus* of the proposed offence, the communication must have been sent without any lawful excuse.

Though initially there was some confusion with the requirement of proving lawful excuse (for some stakeholders, they interpreted this element as a defence), the Law Commission later re-emphasised this was not a defence. Instead, lawful excuse

11 Ibid., c.153(3).
12 Ibid., c.150(4).
13 Ibid., c.150(2).
14 Ibid., c.150(1)b(i).

formed part of the *actus reus* of the offence.[15] Put simply, it would have been for the *prosecution* to prove that the communication sent *was not sent* with a lawful excuse as opposed to the *defence* proving that the communication *was sent* with a lawful excuse. Like that of the other provisions contained in the offence, there was little information given as to what would constitute a reasonable excuse.

7.2.2 Mens Rea

Under first drafts of the proposed offence one of two *mens rea* elements needed to be proven: intent or awareness. Like that of other offences discussed in previous chapters, awareness was considered the situation whereby the person sending the message 'knew' or 'should have known' that harm might have been inflicted upon the likely audience—though as noted above, harm did not need to be proven. However, in an attempt to reduce the scope and reach of the offence, in the final proposal, and was repeated in the OSB, the *mens rea* was reduced to one of 'intent' only,[16] with intent being given its ordinary meaning. I.e,. the sending of a harmful communication in which the aim or purpose was to cause, or likely to cause, harm amounting to at least serious distress.

7.2.3 Summary

Though it is accepted that the repeal of both the MCA and s.127(1) of the CA was a significant step forward in protecting freedom of expression, the proposed replacement, the harms offence, was flawed from its conception. The offence contained significantly vague terminology which would have led to a repeat of how the MCA and s.127(1) of the CA were, and still are, being applied to offences carried out *via* social media. It could not be said that the proposed offence adhered to some of the basic principles of legality, as discussed in Section 7.5 below. Consequently, as has been noted above, the offence was removed from the OSB in January 2023 in a bid to protect the right to freedom of expression. However, as will be shown further, many of the provisions contained in this harms offence, are repeated in other offences contained in the OSA, despite obvious flaws.

7.3 False Communications

As highlighted in the previous chapter, both the MCA and s.127(2) of the CA prohibited the sending of a false communication, with some successful prosecutions under both provisions for doing such an act. However, issues with the use of social media platforms to send mis/disinformation; false advertisements leading to financial loss; and fear-mongering communications, to name but a few, led the Law Commission to note:

15 Law Com. No.399 (n 1) [3.67].
16 Online Safety Bill 2022 c.150(1)b(ii).

> The online environment provides a fertile ground for the spread of false communications, and creates particular challenges for the criminal law in seeking to curtail the most serious conduct.[17]

Many of the challenges in attempting to tackle these issues, were discussed in Chapter 6.

Despite false communications being prohibited under both the MCA and s.127(2) of the CA, the Law Commission, following their 2018 scoping report, recommended the creation of a 'new' false communication offence, which was heavily supported by stakeholders during the consultation period.[18] Since then a 'new' offence of sending a false communication has been created through the enactment of s.179 of the OSA replacing similar provisions in the MCA and s.127(2) of the CA. Under s.179(1) of the OSA it is an offence to intentionally send a knowingly false message, which has the possibility of causing 'non-trivial psychological or physical harm' to a likely audience and is sent without reasonable excuse—mirroring many of the requirements of the proposed harms offence, discussed above. The following section will outline the *actus reus* and *mens rea* of the offence contained in s.179(1) of the OSA.

7.3.1 Actus Reus

The *actus reus* of the offence prohibited under s.179(1) of the OSA consists of the following:

1. A person sends a message.[19] A message under this provision can be sent in several ways:[20]
   (a) Through the sending, transmission, or publishing of an electronic communication; or
   (b) Sending or giving a letter; or
   (c) Causing a letter or electronic communication to be sent. However, it is important to note, that an internet service provider is exempt and is therefore not criminally liable for the sending of a false message under this provision.[21]
2. The message sent conveys false information.[22] No definition is contained in the provision as to the meaning of false, though it is likely that the term false will take its ordinary English meaning. I.e., something that is untrue.

17 Law Com No 381 (n 7) [11.2].
18 Law Com. No 399 (n 1) [3.69].
19 Online Safety Act 2023 s.179(1)a.
20 Ibid., s.182(3).
21 Ibid., s.182(4).
22 Ibid., s.179(1)b.

3. The message sent caused 'non-trivial psychological or physical harm'.[23] It is not clear from the wording of the Act if such harm has to be inflicted or the mere possibility, rendering issues for future interpretation. In addition, both 'non-trivial psychological' and 'physical' harm are left undefined. Once again, this renders issues with interpretation in the future. This is discussed further in Section 7.5.1.2 below.
4. The 'non-trivial psychological or physical harm' inflicted must be to a 'likely audience'.[24] Here, a likely audience is defined as anyone who would encounter the message, including the likelihood that they would encounter the message through another person sharing or forwarding the communication.[25] This creates further issues with the principle of legality, discussed in Section 7.5.2.
5. There must be no 'reasonable excuse' for sending such a message.[26] Like that of the proposed harms offence discussed above, this will be for the prosecution to prove. Similarly, there is no further definition given as to what might be considered a reasonable excuse, giving wide discretionary powers to actors in the criminal justice system.

The OSA also attempts to set some parameters of the offence, including confirming that such an offence includes the sharing of hyperlinks.[27] The issue as to whether the sharing of a hyperlink can constitute an electronic communication has previously caused some judicial discussion, following Alison Chabloz (discussed in Chapter 6) appealing her conviction under s.127(1) of the CA. The premise of her appeal centred on the argument that a hyperlink did not constitute the sending of an electronic communication, even if the content was grossly offensive. This was rejected by the High Court.[28]

Further parameters of the offence include: (1) a statute of limitation period in which prosecutors must bring a case within six months of being notified of such conduct.[29] However, such proceedings cannot be brought more than three years after the commission of the offence.[30](2) 'Recognised news publishers' are exempt from the offence, alongside those holding a licence under the Broadcasting Act 1990 or 1996, those who hold a multiplex licence, a provider of an on-demand service, or 'a film made for cinema to members of the public'.[31]

If all the above elements can be proven and no exemptions contained in the Act are applicable (i.e., falling outside the scope of the limitation period, or the content

23 Ibid., s.179(1)c.
24 Ibid.,
25 Ibid., s.182(5).
26 Ibid., s.179(1)d.
27 Ibid., s.182(7).
28 *Chabloz v Crown Prosecution Service* [2019] EWHC 3094 (Admin).
29 Online Safety Act 2023 s.179(7).
30 Ibid., s.179(8).
31 Ibid., s.180.

is distributed by a 'recognised news publisher', etc,.) the *actus reus* of the offence is present.

7.3.2 Mens Rea

The *mens rea* of the offence contained in s.179(1) of the OSA consists of two elements. First, the message sent must be knowingly false. Under the criminal law framework of England and Wales, knowledge as part of the *mens rea* element is common. For instance, knowledge needs to be proven for an offence of harassment, as discussed in Chapter 5. Therefore, it must be proven that the defendant knows or should have known that the message sent was indeed false. I.e., they knew or should have known that a communication was untrue. Like that of harassment, this will be based on the reasonable person test.

Essentially, it must be established that the average person in the same position as the defendant would have come to the knowledge *or should have* come to the knowledge, that their conduct would result in the sending of a message which was false. At the time of writing, it is unclear if an objective or subjective test will be applied. If the test is subjective, it would result in the characteristics of the accused being taken into consideration when determining if they should have known that the message sent was false. For instance, taking into consideration the religious beliefs of the sender. Whereas an objective test would not, mirroring the law of harassment.

Second, the message sent must be sent with intent, to ensure those who mistakenly share false messages online, do not fall foul of the law. This is an important safeguard given that recent research has uncovered a lack of knowledge by online users in knowing when something online is false:

> OFCOM's study reveals that 30% of UK adults who go online (14.5 million) are unsure about, or don't even consider, the truthfulness of online information. A further 6%—around one in every twenty internet users—believe everything they see online.[32]

Consequently, for the *mens rea* to be present under this offence, the knowingly false message must be sent with the aim or purpose of causing 'non-trivial psychological or physical harm'. Those who share such content recklessly, would not have committed an offence under this provision, therefore providing some safeguards to ensure the overcriminalisation of speech does not occur.

32 OFCOM, 'The genuine article? One in three internet users fail to question misinformation' (*OFCOM*, 22 March 2022) <https://www.ofcom.org.uk/news-centre/2022/one-in-three-internet-users-fail-to-question-misinformation> accessed 7 August 2023.

7.3.3 Summary

It is difficult to see how this 'new' offence differs from previous provisions contained in the MCA and s.127(2) of the CA. A concern that is discussed further in Section 7.5, especially given that the meaning of false still renders issues with legality. An issue which is also relevant when examining the 'new' offence of sending a threatening communication.

7.4 Threatening Communications

Like that of false communications, concerns have previously been raised that the criminal law, in particular the MCA and s.127(1) of the CA, were struggling to keep pace with the use of the internet to send threatening communications to another. Issues often arose between what could be considered a 'credible threat', what is merely menacing or a communication that does not fall within the scope of the criminal law at all, such as that of *Chambers v DPP*.[33] Acknowledged further by the Association of Police and Crime Commissioners in response to the Law Commission's consultation on communication offences:

> Whilst we recognise that existing communications offences explicitly cover threats [...] As commissioners of victims services, we recognise the impact that a communication that contains threatening or menacing language may have on victims, and would argue that in order for the offence to adequately capture and describe the nature of wrongdoing, there is sufficient justification for a specific offence relating to threats to be created.[34]

Similar support was received by other stakeholders who argued that the use of a communications device to send threatening messages was well documented,[35] though as highlighted in the previous chapter, figures varied depending on the study. Indeed, human right's organisations specialising in the right to freedom of expression were in support of such an offence provided it was used to target only *genuine threats* and was not *already prohibited* under the criminal law framework of England and Wales.[36]

A new offence therefore of sending a threatening message has been incorporated into s.181 of the OSA, replacing the sending of a threatening message under the MCA, though as noted below, menacing messages, as prohibited under s.127(1) of the CA, remains. Under s.181(1) of the OSA, it is an offence to send a message which conveys a threat of death or serious harm.

33 *Chambers v DPP* [2012] EWHC 2157 (Admin); [2013] 1 W.L.R. 1833.
34 Law Com. No. 399 (n 1) [3.102].
35 Ibid., [3.103–3.106].
36 Ibid., [3.114].

7.4.1 Actus Reus

Two elements need to be established to prove the *actus reus* of the offence of sending a threatening communication contray to s.181(1) of the OSA. First, the person must send a message.[37] The meaning of a 'message' is given the same definition as discussed above and includes the sending of a hyperlink.[38] Second, the message must convey a threat of death or serious harm.[39] Death needs no further explanation. However, serious harm is defined under s.181(2) of the OSA, as either:

- Serious injury amounting to grievous bodily harm within the meaning of the Offences against the Person Act 1861 (OAPA);[40]
- Rape;[41]
- Assault by penetration within the meaning of section 2 of the Sexual Offences Act 2003 (SOA);[42] or
- Serious financial loss.[43]

The inclusion of 'rape' or 'assault by penetration within the meaning of section 2 of the' SOA as amounting to serious harm under this offence, is arguably in direct response to the growing use of social media platforms to target women online.[44] Many studies highlight how women are subjected to a unique form of abuse online, often grounded in threats of sexual violence.[45] Similarly, serious financial loss[46] has arguably been included due to growing concerns around sextortion.[47] These forms of serious harm will not be discussed any further.

However, defining serious harm as a 'serious injury amounting to [...] GBH' is significantly more complex. GBH is defined in *DPP v Smith*[48] as anything amounting to 'really serious harm' and would include actions such as threatening to break

37 Online Safety Act 2023 s.181(1)a.

38 Ibid., s.182(7).

39 Ibid., s.181(1)b.

40 Ibid., s.181(2)a.

41 Ibid., s.181(2)b.

42 Ibid., s.181(2)c.

43 Ibid., s.181(2)d.

44 Law Com. No. 399 (n 1) [3.106].

45 Amnesty International UK, 'Black and Asian women MPs abused more online' (*Amnesty International*, 2017) <https://www.amnesty.org.uk/online-violence-women-mps> accessed 9 December 2018.

46 Note, there is a defence available under s.181(3) of the Online Safety Act 2023 for this particular 'harm': 'it is a defence for the person to show that the threat was used to reinforce a reasonable demand, and the person reasonably believed that the use of the threat was a proper means of reinforcing the demand'. This does not apply to any other harm contained in the section.

47 Kevin Ashford, '"Sextortion" cases on the increase, police say, leaving victims embarrassed and out of pocket' *ITV News* (London, 7 September 2022) <https://www.itv.com/news/2022-09-07/sextortion-cases-on-the-increase-leaving-victims-embarrassed-and-out-of-pocket> accessed 16 August 2023.

48 *DPP v Smith* [1961] A.C. 290.

another's wrist or ankle, etc. However, the meaning of GBH was extended in 1997 following the case of *R v Ireland*[49] to include psychiatric harm. The meaning of psychiatric harm and the issues it renders with legality is discussed in Section 7.5.1.3.

7.4.2 Mens Rea

The *mens rea* of the offence can be committed in one of two ways:

1. At the time of sending the message the defendant intended that the individual encountering the message would fear that the threat would be carried out;[50] or
2. The defendant '[…] was reckless as to whether an individual encountering the message would fear that the threat would be carried out.'[51]

Put simply, the threatening message must be sent with intent or be sent recklessly. Intent, like that of previous offences discussed, would amount to a defendant's aim or purpose being to cause fear to another that a threat of death or serious harm would be carried out. Whereas recklessness is considered as taking an unjustified risk.

7.4.3 Summary

The inclusion of an offence to specifically criminalise the sending of a threatening message has been welcomed by many, particularly organisations campaigning for better protection for women online.[52] Although the offence under s.181 of the OSA contains more clarity than other provisions discussed above, and in previous chapters, in which Parliament has attempted to set the parameters of the offence during its construction, there are some small, but significant issues as will be demonstrated further in the following sections.

7.5 The 'New' Communication Offences, Freedom of Expression, and Legality

As noted in the introduction, the proposed harms offence and the 'new' communication offences have all been created following an extensive review of communication offences by the Law Commission between 2018 and 2021. However, many of the issues highlighted in the Law Commission's review were not adequately tackled in the proposed harms offence, resulting in its eventual removal, to protect freedom of expression. Of significant worry, though not the only worry, was the use of the terms harm, likely audience and reasonable excuse. Yet, such terminology

49 *R v Ireland* [1998] A.C. 147.
50 Online Safety Act 2023 s.181(1)c(i).
51 Ibid.,
52 Law Com. No.399 (n 1) [3.106].

has continued to be included in the 'new' communication offences which became legally enforceable on the 31 January 2024. These 'new' offences therefore do not tackle many of the issues previously highlighted with communication law and the principle of legality. Of concern, and will be the focus of the remainder of this chapter are:

- The lack of understanding as to the meaning of the types of 'harms' prohibited under all provisions discussed above, in which it cannot be said that the law is sufficiently clear;
- The wide definition given to likely audience and how this is asking the impossible;
- The use of the term reasonable excuse and the wide discretionary powers given to actors in the criminal justice system to establish what constitutes a reasonable excuse; and
- The continued interchangeable nature of the law.

7.5.1 The Types of Harms Prohibited and Lack of Clarity

Harm reduction in the criminal law is not a new phenomenon and arguably underpins the criminal law framework of states across the globe as 'the criminal law system is primary instrumentality for preventing people from intentionally or recklessly harming one another'.[53] But the use of such a principle in determining what should or should not be a criminal offence is contentious as the boundary between what is harmful and what is not is not easily identifiable:

> At first sight, the harm principle seems a straightforward and unproblematic guide to legislative decision-making. Indeed, insofar as our models for understanding harm are broken bones and stolen purses, we can preserve that illusion and think of harm as a simple, determinate, even purely empirical notion [… however …] harm is a very complex concept with hidden normative dimensions, and that partly because of this, the harm principle cannot be applied in a plausible way in large ranges of circumstance without supplementary criteria (or 'mediating maxims'), some of which are provided by independent moral principles.[54]

Put simply, what might be considered as harmful to one person, might not be to another. Mirroring many of the concerns previously raised against the use of the terms offensive and grossly offensive in the criminal law, as was discussed in the

53 Joel Feinberg, *Harm to Others: The Moral Limits of the Criminal Law* (Oxford University Press 1984) 31. For an alternative approach to harm-based reduction, see, Andy Phippen and Louisa Street, 'Addressing online harms in policy - failing to learn from the war on drugs' (2023) 34(2) Ent. L.R. 36.

54 Ibid., 214.

previous chapter. Arguably, the boundaries of what constitutes harmful behaviour become even more complex, when attempting to apply this notion to speech.

Under each provision discussed above, the purpose is, or was, to prohibit some form of harm to another, with each provision being given a different definition of harm. Regardless of how this harm was or is defined under each provision, as will be shown below, each renders significant issues with legality in which it cannot be said that clarity is being maintained in the criminal law.

7.5.1.1 The Meaning of Harm under the Harms Offence

As outlined in Section 7.2.1, harm, under the proposed harms offence, was defined as 'psychological harm amounting to at least serious distress'. Though arguably this was an improvement on the original definition given by the Law Commission—'psychological harm amounting to at least serious *emotional* distress'[55]—issues remained, particularly given that no further explanation was given to the term 'serious distress':

> the meaning of the level of harm in the Law Commission's recommended reform—'serious distress'—is never specifically defined by the Commission. Instead, there just needs to be a 'real or substantial risk of harm'. Consequently, without a clear understanding as to what is actually meant by 'serious distress', particularly in the context of speech, how does the criminal justice system ensure that trivial harms are not criminalised and, in turn, ensure the right to freedom of expression is not infringed?[56]

As a result, it could not be said that the proposed harms offence to replace both the MCA and s.127(1) of the CA brought any form of clarity to this area of the law and instead, merely repeated issues which had previously been raised. I.e., the use of vague terminology with no measurable standard to restrict the right to freedom of expression.

Though the use of the term 'serious distress' is often used in criminal law provisions in England and Wales and therefore could be considered a quantifiable standard by which criminal liability could be measured, the Law Commission made it clear in their proposal that current definitions of the term should not be written into the offence: '[we are] not recommending that all existing definitions of "serious distress" be copied immutably [... into ...] the offence—it is a different offence, and importantly one based on *likely* harm'.[57] The lack of a clear understanding of the term harm became even more concerning given that under the proposed offence, harm did not need to be proven, there just needed to be the possibility

55 Law Commission, *Harmful Online Communications: The Criminal Offences. A Consultation Paper* (Law Com. No.248, 2020) [5.51].

56 Higson-Bliss (n 6) 281.

57 Law Com. No.399 (n 1) [2.52].

that someone from the likely audience, discussed further below, *could* have been harmed by the communication:

> The problem of an inadequate definition is particularly acute because on the drafting there is no need to prove that any harm to any person was caused to that level. It is enough that this level of harm was likely to be caused to anyone likely to see the message. With some forms of communication on the open internet that would mean that it would be enough that the most vulnerable person who might have seen it would be seriously distressed, so long as the message was sent with intent. That would appear to be a threshold that is very easily met.[58]

In essence, there just needed to be the mere possibility that some form of undefined harm could have been inflicted upon another by the sending of the communication.

It is for this main reason that the harms offence was removed from the OSB in January 2023. The lack of a clear understanding as to what would constitute a harmful message meant that there was a real risk that the right to freedom of expression would be infringed:

> In fact, under the Commission's final recommendation those who knowingly express[ed] provocative views online, for instance, individuals who express[ed] controversial views on transgender rights, on both sides of the debate, could well [have found] themselves falling foul of the law.[59]

Yet vague terminology has continued to be used in the 'new' communication offences.

7.5.1.2 The Meaning of Non-trivial Psychological or Physical Harm when Sending a False Communication

It is an offence under s.179(1) of the OSA to send a false communication which has the intention to cause another 'non-trivial psychological or physical harm'. No definition is contained in the Act as to what constitutes this type of harm. Though in defence of lawmakers, the provision directly reflects the recommendation made by the Law Commission, in which no definition was given to this aspect of the *actus reus*. Consequently, a false message sent with the intent to cause 'non-trivial psychological or physical harm' is unlawful; false communications sent with the intent to cause trivial 'psychological or physical harm' is not. However, the line between the two is not easily identifiable. Even non-trivial physical harm, which on the face of it might be considered easy to prove, renders some issues with the interpretation of the offence.

58 Higson-Bliss (n 6) 281.
59 Ibid., 283.

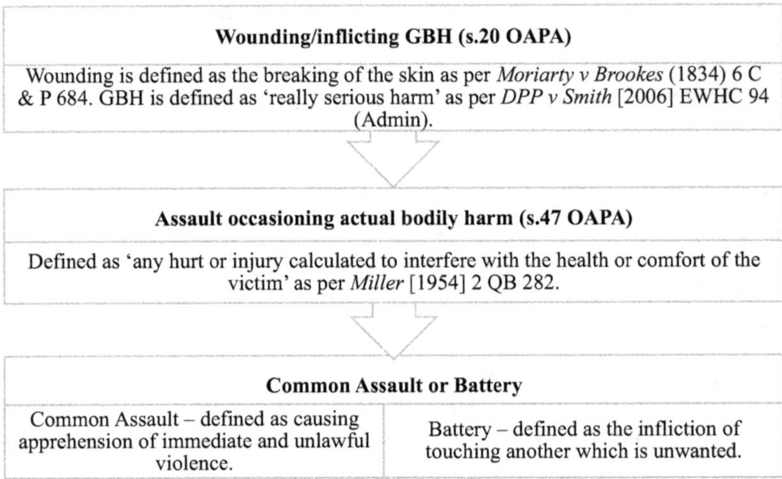

Figure 7.1 Defining non-fatal offences and physical harm.

The use of the criminal law to prohibit the physical harm of another is far from a new phenomenon and exists in many criminal law provisions, particularly in the context of non-fatal offences against the person in England and Wales. This has led to a hierarchy of different types of non-fatal physical harm being created through the enactment of legislation and extensive case law, as shown further in Figure 7.1. At the 'bottom' of this hierarchy is battery, which is defined as 'any intentional touching of another person without the consent of that person and without lawful excuse. It need not necessarily be hostile, rude, or aggressive'.[60] Essentially, the touching of a person on the shoulder, could well constitute battery. In terms of s.179(2)a of the OSA, could it be said that 'battery' would constitute a non-trivial physical harm? Or should the line be drawn at GBH which is defined as 'really serious harm',[61] such as broken or fractured bones? Though, it might be difficult to envision a false communication being sent which causes another some form of physical harm. An example would be the sending of a message which knowingly falsely accuses another of being a paedophile, which is common in the online world,[62] and results in the accused receiving some form of physical injury.

Currently, the difference between a 'non-trivial physical harm' and a 'physical harm' is not clear, creating issues in ensuring the law is action-guiding. Recent events have showcased how the digital world can often merge into the physical

60 *Faulkner v Talbot* [1981] 3 All ER 468 per Lord Lane CJ 471.

61 *Smith* (n 48).

62 Rowena Mason, 'Social media users warned against falsely calling politicians paedophiles' *The Guardian* (London, 8 July 2014) <https://www.theguardian.com/media/2014/jul/08/social-media-users-warned-against-making-false-allegations-mps-paedophiles> accessed 9 August 2023.

world.[63] However, this concern could be easily resolved by clearly stipulating where in the hierarchy of non-fatal offences, a 'non-trivial physical harm' would fall. This will likely be made clearer as cases come before the criminal justice system. Though this does to some degree undermine the principle of legality, in which Fuller notes that we should refrain from case-by-case enlightenment as to the boundaries of the law,[64] this breach is not as significant when compared to the inclusion of the term 'non-trivial psychological' harm.

Though, like that of physical harm, the prohibition of causing someone psychological harm is not new to the criminal law, in which many criminal law provisions prohibit conduct that causes another psychological harm, how this offence is phrased is new. For the Law Commission, during the drafting of the provision on which s.179 of the OSA is based, 'non-trivial psychological harm' was likely 'to include, for example, distress and anxiety, but not annoyance or inconvenience'.[65] It is not quite clear why then, distress or anxiety were not used, as opposed to 'non-trivial psychological harm'. Had distress or anxiety been used, this would have mirrored other criminal law provisions, which in turn would have brought some clarity to this area of the law—whilst at the same time, upholding the principle of legality. For instance, in relation to the Protection from Harassment Act 1997, as discussed in Chapter 5, distress is considered 'oppressive and unreasonable behaviour'.[66] Though it should be noted, when it comes to speech, this could be setting the bar far too low. Nonetheless, there is a definition. Whereas 'non-trivial psychological harm' is not defined.

Like that of 'non-trivial physical harm', it is now for actors in the criminal justice system to set the precedent as to the meaning of this term—which is not easy when there is little case law or previous precedent. Indeed, in the most updated version of the Crown Prosecution Service (CPS) guidelines on communication offences, which were updated following the enactment of the OSA, it simply states, in relation to 'non-trivial psychological harm': 'Prosecutors should be clear when making a charging decision about what the evidence is concerning the suspect's intention and how what was intended was not "trivial", and why not'.[67] Concerns as to where the criminal law should draw the boundaries with psychological harm are further illustrated in how 'serious harm' is defined in s.181(2) of the OSA—the prohibition of sending threatening communications.

63 See, for example, The BBC, 'Rishi Sunak criticises social media craze that led to disorder' *The BBC* (London, 15 August 2023) <https://www.bbc.co.uk/news/uk-england-hampshire-66508164> accessed 15 August 2023.

64 Lon L. Fuller, *The Morality of Law* (Yale University Press 1964) 46.

65 Law Com. No.399 (n 1) [6.46].

66 *Majrowski v Guy's and St Thomas's NHS Trust* [2005] EWCA Civ 251, [2005] Q.B 848 per Auld LJ [82].

67 The Crown Prosecution Service, 'Communication offences' (*CPS.gov*, 2024) <https://www.cps.gov.uk/legal-guidance/communications-offences> accessed 12 March 2024.

7.5.1.3 The Meaning of 'Serious Harm' and Threatening Communications

Whereas the proposed harms offence and the offence of sending a false communication contains or contained no clear definition of the prohibited harm, the provision prohibiting threatening communications does:

> Serious harm means—(a) serious injury amounting to grievous bodily harm (GBH) within the meaning of the Offences against the Person Act 1981, (b) rape, (c) assault by penetration within the meaning of section 2 of the Sexual Offences Act 2003, or (d) serious financial loss.[68]

As noted above, s.181(2)b, c, and d is relatively clear, s.181(2)a—GBH—is less so. GBH is defined in *DPP v Smith*[69] as 'really serious harm'. For instance, a fractured skull or a broken bone would constitute GBH. Though it is likely, in keeping with the extensive case law on the meaning and limits of GBH, the threatening harm does not need to be 'life-threatening, dangerous, or permanent, nor [is it a] requirement that the victim [would] require treatment or that the harm [would] have lasting consequences' to constitute GBH.[70] On a literal interpretation of s.181(2) of the OSA, this may not be of concern. For instance, if someone sends a message online threatening to break another's leg or threatening to 'kick someone's head in' this would amount to serious harm under this provision.

However, as previously noted, in 1997 the meaning of GBH was extended by the House of Lords in *R v Ireland*[71] to include psychiatric injury, which must amount to a recognised psychiatric illness or condition.[72] Though it is important to note that '[h]ysterical and nervous conditions and mere emotions such as fear, distress, or panic do not constitute psychiatric injury'.[73] In the context of communications online, the psychological harm that can be inflicted on another has been well documented.[74] However, communications sent threatening to inflict psychiatric injury less so, though it is not impossible to envision. For example, could it be said that a communication threatening to 'drive someone crazy' or to put another in a 'mental institution' could amount to the psychological harm of another, and if it could, is this foreseeable? What about in the context of a communication which puts a person in fear of their own life but does not directly go far enough to threaten 'really serious harm' or the other prohibited threats under this provision?

68 Online Safety Act 2023 s.181(2).
69 *Smith* (n 48).
70 *Bollom* [2003] EWCA Crim 2846 per Justice Fulford [53].
71 *Ireland* (n 49).
72 *R v D* [2006] EWCA Crim 1139.
73 Michael Allen and Ian Edwards, *Criminal Law* (16th edn, Oxford University Press 2021) 436.
74 Amnesty International, 'Amnesty reveals alarming impact of online abuse against women' (*Amnesty International*, 20 November 2017) <https://www.amnesty.org/en/latest/news/2017/11/amnesty-reveals-alarming-impact-of-online-abuse-against-women/> accessed 9 December 2018.

Like that of the other harms explored above, it will likely be for actors in the criminal justice system to set the parameters of the offence in the wake of vague terminology. This creates significant issues with legality and the criminal law.

7.5.1.4 Summary

Clarity, as noted by Fuller, is an 'essential ingredient' in the criminal law and without it, the law fails in its mission to be 'action-guiding'.[75] As discussed in Chapter 3, the law needs to be action-guiding so that individuals can govern their behaviour in accordance with clear and distinct rules and ultimately not fall foul of the law simply because the legal provision was insufficiently clear. This is of further importance when it comes to criminal provisions which are not necessarily obvious, as is common with offences related to communications, where a balancing act must be made. Or as potently put by Lord Bingham and highlighted at various points in this monograph:

> This is not because bank robbers habitually consult their solicitors before robbing a branch of the NatWest, but because many crimes are a great deal less obvious than robbery, and most of us are keen to keep on the right side of the law if we can.[76]

In essence, we need to strive for the 'maximum clarity which the imperfect medium of language can attain'[77]—something the proposed harms offence failed to do resulting in its quick demise. Yet vague terminology continues to plague the 'new' communication offences.

The use of the terms 'non-trivial psychological or physical harm' and 'serious harm' fails to bring any form of consistency or clarity to this area of the law. In turn, concerns raised previously with the prohibition of false and threatening communications under both the MCA and s.127(1) and (2) of the CA remain. As a result, it cannot be said that legality is being maintained, which like that of other offences examined throughout this monograph, poses a threat to the right to freedom of expression as actors within the criminal justice system attempt to interpret the different meanings given to harm under the 'new' offences.

Failure to create a clear and distinct understanding of any legal provision, particularly when it comes to the coercive nature of the criminal law, further results in personal autonomy being heavily impeded, alongside that of the right to freedom of expression. For Husak,[78] to ensure the protection of personal autonomy against that of the criminal law, 'the law should only intervene where the harm under question

75 Fuller (n 64) 62.

76 Tom Bingham, *The Rule of Law* (Penguin 2011) 37.

77 Law Commission, *Report on Conspiracy and Criminal Law Reform* (1976) Law Com No. 76 [1.8].

78 Douglas Husak, *Overcriminalization: The Limits of the Criminal Law* (Oxford University Press 2008) 82.

prohibits a behaviour which can be defined as a non-trivial harm'.[79] Yet, a lack of understanding as to what would have constituted 'serious distress' in the context of the harms offence and a continued lack of understanding as to what constitutes 'serious harm' or 'non-trivial psychological or physical harm' does not ensure that only non-trivial harms would or could have been criminalised. The lack of clarity as to the meaning of harm under the harms offence and the prohibition of sending false or threatening communications is amplified further when trying to understand the meaning of the likely audience and reasonable excuse.

7.5.2 The Meaning of Likely Audience: Asking the Impossible

Under both the proposed harms offence and the offence prohibiting the sending of a false communication the harm imposed needs to be directed at a likely audience. A likely audience under s.179(2) of the OSA is defined as:

> if, at the time the message is sent, it is reasonably foreseeable that the individuals—(a) would encounter the message, or (b) in the online context, would encounter a subsequent message forwarding or sharing the content of the message.

Similarly, under the proposed harms offence a likely audience was defined as anyone likely to 'encounter' the message.[80] And as briefly discussed in Section 7.2.1 above, in the context of social media, this could have been anyone in the world. Rendering this requirement of the offence significantly broad:

> While this may seem reasonable [the use of the term likely audience], it creates major difficulties on such platforms as Twitter which are open to all. The likely audience is everyone in the world. Given the ease of mass communication, it is a simple matter for a lobby group, such as those asserting the importance of gender identity theory, to organise as part of any audience—making them a 'likely' part of that audience. If they so desire, they can assert the right of transwomen to be potential partners for lesbians and claim that those who disagree are harming them. This is not a fictitious example: it occurs on a regular basis.[81]

The likely audience could therefore be, or could have been under the harms offence, individuals who were more prone to offence; users who are as young as 13 years of age;[82] or political alliances who firmly disagree(d) with the speaker's position. For example, a message sent stating, 'a man cannot become a woman' maybe deemed as false by some. However, for others, this might be considered a true statement but

79 Higson-Bliss (n 6) 280.
80 Online Safety Bill 2022 c.150(4).
81 Law Com. No.399 (n 1) [2.149] (LGB Alliance).
82 In most cases, social media users need to be at least 13 years old.

could be interpreted as causing 'non-trivial psychological harm'.[83] A message sent online is a message sent to the world. Indeed, a likely audience would also include those who are forwarded such content but who might have not necessarily come across it themselves.

The lack of an understanding as to who the likely audience would have been under the harms offence, coupled with the lack of a definitive definition of what constituted harm, was a further reason for its removal from the OSB. However, such a requirement remains in relation to false communications. Not only does its inclusion in s.179(1) of the OSA seriously risk the overcriminalisation of speech, but it also undermines the principle of legality by asking an online user to do the impossible—send a false communication that does not cause 'non-trivial psychological or physical harm' to another—this 'other' being anyone in the world.

Put simply, the false communications offence is asking individuals not to send a message which can be deemed as false, which might cause 'non-trivial psychological or physical harm' to another. In the online world, where context is everything, but is often lost, jokes, banter or distasteful humour could fall within the scope of this offence, given that the likely audience pool is so large. For example, messages sent on April Fool's Day are often false but justified as being a 'joke' or 'banter'. Some of these 'jokes' or 'banter' have the real possibility of causing 'non-trivial psychological or physical harm', such as a 'fake' pregnancy announcement. Where the likely audience could well be anyone in the world, it would not take long to find someone who would be highly upset by such a message, which may go beyond 'trivial psychological harm', especially for those experiencing pregnancy loss or infertility.

Arguably, the example given above of an April Fool's Day joke would be protected under the further requirement placed on the prosecution to prove that the message was sent without reasonable excuse but as explored in Section 7.5.3, issues are also present with this element of the offence. Consequently, it cannot be said that the use of the term likely audience ensures 'the chances of the provision being used arbitrarily is minimal or, indeed, the criminal law will only be invoked as a last resort'.[84]

7.5.3 The Meaning of Reasonable Excuse: Discretion in the Criminal Law

The requirement that a harmful or false message was or is sent without reasonable excuse was contained in both the proposed harms offence and in the offence of sending a false message under s.179(1) of the OSA. During the Law Commission's consultation into these 'new' communication offences, the inclusion of reasonable excuse was hailed by many as safeguarding the right to freedom of expression.[85]

83 This could fall under 'reasonable excuse' but there are issues with this element of the offence also. See Section 7.5.3..

84 Higson-Bliss (n 6) 285.

85 Law Com. No. 399 (n 1) [3.62].

The requirement that the burden of proof is placed on the prosecution to demonstrate, beyond all reasonable doubt, that a message is sent without reasonable excuse was considered as a further aid in protecting the right to freedom of expression: 'In essence, the sender will be entitled to be acquitted unless the prosecution proves that the sender did not have a legitimate or reasonable reason for sending a communication'.[86] Yet, even with this safeguard, the harms offence was still considered a threat to freedom of expression, resulting in its quick demise. And when examining how reasonable excuse has been applied in other areas of the criminal law, it is easy to see why reasonable excuse may not be an adequate safeguard for freedom of expression where the *actus reus* of an offence is so significantly broad.

Reasonable excuse is not new to the criminal law. Similar provisions are found in other areas of the criminal law framework. For instance, reasonable excuse is found in s.1 of the Prevention of Crime Act 1953 whereby a person can rely on reasonable excuse if caught in a public place with a weapon—though this forms part of the defence, rather than the *actus reus*. However, the most well-known connotation of reasonable excuse is its use during the COVID-19 pandemic in England. Under provisions contained in the Health Protection (Coronavirus, Restrictions) (England) Regulations (Health Protection Regulations) 2020, individuals could only leave their homes where they had a 'reasonable excuse to do so'. Although this might have seemed a legitimate requirement—i.e., only to leave one's home when there was no other option—given the global threat to public health, what resulted was an inconsistent application of the criminal law. In some instances, the term was interpreted broadly; in others, a very narrow definition was given.[87] One particular case which caught the national headlines was the issuing of fines to two individuals after they drove five miles to go for a walk by Derbyshire Police who subsequently issued an apology.[88]

Following growing concerns around the inconsistent application of the Health Protection Regulations, the CPS undertook a review of all fines issued under this provision. Concluding that 279 charges (18%) issued under the Health Protection Regulations between March 2020 and March 2021 were unlawful.[89] If such mistakes can take place where a person's basic civil liberties are at risk, how do we ensure similar mistakes are not made with s.179 of the OSA where freedom of expression is at risk?

Put simply, what one police force might see as a reasonable excuse to send a knowingly false message with the intent to cause 'non-trivial psychological or

86 Higson-Bliss (n 6) 287.

87 For an in-depth discussion see, Adam Wagner, *Emergency State: How We Lost Our Freedoms in the Pandemic and Why It Matters* (Penguin 2022).

88 The BBC, 'Covid: Women fined for going for a walk receive police apology' *The BBC* (London, 11 January 2021) <https://www.bbc.co.uk/news/uk-england-derbyshire-55625062> accessed 9 August 2023.

89 Lizzie Dearden, 'All 270 charges brought under Coronavirus Act wrongful, official review finds' *The Independent* (London, 14 May 2021) <https://www.independent.co.uk/news/uk/home-news/coronavirus-act-prosecutions-wrongful-cps-review-b1847194.html> accessed 9 August 2023.

physical harm to another', another may not. This leads to a real possibility that a lack of consistency will be applied in the future interpretation of this offence. Once again, this mirrors concerns with how communication law has previously been applied. For example, what one police force considered grossly offensive another did not.[90] Significant discretion is therefore given to law enforcement, judges, prosecutors, and juries in determining what constitutes a reasonable excuse. Although prosecution guidelines could be created to bring some clarity and consistency to this area of the law, previous attempts to do this with the MCA and s.127(1) and (2) of the CA proves this is easier said than done.[91]

For the Law Commission:

> When deciding whether the defendant had a reasonable excuse for sending or posting the communication, the court must have regard to whether the communication was, or was meant as, a contribution to a matter of public interest.[92]

This was reaffirmed during debates following the inclusion of both the harms offence and the false communications offence in the first draft of the OSB:

> In addition, the court cannot find someone guilty of the harm-based offence or false communications offence if they have a reasonable excuse. A reasonable excuse would include if the communication was or was intended as a contribution to the public interest.[93]

However, what is in the public interest is already a requirement prosecutors need to take into consideration with any criminal offence, including communication offences.[94] Yet, as shown in the previous chapter, there are some cases where it is not always clear why it was in the public interest to pursue a prosecution, *Chambers v DPP* being a prime example of this.[95] Therefore, reasonable excuse does not add any further requirements than already found in the criminal law framework of England and Wales. Further, as noted in Chapter 2, any case that comes before the police, prosecutors or judges, needs to be decided taking into consideration human rights, including the right to freedom of expression, as discussed in Chapter 2. It's difficult to see how a reasonable excuse will provide a better safeguard than

90 As discussed at length in Chapter 6.

91 Ibid,.

92 Law Com. No.248 (n 55) [4.59].

93 Chris Philp, 'Update on the law commission's review of modernising communications offences' (*Gov.uk*, 4 February 2022) <https://questions-statements.parliament.uk/written-statements/detail/2022-02-04/hcws590#:~:text=In%20addition%2C%20the%20court%20cannot,contribution%20to%20the%20public%20interest> accessed 5 August 2023.

94 The Crown Prosecution Service, 'Guidelines on prosecuting cases involving communications sent via social media' (*CPS.gov*, 21 August 2018) [8] <https://www.cps.gov.uk/legal-guidance/social-media-guidelines-prosecuting-cases-involving-communications-sent-social-media> accessed 11 October 2018.

95 *Chambers* (n 33).

human rights law. Therefore, in reality, this element adds very little to ensure the overcriminalisation of speech does not occur and instead gives significant discretion to those working in the criminal justice system to determine what is a reasonable excuse for sending a false communication. For instance, utilising a previous example above, would April Fool's Day be considered a reasonable excuse for sending a false message that amounts to 'non-trivial psychological or physical harm' to another?

As a result, overreliance is therefore still being placed on the discretion of actors in the criminal justice system (the police, prosecutors, and judges) to determine the parameters of this offence. In essence, not tackling the issues raised against previous communication offences where grossly offensive was/is being interpreted narrowly for some but broadly for others.[96]

7.5.4 The Online Safety Act 2023 and Its Place in the Criminal Law Framework of England and Wales: The Interchangeable Nature of the Law

The MCA and s.127(1) and (2) of the CA, as discussed in Chapter 6, have been heavily criticised for their interchangeable nature, where the difference between the two provisions was/is difficult to articulate. This has been made even more complex following the passing of the OSA. For ease the following are criminalised across the MCA, s.127(1) of the CA and s.179 and 181 of the OSA:

- False communications are specifically criminalised under:
  - S.179(1) of the OSA—which prohibits the sending of a knowingly false communication to a likely audience to cause 'non-trivial psychological or physical harm' to another which is sent without reasonable excuse by any form of communication.
- Threatening/menacing communications are prohibited under:
  - S.127(1) of the CA—which prohibits the sending of a menacing message *via* a public electronic communications network with intent or was reckless in the sending of such a message.
  - S.181(1) of the OSA—which prohibits the sending of a threatening message that amounts to a threat of death or serious harm, which is sent recklessly or with intent by any form of communication.
- Indecent communications are prohibited under:
  - S.1(1)(i) of the MCA—which prohibits the sending of an indecent message to another for the purpose of causing 'anxiety or distress' by any form of communication.
  - S.127(1) of the CA—which prohibits the sending of an indecent message *via* a public electronic communications network with intent or was reckless in the sending of such a message.
- Grossly offensive communications are prohibited under:

96 See the previous chapter.

    - S.1(1)(i) of the MCA—which prohibits the sending of a grossly offensive message to another for the purpose of causing 'anxiety or distress' by any form of communication.
    - S.127(1) of the CA—which prohibits the sending of a grossly offensive message *via* a public electronic communications network with intent or was reckless in the sending of such a message.
- Obscene communications are prohibited under:[97]
    - S.127(1) of the CA—which prohibits the sending of an obscene message *via* a public electronic communications network with intent or was reckless in the sending of such a message.

The differences between all these provisions are not obviously clear. Each prohibits very similar behaviour(s) which in turn will lead to continued confusion across the criminal justice system. Mirroring previous concerns around the interchangeable nature of the MCA and s.127 of the CA.[98] For instance, as noted by the CPS, in their current communication offences prosecuting guidelines, following the enactment of the OSA:

> There is a clear overlap with the offence of sending a menacing communication under section 127(1)(a) Communications Act 2003 [and sending threatening communications]. Focus should be on whether the summary section 127 offence reflects the seriousness of the offence and provides adequate powers of sentence. The section 127 offence may also be available where the legal elements of the section 181 offence are not established.[99]

Arguably, the interchangeable nature of the criminal law has been complicated further by the 'new' communication offences.

As it currently stands there is a significant overlap between three communication offences, which is no doubt going to cause issues as cases proceed through the criminal justice system. Put simply, it cannot be said that consistency will be maintained. One police force might pursue a threatening communication under s.181 of the OSA, another might use s.127(1) of the CA, labelling it a menacing communication. This becomes of concern given the difference in punishment; s.181 of the OSA is an either-way offence; s.127(1) is a summary-only offence. It is vital, therefore, that the two are not used interchangeably and if there is a difference between the two offences, this is highlighted clearly in prosecution guidance. Though as was highlighted in the previous chapter, even with prosecution guidance, where legislation is enacted which is embedded in vague terminology mistakes will continue to take place, even with such guidance.

97 Note, obscene material is also prohibited under the Obscene Publications Act 1959 and 1964, though beyond the scope of this monograph.

98 See the previous chapter.

99 Communication Offences (n 67).

This could be easily resolved by amending s.127(1) of the CA to remove reference to menacing communications and removing other overlaps across all three statutes. However, arguably, as has been hinted above, these 'new' communication offences, add very little to our understanding as to when a communication, particularly one sent online where context is everything but is often lost, invokes the criminal law. In essence, many of the issues that have been raised with how the criminal law applies to online communications, even following the passing of the OSA, remain.

7.6 Chapter Summary

The acknowledgement by the Law Commission that previous communication offences were inadequate in dealing with the complexity of online communications, especially those that take place on social media, was a welcomed conclusion. However, it is evident from the discussions above that many of the issues concerning the right to freedom of expression and the principle of legality which have been raised in previous chapters have not been adequately addressed in the passing of these 'new' offences. Instead, many of the issues highlighted throughout this monograph, are also applicable to the OSA.

As discussed above, the 'new' provisions contained in the OSA render significant issues with clarity in the criminal law, particularly around the notion of what constitutes a harmful communication. Even grounding offences around the notion of likely audience or reasonable excuse does not adequately protect the right to freedom of expression. Put simply, it cannot be said that legality is protected under any of these 'new' provisions.

If anything, the law is now more complex than ever. These 'new' offences continue to be grounded in vague terminology, which in turn will result in uncertainty, significant weight being given to the discretion of actors in the criminal justice system to establish the boundaries of the offences and in turn, will lead to inconsistency in the enforcement of the law.

Reference list

Allen M & Edwards I, *Criminal Law* (16th edn, Oxford University Press 2021)

Amnesty International, 'Amnesty Reveals Alarming Impact of Online Abuse against Women' (*Amnesty International*, 20 November 2017) https://www.amnesty.org/en/latest/news/2017/11/amnesty-reveals-alarming-impact-of-online-abuse-against-women/

Amnesty International, 'Black and Asian women MPs abused More Online' (*Amnesty International*, 2017) https://www.amnesty.org.uk/online-violence-women-mps

Ashford K, '"Sextortion" cases on the increase, police say, leaving victims embarrassed and out of pocket' *ITV News* (London, 7 September 2022) https://www.itv.com/news/2022-09-07/sextortion-cases-on-the-increase-leaving-victims-embarrassed-and-out-of-pocket

Bingham T, *The Rule of Law* (Penguin 2011)

Dearden L, 'All 270 charges brought under Coronavirus Act wrongful, official review finds' *The Independent* (London, 14 May 2021) https://www.independent.co.uk/news/uk/home-news/coronavirus-act-prosecutions-wrongful-cps-review-b1847194.html

Department of Digital, Culture, Media & Sport, 'Overview of Expected Impact of Changes to the Online Safety Bill' (*Gov.uk*, 18 January 2021) https://www.gov.uk/government/publications/online-safety-bill-supporting-documents/overview-of-expected-impact-of-changes-to-the-online-safety-bill#:~:text=The%20adult%20safety%20duties%20(%27legal,and%20freedom%20of%20expression%20duties

Feinberg J, *Harm to Others: The Moral Limits of the Criminal Law* (Oxford University Press 1984)

Fuller L L, *The Morality of Law* (Yale University Press 1964)

Higson-Bliss L, 'Prosecuting Communication Offences: Interpreting the Harms Model' (2022) 4 CLR 271

HM Government, 'Internet Safety Strategy – Green Paper' (*HM Government*, 2017) https://assets.publishing.service.gov.uk/government/uploads/system/uploads/attachment_data/file/650949/Internet_Safety_Strategy_green_paper.pdf

Husak D, *Overcriminalization: The Limits of the Criminal Law* (Oxford University Press 2008)

Law Commission, *Modernising Communications Offences: A Final Report* (Law Com. No.399, 2021)

Law Commission, *Harmful Online Communications: The Criminal Offences. A Consultation Paper* (Law Com. No.248, 2020)

Law Commission, *Abusive and Offensive Online Communications: A Scoping Report* (Law Com No 381, 2018)

Law Commission, *Report on Conspiracy and Criminal Law Reform* (Law Com No. 76, 1976)

Mason R, 'Social media users warned against falsely calling politicians paedophiles' *The Guardian* (London, 8 July 2014) https://www.theguardian.com/media/2014/jul/08/social-media-users-warned-against-making-false-allegations-mps-paedophiles

OFCOM, 'The Genuine Article? One in Three Internet Users Fail to Question Misinformation' (*OFCOM*, 22 March 2022) https://www.ofcom.org.uk/news-centre/2022/one-in-three-internet-users-fail-to-question-misinformation

Phippen A & Street L, 'Addressing online harms in policy - failing to learn from the war on drugs' (2023) 34(2) Ent. L.R. 36

Smith G, 'Licence to Chill' (*Cyberleagle*, 22 November 2021) https://www.cyberleagle.com/2021/11/licence-to-chill.html

The BBC, 'Rishi Sunak criticises social media craze that led to disorder' *The BBC* (London, 15 August 2023) https://www.bbc.co.uk/news/uk-england-hampshire-66508164

The BBC, 'Covid: Women fined for going for a walk receive police apology' *The BBC* (London, 11 January 2021) https://www.bbc.co.uk/news/uk-england-derbyshire-55625062

The Crown Prosecution Service, 'Communication Offences' (*CPS.gov*, 2024) https://www.cps.gov.uk/legal-guidance/communications-offences

The Crown Prosecution Service, 'Guidelines on Prosecuting Cases Involving Communications Sent via Social Media' (*CPS.gov*, 21 August 2018) https://www.cps.gov.uk/legal-guidance/social-media-guidelines-prosecuting-cases-involving-communications-sent-social-media

Wagner A, *Emergency State: How We Lost Our Freedoms in the Pandemic and Why It Matters* (Penguin 2022)

Part III

The Criminal Law and Beyond

Whereas Part Two of this monograph focussed primarily on three significant 'harms' associated with the online world, hate speech (Chapter 4), cyberharassment/cyberstalking (Chapter 5) and unlawful communications (Chapters 6 and 7) from a criminal law perspective, Part Three turns to examine the regulation of social media platforms themselves as opposed to individuals. Chapter 8 discusses the latest attempts by the former United Kingdom's government to control unlawful or in some cases, legal but harmful, content online through the creation and implementation of the Online Safety Act 2023. Whereas Chapter 9 explores other countries' approaches to regulating social media. Like that of Part Two, issues with legality and freedom of expression will be critically highlighted. The final chapter, Chapter 10, provides a conclusive summary of the arguments made in the monograph, suggesting recommendations for tackling the 'harms' associated with the online world.

DOI: 10.4324/9781003303688-10

8 Regulating Online Behaviour in the United Kingdom

Beyond the Criminal Law

8.1 Introduction

Whereas Part Two of this monograph focussed primarily on three significant 'harms' associated with the online world, hate speech (Chapter 4), cyberharassment and cyberstalking (Chapter 5), and abusive messages (Chapters 6 and 7) from a criminal law perspective, Part Three turns to examine the regulation of social media platforms themselves as opposed to individuals. This chapter will therefore outline and critically discuss parts of the Online Safety Act 2023 (OSA) and the obligations it places on social media companies to do more to tackle the 'harms' associated with the online world, including those discussed in previous chapters.[1] It is also important to note that, unlike the legal provisions discussed previously, the extent of the OSA extends to Scotland and Northern Ireland, as opposed to just England and Wales.

As will be discussed below, the OSA was born out of the former conservative government's bold plans to become one of the safest places in the world to go online.[2] First envisioned in 2017, the premise of the Act grew significantly; eventually receiving Royal Assent in October 2023. Like many of the legal provisions discussed throughout this monograph, its incorporation into the legal framework of the United Kingdom has been contentious. Many charities and government officials have hailed it as a benchmark for other countries in tackling online 'harms';[3]

1 As noted below, it does regulate more than social media platforms. Arguably however, it has been created with social media in mind.

2 HM Government, 'Internet Safety Strategy – Green Paper' (*Gov.uk*, October 2017) 1 <https://assets.publishing.service.gov.uk/government/uploads/system/uploads/attachment_data/file/650949/Internet_Safety_Strategy_green_paper.pdf> accessed 22 September 2023.

3 See, for example, National Society for the Prevention of Cruelty to Children, 'The Online Safety Bill has been passed in "a momentous day for children"' (*NSPCC,* 19 September 2023) <https://www.nspcc.org.uk/about-us/news-opinion/2023/2023-09-19-the-online-safety-bill-has-been-passed-in-a-momentous-day-for-children/> accessed 22 September 2023; Department for Science, Innovation and Technology and The Rt Hon Michelle Donelan MP, 'Britain makes internet safer, as Online Safety Bill finished and ready to become law' (*Gov.uk*, 19 September 2023) <https://www.gov.uk/government/news/britain-makes-internet-safer-as-online-safety-bill-finished-and-ready-to-become-law> accessed 22 September 2023.

DOI: 10.4324/9781003303688-11

others have considered it a significant threat to the right to freedom of expression.[4] Further, the Act has also been criticised for being unworkable,[5] which in turn breaches the principle of legality as the OSA is, to put it simply, asking the impossible.

Due to the extensive requirements set out under the Act, not all aspects of the OSA will be explored in this chapter—to examine the full requirements under the Act is a book within itself. And even then, the Act is only a very small proportion of the overall reach of this complex piece of legislation. Many of the requirements detailed in the OSA are awaiting further guidance from OFCOM, the United Kingdom's communications regulator, who are essentially the guardians of the OSA, alongside the Secretary of State. It will likely be years before we know the true extent of the OSA and if it has achieved its ultimate aim of ensuring the United Kingdom is one of the safest places in the world to go online.

The discussion below will start by briefly examining the development and history of the OSA. Next, the parameters of the OSA will be outlined, focussing on who falls within its scope. It's important to note, though was often missed in conversations during its passing through Parliament, that the obligations under the OSA extend beyond just social media platforms:

> Almost every online platform that allows user-to-user engagement or search will be caught by the OSB [Online Safety Bill]. From Wikipedia, to Mumsnet, to Minecraft, to Signal, to Tinder, to your local community forum, every online platform or communication channel around the globe which 'targets the United Kingdom' will have to comply with an increasingly onerous array of obligations.[6]

Following on from this, the requirements placed on those who fall within a Category 1 or 2B provider will be discussed—known as the duties. The final parts of this chapter will expose how the Act creates a significant threat to the right to freedom of expression and issues with the principle of legality.

8.2 The Development of the Online Safety Act 2023

Attempting to make the online world safer had been on the former conservative government's agenda since 2017, following a general election in which promises were made to voters:

4 James Baker, 'ORG warns of threat to privacy and free speech as Online Safety Bill is passed' (*Open Rights Group*, 19 September 2023) <https://www.openrightsgroup.org/press-releases/org-warns-of-threat-to-privacy-and-free-speech-as-online-safety-bill-is-passed/> accessed 22 September 2023.

5 Nadia Tymkiw, 'The Online Safety Bill and the risk of unintended consequences' (*The International Forum for Responsible Media Blog*, 11 April 2023) <https://inforrm.org/2023/04/11/the-online-safety-bill-and-the-risk-of-unintended-consequences-nadia-tymkiw/> accessed 6 October 2023.

6 Ibid.,

> to educate today's young people in the harms of the internet and how best to combat them; introduce an industry-wide levy which could in the future be underpinned with legislation; and protect the vulnerable and give people confidence to use the internet without fear through initiatives like a code of practice for social media companies.[7]

Further promising to 'make Britain the best place in the world to setup and run a digital business, while simultaneously ensuring that Britain is the safest place in the world to be online'.[8] The recommendations put forward in the Green Paper focussed on five key areas:

1. A strategic response which would require cooperation between stakeholders, including industry bodies, what was the UK Council for Child Internet Safety (now the UK Council for Internet Safety), government departments and public sector organisations;
2. Working with industry to make the online world safer by encouraging the use of technology to make platforms better, including the creation of a 'social media levy';
3. Embedding the use of safety by design for new and future online platforms;
4. Supporting children, parents, and carers by empathising the critical role education can play in protecting individuals from the 'harms' associated with the online world; and
5. Putting mechanisms in place to respond to online 'harms'.

An extremely modest plan in comparison to what was eventually produced.

In April 2019 the Online Harms White Paper was released, with its recommendations being labelled as 'ambitious'.[9] The key recommendation made in the paper focussed on holding social media companies directly accountable for content on their sites, as opposed to stakeholders working together which was emphasised in the 2017 Green Paper. The paper supported a 'new regulatory framework' to ensure the United Kingdom became 'the safest place in the world to go online'.[10]

What was first envisioned as a modest 20 page piece of legislation imposing a duty of care on some online platforms to protect its users from the 'harms' associated with the online world during its early conception, has changed dramatically. A draft version of the Online Safety Bill (OSB) was made publicly available in 2021 consisting of 145 pages. Since then, the magnitude and reach of the proposed framework has significantly increased, with a final version of the draft Bill being put before Parliament in March 2022. The OSB eventually passed through all

7 The Conservative and Unionist Party Manifesto, 'Forward together: Our plan for a stronger Britain and a prosperous future' (*The Conservative and Unionist Party*, 2017) 79 <https://ucrel.lancs.ac.uk/wmatrix/ukmanifestos2017/localpdf/Conservatives.pdf> accessed 22 September 2023.

8 HM Government (n 2) 3.

9 HM Government, 'Online Harms White Paper' (CP 57, 2019) 1.

10 Ibid.,

stages of the parliamentary process on 19 September 2023, receiving Royal Assent on 26 October 2023. It is now just over 280 pages in length with Paul Scully ex-MP noting at the time of its passing:

> The Bill is world-leading, and the legislative framework established by it will lead to the creation of a profoundly safer online environment in this country. It will kickstart change where that is sorely needed, and ensure that our children are better protected against pornography and other content that is harmful to them.[11]

8.3 The Parameters of the Online Safety Act 2023

The OSA imposes duties on providers of services regulated by the OSA to identify, mitigate, and manage the risks of 'harms' associated with the online world. The OSA applies to two types of online providers: user-to-user services and search services. Search services 'means an internet service that is, or includes, a search engine'.[12] For the purposes of this monograph, search services will not be discussed any further.[13]

Whereas, a user-to-user service is defined as:

> an internet service by means of which content that is generated directly on the service by a user of the service, or uploaded to or shared on the service by a user of the service, may be encountered by another user, or other users, of the service.[14]

With s.2(2) of the Act clarifying:

> (a) For the purposes of subsection (1) it does not matter if content is actually shared with another user or users as long as a service has a functionality that allows such sharing; (b) it does not matter what proportion of content on a service is content described in that subsection.

The scope of user-to-user services includes companies based both inside and outside of the United Kingdom, though the user-to-user service must have links to the United Kingdom. I.e., a significant number of users are based in the United Kingdom[15] or the United Kingdom is a target market.[16] During the parliamentary process, a further element was added to extend the scope of bodies falling within the definition of a user-to-user service to include services

11 HC Deb 12 September 2023, vol 737, col 799.

12 Online Safety Act 2023 s.2(4).

13 Under the Online Safety Act 2023, search services have several different requirements to adhere to as per Chapter 3 of the Act.

14 Online Safety Act 2023 s.2(1).

15 Ibid., s.4(5)a.

16 Ibid., s.4(5)b.

> (a) capable of being used in the United Kingdom by individuals, and (b) there are reasonable grounds to believe that there is a material risk of significant harm to individuals.[17]

Essentially allowing smaller companies who pose significant 'harm' to fall within the scope of the OSA, therefore extending the reach of the obligations under the Act from just the biggest platforms to include, smaller platforms that carry high risks.

However, it is important to note the requirements under the OSA do not extend to services which provide email only, text messaging only or one-to-one telephone calls only.[18] Furthermore, the following are also exempt from its requirements: review websites, internal business communications, public bodies, Parliament, those with foreign sovereign power, or journalistic material from a recognised news publisher.[19] However, it does apply to services which provide pornographic material.[20] As a result of the wide definition given to user-to-user services under the Act, many of the biggest social media platforms we know and use today, will fall within its scope. However, the duties applied to each platform will depend on how the platform is categorised, with the OSA setting out two categories for a user-to-user service:

- Category 1 platform—a user-to-user service which will have the most extensive duties to comply with.
- Category 2B platform—a user-to-user service which will only have to adhere to the minimum requirements set out under the Act.

Arguably, a third category exists, a platform that does not fall within the definition of a user-to-user service under the Act (though might be considered a social media platform) and therefore does not need to adhere to the requirements under the OSA.

As noted above, those who fall within the scope of a Category 1 service will have the most significant duties imposed upon them, as outlined in Section 8.4.2 below. Those who fall within a Category 2B service, will still have duties to adhere to, but these will not be as extensive. The idea is to ensure the protection of competition, whilst also ensuring the state does not overburden small user-to-user services or start-up companies. At the time of writing, who falls within each of these categories is still to be decided by the Secretary of State.[21] In addition, platforms which can be accessed by children (regardless of whether children SHOULD be on the platform) will also have additional duties, as set out in Section 8.4.3 below. And to complicate

17 Ibid., s.4(6).

18 Ibid., Schedule 1.

19 Newspaper publisher is defined under s.56(1) of the Online Safety Act 2023.

20 Online Safety Act 2023 Part 5.

21 Ibid., schedule 11 sets out the parameters that must be followed in determining what is a Category 1 and Category 2B platform.

things further, under provisional guidance created by OFCOM (currently under consultation at the time of writing) these platforms will be split into a further four subgroups (following the outcome of their risk assessment, discussed further in Section 8.4.1.1) to determine how they must adhere to their duties under the Act.[22]

8.4 The Requirements under the Online Safety Act 2023

The OSA is underpinned by three key objectives:[23]

1. Tackling illegal content and activity across user-to-user services;
2. Protecting children from 'harm' (this has become the mantra behind much of the discussions around the OSA during its conception and final passage through Parliament); and
3. Empowering users to make informed decisions about the content they wish to see by giving users greater control, whilst also protecting the right to freedom of expression and the right to privacy.

Failure to comply with the requirements set out under the OSA can have significant consequences for those who fall within its scope. OFCOM can impose a fine of up to £18 million or 10% of annual turnover (whichever is higher) on services for failure to comply with their duties (discussed further below) and in certain situations, company officials can be given a custodial sentence, for instance, for providing false information around child exploitation material online.[24]

The requirements placed on those who fall within the definition of a user-to-user service are extensive with the previous government, in their press release following the passing of the OSA noting:

> Social media platforms will be expected to: remove illegal content quickly or prevent it from appearing in the first place, including content promoting self-harm; prevent children from accessing harmful and age-inappropriate content; enforce age limits and age-checking measures; ensure the risks and dangers posed to children on the largest social media platforms are more transparent, including by publishing risk assessments, [and] provide parents and children with clear and accessible ways to report problems online when they do arise.[25]

22 OFCOM, 'Consultation at a glance: our proposals and who they apply to' (*OFCOM,* 9 November 2023) [1.3–1.4] <https://www.ofcom.org.uk/__data/assets/pdf_file/0023/271175/Consultation-at-a-glance-our-proposals-and-who-they-apply-to.pdf> accessed 1 January 2024.

23 Naomi Kilcoyne, 'The Online Safety Bill: Everything in Moderation?, Parts I and II, Content and Context' (*The International Forum for Responsible Media Blog*, 8 December 2022) <https://inforrm.org/2022/12/08/the-online-safety-bill-everything-in-moderation-parts-i-and-ii-content-and-context-naomi-kilcoyne/> accessed 5 October 2023.

24 Online Safety Act 2023 s.69.

25 Department for Science, Innovation and Technology (n 3).

The extent of these requirements, known as duties, is wholly dependent on how the user-to-user service is categorised.

8.4.1 The Minimum Duties for Category 1 and Category 2B Platforms

S.7(2) of the OSA sets out the minimum duties all user-to-user services must adhere to, regardless of whether they are a Category 1 or 2B platform. As a minimum, all providers must:

1. Complete an illegal content risk assessment;[26]
2. Act upon illegal content on their site, following the risk assessment;[27]
3. Create a content reporting procedure;[28]
4. Create a complaints procedure;[29]
5. Protect, maintain, and balance the right to freedom of expression and privacy;[30] and
6. Make and keep written records of all risk assessments.[31]

8.4.1.1 Complete an Illegal Content Risk Assessment

With guidance and a timeframe set out by OFCOM, all user-to-user services must complete an illegal content risk assessment. They must keep the risk assessment updated (reflecting any changes made by OFCOM as to what is considered illegal content) and before making any significant changes to a platform, the user-to-user service must carry out 'a sufficient illegal content risk assessment relating to the impacts of that proposed change'.[32] This is one of the broadest requirements under the OSA with s.9(5) setting out what should be included in the risk assessment, including, though not limited to, the level of risk to the user in being presented with illegal content, the different ways the service is used, how this can impact online 'harms' and the nature and severity of an online 'harm'.

For this to work, the OSA splits illegal content, for adults,[33] into two subcategories:

26 Online Safety Act 2023 s.9.
27 Ibid., s.10.
28 Ibid., s.20.
29 Ibid., s.21.
30 Ibid., s.22.
31 Ibid., s.23.
32 Ibid., s.9(4).
33 Content is categorised differently for children as discussed in Section 8.4.3.1.

1. Priority illegal content—content that is terrorist related,[34] offences related to child sexual exploitation,[35] or content related to any of the following:[36] suicide assistance; threats to kill; public order offences, including harassment and stalking; drugs or psychoactive substances; firearms or other weapons; assisting illegal immigration; human trafficking; sexual exploitation; sexual images, including extreme pornography and image-based abuse; proceeds of crime; fraud and some matters related to financial services; foreign interference; and inchoate offences. In essence, as highlighted in Section 8.4.1.2, priority content should not be seen by users.
2. Other illegal content—any other material which does not fall within the definition of priority illegal content but is a criminal offence under any of the criminal law frameworks of Scotland, Northern Ireland, England and Wales. In essence, as highlighted in Section 8.4.1.2, users should be limited from seeing other illegal content. The issues this poses with legality, in particular, not asking the impossible, is discussed in Section 8.5.1.2.

Draft guidance, created and issued by OFCOM, is currently under consultation at the time of writing to support user-to-user services in complying with this duty, in the form of a rubrics (labelled as risk profiles by OFCOM). In essence, using these risk profiles, companies will use evidence to determine if their platform poses a low, medium, or high risk of exposure to such content with OFCOM providing a four-step process.[37] Following the risk assessment, services must then act upon reducing illegal content on their sites.

8.4.1.2 Act upon Illegal Content on Their Site, Following the Risk Assessment

All user-to-user services must

> take or use proportionate measures relating to the design and operation of the service to (a) prevent individuals from encountering priority illegal content by means of the service, (b) effectively mitigate and manage the risk of the service being used for the commission or facilitation of a priority offence, as identified in the most recent illegal content risk assessment of the service, and (c) effectively mitigate and manage the risks of harm to individuals, as identified in the most recent illegal content risk assessment of the service.[38]

34 Online Safety Act 2023 Schedule 5.

35 Ibid., Schedule 6.

36 Ibid., Schedule 7.

37 OFCOM, 'Protecting people from illegal harms online. Annex 5: Service Risk Assessment Guidance' (*OFCOM*, 9 November 2023) 10–11 <https://www.ofcom.org.uk/__data/assets/pdf_file/0020/271163/annex-5-illegal-harms-consultation.pdf> accessed 1 January 2024.

38 Online Safety Act 2023 s.10(2).

Put simply, all user-to-user services must act to ensure users do not encounter illegal content and such content is 'swiftly' taken down. Though no definition is given to the term 'swift' under the OSA, or under draft guidance issued by OFCOM. Yet, when it comes to priority illegal content, services must act to 'minimise the length of time' in which such content is present on their site.[39] The problems this causes with legality are discussed further in Section 8.5.2.1. To assist with this duty, codes of practice will be issued by OFCOM, based on whether a platform is considered low, medium, or high risk of exposure to the 'harm' being assessed.

8.4.1.3 Create a Content Reporting Procedure

All services have '[a] duty to operate a service using systems and processes that allow users and affected persons to easily report' illegal content.[40] The procedure must be available to both users of the service and non-users provided the non-user is based in the United Kingdom and is either:

> (a) the subject of the content, (b) a member of a class or group of people with certain characteristic targeted by the content, (c) a parent of, or other adult with responsibility for, a child who is a user of the service or is the subject of the content, or (d) an adult providing assistance in using the service to another adult who requires such assistance, where the other adult is a user of the service or is the subject of the content.[41]

These processes must be easy to use, including for children.

8.4.1.4 Create a Complaints Procedure

A complaints procedure must be created by all user-to-user services. The system created must allow for a complaint to be made in the following situations:[42]

1. Content on a platform that is considered as illegal content;
2. The failure of the platform in not complying with its duties to remove illegal content (s.9), its duties in relation to content reporting (s.16) or not complying with its duties to protect freedom of expression or privacy (s.18(2) and (3));
3. Content that is removed from the platform that has been considered illegal;
4. Complaints with regards to action taken against a user, such as a suspension; and
5. The use of proactive technology in removing or restricting content or the technology has been used in a way that is not compatible with the terms of service.

39 Ibid., s.10(3)a.
40 Ibid., s.20(2).
41 Ibid., s.20(5).
42 Ibid., s.21(4).

The procedure must be 'easy to access, easy to use (including by children), and transparent.'[43]

8.4.1.5 Protect, Maintain, and Balance the Right to Freedom of Expression and Privacy

A duty which has been imposed on all platforms, which was used by the previous government as a counterargument to many of the critics of the OSA, is the duty to protect, maintain and balance the right to freedom of expression and privacy. In essence, every user-to-user service, '[w]hen deciding on, and implementing, safety measures and policies' have a duty to take into account 'the importance of protecting users' right to freedom of expression within the law' whilst also taking into account users' privacy.[44] Put simply, decisions made by user-to-user services must be underpinned by the right to freedom of expression and the right to privacy, including if reported content should be removed from a site, essentially allowing for the privatisation of speech regulation. The issues this creates are discussed further in Section 8.5.1.2.

8.4.1.6 Make and Keep Written Records of All Risk Assessments

The final duty imposed upon all user-to-user services is to keep the following written records:

1. The risk assessment carried out in relation to illegal content (as discussed in Section 8.4.1.1 above) and the children's risk assessment (as discussed in Section 8.4.3.1 below) including details about how the assessment was carried out and its findings;[45] and
2. A written record of how the service has complied with its duties against the recommendations made by OFCOM through codes of practice or if they choose a different route of complying with the duty other than the one recommended by OFCOM, what measures they put in place.[46]

These records must be accurate and made available to OFCOM, with OFCOM having powers under the OSA to enforce user-to-user services to hand these documents over.[47]

43 Ibid., s.21(2)c.
44 Ibid., s.22.
45 Ibid., s.23(2).
46 Ibid., s.23(3).
47 Ibid., Chapter 6.

8.4.2 Category 1

In addition to the duties above, those user-to-user services which are defined as a Category 1 platform, must also adhere to additional duties. As noted earlier, at the time of writing, it is not yet known who will fall within the scope of a Category 1 platform, though it is expected that the biggest platforms, such as Facebook, X, TikTok, etc., will likely be a Category 1 service for the purpose of the OSA. In essence, it will be for the Secretary of State, with guidance from OFCOM to determine the boundaries of a Category 1 platform, considering the number of users, functionalities of the services, how easy content is distributed on the platform and any other factors OFCOM feel are relevant.[48] A Category 1 services must, in addition to the above:

1. Adhere to additional requirements under the illegal content risk assessment duty;[49]
2. Empower adult users;[50]
3. Protect content of democratic importance, protect content generated by a news publisher, and protect journalistic content;[51]
4. Adhere to additional duties around content reporting;[52]
5. Adhere to additional requirements under the duty to protect freedom of expression and privacy;[53] and
6. Adhere to additional requirements under the duty to keep records.[54]

8.4.2.1 Adhere to Additional Requirements under the Illegal Content Risk Assessment Duty

In addition to the duties around illegal content risk assessments, as discussed above in Section 8.4.1.1, Category 1 platforms also have

> [a] duty to summarise in terms of service the findings of the most recent illegal content risk assessment of a service (including as to levels of risk and as to nature, and severity, of potential harm to individuals).[55]

8.4.2.2 Empower Adult Users

The overall purpose of the user empowerment duty is to allow users of a Category 1 service, greater control of the content they see on a platform. In essence, the

48 Ibid., Schedule 11.
49 Ibid., s.10(9).
50 Ibid., s.14.
51 Ibid., s.14; s.18 and s.19.
52 Ibid., s.21(6).
53 Ibid., s.22(4), (6) and (7).
54 Ibid., s.23(9) and (10).
55 Ibid., s.10(9).

attention of all users will be actively drawn to mechanisms on a Category 1 site to reduce the likelihood of seeing, or a user given a warning before viewing, content that may contain any of the following:

- the encouragement, promotion or instructions for suicide, self-harm, or eating disorder material;[56] or
- content that is abusive and targets, or incites hatred against another because of any of the following characteristics: race, religion, sex, sexual orientation, disability, or gender reassignment.[57]

The mechanisms used by a Category 1 service will be proportionate, taking into consideration the size and capacity of the service and the findings of a user empowerment risk assessment.[58] These mechanisms must be clearly stated in the platform's terms of service.[59]

In addition, all users will also be given the option to filter out non-verified users from both interacting with the user and encountering content that has been uploaded by a non-verified user.[60] Consequently, all Category 1 services will now need to give users an option to verify their identity. It is important to note, that this duty is not about putting blame on users for not taking control of their own settings, but instead ensuring platforms allow users to make informed decisions on what they would like to see online.

8.4.2.3 Protect Content of Democratic Importance, Protect Content Generated by a News Publisher, and Protect Journalistic Content

All Category 1 services are also under a duty to protect content of democratic importance. To do this, the platform must have proportionate systems in place (depending on the size and capacity of said platform) to ensure freedom of expression is considered when making decisions on the removal of democratically important content or where action is taken against a user regarding content of democratic importance.[61] S.17(7) defines content of democratic importance as content produced either by a news publisher or a user and 'the content is or appears to be specifically intended to contribute to democratic political debate in the United Kingdom or part or area of the United Kingdom'. This duty should be applied in a 'diverse'[62] manner to a wide array of political opinions and how a service is adhering to this duty must be clearly displayed in its terms of service.[63]

56 Ibid., s.16(3).
57 Ibid., s.16(4) and (5).
58 Ibid., s.16(1).
59 Ibid., s.15(7).
60 Ibid., s.64.
61 Ibid., s.17.
62 Ibid., s.17(3).
63 Ibid., s.17(4).

Similarly, Category 1 services are also under a duty to protect journalistic content to ensure freedom of expression is considered when making decisions on the removal of journalistic content or where action is taken against a user regarding journalistic material.[64] This includes a dedicated complaints procedure for the removal of journalistic material and a complaints procedure for a user who has action taken against them, for content they consider to fall within the scope of journalistic content.[65] For the purposes of this duty, journalistic content is considered material produced by a recognised news publisher or a user which is produced 'for the purpose of journalism; and the content is UK-linked'.[66] For instance, the United Kingdom is a target market or 'content is or is likely to be of interest to a significant number of United Kingdom users'.[67] How a company determines if content falls within the meaning of journalistic content must be clearly noted in its terms of service.[68]

In addition, in a further bid to protect the right to freedom of expression, Category 1 services are also obligated to protect content generated by a recognised news publisher. A recognised news publisher is defined as:

> any of the following entities—(a) the British broadcasting cooperation, (b) Sianel Pedwar Cymru, (c) the holder of a licence under the Broadcasting Act 1990 or 1996 who publishes news-related material in connection with the broadcasting activities authorised under the licence [… and are not excluded under further provisions contained in s.56(2) and (3) of the Act].[69]

In essence, any content that is produced by an organisation that falls within the definition above, is entitled to notice where a platform is considering taking action against them (i.e., removing such content from its site or restricting access). S.18 of the OSA sets out the procedure which must be taken to 'give notice'.[70]

8.4.2.4 Adhere to Additional Duties around Content Reporting

In addition to the requirements set out in Section 8.4.1.4 above, Category 1 services must also have a dedicated complaints procedure for grievances related to their

- User empowerment duty;
- The protection of material of democratic importance, news publisher content or journalistic material; and

64 Ibid., s.19.
65 Ibid., s.19(3).
66 Ibid., s.19(10).
67 Ibid., s.19(11).
68 Ibid., s.19(8).
69 Ibid., s.55(1).
70 There are some situations in which notice does not need to be given, for example, '[i]f a provider of a service reasonably considered that the provider would incur criminal or civil liability'. Ibid., s.18(4).

- Protecting the right to freedom of expression and privacy.

8.4.2.5 Adhere to Additional Requirements under the Duty to Protect Freedom of Expression and Privacy

All Category 1 services, in addition to the duties discussed in Section 8.4.1.5 above, must carry out an assessment on the impact any safety measures or policies will have on the right to freedom of expression and privacy, with particular regard to content produced by news publishers or journalistic content.[71] This assessment must be kept up-to-date and be publicly available,[72] including a statement on the positive steps the platform has taken to protect the right to both privacy and freedom of expression.[73]

8.4.2.6 Adhere to Additional Requirements under the Duty to Keep Records

S.23(9) sets out

> a duty to make and keep written record, in an easily understandable form, of all aspects of every assessment under section 14 (assessments related to adult user empowerment duty set out in section 15(2)), including details about how the assessment was carried out and its findings.

A copy of this written record must also be supplied to OFCOM.[74]

8.4.3 Accessed by Children

All user-to-user services are under a legal obligation to protect children on their platforms with a higher level of protection for children than adults online being considered a priority under the OSA.[75] Therefore, all services will need to carry out a children's access assessment to determine if children can access the platform or part of the platform. In which

> [a] provider is only entitled to conclude that it is not possible for children to access a service, or part of it, if age verification or age estimation is used on the service with the result that children are not normally able to access the service or that part of it.[76]

In essence, all services that fall within the scope of the OSA will need to embed some form of age verification software into their platform. The issues this presents

71 Ibid., s.22(4).
72 Ibid., s.22(6).
73 Ibid., s.22(7).
74 Ibid., s.23(10).
75 Ibid., s.11(1).
76 Ibid., s.13(6).

with legality are discussed further in Section 8.5.1.1. Regardless, many of the social media platforms we use today will have to adhere to additional duties to protect children online as most allow users to access their sites from the age of 13.

OFCOM, in their draft guidance on protecting children from online harms has proposed a two-stage test to adhere to this requirement. First, user-to-user services must determine if a child can access the service; Second, the child user service condition must be met.[77] I.e. a significant number of children can access the site and/or the service is likely to attract children.[78] In which OFCOM endorse a context specific approach in determining if the child user service condition is met.[79]

A user-to-user service will, therefore, be considered as 'likely to be accessed by children' in one of the following three situations:

1. The children's access assessment concludes that it is possible that a significant number of children in the United Kingdom can access all or part of the service or the service 'is a kind likely to attract a significant number of children' and there is no mechanism to stop children accessing the platform;[80]
2. Where a service fails to carry out a children's access requirement;[81] or
3. Following a failure to carry out a children's access requirement OFCOM concludes, after an investigation, that the service is likely to be accessed by children.[82]

The children's access assessment must be done at least once a year,[83] or before any major changes are made to the platform[84] or where concerns have been raised that the age verification software being used, is not working.[85] As noted above, draft guidance is currently under consultation at the time of writing with final guidance due to be published by April 2025, to help platforms adhere to this duty.

Following a children's access assessment, if it is found that a user-to-user service is available to children or is likely to be accessed by children, the platform must then adhere to a further two duties:

1. Carry out a children's risk assessment; and
2. Protect children from the 'harms' associated with the online world.

77 OFCOM, 'Children's Access Assessments: Draft guidance for consultation' (*OFCOM*, 8 May 2024) 11-24 <https://www.ofcom.org.uk/siteassets/resources/documents/consultations/category-1-10-weeks/284469-consultation-protecting-children-from-harms-online/associated-documents/a5-draft-childrens-access-assessments-guidance.pdf?v=336055?> accessed 10 July 2024.

78 Online Safety Act 2023 36(3).

79 OFCOM (n 77) [4.8].

80 Online Safety Act 2023 s.37(2).

81 Ibid., s.37(3).

82 Ibid., s.37(4).

83 Ibid., s.36(3).

84 Ibid., s.36(4)a.

85 Ibid., s.36(4)b.

Failure to adhere to these duties, as noted earlier in this chapter, can result in heavy fines, or in some cases, the imprisonment of company officials.

8.4.3.1 Children's Risk Assessment

A user-to-user service which is likely to be accessed by children is under an obligation to carry out a risk assessment, specifically looking at the risks to children on their site, even if children would not ordinarily be on the site—there needs to just be the mere possibility following the children's access assessment. This risk assessment needs to be kept updated and OFCOM notified of any significant changes.[86] Like that of an illegal content risk assessment, where a user-to-user service wishes to make a change to its platform, it must carry out a fresh children's risk assessment, before any changes are done.[87]

S.11(6) of the OSA outlines what should be considered during a children's risk assessment. This includes taking into account the risks posed by different age groups (because what might be harmful to a 13 year old, might be very different to someone aged 17). In addition, '[t]he level of risk of harm to children presented by content that is harmful to children which particularly affects individuals with a certain characteristic or members of a certain group' must also be considered when carrying out a risk assessment.[88] And like that of an illegal content risk assessment, further guidance and support will be issued by OFCOM to help support user-to-user services in carrying out this duty.

Whereas illegal content in relation to adults, as discussed in Section 8.4.1.1 above is split into two types (priority and illegal harms), for children, three categories of 'harm' are created under the OSA:

1. Primary priority content—as set out in s.61 this includes: pornographic material,[89] and content that encourages, promotes or provides instructions for suicide or an act of deliberate self-injury or an eating disorder. This material should never be seen by children.
2. Priority content which children should be protected from seeing - this includes:[90]
    a. Content that targets a person or incites hatred against another because of their race, religion, sex, sexual orientation, disability, or gender reassignment;
    b. Bullying content which either conveys a serious threat, can be labelled as 'humiliating or degrading' or forms 'part of a campaign of mistreatment';

86 Ibid., s.11(3).
87 Ibid., s.11(4).
88 Ibid., s.11(6)d.
89 Note there are some exceptions as set out in s.61(6) Ibid.,
90 Ibid., s.62.

c. 'Content which promotes or provides instructions for an act of serious violence against people' or depicts such content;
d. Content that promotes violence against animals, including providing instructions;
e. 'Content which encourages, promotes or provides instructions for a challenge or stunt highly likely to result in serious injury to the person who does it or to someone else'; or
f. 'Content which encourages a person to ingest, inject, inhale, or in any other way self administer—(a) physical harmful substance; (b) a substance in such a quantity as to be physically harmful.'

3. Non-designated content that is harmful to children—content that 'presents a material risk of significant harm to an appreciable number of children in the United Kingdom'[91]—come to be known as the lawful but awful clause. Put simply, this is content that is perfectly legal but could be considered as harmful to children, in which platforms will need to notify OFCOM if they come across such material. Examples given by OFCOM include: 'lived experience posts, speaking about anxiety, depression and self-harm' and 'posts portraying feelings of loneliness or inadequacy as helpless and/or deserved'.[92] The issues this presents with the right to freedom of expression and legality are discussed in Section 8.5.2.2.

These 'harms' must be considered during the children's risk assessment and all services likely to be accessed by children must also have a separate content reporting system for the above content.[93] What services must do when they come across these types of 'harms', is discussed in the following section.

8.4.3.2 Duty to Protect Children

Following the children's risk assessment, all platforms are under an obligation to protect children from the harms highlighted during their risk assessment. To do this, they must

> take or use proportionate measures relating to the design or operation of the service to effectively—(a) mitigate and manage the risks of harm to children in different age groups [...] and mitigate the impact of harm to children in different age groups.[94]

91 Ibid., s.60(2)c.

92 OFCOM, 'Protecting children from harms online: Volume 3: The causes and impacts of online harms to children' (*OFCOM*, 8 May 2024) 7.9.64 <https://www.ofcom.org.uk/siteassets/resources/documents/consultations/category-1-10-weeks/284469-consultation-protecting-children-from-harms-online/associated-documents/vol3-causes-impacts-of-harms-to-children.pdf?v=336052> accessed 10 July 2024.

93 Online Safety Act 2003s.20(4).

94 Ibid., s.12(2)a.

In addition, all platforms must

> operate a service using proportionate systems and processes designed to—(a) prevent children of any age from encountering, by means of the service, primary priority content that is harmful to children; (b) protect children in age groups judged to be at risk from other content that is harmful to children.[95]

What will be considered as proportionate will be determined by the outcome of the risk assessment and the size and capacity of the user-to-user service, with support from OFCOM. To aid in these duties, services must use age-verification.[96] Indeed, in draft guidance issued by OFCOM, emphasis is placed on making it harder for children to see 'harmful' content on user-to-user services, even if it can be considered age-appropriate.[97]

All services will also be under a duty to ensure they include in their terms of service details:

- Outlining 'how children of any age are to be prevented from encountering primary priority content';[98]
- 'How children of any age groups judged to be at risk of harm from priority content [...] are protected from encountering it';[99] and
- 'How children in age groups judged to be at risk of harm from non-designated content [...] are prevented from encountering it'.[100]

Furthermore, Category 1 services have '[a] duty to summarise in the terms of service the findings of the most recent children's risk assessment of a service (including as the levels of risk and as to nature, and severity, of potential harm to children)'.[101] Failure to adhere to these requirements can have significant consequences, including the imprisonment of company officials in certain circumstances.

8.4.4 Summary

The passing of the OSA has been hailed by government officials as being the first country in the world to legislate against the 'harms' associated with the online world,[102] though this is not necessarily true, as shown in Chapter 9. Yet, it will not

95 Ibid., s.12(3).
96 Ibid., s.12(4).
97 OFCOM, 'Webinar 3: An Introduction to the Draft Children's Safety Codes of Practice' (*YouTube*, 6 June 2024) <https://www.youtube.com/watch?v=A2mRx5Myj0I&list=PLq5bH2AD0WPmlNP-reUIKf04KkaZ2ZpOA&index=12 accessed 10 July 2024.
98 Online Safety Act 2023 s.12(9)a.
99 Ibid., s.12(9)b.
100 Ibid., s.12(9)c.
101 Ibid., s.10(9).
102 Department for Digital, Culture, Media and Sport and The Rt Hon Nadine Dorries MP, 'World-first online safety laws introduced in Parliament' (*Gov.uk*, 17 March 2022) <https://www.gov.uk/government/news/world-first-online-safety-laws-introduced-in-parliament> accessed 5 January 2023.

be known for several years as to whether the United Kingdom has achieved its aim of becoming one of the safest places in the world to go online, as the OSA is only a small aspect. Full guidance giving life to the OSA is expected in due course from OFCOM, with all guidance not expected to be completed and fully enforced by OFCOM until at least early 2026.

Nonetheless, from the discussions above, it is clear the requirements under the Act are extensive, overly complex and are embedded in vague terminology—despite the duties to protect the right to freedom of expression and the right to privacy. And as will be demonstrated below, we are slowly moving towards the privatisation of speech, in which services that fall within the scope of the OSA, will become the judge and jury of what is, or is not, legal online.

8.5 The Online Safety Act 2023, Freedom of Expression, and Legality

The implementation of the OSA is contentious, to say the least. It was considered by the acting conservative government at its time of passing as a significant step forward in protecting individuals, particularly children, from the 'harms' associated with the online world. Yet 'despite good intentions, the legislation in its current form leaves many open questions and has the potential to lead to unintended and damaging outcomes'.[103] The Act itself is merely a skeleton, with further guidance to come from both the Secretary of State and OFCOM to add meat to its bones.

As will be shown below, the OSA is so overly complex, legality is at risk, and in turn, there is no doubt that freedom of expression is under threat. To demonstrate this, two areas will be of focus (though there is much more that renders issues with legality, such as the discretionary powers given to the Secretary of State and OFCOM—but is beyond the scope of this chapter):

1. Asking the impossible—of focus will be the requirement to use proactive technology to ensure children cannot access a site, or certain areas of a site, and asking social media companies to become the judge and jury in deciding if a post could reasonably be considered as a breach of the law (in either Scotland, Northern Ireland, or England and Wales); and
2. Lack of clarity in the law—of focus will be the requirement to remove illegal content 'swiftly' and 'non-designated content that is harmful to children'.

8.5.1 Asking the Impossible: Proactive Technology and Interpreting the Criminal Law

Throughout various points in the OSA, the requirements being placed on those who fall within its scope is impossible to adhere to. Two significant impossibilities

103 Tymkiw (n 5).

relate to the reliance on proactive technology to verify a user's age and the requirement that platforms, when reviewing flagged content, interpret the criminal law framework of the whole of the United Kingdom—to determine if such content flagged, can reasonably be considered as 'unlawful'. A task which has proven difficult for the courts themselves, as highlighted throughout earlier chapters of this monograph.

8.5.1.1 Proactive Technology and Verification of Age

As noted above, one of the underlying principles of the OSA is to protect young people from the 'harms' associated with the online world. All platforms will therefore be asked to carry out a children's access assessment to see if children can access their platform, even if they are not meant to be on the service. To do this, as required under the OSA, all user-to-user services will need to embed proactive technology, such as facial recognition, into their sites—failure to do so, would mean that a site will automatically be considered as 'likely to be accessed by children'. Essentially, legally enforcing minimum age requirements upon platforms, following their failure to ensure only those who are age appropriate can use their service. I.e., those over the age of 13.[104] To adhere to this requirement, platforms could use their own proactive technology, provided it is adequate, or technology endorsed by OFCOM. Using the technology endorsed by OFCOM would automatically render the platform compatible with this duty.

OFCOM, in their draft guidance which is currently under consultation at the time of writing, emphasis that to meet this duty, the age-assurance/verification software needs to be 'highly effective'.[105] To be considered 'highly effective' such software needs to be technically accurate, robust, reliable, and fair (i.e., ensuring the software is not biased).[106] Yet, such technology, although does exist to some extent, is not 'yet foolproof, or indeed accurate enough to determine someone's exact age'.[107] Indeed, technology endorsed age-verification systems to solve the issues of the digital world are not new. For instance, in 2017 under the Digital Economy Act, Parliament attempted to enforce age-verification on pornographic sites (in a bid to stop young people from accessing such sites).[108] However, this section of the Act was eventually repealed due to the 'complexities of implementation'.[109]

104 OFCOM, 'Children and parents: Media use and attitudes report 2022' (*OFCOM*, 30 March 2022) <https://www.ofcom.org.uk/__data/assets/pdf_file/0024/234609/childrens-media-use-and-attitudes-report-2022.pdf> accessed 31 January 2024.

105 OFCOM (n 77) [3.2].

106 Ibid., [3.4].

107 Andy Phippen, 'Online safety bill: why making the UK the "safest place to go online" is not as easy as the government claims' *The Conversation* (London, 26 September 2023) <https://theconversation.com/online-safety-bill-why-making-the-uk-the-safest-place-to-go-online-is-not-as-easy-as-the-government-claims-214290> accessed 1 January 2024.

108 Digital Economy Act 2017 s.16.

109 Phippen (n 107).

Subsequently, platforms are being required to do something that is currently unfeasible—verify the age of all their users to ensure children cannot access material which they should not be seeing—whilst also upholding the right to freedom of expression, which includes the exchanging of ideas. This could result in some individuals being prevented from accessing perfectly lawful content they are entitled to see, especially given that sites will be forced to prevent those under 18 from seeing lawful but awful material (an issue discussed further in Section 8.5.2.2). Making this aspect of the OSA currently unworkable and even if such technology did exist in the future, '[t]hese measures, if effectively implemented, will make it more difficult for young people to stumble across content meant for adults, but they will not prevent the determined teenager'.[110] Therefore not addressing the issues it set out to do i.e., stopping young people from seeing 'harmful' material online.

8.5.1.2 Interpreting the Criminal Law

Tackling illegal content online, like protecting children online, is another key principle behind the creation and implementation of the OSA. All services, regardless of category, are under a legal obligation to remove illegal content, upon notice of its existence, from its platform. As noted in Section 8.4.1.1 above, illegal content, in relation to adults, is split into two categories: priority illegal content and 'other' unlawful content—with significant weight being given to the ideal that priority illegal content should not be seen by users, but both being subject to the same takedown requests under the OSA. Similarly, for those platforms that are likely to be accessed by children, illegal content—primary priority content, priority content and 'non-designated content that is harmful to children' (discussed further in Section 8.5.2.2)—also needs to be removed/restricted from platforms. Current draft guidance from OFCOM attempts to clarify how this duty will work for content likely to be accessed by children. However, the focus of this section will be on the removal of illegal content for adults.[111]

Under current draft guidance, to adhere to this duty in relation to adults, platforms will be required to essentially interpret priority illegal content in line with the criminal law framework of the whole of the United Kingdom, to determine if a complained about post, or a post flagged by AI technology, could be considered as reasonably unlawful. To do this platforms must have 'reasonable grounds to infer that content is illegal content' based on 'reasonably available information'.[112] Reasonable grounds, as set out in s.192 of the OSA, might exist where a platform:

110 Ibid.,

111 OFCOM, 'Protecting people from illegal harms online. Volume 5: How to judge whether content is illegal or not? (Illegal Content Judgements Guidance)' (*OFCOM*, 9 November 2023) <https://www.ofcom.org.uk/__data/assets/pdf_file/0023/271148/volume-5-illegal-harms-consultation.pdf> accessed 31 January 2024.

112 Online Safety Act 2023 s.192.

> a) has reasonable grounds to infer that the conduct or behaviour element (the act which constitutes the offence) is present and satisfied; b) has reasonable grounds to infer that the mental element (the state of mind when committing the offence) is present and satisfied, and; c) does not have reasonable grounds to infer that a defence to the offence may be successfully relied upon.[113]

Though,

> [i]t is important to note that 'reasonable grounds to infer' is a new legal threshold and is different from the 'beyond reasonable doubt' threshold used by the criminal courts. The 'beyond reasonable doubt' threshold is a finding that only UK courts can reach. When the 'beyond reasonable doubt' threshold is found in UK courts, the person(s) responsible for the relevant illegal activity will face criminal conviction. However, when services have established 'reasonable ground to infer' that content is illegal according to the Act, this does not mean that the user will necessarily face any criminal liability for the content and nor is it necessary that any user has been prosecuted or convicted of a criminal offence in respect of such content. When services make an illegal content judgement in relation to particular content and have reasonable grounds to infer that the content is illegal, the content must however be taken down.[114]

'Reasonably available information' could include content information, complaints information, user profile information, user profile activity, and published information.[115]

Essentially, a burden of proof less than the balance of probabilities has been created. To aid with this process, OFCOM proposes, in relation to restricting content for adults, providing in-depth guidance on the interpretation of the priority offences set out in Schedules 5 to 7 of the OSA only, with some minor exceptions.[116] Whereas when it comes to 'other' illegal content, this only needs to be removed by services when a reasoned decision is put to them by law enforcement, or the material is found unlawful by a court of law.[117]

Put simply, under this duty, platforms, with some support from OFCOM (depending on whether the complained about conduct is a priority offence or another offence), in legal terms, will need to interpret the *actus reus, mens rea*, and defences of a specific criminal act, against a piece of content that has come to their attention. A complex task for those working in the criminal justice system, let alone

113 OFCOM (n 111) [26.12].

114 Ibid., [26.14].

115 Ibid., [26.26].

116 OFCOM anticipate creating guidelines for the following non-priority offences: false communications; epilepsy trolling; assisting another to self-harm; and cyberflashing. Ibid., [26.72].

117 Ibid., [26.281].

private entities, with OFCOM noting that: 'some areas the law is uncertain and in others it is highly technical'.[118]

This includes interpreting all the provisions which have been discussed in previous chapters of this monograph. With hate related speech, cyberharassment and cyberstalking being defined under the Act as priority illegal content, with guidance for these offences being issued from OFCOM. Communication offences as set out in Chapter 6, including the 'new' offences discussed in Chapter 7, fall within the definition of 'other' illegal content and therefore no guidance will be available, with the exception of false communications. Instead, platforms will be required to remove 'other' illegal content when a reasoned decision is put to them by law enforcement, or the material is found unlawful by a Court of Law.[119] Despite, as an example, as highlighted in Chapter 6, the continued difficulties the criminal justice system has experienced in determining what is a 'grossly offensive' communication.

As highlighted throughout this monograph, often those working in the criminal justice system, have found it difficult to interpret these provisions accurately due to the vague terminology used in each provision. For instance, as discussed in Chapter 5, the European Court of Human Rights found the United Kingdom in breach of Article 10 of the European Convention on Human Rights, for its failure to consider the right to freedom of expression in the pursuement of another for harassment.[120] If judicially trained minds can come to diametrically opposite opinions on a set of facts, where the burden of proof is much higher (beyond all reasonable doubt) how are social media platforms supposed to adhere to these requirements? Yet, repeated failure to remove such content, will result in further action being taken. Leading essentially to the privatisation of speech as platforms are asked to do the impossible—police speech based on provisions grounded in vague terminology.

This will no doubt lead to unintended consequences. As eloquently put by Tymkiw:

> Would algorithms remove all tweets promoting an environmental protest, on the basis that they are procuring a Public Order offence? Would the UK population be banned from discussing the unofficial '420 Day', where cannabis producers, consumers, and advocates around the world celebrate marijuana use? Would discussion online about the pros and cons of buying shares be removed for potential violation of financial services legislation?[121]

Concerns which have been echoed in other jurisdictions that have used similar approaches to regulating the online world, such as Germany, as discussed further in the following chapter. McMillan highlights, with regards to Germany, that without

118 Ibid., [26.61].
119 Ibid., [26.281].
120 *Pal v The United Kingdom* (44261/19) [2021] 11 WLUK 603 Times, 9 February 2022 (ECHR).
121 Tymkiw (n 5).

legal expertise, private companies have 'suddenly become the investigator, judge, and executioner' of what is or is not lawful to say online.[122]

8.5.1.3 Summary

The requirements that user-to-user services use proactive technology and the further requirement to interpret the criminal law framework of the United Kingdom are, put simply, asking platforms to do the impossible. And as discussed in Chapter 3, the law should not, and cannot, in accordance with the principle of legality, ask the impossible. But the OSA does. It emphasises the importance of proactive technology in protecting young people from the 'harms' associated with the online world. Yet such technology is not yet 'foolproof' and failure to adhere to these requirements can invoke significant consequences, including prison sentences for company officials in certain circumstances.

In addition to this, private companies are being asked to do the work of the courts, in determining if certain content breaches the criminal law framework of the United Kingdom, whilst also balancing the right to freedom of expression. A duty, like ensuring children cannot access material they should not, that needs to be adhered to, otherwise, a platform could be in breach of the OSA. However, this monograph has proven the difficulties for judicially trained minds in determining if a message is unlawful or indeed, protected under the right to freedom of expression. A clear example of this is *Chambers v DPP*,[123] discussed in Chapter 6. Both the Magistrates' Court and the Crown Court concluded that Chambers had sent a menacing message contrary to s.127(1) of the Communications Act 2003. The High Court quashed his conviction.

Now, under the OSA, companies such as Meta, X, and Snapchat will have to make these decisions. And although the takedown of material user-to-user services deem unlawful will not necessarily meet the threshold of a criminal offence (as it's based on 'reasonableness' as opposed to 'beyond all reasonable doubt') private entities are now the gatekeepers of the right to freedom of expression. Though it could be suggested that since the creation of social media, this has always been the case, as platforms have always been able to determine what is and is not acceptable on their services in accordance with their own terms of service, there are ample examples of platforms getting this wrong. For example, Facebook has previously come under heavy criticism for removing the American Declaration of Independence, after AI technology flagged it as hate speech.[124] If platforms have struggled to interpret their own terms of service against the right to freedom of

122 Robert Gorwa, 'Elections, institutions, and the regulatory politics of platform governance: The case of the German NetzDG' (2021) 45(6) Telecommun. Policy 1, 7.

123 *Chambers v DPP* [2012] EWHC 2157 (Admin), [2013] 1 W.L.R. 183.

124 The BBC, 'Facebook finds Independence document "racist"' *The BBC* (London, 5 July 2018) <https://www.bbc.co.uk/news/technology-44722728> accessed 1 January 2024.

expression, how are they now expected to interpret the criminal law framework of the whole of the United Kingdom? And to complete this task 'swiftly'?

8.5.2 The Repetition of Vague Terminology

Similar to other provisions discussed in this monograph, the OSA is grounded in vague terminology, with this being a deliberate and considered choice by lawmakers, to ensure the OSA is as future proofed as possible.[125] Though it is accepted that the OSA needs to be able to adapt to future changes in technology, especially as we move away from Web 2.0 into Web 3.0 and the Metaverse, some elements are so inherently vague, it renders significant issues with legality. Of concern, and will be the focus of this section, are the meanings, or in some cases, lack of meaning, given to the terms 'swiftly' and 'harmful material to children'.

8.5.2.1 The Meaning of Swiftly

As noted in Section 8.4.1.2 above, platforms will be under a duty to remove unlawful content, which has come to the company's attention, either by AI technology or being flagged by users, 'swiftly'. The OSA does not define the term 'swiftly' and provisional guidance from OFCOM indicates that they too, will not define what it considers as 'swift'. Justifying this decision by stating:

> we are conscious of the risk of perverse outcomes if the regulator were to suggest a one size fits all approach to deadlines for content moderation processes, including those for complaints. It could lead to resources being diverted from types of illegal content which due to their virality cause harm to very many people, resources being diverted from very serious harms which are not illegal (for example, harms to children), or to decisions being made incorrectly due to time pressures.[126]

Instead, it will be for platforms themselves, to determine in their own risk assessments (as part of additional duties under the OSA) what they consider to be 'swift' in the takedown of illegal content:

> To comply with these duties, OFCOM recommends that all large and multi-risk services set and record internal content policies, measure their performance against recorded targets, adequately resource their moderation

125 HC Deb 12 September 2023, vol 737, col 802.

126 OFCOM, 'Protecting people from illegal harms online. Volume 4: How to mitigate the risk of illegal harms – the illegal content Codes of Practice' (*OFCOM*, 9 November 2023) [16.100] <https://www.ofcom.org.uk/__data/assets/pdf_file/0022/271147/volume-4-illegal-harms-consultation.pdf> accessed 1 January 2024.

functions and ensure employees involved in content moderation receive appropriate training.[127]

An interesting approach, given in the past, Facebook has been heavily criticised for its failure to act 'swiftly' in the takedown of a video livestreaming a terrorist attack in Christchurch, New Zealand in 2019.[128] The attack was livestreamed on Facebook, later being removed by the company around an hour after the event occurred. However, other Facebook users continued to reupload the video to the platform, along with the video being uploaded on other sites. In the first, 24 hours after the Christchurch attack, Facebook removed 1.5 million copies of the video from its site.[129] Though not considered by many, as quick enough.[130]

Even in other jurisdictions outside of the United Kingdom, there are inconsistencies in what is considered a reasonable time limit to remove unlawful content online. For example, in France, legislation was struck down by the French Constitutional Court for its requirement that social media platforms remove 'manifestly unlawful content' within 24 hours.[131] Yet in Germany, similar legislation requires platforms to remove such material within 24 hours of being notified of its existence.[132] Both approaches are discussed further in Chapter 9.

The ambiguous nature of the term 'swiftly'—which is defined by the Cambridge English Dictionary as 'quickly or immediately'[133]—does not ensure the law is action-guiding. What one platform might consider as 'swift' another may not. What OFCOM might consider 'swift' in one incident, might not be the same in another. Yet, consistent failure to remove unlawful content in a 'swift' manner can result in heavy fines under the OSA. This becomes of even more concern when platforms will be required to remove 'harmful content' for children, 'swiftly', given that what constitutes harmful in this instance, also lacks any form of clarity in the law.

127 Jessica Kingsbury, 'Ofcom's "Roadmap to Regulation" underway with its consultation on illegal harms duties under the Online Safety Act' (*The International Forum for Responsible Media Blog*, 17 January 2024) <https://inforrm.org/2024/01/17/ofcoms-roadmap-to-regulation-underway-with-its-consultation-on-illegal-harms-duties-under-the-online-safety-act-jessica-kingsbury/> accessed 17 January 2024.

128 Paul Karp, 'Australia passes social media law penalising platforms for violent content' *The Guardian* (London, 4 April 2019) <https://www.theguardian.com/media/2019/apr/04/australia-passes-social-media-law-penalising-platforms-for-violent-content> accessed 30 April 2019.

129 Jim Waterson, 'Facebook removed 1.5m videos of New Zealand terror attack in first 24 hours' *The Guardian* (London, 17 March 2019) <https://www.theguardian.com/world/2019/mar/17/facebook-removed-15m-videos-new-zealand-terror-attack> accessed 26 March 2019.

130 Karp (n 128).

131 Online Hate Bill (2020) Article 1. See, Chapter 9 for an in-depth discussion on the French approach to regulating the online world.

132 Act to Improve Enforcement of the Law in Social Networks (2017) s.3(2). See, Chapter 9 for an in-depth discussion on the German approach to regulating the online world.

133 Cambridge Dictionary, 'Swiftly' (*Cambridge Dictionary*, 2024) <https://dictionary.cambridge.org/dictionary/english/swiftly> accessed 29 January 2024.

8.5.2.2 Harmful Material to Children

For those platforms which can be accessed by those under the age of 18, they will be under a further duty to remove material that presents 'a material risk of significant harm to an appreciable number of children in the United Kingdom'.[134] In essence, material which is essentially legal but could be considered harmful, may, in some instances, be requested to be removed from user-to-user services. Some aspects of this provision are defined under the OSA, others, at the time of writing, are under consultation.[135]

The OSA defines harm under this provision as 'physical or psychological harm' taking into consideration '(a) the nature of the content; (b) the fact of its dissemination; (c) the manner of its dissemination', under s.234(2) and (3) of the Act. A significantly broad definition, in which platforms will also have to interpret 'non-designated content that is harmful to children' considering different characteristics of child users, such as age, race, disabilities, etc., with company officials facing imprisonment for repeated failures to protect children from the online world.[136] Current draft guidance issued by OFCOM has also attempted to bring some further clarity to this provision, by defining the following:[137]

- 'significant harm to an appreciable number of children in the United Kingdom' is to be interpreted as causing 'lasting or severe impacts on children's wellbeing, attitudes or behaviour, or attitudes or behaviours likely to cause harm to others'; and
- Material risk means the likelihood of it occurring.

In essence, it will be for platforms, with some support from OFCOM to determine what might be completely lawful, but harmful for children, rendering issues with the over-censorship of speech, using a 4 stage test:[138]

1 What harms are arising from children viewing online content?
2 Is the harm identified significant?
3 Is there a material risk of that harm occurring?
4 Are an 'appreciable' number of children in the United Kingdom affected?

Even with this further draft guidance from OFCOM, issues remain. For example, the following could all fall within the 'lawful but awful' clause for children:

- Material promoting gambling;
- Material discussing current events, for instance, ongoing wars, terrorist attacks, or criminal behaviour; or
- The promotion of unhealthy food.

134 Online Safety Act 2023 s.60(2)c.
135 OFCOM (n 92).
136 Online Safety Act 2023 s.11(6)d.
137 OFCOM (n 92) [7.9.13 - 7.9.14].
138 Ibid., [7.9.16].

This is just a small list of examples which could fall within the scope of the wide discretion given to platforms to consider what is lawful, but harmful to children as

> [p]latforms will be expected to make rules around content they deem might be harmful to certain users, and censor it before it can be published. As a result, this might also prevent children from accessing information related to gender and sexuality that could be caught up in the filtering and monitoring systems platforms will put in place. Without a clear definition of what harmful content is, it will be down to platforms to guess—and with moving goalposts, depending on the government of the day.[139]

As noted above, examples given by OFCOM which can amount to 'lawful but harmful' content to children could include: 'lived experience posts, speaking about anxiety, depression and self-harm' and 'posts portraying feelings of loneliness or inadequacy as helpless and/or deserved'. I.e., depressive content.[140] Of greater concern, is the recent discussions around the banning of under 16s from all social media platforms, which at the time of writing, was being mooted by some MPs[141] and being discussed in the media.[142] This has since been dismissed by the Labour Government, following a change in leadership.[143] However, the wide-reaching nature of the OSA and its grounding in vague terminology leaves the real possibility of it being open to abuse in the future.

8.5.2.3 Summary

Vague terminology is an issue that has been raised throughout this monograph and although the OSA was purposely created to be as broad as possible, to future-proof the Act, legality is clearly undermined. Platforms will be required to Act 'swiftly' to remove unlawful content, but no parameters have been set, either in statute or guidance as to what constitutes 'swiftly'. If user-to-user services are to adhere to the extensive duties to remove illegal content from their sites, they need to understand the full scope of their requirements, including, how long platforms have to remove such unlawful content. This is particularly acute where a law is complex and right and wrong are not easily identifiable and at the heart of decisions, is the right to freedom of expression. Indeed,

139 Phippen (n 107).

140 OFCOM (n 97).

141 The BBC, 'MP urges social media ban for under 16s' *The BBC* (London, 25 January 2024) <https://www.bbc.co.uk/news/av/uk-politics-68085378> accessed 31 January 2024.

142 Aletha Adu and Dan Milmo, 'Rishi Sunak considers curbing social media use for under-16s' *The Guardian* (London, 14 December 2023) <https://www.theguardian.com/media/2023/dec/14/rishi-sunak-considers-curbing-social-media-use-under-16s> accessed 31 January 2024.

143 Nathan Standley, 'Starmer against "simply banning" children's phones' *The BBC* (London, 12 July 2024) <https://www.bbc.co.uk/news/articles/cd1rklm6433o#:~:text=Prime%20Minister%20Sir%20Keir%20Starmer,dangers%22%20posed%20to%20children%20online> accessed 12 July 2024.

> Free speech as we understand it today relies on specific legal processes of protection that have developed over centuries. It's not an abstract idea, but one grounded in very particular social and legal practices.[144]

To understand these 'social and legal practices', time is needed. Time which platforms might not necessarily have, depending on how 'swiftly' is interpreted in future complaints that come to the attention of OFCOM. Although OFCOM will not be reviewing individual complaints, they will be making decisions on whether a platform has adhered to its duties under the Act, including the requirement to remove illegal content 'swiftly' even if we do not know what constitutes 'swift'. With the notion of 'swiftly' becoming even more complex in the requirement to remove legal, but harmful content from services.

Under initial drafts of the OSA, the 'lawful but awful' clause, as it became known, applied to both adults and children, with a decision later being made to remove this requirement in relation to adults, due to concerns over the right to freedom of expression.[145] Yet, it remains in place for children and what constitutes 'harmful' under this provision is anything that can amount to 'physical or psychological harm' with some, though inherently vague, parameters being set. For instance, considering the nature of the content of the communication. The justification for such vagueness is to allow for action to be taken quickly to protect young people from the 'harms' associated with the online world. But like that of adults, children are entitled to the right to freedom of expression, regardless of frontiers and to disseminate information.

8.6 Chapter Summary

Only time will tell if the OSA will ultimately achieve its aim of the United Kingdom becoming one of the safest places in the world to go online. But what this chapter has demonstrated is the complex nature of this piece of legislation, with only a small glimpse of just some aspects of the Act. As noted at the start of this chapter, to examine every aspect of the Act would be a book in itself. And yet, there is still so much unknown around the Act, as we await further concrete guidance from OFCOM to bring the OSA to life.

However, from what we do know about the Act thus far, it's overly complex, asking the impossible in some instances and grounded in vague terminology—risking the real possibility of the over-censorship of speech as we allow private entities

144 Phillip Seargeant, 'How AI threatens free speech – and what must be done about it' *The Conversation* (London, 18 January 2024) <https://theconversation.com/how-ai-threatens-free-speech-and-what-must-be-done-about-it-221330> accessed 31 January 2024.

145 Department of Digital, Culture, Media and Sport, 'Overview of expected impact of changes to the Online Safety Bill' (*Gov.uk*, 18 Jan 2022) <https://www.gov.uk/government/publications/online-safety-bill-supporting-documents/overview-of-expected-impact-of-changes-to-the-online-safety-bill#:~:text=The%20adult%20safety%20duties%20(%27legal,and%20freedom%20of%20expression%20duties> accessed 7 August 2023.

to do the work of public organisations. Of particular concern, as highlighted above, is the requirement for platforms to use proactive technology that does not yet fully exist, therefore asking platforms to do the impossible—embed proactive technology in their platforms which stops young people from accessing information or content they are not entitled to see. As noted by Seargeant, in relation to AI technology in general: 'The consequences of this are that AI-driven filters can often lean towards censoring content which is neither illegal or offensive'.[146] In which 'it's entirely possible that many young adults would be falsely identified as being minors—which might prevent them from accessing legal content'.[147]

Further concerns have been raised with the requirement for user-to-user services to remove unlawful content from their sites in line with the criminal law framework of Scotland, Northern Ireland, and England and Wales, swiftly. And when it comes to children, removing harmful, but legal content from their view. All of which threatens the right to freedom of expression.

But despite the former government preaching that the United Kingdom is the first country in the world to legislate against the 'harms' associated with the online world, this is not necessarily true, as shown in the following chapter. Many of the issues highlighted in this chapter, also apply to other countries' approaches to regulating the online world, in particular, social media platforms.

Reference list

Adu A & Milmo D, 'Rishi Sunak considers curbing social media use for under-16s' *The Guardian* (London, 14 December 2023) https://www.theguardian.com/media/2023/dec/14/rishi-sunak-considers-curbing-social-media-use-under-16s

Baker J, 'ORG Warns of Threat to Privacy and Free Speech as Online Safety Bill Is Passed' (*Open Rights Group*, 19 September 2023) https://www.openrightsgroup.org/press-releases/org-warns-of-threat-to-privacy-and-free-speech-as-online-safety-bill-is-passed/

Cambridge Dictionary, 'Swiftly' (*Cambridge Dictionary*, 2024) https://dictionary.cambridge.org/dictionary/english/swiftly

Department for Science, Innovation and Technology & The Rt Hon Michelle Donelan MP, 'Britain makes internet safer, as Online Safety Bill finished and ready to become law' (*Gov.uk*, 19 September 2023) https://www.gov.uk/government/news/britain-makes-internet-safer-as-online-safety-bill-finished-and-ready-to-become-law

Department for Digital, Culture, Media & Sport & The Rt Hon Nadine Dorries MP, 'World-first Online Safety Laws Introduced in Parliament' (*Gov.uk*, 17 March 2022) https://www.gov.uk/government/news/world-first-online-safety-laws-introduced-in-parliament

Gorwa R, 'Elections, institutions, and the regulatory politics of platform governance: The case of the German NetzDG' (2021) 45(6) Telecommun Policy 102

HC Deb 12 September 2023, vol 737, col 799 - 802

HM Government, *Online Harms White Paper* (CP 57, 2019)

HM Government, 'Internet Safety Strategy – Green Paper' (*Gov.uk*, October 2017) https://assets.publishing.service.gov.uk/government/uploads/system/uploads/attachment_data/file/650949/Internet_Safety_Strategy_green_paper.pdf

146 Seargeant (n 144).
147 Phippen (n 107).

Karp P, 'Australia passes social media law penalising platforms for violent content' *The Guardian* (London, 4 April 2019) https://www.theguardian.com/media/2019/apr/04/australia-passes-social-media-law-penalising-platforms-for-violent-content

Kilcoyne N, 'The Online Safety Bill: Everything in Moderation? Parts I and II, Content and Context' (*The International Forum for Responsible Media Blog*, 8 December 2022) https://inforrm.org/2022/12/08/the-online-safety-bill-everything-in-moderation-parts-i-and-ii-content-and-context-naomi-kilcoyne/

Kingsbury J, 'Ofcom's "Roadmap to Regulation" Underway with Its Consultation on Illegal Harms Duties Under the Online Safety Act' (*The International Forum for Responsible Media Blog*, 17 January 2024) https://inforrm.org/2024/01/17/ofcoms-roadmap-to-regulation-underway-with-its-consultation-on-illegal-harms-duties-under-the-online-safety-act-jessica-kingsbury/

National Society for the Prevention of Cruelty to Children, 'The Online Safety Bill Has Been Passed in "a Momentous Day for Children"' (*NSPCC*, 19 September 2023) https://www.nspcc.org.uk/about-us/news-opinion/2023/2023-09-19-the-online-safety-bill-has-been-passed-in-a-momentous-day-for-children/

OFCOM 'Children's Access Assessments: Draft guidance for consultation' (*OFCOM*, 8 May 2024) https://www.ofcom.org.uk/siteassets/resources/documents/consultations/category-1-10-weeks/284469-consultation-protecting-children-from-harms-online/associated-documents/a5-draft-childrens-access-assessments-guidance.pdf?v=336055

OFCOM, 'Protecting children from harms online: Volume 3: The causes and impacts of online harms to children' (*OFCOM*, 8 May 2024) https://www.ofcom.org.uk/siteassets/resources/documents/consultations/category-1-10-weeks/284469-consultation-protecting-children-from-harms-online/associated-documents/vol3-causes-impacts-of-harms-to-children.pdf?v=336052

OFCOM, 'Consultation at a Glance: Our Proposals and Who they Apply to' (*OFCOM*, 9 November 2023) https://www.ofcom.org.uk/__data/assets/pdf_file/0023/271175/Consultation-at-a-glance-our-proposals-and-who-they-apply-to.pdf

OFCOM, 'Protecting People from Illegal Harms Online. Volume 4: How to Mitigate the Risk of Illegal Harms – the Illegal Content Codes of Practice' (*OFCOM*, 9 November 2023) https://www.ofcom.org.uk/__data/assets/pdf_file/0022/271147/volume-4-illegal-harms-consultation.pdf

OFCOM, 'Protecting People from Illegal Harms Online. Volume 5: How to Judge Whether Content Is Illegal or Not? (Illegal Content Judgements Guidance)' (*OFCOM*, 9 November 2023) https://www.ofcom.org.uk/__data/assets/pdf_file/0023/271148/volume-5-illegal-harms-consultation.pdf

OFCOM, 'Protecting People from Illegal Harms Online. Annex 5: Service Risk Assessment Guidance' (*OFCOM*, 9 November 2023) https://www.ofcom.org.uk/__data/assets/pdf_file/0020/271163/annex-5-illegal-harms-consultation.pdf

OFCOM, 'Children and Parents: Media Use and Attitudes Report 2022' (*OFCOM*, 30 March 2022) https://www.ofcom.org.uk/__data/assets/pdf_file/0024/234609/childrens-media-use-and-attitudes-report-2022.pdf

Phippen A, 'Online safety bill: why making the UK the 'safest place to go online' is not as easy as the government claims' *The Conversation* (London, 26 September 2023) https://theconversation.com/online-safety-bill-why-making-the-uk-the-safest-place-to-go-online-is-not-as-easy-as-the-government-claims-214290

Seargeant P, 'How AI threatens free speech – and what must be done about it' *The Conversation* (London, 18 January 2024) https://theconversation.com/how-ai-threatens-free-speech-and-what-must-be-done-about-it-221330

Standley N, 'Starmer against "simply banning" children's phones' *The BBC* (London, 12 July 2024) https://www.bbc.co.uk/news/articles/cd1rklm6433o#:~:text=Prime%20Minister%20Sir%20Keir%20Starmer,dangers%22%20posed%20to%20children%20online

The BBC, 'MP urges social media ban for under 16s' *The BBC* (London, 25 January 2024) https://www.bbc.co.uk/news/av/uk-politics-68085378

The BBC, 'Facebook finds Independence document "racist"' *The BBC* (London, 5 July 2018) https://www.bbc.co.uk/news/technology-44722728

The Conservative and Unionist Party Manifesto, 'Forward Together: Our Plan for a Stronger Britain and a Prosperous Future' (*The Conservative and Unionist Party*, 2017)

Tymkiw N, 'The Online Safety Bill and the Risk of Unintended Consequences' (*The International Forum for Responsible Media Blog*, 11 April 2023) https://inforrm.org/2023/04/11/the-online-safety-bill-and-the-risk-of-unintended-consequences-nadia-tymkiw/

Waterson J, 'Facebook removed 1.5m videos of New Zealand terror attack in first 24 hours' *The Guardian* (London, 17 March 2019) https://www.theguardian.com/world/2019/mar/17/facebook-removed-15m-videos-new-zealand-terror-attack

9 International Perspectives on Social Media and the Law

9.1 Introduction

The issues discussed throughout this monograph thus far on the problems the digital world has created are not unique to the United Kingdom as 'free speech is not restricted by geographical boundaries any longer: with both positive and negative developments having a spill over effect worldwide'.[1] At the time of writing, governments across the globe are attempting to tackle the 'harms' associated with the digital age, through both the criminal law and social media regulation. This chapter explores the regulation of social media beyond the United Kingdom, focussing on France, Germany, and India. Each of these states, including the United Kingdom, have taken similar approaches to regulating (mis)behaviours online. However, the outcome of each approach has been significantly different—the rationale as to why these examples have been chosen.

In France, many provisions contained in the Online Hate Bill 2020 (OHB) were struck down by the French Constitutional Court for breaching the right to freedom of expression as guaranteed under both Article 10 of the European Convention on Human Rights (ECHR) and Article 11 of the Declaration of the Rights of Man and of the Citizen of 1789 (DRMC). Whereas in Germany the Act to Improve Enforcement of the Law in Social Networks 2017 (NetzDG), which inspired France's OHB, proved highly controversial when it was first enacted. Yet, NetzDG remains good law, despite continued concerns that the provision breaches both the right to freedom of expression and legality. Finally, India's Information Technology Act 2008 (IT Act) and the most recent enactment of the Information Technology (Intermediary Guidelines and Digital Media Ethics Code) Rules 2021 (the Rules), will be examined, providing a clear example as to why we should be careful when it comes to regulating the online world; whether through the criminal law or the regulation of platforms.

1 Raghav Mendiratta, 'India's IT Rules, 2021: Incompatible with the ICCPR and a fatal blow to democratic discourse' (*The International Forum for Responsible Media Blog*, 19 May 2021) <https://inforrm.org/2021/05/19/indias-it-rules-2021-incompatible-with-the-iccpr-and-a-fatal-blow-to-democratic-discourse-raghav-mendiratta/> accessed 31 July 2023.

DOI: 10.4324/9781003303688-12

9.2 France: Regulating Hate Speech

Like that of the United Kingdom, French officials have attempted to be proactive in trying to combat online hate, particularly in the wake of several terrorist attacks in and around France. France, again like the United Kingdom, is party to the ECHR and therefore is lawfully obliged to protect the right to freedom of expression, as guaranteed under Article 10. In addition, the right to freedom of expression and communication, as noted in the introduction, is further protected under Article 11 of the DRMC which states that:

> The free communication of ideas and of opinions is one of the most precious rights of man. Any citizen may therefore speak, write and publish freely, except what is tantamount to the abuse of this liberty in the cases determined by Law.

This right extends to internet communications.[2]

However the right to freedom of expression and communications is not absolute under Article 11 of the DRMC, and it can, and has been limited, but it must be necessary, appropriate, and proportionate to the objective being pursued.[3] For the Constitutional Council of France the right to freedom of expression constitutes 'a fundamental freedom, all the more precious as its exercise is one of the essential guarantees of respect for other rights and freedoms and for national sovereignty'.[4]

A balance must therefore be struck between a person's right to freedom of expression and communication and conduct that undermines public order and the rights of third parties.[5] A balance which was not struck during the creation and implementation of the OHB by the French officials resulting in its quick demise following the Constitutional Court of France concluding that many of the provisions set out in the Bill were unconstitutional. Indeed, for Senate Bruno Retailleau , the decision of the French Constitutional Court represented a total 'decapitation of the law' after six Articles were struck down and five were amended by the Court.[6]

9.2.1 The Online Hate Bill: Creation and Purpose

The OHB stemmed from a 2018 report into tackling racism and Antisemitism online.[7] The report recommended the creation of stronger laws to impose stricter requirements on social media platforms to report online hate, without any delay,

2 Decision no. 2020-801 DC of 18 June 2020 [4].

3 French Constitution Article 34.

4 Decision no. 84-181 DC of 11 October 1984.

5 French Constitution Article 34.

6 Decision no. 2020-801 (n 2)

7 Karim Amellal, Laetitia Avia and Gil Taïeb, 'Strengthen the fight against racism and antisemitism on the internet' (*gouvernement.fr*, 20 September 2018) <https://www.gouvernement.fr/sites/default/files/contenu/piece-jointe/2018/09/rapport_visant_a_renforcer_la_lutte_contre_le_racisme_et_lantisemitisme_sur_internet_-_20.09.18.pdf> accessed 6 June 2023 (translated 6 June 2023).

following growing concerns around the radicalisation of young people and terrorist, racist, antisemitic, and hateful content on the internet:[8]

> In this mechanism of hatred, the internet plays a key role, both by offering an unlimited number of spaces for expression, by ensuring the longevity of hate speech, but also as an instrument of propagation, 'virality', and amplification of hate speech.[9]

Such content as listed above, was seen not only as harmful to those who were subjected to such abuse but also posed a significant threat to democracy.

The purpose behind the OHB, following the 'Strengthen the fight against racism and antisemitism on the internet' report was to impose specific rules upon social media platforms to do more to tackle content that 'incited hatred and discrimination based on race, religion, gender, sexual orientation, or disability'.[10] In essence, pushing 'technology companies to regulate hate content more forcefully and to repress certain types of behaviours more quickly'.[11] Many of the proposed elements of the Bill would have made reforms to Article 6 of the 2004 Digital Economy Act in France. The Bill passed on 13 May 2020, with 255 officials in favour, 155 opposing, and 47 abstaining its passing.[12] Five days after its passing, 60 Senators appealed its implementation before the French Constitutional Court.[13]

The Bill itself imposed several obligations on social media platforms,[14] including though not limited to, the creation of more formalised notification methods which must be easily accessible and useable for all social media users in France; and increased transparency over content removal decisions and blocking content on mirror sites.[15] However, the most controversial obligation imposed under the OHB, under Article 1, was the removal of manifestly unlawful content from platforms within 24 hours of notification that such content existed, or in the case of child sexual abuse or terrorist content, one hour. Failure to comply could have

8 Ibid.,

9 Ibid.,

10 Giovanni Ziccardi, *Online Political Hate Speech in Europe: The Rise of New Extremisms* (Edward Elgar Publishing 2020) 153.

11 Ibid.,

12 Assemblée nationale, 'PPL visant à lutter contre les contenus haineux sur internet: adoption en lecture définitive' (*Assemblée nationale*, 13 May 2020) <https://www.assemblee-nationale.fr/dyn/actualites-accueil-hub/ppl-visant-a-lutter-contre-les-contenus-haineux-sur-internet-adoption-en-lecture-definitive> accessed 6 June 2023 (translated 6 June 2023).

13 Jacob Schulz, 'What's going on with France's online hate speech law?' (*LawFare*, June 23 2020) <https://www.lawfareblog.com/whats-going-frances-online-hate-speech-law> accessed 6 June 2023.

14 At the time in which the Bill was passed, and subsequently stuck down, it was not exactly known which internet platforms would fall within its scope. The law stipulated that only sites that surpassed a certain metric of monthly traffic would have been subjected to its provisions, but the figures were never determined. However, it is very likely it would have covered many of the social media platforms we use today. See, Assemblée nationale (n 12).

15 Ibid.,

resulted in the imprisonment of company officials or fines of up to 250,000 euros for each breach.[16] It is Article 1, which will be the focus of the remaining conversation on France's OHB.

9.2.2 The Online Hate Bill and Its Demise

As noted above, Article 1 of the OHB imposed significant obligations on platforms, including the removal of manifestly unlawful content within 24 hours. In essence, content that was considered manifestly unlawful, either by users or AI technology, *had to be removed.* Content that did not reach the threshold to be considered as manifestly unlawful could legally remain on the site (though platforms could have still removed such content, particularly if it breached a platforms community guidelines). Manifestly unlawful content included:

> Hate related content, which targeted an individual or a group on their origin, ethnicity, race, religion, gender, or gender identity, sexual orientation, or disability; or content that glorified criminal offences; or material that either denied or trivialised genocide, war crimes, slavery, or crimes against humanity; or sexual harassment, including the removal of pornography which could be accessed by minors.[17]

Like that of the United Kingdom's Online Safety Act (OSA), a hierarchy of illegal content was created. In the scenarios listed above, such content, under the OHB, had to be removed—there were no exceptions. So even in the hypothetical situation that content was not removed in the short timeframe due to technical issues, this would have still rendered a breach of Article 1 of the OHB. In addition, child pornography and terrorist content had to be removed, once reported, within one hour (under previous provisions, platforms were already under a legal duty to remove such content within 24 hours).[18] As with 'manifestly unlawful' content, there were no exceptions. Following the passing of the Bill, the French Constitutional Court was asked to consider Articles 1, 4, 5, 7, and 8.

The premise of the argument before the Constitutional Court, primarily focussed on the right to freedom of expression and communication, as protected under Article 11 of the DRMC. Considerable concern was raised against Article 1 of the OHB, with arguments being put forward that the lack of safeguards, such as there being no extension to the 24 hour rule, posed a significant threat to freedom of expression. In addition, arguments were put forward that the Bill created legal provisions which were, simply put, asking the impossible, which as explored in further detail in Section 9.2.4 below, is a fundamental breach of the principle of legality. These were concerns, which were echoed in the local media following the passing of the Bill, with ARTICLE 19 (a human rights organisation) being highly critical:

16 Schulz (n 13).
17 Assemblée nationale (n 12).
18 Decision no. 2015-125 DC of 5 February 2015.

> ARTICLE 19 is concerned that the French proposal of a Bill on Countering Online Hatred [...] fails to comply with international free expression standards. We warn that the Bill entrenches private censorship of a wide range of illegal content at the expense of the courts, the 24 hour-time limit on content removals is too short and the sanctions meted out to eradicate online 'hatred' are disproportionate.[19]

Other arguments put to the Court included a lack of understanding in some of the language used in the provision; some of the provisions contained in the Bill, already existing in the legal framework of France, creating contradictory law; and the possibility of excessive removal of online content—all of which threatened the right to freedom of expression.

Though the French Constitutional Court accepted that the OHB was enacted with good intention, they found that many of the prohibited types of content under the Bill undermined the right to freedom of expression and communication.[20] The Court concluded that in many of the Articles under scrutiny: 'the legislator ha[d] made an attack on [...] freedom of expression and communication which [was] not appropriate, necessary, and proportionate to the aim pursued'.[21] Many of the Articles contained in the provision, including that of manifestly unlawful content, were struck down as being unconstitutional with the Court noting:

> However, on the one hand, the determination of the unlawful nature of the content in question is not based on its manifest nature. It is subject to the sole discretion of the administration. On the other hand, the initiation of an appeal against the withdrawal request is not suspensive and the one-hour period given to the publisher or the host to withdraw or make inaccessible the targeted content does not allow him to obtain a decision from the judge before being forced to withdraw it. Finally, the host or publisher who does not comply with this request within this period may be sentenced to one year's imprisonment and a fine of 250,000 euros.[22]

Consequently, the Bill itself only made some very modest reforms after the judgment of the French Constitutional Court.[23]

9.2.4 The French Approach, Legality, and Freedom of Expression

The French approach to attempting to tackle the 'harms' associated with the online world posed significant issues with the right to freedom of expression. The Bill itself was highly controversial both inside and outside of France, with the European

19 ARTICLE 19, 'France: Analysis of draft hate speech bill' (*article19.org*, 3 July 2019) <https://www.article19.org/resources/france-analysis-of-draft-hate-speech-bill/> accessed 4 July 2023.

20 Decision no. 2020-801 (n 2) [13].

21 Ibid., [8].

22 Ibid., [7].

23 Schulz (n 13).

Commission warning that implementation of the Bill was 'likely [a] violation of the e-commerce directive and the Charter of Fundamental Rights of the European Union'.[24] Although the case before the Constitutional Court primarily focussed upon the right to freedom of expression and communication, as protected under Article 11 of the DRMC and Article 10 of the ECHR, there were also issues with the principle of legality—an argument supported further by ARTICLE 19.[25]

For example, the OHB was, at times, asking the impossible: 'these provisions would impose constraints on all publishers and hosts that are impossible to satisfy and would in doing so disregard the principle of equality before public charges'.[26] Under the principle of legality for a legal provision to adhere to this principle, it cannot ask the impossible, with Fuller giving the example of legally obliging someone to do something in one Act of Parliament but prohibiting them from doing the same in another.[27] In this case, it was put to the Court, that the requirements imposed under the Bill were impossible for some organisations to meet, and in turn, not only did this undermine the principle of legality but also equity before the law. An argument, that was accepted by the French Constitutional Court. Yet, as noted in Chapter 8, impossibility remains present in the United Kingdom's OSA.

Further, the requirement that content which could have been considered as 'manifestly unlawful' having to be removed within 24 hours, was also asking the impossible. During these 24 hours, moderators on platforms, or perhaps in some cases AI technology, would have had to determine, by reference to the criminal code of France, if the content flagged did constitute something that can be considered as manifestly unlawful. An impossible task to be completed in one 24 hour period. This therefore raises further legitimate concerns with how the United Kingdom have attempted to regulate the online world, through the creation and implementation of the OSA, as discussed in the previous chapter. Put simply, where a platform is given a time limit and failure to adhere to that time limit can result in heavy fines, there is a real and significant threat that platforms will remove such content anyway, to avoid punishment:

> given the difficulties in assessing the manifestly illegal nature of the content reported within the time limit, the penalty incurred from the first breach and the absence of any specific cause for exoneration from liability, the contested provisions can only encourage online platform operators to withdraw the content reported to them, whether or not it is manifestly illegal.[28]

24 European Union Agency for Fundamental Rights, 'French Bill on combating hate content on the internet' (*FRA*, 2019) <https://fra.europa.eu/en/content/french-bill-combating-hate-content-internet> accessed 4 July 2023.

25 ARTICLE 19 (n 19).

26 Decision no. 2020-801 (n 2) [3].

27 Lon L. Fuller, *The Morality of Law* (Yale University Press 1964) 70.

28 Decision no. 2020-801 (n 2) [19].

In essence, we run the real risk of lawful content being taken down when companies are asked to do the work of the Courts, without the expertise and coercive punishment is implemented. Indeed, as noted by Ziccardi in relation to the OHB:

> The approach of entrusting exclusively to platforms the duty to discipline and deciding on content had long been criticised, and raises problems of censorship with the risk that platforms under threat of sanction will be led to delete as much content as possible.[29]

The OHB also failed to adequately set the boundaries of the law, with it being suggested, using the provision of hateful and sexual material as an example (content which under the Bill was labelled as manifestly unlawful), before the Court that the offence was not 'defined in sufficiently clear and precise terms [... and ...] it could result from simple negligence'.[30] Similarly, in other parts of the provision, the word 'promptly' was included. For instance, under the Bill, platforms were under an obligation to promptly inform 'competent authorities about illegal content notified to them'.[31] Failure to adhere to this could have resulted in fines or in some cases imprisonment. However, no meaning was given to this term, with little clarity found elsewhere in the legal framework of France, as to the meaning of 'promptly'. For example, in a copyright case in 2012, five days were seen to fall outside the scope of 'promptly'.[32]

Despite the OHB no longer being legally enforceable, if it ever was, this Bill provides a leading example of why we need to be careful when it comes to regulating the online world, whether regulating platforms or individuals. Many of the concerns raised against this provision in France, resulting in its ultimate demise, applies to the OSA in the United Kingdom. As potently put by the Constitutional Court:

> The attack on the freedom of expression and communication therefore did not result from the fact that the unlawful remarks had to be withdrawn by the operators of the online platform, but from the fact that the system adopted by the legislator could only lead to also entail the withdrawal of lawful remarks for the sole reason that they have been the subject of a report.[33]

Concerns which have been echoed in Germany, following the creation and implementation of NetzDG, the inspiration behind France's attempt, and failure to regulate the online world through the OHB.

29 Ziccardi (n 10) 152.
30 Decision no. 2020-801 (n 2) [11].
31 ARTICLE 19 (n 19).
32 Schulz (n 13).
33 Decision no. 2020-801 (n 2) [8].

9.3 The German Approach: NetzDG

The French approach to online regulation, as noted above, was highly influenced by legislation passed in Germany in 2017: Gesetz zur Verbesserung der Rechtsdurchsetzung in sozialen Netzwerken (The Act to Improve Enforcement of the Law in Social Networks), commonly referred to as NetzDG. The rationale behind the implementation of the Act was to attempt to force companies to be more proactive, rather than reactive to the 'harms' associated with the online world, in particular hate speech, whilst also finding the balance between regulation and the right to freedom of expression.

Like France and the United Kingdom, Germany is party to the ECHR and therefore must comply with the protection of both the right to freedom of expression and the right to privacy, as outlined in Chapter 2. In addition, freedom of expression is further protected under Article 5(1) of the German Constitution:

> Every person shall have the right freely to express and disseminate his opinions in speech, writing and pictures and to inform himself without hindrance from generally accessible sources.

This right is not absolute and can be limited, as noted in Article 5(2): 'These rights shall find their limits in the provisions of general laws, in provisions for the protection of young persons and in the right to personal honour'. A clear example of this is NetzDG, which imposes several obligations on social media companies to combat hate speech, amongst other illegal behaviours, on their platforms. Most notably, NetzDG forces platforms to remove or block 'manifestly unlawful content' from its site in Germany within 24 hours of being 'flagged'[34]—a requirement which will be the focus of this section. Although this approach is similar to the OHB in France, as discussed in Section 9.2 above, unlike in France, NetzDG has stood the test of time and remains good law to this day—despite concerns being raised at the time that the right to freedom of expression and legality would be impinged. NetzDG is an important and significant legal provision as it is 'probably the first regulation in the world to directly proscribe how large user-generated content platforms moderated harmful content'.[35]

9.3.1 NetzDG: Creation and Purpose

In 2017 the Federal Government of Germany passed NetzDG which became legally binding on 1 January 2018,[36] following voluntary codes of practise failing to tackle

34 'Flagged' is a term used to describe when a communication online has been reported to the network host.

35 Robert Gorwa, 'Elections, institutions, and the regulatory politics of platform governance: The case of the German NetzDG' (2021) 45(6) Telecommun. Policy 1.

36 The Act was implemented in October 2017 however social media sites had three months from the implementation of the Act to comply with its conditions, before it became legally enforceable on 1 January 2018.

the ever-growing presence of online hate in Germany.[37] There were several aims behind the creation of the Act, most notably, forcing social media companies to be more proactive in removing illegal content from their sites, in particular, hate speech; impose punishments, including fines and in some cases imprisonment upon platforms who were slow to remove such content; and attempt to tackle the growing issue of 'fake' online news—which was being used as justification to target minority groups in and around Germany.[38] Leading the Federal Government of Germany to decide to legislate against fake news and online hate,[39] after finding that:

> Online discussions are often aggressive, abusive and hateful [...] Hate crime may seriously threaten the peace in a liberal, open, and democratic society if it's not suppressed and prosecuted effectively.[40]

As a direct result, the German government created and passed NetzDG through Bundestag in less than five months.[41]

NetzDG specifically applies:

> to telemedia service providers which, for profit-making purposes, operate internet platforms which are designed to enable users to share any content with other users or to make such content available to the public.[42]

This includes social media platforms, with over 2 million users, though like that of the OSA in the United Kingdom, journalistic content is exempt. Systematic breaches of the NetzDG by a platform can result in fines of up to 50 million euros.[43]

9.3.2 NetzDG: Initial Concerns

The Act itself imposes several obligations on those who fall within its scope including, though not limited to, transparent reporting systems for both users and non-users; a designated domestic point of contact to receive information requests from

37 Gorwa, (n 35) 4.

38 Fake news can be defined 'as information distributed via a medium – often for the benefit of specific social actors – that then proves unverifiable or materially incorrect'. See, Simeon Yates, '"Fake news" – why people believe it and what can be done to counter it' *The Conversation* (London, 13 December 2016) <https://theconversation.com/fake-news-why-people-believe-it-and-what-can-be-done-to-counter-it-70013> accessed 31 July 2018.

39 Lizzie Dearden, 'Germany to fine social networks up to €50m for not taking down illegal "fake news" posts' *The Independent* (London, 5 April 2017) <https://www.independent.co.uk/news/world/europe/germany-fake-news-social-networks-fine-facebook-50-million-euros-illegal-content-hate-speech-angela-a7668731.html> accessed 31 July 2018.

40 Federal Ministry of Justice and Consumer Protection, 'Questions and answers: Act to Improve Enforcement of the Law in Social Networks' (*German Government*, 2017) <https://www.bmjv.de/SharedDocs/FAQ/EN/NetzDG/NetzDG.html> accessed 31 July 2018.

41 This was arguably rushed through Bundestag due to an upcoming election.

42 Act to Improve Enforcement of the Law in Social Networks (2017).

43 If an honest mistake is made or a platform overlooks an item by error, there is no liability.

German law enforcement (with responses expected within 48 hours); six monthly transparency reports; and most notably the removal of unlawful types of content in a specified time period—the focus of this section.

For content to be considered unlawful under NetzDG, the conduct itself must breach the German Criminal Code. Under the German Criminal Code, multiple offences are prohibited which apply to the online world. Where a behaviour can constitute a criminal offence under the Penal Code, platforms must remove or block such content within a specified time limit. Put simply, platforms when making decisions on what content can be viewable in Germany, must make these decisions taking into account the German Criminal Code.

The specified time limit for social media companies to remove illegal content from their sites in Germany was, and still is, dependent upon the classification of the unlawful content. The Act places different time constraints on the removal of 'manifestly unlawful content' and content which is simply 'unlawful'. 'Manifestly unlawful content' must be removed or blocked from sites within 24 hours of being 'flagged'. Whereas content which is considered as 'unlawful' contrary to the German Criminal Code, must be removed within seven days.[44] Though unlike France's OHB, this seven day period can be extended.[45] Yet the Act did not, and still does not, clarify the difference between 'manifestly unlawful content' and 'unlawful content'—which raised significant concerns for many human rights organisations following the passing of the Act:

> The distinction between 'manifestly unlawful' and 'unlawful' is not clear, and difficult for a private enterprise to accurately predict: the Act provides no guidance to social networks on how they should differentiate 'manifestly unlawful content' from 'unlawful content', and contains no duty on the part of social networks to consider user's rights to freedom of expression when making these (even though law enforcement authorities are required to consider this when acting to restrict freedom of expression pursuant to the GCC [German Criminal Code]).[46]

Unlike that of the United Kingdom's OSA, there are no provisions contained in NetzDG protecting the right to freedom of expression. Indeed, there is no punishment for platforms that block or delete content which is *not* unlawful, only for systematically *failing* to block or delete content that is contrary to the German Criminal Code.

44 Act to Improve Enforcement of the Law in Social Networks (2017) s.3(3).

45 William Echikson and Olivia Knodt, 'Germany's NetzDG: A key test for combatting online hate' (*CEPS*, November 2018) 3 <https://papers.ssrn.com/sol3/papers.cfm?abstract_id=3300636> accessed 4 July 2023.

46 ARTICLE 19, 'Germany: The Act to Improve Enforcement of the Law in Social Networks' (*article19.org*, August 2017) 19 <https://www.article19.org/wpcontent/ uploads/2017/09/170901-Legal -Analysis-German-NetzDG-Act.pdf> accessed 13 July 2018.

For the campaign group ARTICLE 19, the passing of NetzDG was a clear violation of the right to freedom of expression:

> ARTICLE 19 finds the Act, taken overall, to be dangerous to the protection of freedom of expression in Germany, and we are particularly concerned that countered with much weaker institutional and legal safeguards for the protection of human rights are looking at this Act as a model for increasing intermediary liability.[47]

In essence, for ARTICLE 19, the requirements placed on platforms under NetzDG would mean that social media sites would have to act *too* quickly in the removal of content from their servers as there was (and remains) no guidance in place to protect freedom of speech. Consequently, arguments were raised suggesting social media sites would be more likely to be over-cautious creating an 'environment wherein lawful content is routinely blocked or removed as a precaution'.[48] This perspective was supported further by David Kaye, the former United Nations Special Rapporteur on Freedom of Expression:

> With these 24 hour [to] seven day deadlines—if you are a company you are going to want [to] avoid fines and bad public branding of your platform. If there is a complaint about a post you are just going to take it down. What is in it for you to leave it up? I think the result is likely to be greater censorship.[49]

Put bluntly, concerns were raised that a 'deletion orgy' would be an inevitable consequence of such vague terminology.[50] A concern which was echoed by the French Constitutional Court when striking down similar provisions in the French OHB.

These concerns surrounded the lack of clarity contained in the Act, in particular, the difference between unlawful content (which needs to be removed within seven days) and manifestly unlawful content (which needs to be removed within 24 hours). Neither were defined, therefore undermining the principle of legality. Though it is accepted that some form of vagueness is inherent in the law, as it would be impossible to legislate for all matters, citizens, or in the case of NetzDG social media platforms, must be able to govern their behaviour in accordance with law. In turn, the law must not ask the impossible. Here, arguably the requirements under NetzDG could be seen as breaching key components of the principle of legality, in particular, clarity, the action-guiding nature of the law and not asking the impossible. Indeed, following the implementation of NetzDG, several individuals in Germany had their social media accounts blocked by social media companies,

47 Ibid., 24.

48 Ibid., 1.

49 David Kaye, the UN's Special Rapporteur on Freedom of Expression. See, Patrick Evans, 'Will Germany's new law kill free speech online?' *The BBC* (London,18 September 2017) <https://www.bbc.co.uk/news/blogs-trending-41042266> accessed 31 July 2018.

50 Gorwa (n 35) 7.

who had perhaps been overcautious in their approach to interpreting the German Criminal Code, due to the vague requirements contained in NetzDG.[51]

9.3.3 NetzDG: Initial Concerns versus Reality

The passing of NetzDG has been described by Gorwa, as 'the best of bad options [*sic*]'[52], though since its enactment, 26 countries have passed similar legislation.[53] Yet, roughly six years since the implementation of NetzDG responses have been mixed:

> Supporters see the legislation as a necessary and efficient response to the threat of online hatred and extremism. Critics view it as an attempt to privatise a new 'draconian' censorship regime, forcing social media platforms to respond to this new painful liability with unnecessary takedowns.[54]

Some studies have shown that mass removal of content, which was the biggest fear following the enactment of NetzDG has not been proven.[55] Whilst on the other hand, arguments have been put forward that:

> Technology companies have no doubt acted cautiously under [N]etzDG by removing infringing content to avoid possible sanctions, which has led to satire material being incorrectly removed.[56]

At the point of writing, no consensus has been reached as to whether NetzDG has restricted the right to freedom of expression, or indeed, if the legislation has ultimately achieved its aim of reducing hate speech online. The German government has promised a study exploring the impact of this piece of legislation, but this is still forthcoming. To date, only two fines have been issued under the provision, both against Facebook and neither related to manifestly illegal or unlawful content.[57]

51 Philip Oltermann, 'Tough new German law puts tech firms and free speech in spotlight' *The Guardian* (London, 5 January 2018) <https://www.theguardian.com/world/2018/jan/05/tough-new-german-law-puts-tech-firms-and-free-speech-in-spotlight> accessed 6 August 2018; Joseph Nasr, 'Beatrix von Storch: German police accuse AfD politician of hate incitement over anti-Muslim tweet' *The Independent* (London, 2 January 2018) <https://www.independent.co.uk/news/world/europe/beatrix-von-storch-germany-afd-anti-muslim-twitter-north-rhine-westphalia-new-years-eve-a8138086.html> accessed 31 July 2018.

52 Gorwa (n 35) 10.

53 Rachel Griffin, 'New school speech regulation as a regulatory strategy against hate speech on social media: The case of Germany's NetzDG' (2022) 46(9) Telecommun. Policy 1, 6.

54 Echikson and Knodt (n 45) i.

55 Ibid.,

56 Written evidence from techUK (FEO0062). See, House of Lords, *Select Committee on Communications and Digital: Freedom of Expression Online* (HL Deb 2021-04, 23).

57 One fine related to misleading users into reporting content under Facebook's community guidelines as opposed to NetzDG (arguably to mislead officials on figures) and the other fine related to transparency reports.

Since its initial implementation, NetzDG has undergone multiple amendments, including additional transparency requirements; expanding the reach of the Act to include video sharing websites; and most controversially, requiring companies to send the personal information of users to the Federal German Police, who have had content removed for hate speech violations. This controversial amendment to NetzDG was reviewed by the German Courts, following Google, the owner of YouTube, taking legal action.[58] The German Administrative Court granted interim relief.

For Bayer, NetzDG has failed in its mission to stop extremist online behaviour, arguing that 'simply deleting or blocking this [extremist] content did not help to stop the tide of increasing extremist expressions in Germany'.[59] With Facebook, in the six months following the implementation of NetzDG, removing 21.2% of material reported for breaching the German Criminal Code; YouTube 27.1%; and Twitter 10.8%.[60] Put simply, NetzDG has not necessarily resulted in the mass take-down of content. To put this into context:

> Facebook's NetzDG transparency report shows that 74 pieces of content were blocked in Germany for inciting hatred. Within the same period, it removed a total of 6 million pieces of content globally for violating its community rules on hate speech.[61]

However, despite changes made to the law, NetzDG still offers no definitive definition of 'manifestly illegal content' and content that is simply 'unlawful'. With the list of criminal offences covered under this provision still being significantly broad, and continues to grow, as new criminal provisions make their way onto the statute book.[62]

9.3.4 NetzDG, Legality, and Freedom of Expression

NetzDG has created mixed debates since its implementation into the legal system of Germany. The law tackles the hosts of unlawful content, rather than the publisher, putting the onus on companies to remove illegal content from their sites rather than pursuing the individual who posted such commentary. A notion which Balkin defines as 'new school speech regulation'.[63] Put simply, new school speech

58 Reuters, 'Google takes legal action over Germany's expanded hate-speech law' (*Reuters*, 27 July 2021) <https://www.reuters.com/technology/google-takes-legal-action-over-germanys-expanded-hate-speech-law-2021-07-27/> accessed 1 January 2024.

59 Judit Bayer, 'Germany: New law against right-wing extremism and hate crime' (*The International Forum for Responsible Media Blog*, 24 April 2021) <https://inforrm.org/2021/04/24/germany-new-law-against-right-wing-extremism-and-hate-crime-judit-bayer//> accessed 7 July 2023.

60 Echikson and Knodt (n 45) 7.

61 Ibid., 8.

62 For instance, the criminal code has been updated to include explicitly criminalising threats of sexual assault.

63 Jack M. Balkin, 'Old-School/New-School Speech Regulation' (2014) 127(8) Harv. Law Rev. 2296.

regulation describes 'state regulation which coerces intermediaries into restricting speakers instead of coercing speakers directly'.[64] In essence, we have moved away from the regulation of individuals (old-school regulation), as discussed in Part Two of this monograph, to the regulation of platforms themselves (new school speech regulation). Yet this approach to regulation is contentious, with NetzDG providing a leading example with its compliance with the right to freedom of expression, and in turn, legality, being debatable.

For McMillian, although NetzDG is compatible with Article 5 of the German Constitution, due to the previous jurisprudence of the German courts, the provision itself remains incompatible with Article 10 of ECHR for two significant reasons. First, the vague language contained in the provision does risk the probability of over-blocking or the removal of lawful speech, without due process.[65] The vagueness inherent in the provision means that platforms are unable to guide their actions in accordance with clear and definitive laws, which in turn, risks them being overly cautious. McMillian further argues that the requirements imposed on platforms under NetzDG are not proportionate and in turn, are not taking the least intrusive method possible, to render it compatible with the right to freedom of expression:

> [NetzDG] suffers from the issues all laws passed with short notice and out of fear suffer from: it is vague, overbroad, and pins the moral blame for very real issues on the wrong individuals [...] The ECtHR should find that this law violates Article 10 for all criminal provisions other than those which implicate imminent violence or threats to government agencies.[66]

Second, the privatisation of the administration of justice is taking place: 'Now, without the guidance that years of judicial experience would provide, tech companies are sent out to sea to determine what content is manifestly unlawful'.[67] As potently put by McMillian

> whether something is insulting or defamatory to an individual is hard enough to determine [by the courts]. Whether it is insulting or defamatory enough to fine an intermediary is another question altogether.[68]

Without legal expertise, private companies have 'suddenly become the investigator, judge, and executioner' of what is or is not illegal to say or do online.[69] In turn, risking freedom of expression.

But as noted above, these concerns could arguably be misleading, with arguments raised by Griffin that privatisation concerns, such as those raised by

64 Griffin (n 53) 4.

65 Imara McMillan, 'Enforcement Through the Network: The Network Enforcement Act and Article 10 of the European Convention on Human Rights' 2019 20(1) Chic. J. Int. Law 252, 289.

66 Ibid.,

67 Ibid., 265.

68 Ibid., 284.

69 Gorwa (n 35) 7.

McMillian and Gorwa, are overstated.[70] Further, the lack of evidence available on the outcome of the implementation of NetzDG, means that conclusions are unable to be drawn. Although broadly speaking 'complaints are typically resolved within 24 hours and around a quarter result in removal; this has been interpreted as evidence both for overblocking and against it'.[71] In essence, a firm consensus cannot be drawn, though Griffin goes as far as suggesting that NetzDG, put simply, does not work.[72]

9.4 India: When Things Go Really Wrong

Like that of other jurisdictions examined throughout this monograph, the Indian government has also followed suit in attempting to regulate the online world. The Indian government has taken a two-stage approach to regulating unacceptable behaviour online in particular, unacceptable behaviour on social media platforms. First through the implementation of criminal law provisions to regulate individual conduct. Of note and will be the focus in the first part of this section, is the IT Act, which was amended in 2008 to include an offence of sending grossly offensive, menacing or false messages.[73] Second, through the regulation of intermediaries, including social media platforms, following the creation and implementation of the Rules, which will be the focus towards the end of this section. Though India is a very different jurisdiction compared to the European countries which have previously been examined, India has been chosen as a case study to illustrate why we need to be careful when it comes to regulating the online world, particularly when the rest of the globe are looking for inspiration in their own fight against the 'harms' associated with the internet.

In a well-functioning democracy such as France, Germany, and the United Kingdom (as discussed above and in the previous chapters) the use of vague terminology in legal provisions, might not necessarily be a cause for serious concern (though as highlighted throughout this monograph the author disputes this). However, when less functioning democracies take inspiration from these more 'stable' jurisdictions, the issues presented throughout this monograph become even more glaringly apparent, with India being a clear example of this, where there has been a growing trend in silencing voices across the state, particularly those online.[74]

Whereas Germany, France, and the United Kingdom, are all party to the ECHR, India is not. However, India is a signatory to the United Nations Universal

70 Griffin (n 53) 1.

71 Ibid., 10.

72 Ibid., 11.

73 Information Technology Act 2000 s.66A.

74 Toshaar Trivedi and Achyutam Bhatnagar, 'India: The dubious dilemma, muzzling fake news or gagging freedom of speech and expression' (*The International Forum for Responsible Media Blog*, 12 May 2021) <https://inforrm.org/2021/05/12/india-the-dubious-dilemma-muzzling-fake-news-or-gagging-freedom-of-speech-and-expression-toshaar-trivedi-and-achyutam-bhatnagar/> accessed 7 July 2023.

Declaration of Human Rights (UDHR) and acceded to the International Covenant on Civil and Political Rights (ICCPR) in 1948 and 1979 respectively. These provisions were discussed in Chapter 2. Both the UDHR and the ICCPR have had significant influence on the Indian Constitution—the supreme law of India—which amongst other protected rights, includes the protection of the right to freedom of expression: 'All citizens shall have the right (a) to freedom of speech and expression'.[75] There are however limits:

> Nothing in sub clause (a) of clause (1) shall affect the operation of any existing law, or prevent the state from making any law, in so far as such law imposes reasonable restrictions on the exercise of the right conferred by the said sub clause in the interests of the sovereignty and integrity of India, the security of the state, friendly relations with foreign states, public order, decency, or morality or in relation to contempt of court, defamation, or incitement to an offence.[76]

Of note, is the limitation on expressions which have the possibility to create public disorder or can be considered to impede on the decency or morality of Indian citizens, with the government of India using these limitations to justify the wide-reaching nature of the law under s.66A of the IT Act and most recently, during the enactment of the Rules in 2021.

9.4.1 The Information Technology Act 2000/2008

The construction of the IT Act in India is loosely based on the United Nations Model Law on Electronic Commerce 1996, with India at the time of passing the IT Act, being the 12th country in the world to pass legislation aimed at combatting the 'harms' associated with the online world. The Act itself was significantly updated in 2008 and contains more than just criminal law provisions—somewhat similar to the OSA in the United Kingdom. It covers, though not limited to, updating the law to recognise the importance of digital signatures; computer misuse; data offences; and specific criminal offences *akin* to communication offences which were found in the criminal law framework of England and Wales, as critically examined in Chapter 6. Of all the provisions contained in the IT Act, the most controversial was s.66A, which was written into the Act in 2008, after arguments were made that the law in India did not adequately protect individuals from online abuse.

S.66A of the IT Act stated:

> Any person who sends, by means of a computer resource or a communication device (a) any information that is grossly offensive or has [a] menacing character; or (b) any information which he knows to be false, but for the purpose of causing annoyance, inconvenience, danger, obstruction, insult, injury,

75 Indian Constitution Article 19(1).
76 Ibid., 19(2).

> criminal intimidation, enmity, hatred, or ill will, persistently by making use of such computer resource or a communication device [will be prosecuted].

A provision *akin* to s.127 of the Communications Act 2003 (CA) and the Malicious Communications Act 1988 (MCA) in their original format. However, there was a small, but significant difference between this provision and the provisions which were found in the law of England and Wales; the sending of false communications goes beyond annoyance or inconvenience, to include, amongst other situations, insult, hatred, or ill-will in India. In essence, the purpose of the provision was to criminalise the conduct of sending grossly offensive, menacing, or false messages online, to help reduce the use of the internet being used to abuse others.

The implementation of this provision into the IT Act was contentious. The lack of understanding as to what constituted a grossly offensive, menacing, or false message left some commentators concerned it would be abused.[77] A substantial concern given that the criminal justice system in India is overly slow, and open to abuse.[78] Concerns which quickly became a reality as s.66A of the IT Act proved to be 'totally subjective and depend[ed] upon individual judges'.[79] Consistency was therefore lost, and discretion, resulting in the abuse of s.66A, was rampant, which in turn, infringed dramatically on the right to freedom of expression across India. In many cases, individuals were often charged for an offence under s.66A of the IT Act, with other offences being tagged on, such as 'offending religious feelings'[80] or 'defiling sacred objects'.[81]

An example of the abuse of s.66A of the IT Act can be seen in the prosecution of Shaheen Dhada who, in 2012, posted the following, after the death of a controversial political figure in India:

> Every day thousand[s] of people die. But still the world moves on […] Just due to one politician dead. A natural death. Everyone goes crazy […] Respect is earned not given out, definitely not forced. Today Mumbai shuts down due to fear not due to respect.[82]

Soon after she posted the message on Facebook Dhada received phone calls from friends telling her to remove the message for fear of retaliation by authorities. Later the same day, she was arrested for her own safety after supporters of the political

77 Nikhil Moro, 'Social Media and Criminal Libel in India: A Case for Reform' (2020) 25(4) Comms L 209.

78 Madan B. Lokur, 'Justice Lokur: Our fundamental rights to free speech and protest are being eroded and mauled' *The Wire* (India, 12 October 2020) <https://thewire.in/rights/fundamental-rights-free-speech-protest> accessed 30 July 2023.

79 Moro (n 77) 218.

80 Indian Penal Code of 1860 s.295.

81 Ibid., s.295A.

82 Rajini Vaidyanathan, 'India Facebook arrests: Shaheen and Renu speak out' *The BBC* (London, 26 November 2012) <https://www.bbc.co.uk/news/world-asia-india-20490823> accessed 8 August 2018.

figure, took offence to the Facebook post. The next day after being held in a police cell overnight, Dhada was rearrested for violating s.295a of the Indian Penal Code, later being charged with a subsequent offence under s.66A of the IT Act. In addition, a friend of Dhada, Renu Srinivasan, was also charged with the same offence under the IT Act for liking, sharing, and commenting on the original post.[83] This is one of many examples in which s.66A, since its implementation into the IT Act in 2008, was used to limit the right to freedom of expression in India with the provision often being considered to be on 'shaky ground[s] constitutionally' due to the ambiguous terminology used in the provision.[84]

In 2013, the Supreme Court of India was asked to consider the compatibility of s.66A of the IT Act against the Indian Constitution, with significant weight being placed on its incompatibility with the right to freedom of expression in *Shreya Singhal v Union of India*.[85] In addition, the Court also examined if the provision complied with the principle of legality, in that could it be said that the provision was clear and predictable:

> a penal law is void for vagueness if it fails to define the criminal offence with sufficient definiteness. Ordinary people should be able to understand what conduct is prohibited and what is permitted. Also, those who administer the law must know what offence has been committed so that arbitrary and discriminatory enforcement of the law does not take place.[86]

The Supreme Court of India therefore looked at the language contained in s.66A including the meaning of the terms 'grossly offensive' and 'menacing', which as discussed in Chapter 6, has been of significant judicial debate in England and Wales.

The lack of a clear understanding as to what was meant by these terms for the Supreme Court of India raised legitimate concerns that the terms were too ambiguous, and consequently did not comply with the principle of legality and in turn, were incompatible with Article 19 of the Indian Constitution:

> Quite apart from this, as has been pointed out above, every expression used is nebulous in meaning. What may be offensive to one may not be offensive to another. What may cause annoyance or inconvenience to one may not cause annoyance or inconvenience to another. Even the expression 'persistently' is completely imprecise—suppose a message is sent twice, can it be said that it was sent 'persistently'? Does a message have to be sent (say) at least eight times, before it can be said that such message is 'persistently' sent? There is

83 Ibid.,
84 Moro (n 77) 220.
85 *Shreya Singhal v Union of India* (2013) 12 S.C.C. 73.
86 Ibid., [52].

> no demarcating line conveyed by any of these expressions—and that is what renders the Section unconstitutionally vague.[87]

Interestingly, the Supreme Court of India was concerned about the term 'persistently' and its lack of a definitive definition, a concern which has been echoed by ARTICLE 19 concerning Germany's NetzDG, as noted earlier in this chapter. To further examine the principle of legality and the prohibited behaviours under s.66A of the IT Act, the Indian Supreme Court examined in detail two cases stemming from English Law: *DPP v Collins*[88] and *Chambers v DPP*[89]—both of which were discussed in Chapter 6.

For the Supreme Court of India, the cases of *Collins* and *Chambers* provided undisputable evidence of the ambiguity of the terms grossly offensive and menacing and their lack of compatibility with the basic fundamental principles of legality, and in turn, threatened the right to freedom of expression:

> These two cases illustrate how judicially trained minds would find a person guilty or not guilty depending upon the Judge's notion of what is 'grossly offensive' or 'menacing'. In *Collins'* case, both the Leicestershire Justices and two Judges of the Queen's Bench would have acquitted Collins whereas the House of Lords convicted him. Similarly, in the *Chambers* case, the Crown Court would have convicted Chambers whereas the Queen's Bench acquitted him. If judicially trained minds can come to diametrically opposite conclusions on the same set of facts it is obvious that expressions such as 'grossly offensive' or 'menacing' are so vague that there is no manageable standard by which a person can be said to have committed an offence or not to have committed an offence.[90]

The clear lack of a definition as to what constituted a menacing or grossly offensive communication, led the Supreme Court of India to conclude that s.66A of the IT Act did not comply with the notion of legality in the criminal law and ran the real risk of breaching the right to freedom of expression. In essence, alongside the lack of clarity contained in the provision, s.66A provided no safeguards to protect the right to freedom of expression, therefore conflicting with Article 19 of the Indian Constitution. Consequently, this section of the IT Act was considered void by the Indian Supreme Court and struck down in 2015.[91] This was a most welcomed decision: '[t]he ruling is a huge victory for free speech in India.'[92] However, though

87 Ibid., [76].

88 *DPP v Collins* [2006] UKHL 40.

89 *Chambers v DPP* [2012] EWHC 2157 (Admin), [2013] 1 W.L.R. 183.

90 *Shreya Singhal* (n 85) [82].

91 Ibid., [119]. Other provisions were also struck down including the Kerala Police Act 2011. In addition, the Indian Supreme Court read down the meaning of s.79 of the Information Technology Act 2008.

92 Stephen Mathias, 'Section 66A Judgment' (2015) 31(4) C.L.S. Rev 573.

'widely celebrated as a landmark judgment on free speech',[93] in reality, this was not necessarily the case.

Research undertaken by the People's Union for Civil Liberties uncovered that five years after the Supreme Court struck down the provision, 800 cases related to s.66A, were pending before the Indian Courts.[94] This was despite s.66A technically no longer being on the statute book: 'right from the police station, to trial courts, and all the way to High Courts, one finds that s.66A is still in use despite it being denied a place on the statute book'.[95]

The research conducted by the People's Union for Civil Liberties provided concrete evidence that the change in law was not being implemented on the ground, particularly by law enforcement, with numerous examples being given in the report of the provision still being enforced even by the courts:

> We conducted advanced searches over two online databases; a popular public access platform (IndianKanoon) and another requiring subscription (Supreme Court Cases Online), to survey the extent to which Section 66-A continues to haunt the legal system. The data range for the period between January 2018 to September 2018 (till date) from IndianKanoon lists a total of 45 cases, while that for Supreme Court Cases Online from March 2015 till September 2018 is a total of 21 cases.[96]

As a consequence of these findings, the People's Union for Civil Liberties approached the Indian Supreme Court in 2021 with a writ asking for further directions as to the constitutional compatibility of the continued use of s.66A of the IT Act, with the Supreme Court ordering in October 2022 all pending cases, investigations and prosecutions under s.66A to be closed.[97]

It is not fully known why s.66A of the IT Act continued to be used across the criminal justice system in India, despite it being struck down. To explore this further, would be beyond the scope of this monograph. However, what is demonstrated is the importance of restricting the implementation of ambiguous legislation, which renders the possibility of abuse, especially when less democratic countries are taking inspiration from other jurisdictions. Illustrated further in the Indian government's attempt to directly regulate platforms, in particular social media companies through the creation of the Rules.

93 Sanjana Srikumar and Tanmay Singh, 'Third time lucky?: Section 66A and the afterlife of strategic litigation' (*Global Freedom of Expression*, 6 January 2023) <https://globalfreedomofexpression.columbia.edu/updates/2023/01/third-time-lucky-section-66a-and-the-afterlife-of-strategic-litigation/> accessed 1 July 2023.

94 Ibid.,

95 Abhinav Sekhri and Apar Gupta, 'Section 66A and other legal zombies' (*Global Freedom of Expression*, 6 January 2023) 3 <https://globalfreedomofexpression.columbia.edu/wp-content/uploads/2015/06/Sec.-66A-and-Other-Legal-Zombies.pdf> accessed 2 July 2023.

96 Ibid.,

97 Srikumar and Singh (n 93).

9.4.2 The Misguided War: Protecting Freedom of Expression

In recent years, the citizens of India have witnessed a decline and breakdown in civil liberties and the right to freedom of expression across India with a 'particularly disturbing trend [in] the silencing of voices through targeted prosecutions of activists, students, academics, protesters, and journalists'.[98] Most recently though, through the creation and implementation of the Rules in 2021, which, unlike India's previous approaches to regulating the online world, as discussed above, targets platforms as opposed to individuals, with criminal sanctions imposed on platforms for a failure to adhere to these new obligations. Although arguably this approach is *akin* to NetzDG and the OSA, the Rules do not contain any safeguards to ensure the protection of the right to freedom of expression. In turn, the provision has been drafted so significantly broad in places, that it renders issues with the principle of legality, posing a further threat to democracy across India.

The Rules, which became legally binding on 25 May 2021, were created by the Central Government of India through secondary legislation. In essence, the Rules were created by the government as opposed to Parliament, using the provision laid out in s.87(1) of the IT Act which states that: 'The Central Government may, by notification in the Official Gazette and in the Electronic Gazette, make rules to carry out the provisions of this [IT] Act'. Put simply, the Rules did not have any parliamentary oversight or debate before their implementation and although perfectly legal, this approach has been heavily criticised, particularly given the number of bodies who find themselves within the scope of the Rules. Alongside the vague nature of the provision which leaves the real possibility of the provision being abused by the state, as legality is not being maintained.

Like the OSA and NetzDG, the Rules impose extensive obligations on platforms within its scope to remove certain types of content within a specified time limit. Such content includes, though not limited to: discrimination; depiction of illegal or harmful substances; imitable behaviour; nudity; language; and sex.[99] Though, unlike the OSA and NetzDG, the Rules extend beyond intermediaries such as social media platforms and search services, to include traditional forms of media, such as news sites and on demand platforms, for instance, Netflix and Amazon.[100] Consequently, the platforms which fall within the scope of the Rules have been heavily criticised for their failure to protect and maintain the right to freedom of expression.[101]

98 Mendiratta (n 1).

99 Information Technology (Intermediary Guidelines and Digital Media Ethics Code) Rules 2021 rule 2H.

100 Ibid., rule 3. Although the use of the Rules to regulate the press and on demand services is of serious concern, this will not be explored any further here as it is beyond the scope of this monograph. Though it is important to note, some of the provisions which are of most concern when it comes to the regulation of social media platforms, are also applicable to these other types of intermediaries.

101 For example, Trivedi and Bhatnagar (n 74).

The Rules were created to specifically deal with the 'harms' associated with the online world, in particular, the 'harms' carried out on social media platforms. The Rules split social media companies into two categories: (1) a 'social media intermediary' and (2) a 'significant social media intermediary'. A 'social media intermediary' is defined as:

> an intermediary which primarily or solely enables online interaction between two or more users and allows them to create, upload, share, disseminate, modify, or access information using its services.[102]

A 'significant social media intermediary' is defined as a: 'social media intermediary having number of registered users in India above such threshold as notified by the Central Government'.[103] With the Internet Freedom Foundation noting that '[t]hese categories bring a high level of government discretion in determining which platforms need to comply with what regulations'.[104] Since the Central Government of India has set this bar at 5 million users. A number which has been set, with no parliamentary oversight. Of even more concern, the Central Government of India, under Rule 6(1) can declare a 'social media intermediary' as a 'significant social media intermediary' even if they do not reach the 5 million user threshold. In essence, the Indian government is free to declare a platform a 'significant social media intermediary' giving the Central Government of India wide discretionary powers, which undermines the principle of legality:

> The most subtle element in the task of maintaining congruence between law and official actions lies, of course, in the problem of interpretation. Legality requires that judges and other officials apply statutory law, not according to their fancy or with crabbed literalness, but in accordance with the principle of interpretation.[105]

Without clear and distinct rules as to when a body is considered a 'significant social media intermediary' platforms are under a continued arbitrary threat and accordingly, it cannot be said, that the law is action-guiding.

This is of particular concern because, like that of the OSA, those platforms which can be defined as a 'significant social media intermediary' have considerably more obligations to adhere to. As a minimum all social media intermediaries must, though not limited to:

- Publish all policies on their website;

102 Information Technology (Intermediary Guidelines and Digital Media Ethics Code) Rules 2021 rule 2W.

103 Ibid., rule 2V.

104 Krishnesh Bapat, Anushka Jain, Apar Gupta and Tanmay Singh, 'Deep dive: How the intermediaries rules are anti-democratic and unconstitutional' (*Internet Freedom Foundation*, 27 February 2021) <https://internetfreedom.in/intermediaries-rules-2021/> accessed 31 July 2023.

105 Fuller (n 27) 82.

- Have rules that prohibit 'the display, upload, modify, publish, transmit, store, update, or share any information that':[106]
  - Belongs to another;
  - 'is obscene, pornographic, paedophilic, invasive of another's privacy including bodily privacy, insulting, or harassing on the basis of gender, racially or ethnically objectionable, relating or encouraging money laundering or gambling';[107]
  - Is harmful to children;
  - Can be labelled as mis/disinformation; and
  - 'Threatens the unity, integrity, defence, security, or sovereignty of India, friendly relations with foreign states, or public order, or causes incitement to the commission of any cognisable offence, or prevents investigation of any offence, or is insulting to other nation'.[108]
- Produce yearly reports;
- Keep on file any material removed for 180 days for use by law enforcement; and
- Assist law enforcement within 72 hours.

In addition, where such material is reported, the platform must remove such material within 24 hours. Failure to adhere can result in heavy fines and like that of the OHB in France, there are no exceptions. Running the real risk of the over-removal of lawful speech, for fear of repercussions for leaving unlawful content viewable. This approach was seen as incompatible with the right to freedom of expression in France and is of great concern in India, due to continued evidence that democracy is slowly being eroded in this state.

Further additional requirements for a 'significant social media intermediary' include, though not limited to:[109]

- Appointing a chief complaints officer in India;
- Nominating a contact person in India who can help support the police and must be available 24 hours a day, seven days a week. They must also be different from the chief complaints officer and be based in India; and
- Publishing monthly compliance reports.

The requirements, therefore, placed on social media platforms are extensive, whether a 'social media intermediary' or a 'significant social media intermediary'. No further information is given in the Rules as to the meaning of the prohibited content. For example, it is not known what is harmful to children, what

106 Information Technology (Intermediary Guidelines and Digital Media Ethics Code) Rules 2021 rule 3(1)b.
107 Ibid., rule 3(1)b(ii).
108 Ibid., rule 3(1)b(vii).
109 Ibid., rule 4.

would constitute nudity as opposed to art or what would be considered fake news. These are left to the interpretation of the Indian Authorities, mainly the Central Government of India, The Ministry of Electronics and Information Technology, and the Ministry of Information and Broadcasting, with no parliamentary oversight. Once again, giving significant discretionary powers to government bodies, which in turn risks the law being unfairly enforced, especially where clear and distinct legal rules are lacking. All of which do not comply with the principle of legality.

The lack of understanding as to the extent and boundaries of many of the provisions contained in the Rules has led to significant criticism.[110] Many commentators are heavily critical of the Rules, for fear, like that of s.66A of the IT Act, the provision will lead to an abuse of power, particularly given the lack of legality contained throughout.[111] Concerns which are slowly starting to become a reality, following the Ministry of Information and Broadcasting asking social media platforms to remove adverts for a BBC documentary which was critical of the Indian Prime Minister, Narendra Modi, under the proviso that it threatened the 'unity, integrity, defence, security, or sovereignty of India' contrary to Rule 3(1)b(ii). In response

> [b]oth Twitter and YouTube quickly complied with the government's censorship requests. Posts on about 50 Twitter accounts were removed, with activists, politicians and even Hollywood actors among those affected, as well as an unspecified number of YouTube channels.[112]

By January 2023, action had been taken 'against 94 YouTube channels, 19 social media accounts and 747 URLs on the government's request' for failure to adhere to the Rules.[113] Indeed, at the time of writing more than 18 petitions challenging the constitutionality of the Rules before the Indian High Courts have been submitted,[114] with the Foundation for Independent Journalism wishing to get a Supreme Court decision declaring the Rules void due to their incompatibility with Article 19 of the Indian Constitution. Due to the inherently slow nature of the justice system in India, only time will tell if these Rules will remain legally binding.

110 See for instance, Bapat, Jain, Gupta and Singh, (n 104); Devdutta Mukhopadhyay, 'Now streaming: The chilling effect of the new IT rules' *The Indian Express* (India, 11 March 2021) <https://indianexpress.com/article/opinion/columns/new-it-rules-ott-platforms-content-youtube-netflix-amazon-7222873/> accessed 31 July 2023; Trivedi and Bhatnagar (n 74).

111 Mendiratta (n 1).

112 Hannah Ellis-Petersen, 'Indian ban on BBC Modi film puts Musk's Twitter "free speech" to the test' *The Guardian* (London, 25 January 2023) <https://www.theguardian.com/world/2023/jan/25/india-ban-on-bbc-modi-film-elon-musk-twitter-free-speech-emergency-laws#:~:text=The%20response%20by%20the,be%20banned%20on%20social%20media> accessed 31 July 2023.

113 Ibid.,

114 Apar Gupt, 'The IT Rules fail the test of constitutionality' *The Indian Express* (India, 1 October 2021) <https://indianexpress.com/article/opinion/columns/the-it-rules-fail-the-the-test-of-constitutionality-7542621/> accessed 31 July 2023.

9.4.3 The Indian Approach, Legality, and Freedom of Expression: Why We Should Care

The inclusion of India as a case study in this monograph as opposed to another European state may seem out of the ordinary, but it provides a prime example as to why states across the globe need to be careful when it comes to the regulation of the online world. Those countries which are more 'democratic' or 'stable' need to be careful they do not set a precedent, by using vague terminology in their own provisions, which could be abused by other states, looking for 'inspiration' in attempting to tackle the 'harms' associated with the digital world. The approach by officials in India reflects many approaches undertaken across Europe, with s.66A of the IT Act directly mirroring, in their original format, both the MCA and s.127(1) and (2) of the CA in England and Wales. Yet, in India this provision was heavily abused in restricting the right to freedom of expression, resulting in s.66A eventually being declared unconstitutional by the Indian Supreme Court. However, it remained on the statute book until very recently.[115]

A significant justification for s.66A being struck down by the Indian Supreme Court was the inherent vagueness contained in the provision:

> The court found that the provision was vague and overbroad—a significant finding given that the provision was overwhelmingly used to crush political dissent, and silence social and political commentary on social media and the internet.[116]

At no point could it be said that the provision complied with any of the requirements of the principle of legality. The vagueness in the terms contained in the provision lead to an abuse of power and in India, '[a]ny law which does not strike a proper balance between freedoms guaranteed and social control permitted by the clauses in Article 19 is an unreasonable restriction'.[117] Yet, such laws remain in England and Wales. But most concerningly the Indian government continues to create provisions similar to European approaches, which are so inherently vague they render incompatible with the basic principles of legality. Nothing demonstrates this more than the recent enactment of the Rules by the Central Government of India.

9.5 Chapter Summary

Regulating the online world, in particular, social media has proven a headache for governments across the globe, with there being no general consensus on how the digital world *should* be regulated. The countries discussed in this chapter were all chosen because of the similarities in approaches each has taken in regulating social media platforms. Yet the outcomes have differed dramatically. In addition,

115 Srikumar and Singh (n 93).

116 Ibid.,

117 *Chintaman Rao v State of Madhya Pradesh*, 1950 SCC 118.

the issues highlighted above, have also been raised against the United Kingdom's OSA—as discussed at length in Chapter 8.

In France, the French Constitutional Court struck down the OHB, following its failure to adequately set limitations to ensure the law was not abused and in turn, protected the right to freedom of expression. Significant weight was also given to the lack of legality within the provision, which was open to abuse. Whereas in Germany, similar provisions, despite initial concerns around freedom of expression and legality, remains legally enforceable. Indeed, research into NetzDG since its enactment has been mixed—neither confirming nor denying if the provision has hindered the right to freedom of expression. In India, similar legislation to both France, Germany, and the United Kingdom has been implemented into the legal framework of India, but such use of these provisions, many of which mirror European approaches to regulating the online world, have been heavily abused.

Without a consensus as to how the online world should be regulated, the issues highlighted above are going to remain and perhaps this is not an issue one country can tackle on its own. However, what is clear though, from the discussions above, is the need to ensure less 'stable' societies do not follow suit in enacting legislation grounded in vagueness and discretion, as has been the case in the United Kingdom, France, and Germany. India is a prime example of why we need to be careful when enacting legislation which does not comply with the principle of legality when the rest of the world is looking for inspiration in their own fight against tackling the 'harms' associated with the online world.

Reference list

Amellal K, Avia L & Taïeb G, 'Strengthen the Fight against Racism and Antisemitism on the Internet' (*gouvernement.fr*, 20 September 2018) https://www.gouvernement.fr/sites/default/files/contenu/piece-jointe/2018/09/rapport_visant_a_renforcer_la_lutte_contre_le_racisme_et_lantisemitisme_sur_internet_-_20.09.18.pdf

ARTICLE 19, 'France: Analysis of Draft Hate Speech Bill' (*article19.org*, 3 July 2019) https://www.article19.org/resources/france-analysis-of-draft-hate-speech-bill/

ARTICLE 19, 'Germany: The Act to Improve Enforcement of the Law in Social Networks' (*article19.org*, August 2017) https://www.article19.org/wpcontent/ uploads/2017/09/170901-Legal-Analysis-German-NetzDG-Act.pdf

Assemblée nationale, 'PPL visant à lutter contre les contenus haineux sur internet: adoption en lecture définitive' (*Assemblée nationale*, 13 May 2020) https://www.assemblee-nationale.fr/dyn/actualites-accueil-hub/ppl-visant-a-lutter-contre-les-contenus-haineux-sur-internet-adoption-en-lecture-definitive

Balkin J M, 'Old-School/New-School Speech Regulation' (2014) 127(8) Harv Law Rev 2296

Bapat K, Jain A, Gupta A & Singh T, 'Deep Dive: How the Intermediaries Rules Are Anti-Democratic and Unconstitutional' (*Internet Freedom Foundation*, 27 February 2021) https://internetfreedom.in/intermediaries-rules-2021/

Bayer J, 'Germany: New Law against Right-Wing Extremism and Hate Crime' (*The International Forum for Responsible Media Blog*, 24 April 2021) https://inforrm.org/2021/04/24/germany-new-law-against-right-wing-extremism-and-hate-crime-judit-bayer//

Dearden L, 'Germany to fine social networks up to €50m for not taking down illegal "fake news" posts' *The Independent* (London, 5 April 2017) https://www.independent.co.uk

/news/world/europe/germany-fake-news-social-networks-fine-facebook-50-million-euros-illegal-content-hate-speech-angela-a7668731.html

Echikson W & Knodt O, 'Germany's NetzDG: A Key Test for Combatting Online Hate' (*CEPS*, November 2018) https://papers.ssrn.com/sol3/papers.cfm?abstract_id=3300636

Ellis-Petersen H, 'Indian ban on BBC Modi film puts Musk's Twitter "free speech" to the test' *The Guardian* (London, 25 January 2023) https://www.theguardian.com/world/2023/jan/25/india-ban-on-bbc-modi-film-elon-musk-twitter-free-speech-emergency-laws#:~:text=The%20response%20by%20the,be%20banned%20on%20social%20media

European Union Agency for Fundamental Rights, 'French Bill on Combating Hate Content on the Internet' (*FRA*, 2019) https://fra.europa.eu/en/content/french-bill-combating-hate-content-internet

Evans P, 'Will Germany's new law kill free speech online?' *The BBC* (London, 18 September 2017) https://www.bbc.co.uk/news/blogs-trending-41042266

Federal Ministry of Justice and Consumer Protection, 'Questions and answers: Act to Improve Enforcement of the Law in Social Networks' (*German Government*, 2017) https://www.bmjv.de/SharedDocs/FAQ/EN/NetzDG/NetzDG.html

Fuller L L, *The Morality of Law* (Yale University Press 1964)

Gorwa R, 'Elections, Institutions, and the Regulatory Politics of Platform Governance: The Case of the German NetzDG' (2021) 45(6) Telecommun Policy 1

Griffin R, 'New School Speech Regulation as a Regulatory Strategy against Hate Speech on Social Media: The Case of Germany's NetzDG' (2022) 46(9) Telecommun Policy 1

Gupt A, 'The IT Rules fail the test of constitutionality' *The Indian Express* (India, 1 October 2021) https://indianexpress.com/article/opinion/columns/the-it-rules-fail-the-the-test-of-constitutionality-7542621/

House of Lords, *Select Committee on Communications: Freedom of Expression Online* (HL Deb 2021-04, 23)

Lokur M B, 'Justice Lokur: Our fundamental rights to free speech and protest are being eroded and mauled' *The Wire* (India, 12 October 2020) https://thewire.in/rights/fundamental-rights-free-speech-protest

Mathias S, 'Section 66A Judgment' (2015) 31(4) CLS Rev 573

McMillan I, 'Enforcement Through the Network: The Network Enforcement Act and Article 10 of the European Convention on Human Rights' 2019 20(1) Chic J Int Law 252

Mendiratta R, 'India's IT Rules, 2021: Incompatible with the ICCPR and a Fatal Blow to Democratic Discourse' (*The International Forum for Responsible Media Blog*, 19 May 2021) https://inforrm.org/2021/05/19/indias-it-rules-2021-incompatible-with-the-iccpr-and-a-fatal-blow-to-democratic-discourse-raghav-mendiratta/

Moro N, 'Social Media and Criminal Libel in India: A Case for Reform' (2020) 25(4) Comms L 209

Mukhopadhyay D, 'Now streaming: The chilling effect of the new IT rules' *The Indian Express* (India, 11 March 2021) https://indianexpress.com/article/opinion/columns/new-it-rules-ott-platforms-content-youtube-netflix-amazon-7222873/

Narayan V, 'Man booked under IT Act for "defaming" CM Devendra Fadnavis' *The Times of India* (Mumbai, 10 July 2015) https://timesofindia.indiatimes.com/india/Manbooked-under-IT-Act-for-defaming-CM-Devendra-Fadnavis-intweet/articleshow/48011122.cms

Nasr J, 'Beatrix von Storch: German police accuse AfD politician of hate incitement over anti-Muslim tweet' *The Independent* (London, 2 January 2018) https://www.independent.co.uk/news/world/europe/beatrix-von-storch-germany-afd-anti-muslim-twitter-north-rhine-westphalia-new-years-eve-a8138086.html

Oltermann P, 'Tough new German law puts tech firms and free speech in spotlight' *The Guardian* (London, 5 January 2018) https://www.theguardian.com/world/2018/jan/05/tough-new-german-law-puts-tech-firms-and-free-speech-in-spotlight

Reuters, 'Google Takes Legal Action over Germany's Expanded Hate-Speech Law' (*Reuters*, 27 July 2021) https://www.reuters.com/technology/google-takes-legal-action-over-germanys-expanded-hate-speech-law-2021-07-27/

Schulz J, 'What's Going on with France's Online Hate Speech Law?' (*LawFare*, 23 June 2020) https://www.lawfareblog.com/whats-going-frances-online-hate-speech-law

Sekhri A & Gupta A, 'Section 66A and Other Legal Zombies' (*Global Freedom of Expression*, 6 January 2023) https://globalfreedomofexpression.columbia.edu/wp-content/uploads/2015/06/Sec.-66A-and-Other-Legal-Zombies.pdf

Srikumar S & Singh T, 'Third Time Lucky?: Section 66A and the Afterlife of Strategic Litigation' (*Global Freedom of Expression*, 6 January 2023) https://globalfreedomofexpression.columbia.edu/updates/2023/01/third-time-lucky-section-66a-and-the-afterlife-of-strategic-litigation/

The Local, 'This is what Facebook moderators in Germany have to deal with' *The Local* (Stockholm, 16 December 2016) https://www.thelocal.de/20161216/this-is-what-facebook-moderators-in-berlin-have-to-deal-with

Trivedi T & Bhatnagar A, 'India: The Dubious Dilemma, Muzzling Fake News or Gagging Freedom of Speech and Expression' (*The International Forum for Responsible Media Blog*, 12 May 2021) https://inforrm.org/2021/05/12/india-the-dubious-dilemma-muzzling-fake-news-or-gagging-freedom-of-speech-and-expression-toshaar-trivedi-and-achyutam-bhatnagar/

Vaidyanathan R, 'India Facebook arrests: Shaheen and Renu speak out' *The BBC* (London, 26 November 2012) https://www.bbc.co.uk/news/world-asia-india-20490823

Yates S, '"Fake news" – why people believe it and what can be done to counter it' *The Conversation* (London, 13 December 2016) https://theconversation.com/fake-news-why-people-believe-it-and-what-can-be-done-to-counter-it-70013

Ziccardi G, *Online Political Hate Speech in Europe: The Rise of New Extremisms* (Edward Elgar Publishing 2020)

10 Conclusion

10.1 Introduction

There is no doubt that there is a 'darker' side to the online world, that is not under dispute in this monograph. But what is under dispute, is the continuous rhetoric that the only way to tackle these issues is by using the criminal law. The criminal law is a coercive tool and when embedded in vague terminology, is open to abuse. What is often lost in these conversations, as was highlighted in Chapter 2, is the 'good' that can come from engaging with the online world. The continued echo that there 'should be a law against that' is never going to tackle societal norms. Indeed, as noted by Reed and Murray, there seems to be a clash between legal norms and the norms of cyberspace:

> From a lawmaker's perspective, legal norms are by definition supremely authoritative in the geographical territory of their law systems. But does this weight of authority carry over into cyberspace? How well does the law compete with other norms we have described? The answer seems to be: not terribly well.[1]

This is complicated further when legal norms are being applied to online abuse, an ambiguous term, as discussed in Chapter 6, that often invokes strong opinions on both sides of the debate.

Throughout various chapters of this monograph, it has been shown that many of the provisions currently used to tackle behaviours such as racist commentary on social media sites (Chapter 4), the use of such sites to subject another to cyber-harassment and/or cyberstalking (Chapter 5), or just to abuse another (Chapters 6 and 7), are currently not adhering to the principle of legality. And as highlighted in Chapter 3, and reflected throughout this monograph, legality needs to be maintained because 'legality offers the most just, most effective, most coherent, most persuasive, most legitimate and even the most moral approach'[2] to the regulation of individual behaviour. Something that is of utmost importance when it comes to

1 Chris Reed and Andrew Murray, *Rethinking the Jurisprudence of Cyberspace* (Elgar 2018) 120.

2 Jessica Lynn Corsi, 'An Argument for Strict Legality in International Criminal Law' [2018] 49 Geo. J. Int'l L. 1321.

DOI: 10.4324/9781003303688-13

restricting a fundamental democratic right, such as the right to freedom of expression. Indeed, the current approach to regulating the online world clearly highlights that 'this inconsistent over-action, under-action, lack of action, shows that we need a principled framework, centred in human rights',[3] including maintaining the principle of legality.

The following discussion highlights the importance of tackling societal norms to combat the 'harms' associated with the online world. It is only when societal norms are on par with what is expected of human behaviour, that legal norms will take effect. To do this, Chapter 10 provides a keyword analysis of the National Education Curriculum in England for both primary and secondary school students. It highlights the lack of emphasis placed on education to improve digital etiquette within society and how, instead, emphasis is being placed on the criminal law to tackle these issues. Final discussions outline recommendations for the issues highlighted throughout this monograph on how we can appropriately regulate online behaviour, whilst adhering to the principle of legality and protecting freedom of expression.

10.2 Applying the Criminal Law to the Online World

As noted in Chapter 1, there does not seem to be a day that goes by where there is not a news story highlighting the 'darker' side of the online world, followed by the cry 'there should be a law against that'. In turn, as demonstrated in previous chapters, the criminal law framework has been adapted to fit the digital age—and in many cases, resulting in the principle of legality being undermined and freedom of expression being threatened. Yet, there seems to be something about the online world, where societal and legal norms come into direct conflict with one another.

Using child sexual abuse material as an example, Reed and Murray demonstrate the difficulties in applying legal norms to cyberspace. The conduct, the sharing of child sexual abuse material, is a behaviour where there is a general consensus, internationally, that 'the creation, communication and (in most countries) possession of such images should be a serious criminal offence'.[4] Indeed, as noted by Reed and Murray, it is a type of online harm that is often reported in the mainstream press, especially in the United Kingdom. As a result, 'it seems likely that most UK residents know that child sexual abuse images contravene the law'.[5] For instance, as noted in Chapter 8 one of the key objectives of the United Kingdom's Online Safety Act 2023 (OSA), is to protect children from the 'harms' associated with the online world, including child sexual abuse material. Yet, the sharing of such material online is, and continues to be, common. Leading Reed and Murray to conclude:

3 Ellie Judson, 'The Online Safety Bill: Demos Position Paper' (*Demos*, April 2022) 7 <https://demos.co.uk/wp-content/uploads/2023/02/OSB-position-paper.pdf> accessed 14 March 2024.

4 Reed and Murray (n 1) 121.

5 Ibid.

> It is clear that legal norms are losing out to technically mediated cyberspace norms even in this field, which is normally seen as the most heinous of criminal offences. [...] it seems clear that technology is driving a whole new set of online social norms. Whereas there is a strong legal (and offline social) norm against the production and distribution of child sexual abuse images, the ready availability of high quality cameras and the prevalent cyber-norm of producing and sharing sexualised images digitally has led to cyber-normalisation of sharing of indecent images irrespective of whether these are images of adults or minors.[6]

Similar arguments can be raised about copyright material, where there seems to be a genuine consensus amongst online users, that the illegal distribution, downloading and uploading of copyright material, is acceptable online behaviour but stealing property in the physical world is not, and in many cases, would constitute theft.

If legal norms are struggling to take effect in the online world against behaviour(s) where there is a genuine offline norm that such conduct is unacceptable, such as the sharing of child sexual abuse imagery, why would this be any different in relation to behaviour(s) where there is no genuine consensus that such behaviour is unacceptable, either offline or online? A prime example of this would be the sending of grossly offensive communications, which are prohibited, as outlined in Chapter 6, under both the Malicious Communications Act 1988 (MCA) and s.127(1) of the Communications Act 2003 (CA). Though it is illegal to send such a communication that can be defined as grossly offensive, there is no genuine societal norm that such behaviour is unacceptable both in the offline world and the online world. Whereas, as discussed above, in the offline world, when it comes to child sexual abuse imagery, there is a consensus that such conduct is wholly unacceptable—yet such behaviour continues to take place online.

What is therefore missing from many of the discussions around tackling the 'harms' associated with the online world, is the importance of changing societal norms. Instead, especially in England and Wales, and arguably societies across the globe we have seen a call for stronger legal provisions because after all, 'there should be a law against that'. Arguably because the law can be considered a 'quick fix' as it is perceived that something is being done as opposed to tackling the root cause of the problem.[7] This is despite, as was discussed and highlighted in Chapter 2 the importance of tackling social norms first: 'day to day we are more likely to alter our behaviour to comply with social norms in preference to legal norms or legal rules'.[8]

This is evidently clear when it comes to the use of the criminal law to tackle racist conduct, both online and offline, as highlighted in Chapter 4. The use of the internet, in particular, social media to send racist abuse to another is a prevalent

6 Ibid., 122–123.

7 Stephen L. Newman, 'Finding the Harm in Hate Speech: An Argument against Censorship' (2017) 50(3) CJPS 679, 687.

8 Reed and Murray (n 1) 103.

issue for governments across the globe. For instance, as outlined in Chapter 4, year-on-year, police forces in England and Wales have witnessed an increase in crimes where there is a hate crime element, with race being the most recorded hate crime characteristic.[9] Similar trends have also been mirrored on social media platforms.[10] Yet, such conduct is not unique to the digital world, racist behaviour is inherent within society, social media has just magnified the problem for the world to see. No longer, is it easy to ignore that such traits exist amongst humankind. Yet, no matter how much criminal law is enacted to tackle the problem of racist speech online, without changing societal norms, such behaviour will continue to flourish. Indeed, '[o]ne cannot blame Facebook for the dark side of human nature'.[11]

But how then do we tackle societal norms, to ensure we are getting the best out of legal provisions? The answer is simple, but not an overnight fix, nor something that can necessarily be pointed to by policymakers to state: 'look what we have done'—which we have seen with the previous UK government's stance following the passing of the OSA. The answer is simply, better, and stronger digital education:

> One way of shifting the social norm in the direction of law is via education. If cyberspace actors can be convinced that their conduct is morally wrong, rather than merely unlawful, enough of them may change their behaviour in the direction of the legal norm to start change in the social norm.[12]

Reed and Murray give the example of education programmes being run by the music industry to equate 'file sharing with crimes against physical property, such as theft which are widely accepted as being morally wrong'.[13] The belief that education plays an important role in tackling social and legal norms is supported further by Newman. Newman, using hate speech as an example, suggests that if the censorship of such conduct is about supporting 'public good', which is the notion often used to support the use of legal provisions to prohibit such conduct, then surely, education is better than the coercive nature of the criminal law? As echoed in Chapter 2:

> Words can be hurtful. They can antagonize [*sic*], they can wound. But words also inform and educate. They can dispel prejudice and reveal unanticipated

9 Home Office, 'Hate crime, England and Wales, 2021 to 2022' (*Gov.uk*, 6 October 2022) <https://www.gov.uk/government/statistics/hate-crime-england-and-wales-2021-to-2022/hate-crime-england-and-wales-2021-to-2022> accessed 1 February 2023.

10 Matthew L. Williams, Pete Burnap, Amir Javed, Han Liu and Sefa Ozalp, 'Hate in the Machine: Anti-Black and Anti-Muslim Social Media Posts as Predictors of Offline Racially and Religiously Aggravated Crime' 60(1) BJC 93.

11 Hugh Stephens, 'Those problematic comments on Facebook – Who bears responsibility for them?' (*Hugh Stephens Blog*, 22 November 2021) <https://hughstephensblog.net/2021/11/22/those-problematic-comments-on-facebook-who-bears-responsibility-for-them%EF%BF%BC/> accessed 14 March 2024.

12 Reed and Murray (n 1) 129.

13 Ibid., 129.

Table 10.1 Keyword and phrase search National Primary Curriculum for England

Keyword/phrase	*Mentions in the National Primary Curriculum for England*	*Why it was mentioned*
Social Media	0	NA
Internet	4	Privacy and safety – 1 How the internet works – 1 Using the internet – 1 Miscellaneous reference – 1
Computer	7	Computer science – 2 Writing computer programmes – 1 Computer networks – 1 Computer design – 1 Computer mapping – 1 Miscellaneous reference – 1
Online	5	Online technology and privacy – 1 Miscellaneous reference – 4
Technology	27	Design and technology – 14 Using technology – 7 Communication and Technology – 2 Respect and technology – 2 Miscellaneous reference – 2

Note: Department for Education, 'The National Curriculum in England: Key stages 1 and 2 framework document' (*Gov.uk*, September 2013) <https://assets.publishing.service.gov.uk/media/5a81a9abe5274a2e8ab55319/PRIMARY_national_curriculum.pdf> accessed 14 March 2024.

> affinities. We need strong laws to protect us from violence and discrimination, but laws that protect us from hurtful words tend to silence us as well as our antagonists, because they close down rather than open conversations and because they teach good citizens to call the police rather than do the hard work of combating hateful ideas.[14]

Yet, education is given very little consideration in debates surrounding the 'harms' associated with the online world. For instance, the National Educational Curriculum for primary school children (aged 4–11) in England does not contain the phrase 'social media' in any of its 201 pages, as shown further in Table 10.1. Similarly, the National Educational Curriculum for England for secondary school students (aged 11–16) does not mention the phrase 'social media' anywhere in its 105 pages, as demonstrated in Table 10.2.

Indeed, as shown in Tables 10.1 and 10.2, little consideration is given to digital etiquette compared to technology usage in general. For instance, in the primary school National Curriculum, reference is made only once that students should be

14 Newman (n 7) 693.

Table 10.2 Keyword and phrase search National Secondary Curriculum for England

Keyword/phrase	*Mentions in the National Secondary Curriculum for England*	*Why it was mentioned*
Social Media	0	NA
Internet	0	NA
Computer	10	Computer science – 4 Writing computer programmes – 1 Understanding computer systems – 3 Creativity and computers – 1 Miscellaneous reference – 1
Online	3	Online technology and privacy – 1 Miscellaneous reference – 2
Technology	22	Design and technology – 13 Using technology – 2 Communication and Technology – 2 Safety and technology – 2 Creativity and technology – 1 Development of technology – 1 Miscellaneous reference – 1

Note: Department for Education, 'The National Curriculum in England: Key stages 3 and 4 framework document' (*Gov.uk*, December 2014) <https://assets.publishing.service.gov.uk/media/5da7291840f0b6598f806433/Secondary_national_curriculum_corrected_PDF.pdf> accessed 14 March 2024.

able to 'use technology safely, respectfully and responsibly; recognise acceptable/unacceptable behaviour; identify a range of ways to report concerns about content and contact'.[15] For secondary school children, they should

> understand a range of ways to use technology safely, respectfully, responsibly, and securely, including protecting their online identity and privacy; recognise inappropriate content, contact and conduct and know how to report concerns.[16]

This is mentioned twice in the document. Whereas, how to use new technology more broadly is referenced fourteen times for primary school children; and eleven times for secondary school children. Given the extent of new technology and its impact on every aspect of everyday life, as highlighted in Chapter 1, it is regrettable

15 Department for Education, 'The National Curriculum in England: Key stages 1 and 2 framework document' (*Gov.uk*, September 2013) accessed 14 March 2024.

16 Department for Education, 'The National Curriculum in England: Key stages 3 and 4 framework document' (*Gov.uk*, December 2014) 86 <https://assets.publishing.service.gov.uk/media/5da7291840f0b6598f806433/Secondary_national_curriculum_corrected_PDF.pdf> accessed 14 March 2024.

that more emphasis is not placed on the importance of digital education, beyond just how to use new technology, to encompass more discussions on how individuals present themselves and interact with others online. Whereas in Australia, for example, significant emphasis has been placed on education to help tackle online 'harms', through the creation and implementation of the eSafety Commissioner.

In Australia, educational initiatives to combat inappropriate conduct online is regarded as 'one of the most important elements of crime prevention'.[17] Programmes have been created by the federal government such as 'Thinkuknow', targeting both school-aged children and the wider public in digital etiquette.[18] An approach endorsed further in the work of the e-Safety Commissioner, who has the power to investigate complaints related to conduct carried out online, and report the most serious incidents to the police, whilst tackling the less serious complaints by working with online platforms. The e-Safety Commissioner also has significant responsibility for the education of Australian Citizens to 'have safer, more positive online experiences'.[19] This includes, though not limited to:[20]

- Free presentations to pre-service teachers in their final year of tertiary study;
- Free webinars to upskill university support staff about the latest online safety risks to young adults and strategies to deal with them;
- Creating best practice frameworks;
- Classroom resources; and
- Specific training tools for schools and universities.

Whereas education has been placed at the center of combatting online 'harms' in Australia, in the United Kingdom, significant weight has been placed on the criminal law to tackle such issues, as noted in various chapters of this monograph, and clearly demonstrated during the passing of the OSA where weight was placed on regulating social media companies through coercive enforcement,[21] as opposed to tackling the societal issues and education. This has been reflected further in other countries approaches to tackling online abuse, as shown in Chapter 9.

At the time of writing, the Department of Education for England is consulting on draft guidance for those working in the education system on 'Relationships

17 Parliament of Australia, *Cyber Safety – Joint Select Committee High-wire act: Cyber-safety and the young Interim report* (June 2011) [11.18].

18 Thinkuknow, 'What we see, say, do online' (*Thinkuknow.org.au*, 2018) <https://www.thinkuknow.org.au/what-we-see-say-do-online> accessed 27 July 2018.

19 eSafety Commissioner, 'eSafety Education' (*Australian Government*, 2024) <https://www.esafety.gov.au/educators#:~:text=eSafety%27s%20education%20and%20training%20team,strategies%20to%20deal%20with%20them.> accessed 14 March 2024.

20 Ibid.,

21 Department for Science, Innovation and Technology and The Rt Hon Michelle Donelan MP, 'Overwhelming support for Online Safety Act as rules making UK the safest place in the world to be online become law' (*Gov.uk*, 27 October 2023) <https://www.gov.uk/government/news/overwhelming-support-for-online-safety-act-as-rules-making-uk-the-safest-place-in-the-world-to-be-online-become-law> accessed 14 March 2024.

Education, Relationships and Sex Education and Health education.'[22] The guidance covers an array of topics, including some aspects of online 'harms'. However, much of the focus in the guidance is placed on teaching young people the legal provisions prohibiting 'harms' such as the sharing of sexual imagery, cyberharassment and violent material as opposed to digital citizenship, with strict age-limits being imposed on teachers as to when certain content can be discussed.[23] A similar approach is endorsed in the Department of Education's 'Teaching online safety it schools' guidance, where significant emphasis is placed on the 'bad' rather than the 'good' when it comes to interacting with the online world. In essence, what digital education we have is extremely limited.[24]

Education is vital in the discussion of online behaviours, a discussion that is often missing in wider discourse around our online interactions. That is not to say there is no place for the criminal law when it comes to conduct carried out online. There will always be certain behaviours that warrant criminal law intervention. However, where the criminal law is used, it needs to be grounded in legal provisions which comply with the principle of legality—something we are currently failing to do.

10.3 Protecting Legality in the Criminal Law on Social Media

The previous chapters have examined several 'harms' associated with the online world, and the criminal law's application to prohibit such conduct, from the principle of legality. This monograph started by setting the theoretical background to the thesis of this book—the criminal law framework, as it currently stands, when applied to certain conduct carried out on social media does not uphold the very basics of legality. In turn, the right to freedom of expression, as protected under both national and international law, as outlined in Chapter 2, is under threat. As discussed in Chapter 3, legality comprises of several underlying principles, though there is no true consensus as to what these underlying principles are, there are significant overlaps. As noted in Chapter 3, '[a]mongst the best known'[25] approaches to legality, is Lon Fuller.[26] And it was Fuller's understanding of legality which was

22 Department for Education, 'Draft Relationships Education, Relationships and Sex Education (RSE) and Health education: Statutory guidance for governing bodies, proprietors, head teachers, principals, senior leadership teams, teachers' (*Gov.uk*, 16 May 2024) <https://consult.education.gov.uk/rshe-team/review-of-the-rshe-statutory-guidance/supporting_documents/Draft%20RSE%20and%20Health%20Education%20statutory%20guidance.pdf> accessed 10 July 2024. Note, this guidance was produced under the previous government and therefore might not be implemented by the new Labour government.

23 For example, 'the concepts and laws relating to harmful sexual behaviour' cannot be taught before the age of 11. Ibid., 27.

24 Department for Education, 'Teaching online safety in schools' (*Gov.uk*, 12 January 2023) <https://www.gov.uk/government/publications/teaching-online-safety-in-schools/teaching-online-safety-in-schools#curriculum-context> accessed 10 July 2024.

25 Reed and Murray (n 1) 202.

26 Lon L. Fuller, *The Morality of Law* (Yale University Press 1964) 202.

used to critique the current use of law to govern individual conduct online, in Part Two and Three of this monograph. As a reminder to the reader, Fuller argued that legality encompassed eight key principles:[27]

1. The law must be general;
2. The law must be prospective;
3. The prohibition of retrospective law;
4. The law must be clear;
5. The prohibition of contradictory law;
6. The law must not ask the impossible;
7. Consistency must be maintained in the law; and
8. The law must be fairly enforced.

Each chapter that followed, exposed, with examples, the current problems in applying the criminal law to conduct carried out on social media platforms.

Chapter 4 discussed the issues of attempting to tackle racist behaviour on social media platforms, through the application of s.66 of the Sentencing Act 2020 (SA), s.31 and 32 of the Crime and Disorder Act 1988 (CDA) and s.18 and 19 of the Public Order Act 1986 (POA) to a social media context. Though, as noted in Chapter 4, the arguments made in this chapter, are not unique to conduct carried out on social media, social media has made the issue more complex, where context is everything but is often lost in the virtual world. Indeed, the Law Commission, during their extensive review of hate crimes more generally, stated:

> [we] are deeply concerned that misrepresentation as to the sort of conduct which are caught by the stirring up offences may lead people to avoid saying things that they are perfectly entitled to express.[28]

An issue that gained significant conversation in April 2024, following a new criminal provision being enacted in Scotland, the Hate Crime and Public Order (Scotland) Act 2021, which 'introduces the offence of "stirring up hatred" – either in person or online – related to age, disability, religion, sexual orientation, transgender identity or being intersex.'[29]

Three significant concerns with legality were raised in Chapter 4: (1) the inherent vagueness of key aspects of s.66 of the SA, s.31 and 32 of the CDA and s.18 and 19 of the POA; (2) consistency being lost; and (3) retrospective law, following the application of stirring up offences to the online world, going beyond Parliament's original intent. In recent years, calls have been made to make significant changes

27 Ibid., 33–94.

28 Law Commission, *Hate Crime Laws: Final Report* (Law Com No 401, 2021) [10.12].

29 Laura Higson-Bliss, 'Scotland's hate crime law: the problem with using public order laws to govern online speech' *The Conversation* (London, 23 April 2024) <https://theconversation.com/scotlands-hate-crime-law-the-problem-with-using-public-order-laws-to-govern-online-speech-227951> accessed 10 July 2024.

to this area of the law, to ensure a better balance between freedom of expression and the criminal law.[30] Most notably, to remove reference to insulting behaviour, following a general consensus that such conduct falls within the realms of freedom of expression.[31] But if we want to strive for the 'maximum clarity which the imperfect medium of language can attain',[32] we also need to consider the continued use of the terms hostile and abusive. Both terms are inherently vague and impossible to quantify in the online world where, as echoed earlier, context is everything but is often lost. Indeed, in today's liberal and democratic society, where free speech needs to be protected, it is legitimate to ask if we should even criminalise hostile and abusive speech.

The lack of consensus as to the meaning of key terms in the provisions discussed in Chapter 4, has led to inconsistency in the criminal law. As highlighted in Chapter 4, it is not quite clear why in one case, as an example, the POA was used, as seen in *R v Liam Stacey*.[33] Whereas in another matter, such as *R v Alison Chabloz*,[34] s.127(1) of the CA was applied. Both cases could be considered abusive, at the very least, and arguably demonstrated racial hatred—yet different legal provisions were applied and the reasoning as to why, is unclear. In fact, it is of concern that provisions such as the POA are being used in a social media context, as arguably this is creating retrospective criminal law. The purpose of the POA is to regulate public disorder, in particular, riots, football hooliganism, protests, etc. Yet the Act has been used to cover social media related offences, where public disorder is not under threat.

Similar issues were raised in Chapter 5 over the use of vague terminology, most notably, a course of conduct, harassment and stalking in the Protection from Harassment Act (PfHA). And like that of Chapter 4, these arguments are not unique to the digital world but have become more complex in the wake of new technology. Following significant amendments to the PfHA to include stalking as a separate offence under the Act in 2012, arguments were made at the time that cyberstalking should be included as a separate offence, with MacEwan noting that it was 'naïve, to view it simply as "old behaviour using new technologies"'.[35] As new technology has advanced it has become easier to harass and stalk another. Further, given the added complex notion that 'the general monitoring of a person's social media page, is expected, and somewhat consented to',[36] we are at an opportune moment to consider the specific criminalisation of cyberharassment and cyberstalking, to address the issues highlighted in Chapter 5. Ensuring that any provisions created,

30 Ibid.,

31 Law Com No 401 (n 28) [10.305].

32 Law Commission, *Report on Conspiracy and Criminal Law Reform* (1976) Law Com No. 76 [1.8].

33 *R v Liam Stacey*, Swansea Crown Court On Appeal From The Magistrates' Court, A20120033.

34 *R v Alison Chabloz*, Westminster Magistrates' Court, 11 January 2018 (unreported).

35 Neil MacEwan, 'The New Stalking Offences in English Law: Will They Provide Effective Protection from Cyberstalking?' (2012) 10 Crim.L.R. 767, 768.

36 Law Commission, *Abusive and Offensive Online Communications: A Scoping Report* (Law Com No 381, 2018) [8.174].

are not grounded in vague terminology, and are targeting the most extreme cases. This is not creating new law; it is simply bringing clarity to this area of the law.

In turn, as highlighted in Chapter 5, to protect legality further, we need to reconsider what constitutes the reasonable person in a social media context and ensure the law is not asking the impossible. Though a longstanding provision in the criminal law, the use of the reasonable person test, as discussed at length in Chapter 5, when applied in a social media context significant issues can be raised. To better protect the right to freedom of expression and adhere to the principle of legality, it is suggested that we should, when considering online behaviours, ground the reasonable person test into that of the reasonable social media user.

Of all the provisions used to govern conduct carried out on social media, the most controversial is the continued usage of the MCA and s.127(1) of the CA, as it cannot be said that generality in the law is being adhered to. Significant concern was raised in Chapter 6 with the terms threatening, indecent, obscene, false, menacing, and grossly offensive. Concerns that have not gone unnoticed with the Law Commission in 2021, calling for the repeal of both provisions.[37] Both provisions are grounded in terminology that is difficult to define, and even with the modest changes made by the passing of the OSA, the issues raised in Chapter 6 have not been addressed. As a result, heavy reliance is being placed on the discretion of law enforcement, Crown Prosecutors, judges, and juries on what constitutes, as an example, a menacing, or indeed, grossly offensive communication—resulting in inconsistent application of the law. Even prosecuting guidelines have not brought generality to this area of the law. For instance, as discussed in Chapter 6, even with prosecuting guidelines being in place, mistakes continue to be made by those working in the criminal justice system, such as in the case of *Alison Chabloz*.[38]

The Law Commission's recommendation to repeal both the MCA and s.127(1) of the CA was welcomed by many,[39] after they concluded that both provisions were not suited for the digital world.[40] This is something that needs to be revisited, and although their recommended replacement, the harms model, did not necessarily address previous concerns with communication offences—it is clear that both the MCA and s.127(1) of the CA pose such significant issues with legality, they need to be replaced to ensure fair enforcement of the law in the future. Currently, what one police force, Crown Prosecutor, judge, or jury may consider, as an example, grossly offensive, another may not—it cannot be said, that the MCA and s.127(1) of the CA are action-guiding.

If history has taught us anything, it is that creating communication offences, grounded in vagueness only undermines freedom of expression and does not protect those who are subjected to the most horrific forms of abuse. And even

37 Law Commission, *Modernising Communications Offences: A Final Report* (Law Com. No.399, 2021) [2.1].

38 *Chabloz* (n 34).

39 Law Commission, *Harmful Online Communications: The Criminal Offences. A Consultation Paper* (Law Com. No.248, 2020) Chapter 5.

40 Law Com No 399 (n 37).

with prosecuting guidelines in place, overreliance on discretion results in unfair enforcement of the law and in turn prospectivity being threatened. Yet, the 'new' communication offences, as outlined in Chapter 7, still pose significant issues with legality. All the provisions discussed in Chapter 7, are embedded in vague terminology, most notably what constitutes 'harm' under each of the offences discussed in Chapter 7. 'Harm' under the harms-offence was defined as 'psychological harm amounting to at least serious distress'[41]—a significantly wide definition and one of the reasonings for its removal from the Online Safety Bill 2022 before its passing through Parliament.[42] Nonetheless, both s.179 and 181 of the OSA, lack clarity in relation to the 'harms' they prohibited. Under s.179 'harm' is defined as 'non-trivial psychological or physical harm'.[43] Whereas s.181(2) defines harm as:

> (a) serious injury amounting to grievous bodily harm (GBH) within the meaning of the Offences against the Person Act 1981, (b) rape, (c) assault by penetration within the meaning of section 2 of the Sexual Offences Act 2003, or (d) serious financial loss.[44]

All of these render issues with legality and do not sufficiently overcome the arguments made against previous communication offences, most notably the MCA and s.127(1) of the CA. Clarity, as noted by Fuller, is an 'essential ingredient'[45] in legality and yet, it's a significant issue highlighted throughout each chapter of this monograph, and should have been at the forefront of lawmakers' minds, when creating and implementing these 'new' communication offences.

The lack of understanding as to the meaning of 'harm' is also reflected in the notion of 'likely audience'. A term used in the recommended harms-offence and repeated in s.179 of the OSA—despite concerns over how inherently broad the term was, leading to individuals being asked to do the impossible—send a communication that does not cause 'psychological harm amounting to at least serious distress' to a likely audience, with this likely audience being anyone in the world.[46] In turn, many of the issues highlighted in Chapter 6 remain, and in fact, are complicated further, given that we now have a range of communication offences which overlap, as opposed to just two offences. The interchangeable nature of communication-based law therefore remains, despite the passing of the OSA.

41 Online Safety Bill 2022 c.150(4).

42 Department of Digital, Culture, Media and Sport, 'Overview of expected impact of changes to the Online Safety Bill' (*Gov.uk*, 18 Jan 2022) <https://www.gov.uk/government/publications/online-safety-bill-supporting-documents/overview-of-expected-impact-of-changes-to-the-online-safety-bill#:~:text=The%20adult%20safety%20duties%20(%27legal,and%20freedom%20of%20expression%20dutie> accessed 7 August 2023.

43 Online Safety Act 2023 s.179(1)c.

44 Ibid., s.181(2).

45 Fuller (n 26) 62.

46 Laura Higson-Bliss, 'Prosecuting Communication Offences: Interpreting the Harms Model' (2022) 4 CLR 27, 284.

These 'new' provisions need to be applied carefully going forwards and where issues remain, these are highlighted to lawmakers, to ensure future amendments can address the concerns raised in Chapter 7. The 'harms' prohibited under the remaining offences need to be clarified further, to ensure discretion in the criminal justice system is not being heavily relied upon, and the notions of 'reasonable excuse' and 'likely audience' need to be replaced with concepts which create consistency within the law and are not open to abuse. As shown during the COVID-19 pandemic, 'reasonable excuse' creates more issues than it seeks to resolve, resulting in negative attitudes towards the law and those enforcing it.

The concerns raised in Part Two of this monograph, are not just unique to the United Kingdom, or indeed, the criminal law. Legality is also a significant issue in the recent attempt to regulate user-to-user services, in particular, social media platforms through the creation and implementation of the OSA—the previous UK government's attempt to become one of the 'safest places in the world to go online',[47] as discussed in Chapter 8. The OSA is an extensive piece of legislation which will have far-reaching consequences, that are still not yet fully understood. The Act is grounded in vagueness and at times, asking the impossible. Of significant concern, is the requirement that user-to-user services do the work of law enforcement, judges, and juries in interpreting the criminal law framework of Scotland, Northern Ireland, England and Wales in determining if a complained about behaviour constitutes an offence in any of these jurisdictions. This includes all the provisions discussed in previous chapters of this monograph—despite, as highlighted in Chapter 8, those working in the criminal justice system, who have significant expertise that private platforms do not, struggling to apply the law correctly at times. In turn, we are seeing the privatisation of speech. The issues this presents with legality are further amplified by the vagueness and lack of clarity contained in many of the provisions in the OSA.

But despite the previous UK government suggesting we are world-leading in the fight against the 'harms' associated with the online world, this is not necessarily true and many of the issues highlighted in Chapter 8 have also been raised against other countries' approaches to regulating the internet, in particular, social media platforms, as shown in Chapter 9. Chapter 9 examined three other countries' attempts to regulate social media platforms: France, Germany, and India. And as highlighted in Chapter 9, each was chosen due to their similarities, not only with each other but also with the United Kingdom's OSA and each posed, or still poses, significant issues with legality.

In France, the French Constitutional Court struck down the Online Hate Bill, following its failure to adequately set limitations to ensure the law was not abused and in turn, protected the right to freedom of expression.[48] Significant weight was

47 HM Government, 'Internet Safety Strategy – Green paper' (*Gov.uk*, October 2017) 1 <https://assets.publishing.service.gov.uk/government/uploads/system/uploads/attachment_data/file/650949/Internet_Safety_Strategy_green_paper.pdf> accessed 22 September 2023.

48 Decision no. 2020-801 DC of June 18, 2020.

also given to the lack of legality within the provision. In particular, like that of the United Kingdom's OSA, asking platforms to do the impossible by requiring them to interpret the criminal code of France against reported content to determine if such content should be removed—giving platforms 24 hours to make such a determination. Whereas in Germany, a similar provision, NetzDG, despite initial concerns around freedom of expression and legality, remains legally enforceable. Indeed, research into NetzDG since its enactment has been mixed—neither confirming nor denying if the provision has hindered the right to freedom of expression,[49] though it is accepted that legality is still a significant issue. In India, similar legislation to both France, Germany, and the United Kingdom has been implemented into the legal framework of India, but these provisions, many of which mirror European approaches to regulating the online world, have been heavily abused due to its lack of legality.

Of significant concern, as was discussed at length in Chapter 9, was the abuse of s.66A of the Information Technology Act 2000/2008 (IT Act) which mirrored both the MCA and s.127(1) and (2) of the CA (in their original enactment) by Indian authorities. The lack of understanding as to what constituted, as an example, a grossly offensive communication under the IT Act, led to significant abuse by authorities across India, leading the Supreme Court of India to strike down the provision for being incompatible with both the right to freedom of expression and legality.[50] Yet, legal provisions continue to be created in India, mirroring many European approaches to regulating the online world, which are being heavily abused, such as the recent creation and implementation of the Information Technology (Intermediary Guidelines and Digital Media Ethics Code) Rules 2021—which is very similar to the OSA and NetzDG. India is a prime example of why we need to be careful when enacting legislation which does not comply with the principle of legality when the rest of the world is looking for inspiration in their own fight against the 'harms' associated with the online world.

The principle of legality is fundamental in any legal framework but is of particular importance in criminal law provisions. It is vital, that when criminal law is produced, it is created with as much legal certainty as possible, especially when it's being used to restrict a fundamental right such as the right to freedom of expression. A balance we are struggling to make when it comes to conduct carried out on social media. Many of the discussions, as highlighted throughout this monograph, when it comes to social media, focus on the 'darker' side, and it is this 'darker' side that is used to justify the coercive nature of the criminal law. But if we really do want to become one of the 'safest places in the world to go online' whilst also protecting democracy and the right to freedom of expression, we need to ensure that the criminal law is only used in the most extreme circumstances, and where it is used, it is grounded in the principle of legality. Whilst also acknowledging the criminal

49 Rachel Griffin, 'New school speech regulation as a regulatory strategy against hate speech on social media: The case of Germany's NetzDG' (2022) 46(9) Telecommun. Policy 1, 10.

50 *Shreya Singhal v Union of India* (2013) 12 S.C.C. 73.

law cannot be used to send social signals about what is or is not acceptable online, education needs to play a part—an element that is heavily missing across wider conversations on regulating the online world, in particular, social media platforms.

Reference list

Corsi J L, 'An Argument for Strict Legality in International Criminal Law' (2018) 49 Geo J Int'l L 1321

Department for Education, 'Draft Relationships Education, Relationships and Sex Education (RSE) and Health education: Statutory guidance for governing bodies, proprietors, head teachers, principals, senior leadership teams, teachers' (*Gov.uk*, 16 May 2024) https://consult.education.gov.uk/rshe-team/review-of-the-rshe-statutory-guidance/supporting_documents/Draft%20RSE%20and%20Health%20Education%20statutory%20guidance.pdf

Department for Education, 'Teaching online safety in schools' (*Gov.uk*, 12 January 2023) https://www.gov.uk/government/publications/teaching-online-safety-in-schools/teaching-online-safety-in-schools#curriculum-context

Department for Education, 'The National Curriculum in England: Key Stages 3 and 4 Framework Document' (*Gov.uk*, December 2014) https://assets.publishing.service.gov.uk/media/5da7291840f0b6598f806433/Secondary_national_curriculum_corrected_PDF.pdf

Department for Education, 'The National Curriculum in England: Key Stages 1 and 2 Framework Document' (*Gov.uk*, September 2013) https://assets.publishing.service.gov.uk/media/5a81a9abe5274a2e8ab55319/PRIMARY_national_curriculum.pdf

Department for Science, Innovation and Technology and The Rt Hon Donelan M MP, 'Overwhelming support for Online Safety Act as rules making UK the safest place in the world to be online become law' (*Gov.uk*, 27 October 2023) https://www.gov.uk/government/news/overwhelming-support-for-online-safety-act-as-rules-making-uk-the-safest-place-in-the-world-to-be-online-become-law

Department of Digital, Culture, Media & Sport, 'Overview of expected impact of changes to the Online Safety Bill' (*Gov.uk*, 18 Jan 2022) https://www.gov.uk/government/publications/online-safety-bill-supporting-documents/overview-of-expected-impact-of-changes-to-the-online-safety-bill#:~:text=The%20adult%20safety%20duties%20(%27legal,and%20freedom%20of%20expression%20duties

eSafety Commissioner, 'eSafety Education' (*Australian Government*, 2024) https://www.esafety.gov.au/educators#:~:text=eSafety%27s%20education%20and%20training%20team,strategies%20to%20deal%20with%20them

Fuller L L, *The Morality of Law* (Yale University Press 1964)

Griffin R, 'New School Speech Regulation as a Regulatory Strategy against Hate Speech on Social Media: The Case of Germany's NetzDG' (2022) 46(9) Telecommun Policy 1

Higson-Bliss, 'Scotland's hate crime law: the problem with using public order laws to govern online speech' *The Conversation* (London, 23 April 2024) https://theconversation.com/scotlands-hate-crime-law-the-problem-with-using-public-order-laws-to-govern-online-speech-227951

Higson-Bliss L, 'Prosecuting Communication Offences: Interpreting the Harms Model' (2022) 4 CLR 271

HM Government, 'Internet Safety Strategy – Green Paper' (*Gov.uk*, October 2017) https://assets.publishing.service.gov.uk/government/uploads/system/uploads/attachment_data/file/650949/Internet_Safety_Strategy_green_paper.pdf

Home Office, 'Hate Crime, England and Wales, 2021 to 2022' (*Gov.uk*, 6 October 2022) https://www.gov.uk/government/statistics/hate-crime-england-and-wales-2021-to-2022/hate-crime-england-and-wales-2021-to-2022

Judson E, 'The Online Safety Bill: Demos Position Paper' (*Demos*, April 2022) https://demos.co.uk/wp-content/uploads/2023/02/OSB-position-paper.pdf

Law Commission, *Hate Crime Laws: Final Report* (Law Com No 401, 2021)

Law Commission, *Modernising Communications Offences: A Final Report* (Law Com. No.399, 2021)

Law Commission, *Harmful Online Communications: The Criminal Offences. A Consultation Paper* (Law Com. No.248, 2020)

Law Commission, *Abusive and Offensive Online Communications: A Scoping Report (Law Com No 381, 2018)*

Law Commission, *Report on Conspiracy and Criminal Law Reform* (Law Com No. 76. 1976)

MacEwan N, 'The New Stalking Offences in English Law: Will They Provide Effective Protection from Cyberstalking?' (2012) 10 Crim.L.R. 767

Newman S L, 'Finding the Harm in Hate Speech: An Argument against Censorship' (2017) 50(3) CJPS 679

Parliament of Australia, *Cyber Safety - Joint Select Committee High-wire act: Cyber-Safety and the Young Interim Report* (June 2011)

Reed C & Murray A, *Rethinking the Jurisprudence of Cyberspace* (Elgar 2018)

Stephens H, 'Those Problematic Comments on Facebook—Who Bears Responsibility for Them?' (*Hugh Stephens Blog*, 22 November 2021) https://hughstephensblog.net/2021/11/22/those-problematic-comments-on-facebook-who-bears-responsibility-for-them%EF%BF%BC/

Thinkuknow, 'What We See, Say, Do Online' (*Thinkuknow.org.au*, 2018) https://www.thinkuknow.org.au/what-we-see-say-do-online

Williams M L, Burnap P, Javed A, Liu H & Ozalp S, 'Hate in the Machine: Anti-Black and Anti-Muslim Social Media Posts as Predictors of Offline Racially and Religiously Aggravated Crime' 60(1) BJC 93

Index

For Product Safety Concerns and Information please contact our EU
representative GPSR@taylorandfrancis.com
Taylor & Francis Verlag GmbH, Kaufingerstraße 24, 80331 München, Germany

www.ingramcontent.com/pod-product-compliance
Lightning Source LLC
LaVergne TN
LVHW021120300926
849160LV00010B/801

* 9 7 8 1 0 3 2 3 0 1 5 6 3 *